SHAKSPERIAN STUDIES

BY

MEMBERS OF THE DEPARTMENT
OF ENGLISH AND COMPARATIVE LITERATURE
IN COLUMBIA UNIVERSITY

SHAKSPERIAN STUDIES

BY

MEMBERS OF THE DEPARTMENT
OF ENGLISH AND COMPARATIVE LITERATURE
IN COLUMBIA UNIVERSITY

EDITED BY

BRANDER MATTHEWS
AND
ASHLEY HORACE THORNDIKE

NEW YORK

RUSSELL & RUSSELL · INC

1962

6871

PREFATORY NOTE

The papers in this volume were prepared by the professors of the Department of English and Comparative Literature in Columbia University, as the contribution of this institution to the celebration of the tercentenary of Shakspere's death; and no effort has been made to conform them to a general plan or to harmonize conflicting opinions.

That so varied a collection of studies comes from a single department in a single university is testimony to the importance and to the significance of the position which Shakspere holds in our education. It may serve also in some slight measure to represent the widespread appreciation and the deepseated affection felt for Shakspere on our side of the Western Ocean and on this three hundredth year of his immortality.

B. M.
A. H. T.

April 1, 1916.

CONTENTS

SHAKSPERE DEAD

PERFORM NO SIGHING FUNERALS: HE LIVES
THE GOD IN HIS OWN CREATURES IMMANENT,
WHICH, RIGHTLY GAZED ON, PROVE TRUE PÉRSPECTIVES
WHEREIN TO SCAN HIS NATURE'S FIRMAMENT
AND CHART THE CONSTELLATIONS OF HIMSELF,
BE IT ECLIPSÈD IN SWART CALIBAN,
OR TWINKLING BRIGHT IN PROSPER'S AIR-BORN ELF,
OR AS A GLORY IN THE HEART OF MAN;
IN THREE, LIKE MORNING STARS WHICH SANG TOGETHER,—
A MAID, THE ABSTRACT OF ALL LOVE IN YOUTH,
AN OLD MAD KING FOOL-FRIENDED IN FOUL WEATHER,
A PRINCE ENTANGLED IN THE VEILS OF TRUTH.
    HIS IS THEIR GLORY; OF THEIR BEAMS HIS SOUL
    WEAVETH IN HEAVEN HER OWN CLEAR AUREOLE.

I

SHAKSPERIAN STAGE TRADITIONS

By Brander Matthews

Professor of Dramatic Literature

SHAKSPERIAN STAGE TRADITIONS

I

It is unreasonable to expect that a financier, an artist or an actor should be able to talk entertainingly or to write instructively about his work in life. Sufficient is it if he can do this work satisfactorily, by dint of native gift; and we have no right to demand that he should always be conscious of his processes. It is the business of the financier to make money useful—of the artist to paint pictures or to model statues, to design buildings or to lay out gardens,—of the actor to delight us by the impersonation of character involved in situation; and it is not necessary that any one of them should be a theorist of the art whereby he earns his living. Yet now and again artists appear who happen to possess the critical faculty as well as the creative; and whenever one thus doubly endowed is moved to discuss the practise of his calling and the principles of his craft, the rest of us will do well to listen attentively on the likely chance of picking up suggestions from which we may profit. What Reynolds and Fromentin and La Farge said about painting has an abiding value; and so have the less elaborate considerations of acting for which we are indebted to Talma, to Coquelin and to Jefferson.

In 'Art and the Actor,' Coquelin's plea for a fuller recognition of the importance and dignity of the histrionic profession, we are told that "there are but few masterpieces [of dramatic literature] so perfect that the actor cannot find something to add to them, if so inclined." This assertion will seem boastful only to those belated expounders who still seem to think that Sophocles and Shakspere and Molière wrote their plays solely for us moderns to peruse and who appear to believe blindly that these plays, composed expressly for the stage, will yet render up their full content to a lonely reader in the study. The perusal of the text will put us in possession of all the words of the dramatic poet; but only by performance in the theater itself is the spirit of a true drama made manifest and only before an actual audience can we gage its appeal to the soul of the multitude. The more familiar an open-minded reader may be with the printed lines of a dramatic masterpiece, the more likely is he to be delightedly surprised by the richness of detail and the fresh revelation of meaning when at last he has the privilege of seeing the play performed; and this rich revelation is always more or less due to the inventive skill of the performers in elaborating the latent possibilities of the dialog, in short, to the "something added by the actor."

The devoted student who dwells remote from theaters and who is thereby deprived of all opportunity to see Shakspere's comedies and tragedies on the stage itself, may worship the poet with unquestioning idolatry; but he is in no position to estimate the full power of the playwright. He does not suspect how much more varied and colored and moving these comedies and these tragedies are when their characters are sustained by flesh-and-blood performers, when the words take on a new magic by the modulated tones of the human voice, and when the action is illustrated and illuminated by the appropriate by-play of the actors. This by-play, which is often team-play, this stage-business, as it is called, has been devised by successive generations of ingenious performers, every generation retaining the best of the inventions of its predecessors and handing these along (augmented by its own contributions) to the generation that comes after. To-day the stage-manager who undertakes to produce a play of Shakspere's has at his command an immense body of these traditions, many of which he may prefer not to utilize, although he is certain to preserve others which serve to bring into high relief the inner significance of vital episodes.

Such a body of gestures and actions is cherished by the Comédie-Française and utilized in its performances of Molière's comedies. "There are certain traditions at the Théâtre-Français," so Coquelin told us in his address on the actor's art, "without which Molière is never played, and which the spectator, becoming a reader, mentally supplies as he sits by his fireside, as one supplies omissions in an incomplete copy." Some of these traditions are possibly derived directly from the original performances when the author-actor was the manager of the company; and some of them are the contribution of comedians as recent as Coquelin himself. They are so many, and they aid so amply in the interpretation of the plays, that Regnier brought out an edition of 'Tartuffe' wherein the best of the traditions which cluster around Molière's masterpiece were all carefully and elaborately set down to vivify the dialog. Regnier called this the 'Tartuffe des Comédiens'; and Coquelin once told me that he proposed to continue his teacher's task and to edit other of Molière's more important comedies with a similar amplitude of histrionic annotation. It is greatly to be regretted that the project was never carried out; no existing edition of Molière would surpass this in interest or in utility, if it had been prepared with the skill, the tact, and the scholarship displayed by Regnier in his single volume.

Coquelin asserted that the spectator of Molière, becoming a reader, supplied mentally the illustrative actions which he could not find in the text. But how about the reader of Molière who has never been a spectator? His memory cannot supply this material; and even if his imagination is active, he can never invent as adroitly or as abundantly as the actors themselves, charged with the high responsibility of actual performance and trained to scrutinize the dialog assiduously in search of histrionic opportunity. The task which Regnier began and which Coquelin failed to carry out, may yet be completed by one or another of the comedians of the Théâtre Français; and even before it is finally accomplished for Molière, it may be undertaken for Shakspere. The Shaksperian traditions are as many, as varied and as helpful; and they are now kept alive only by word of mouth, descending orally from actor to actor or preserved by the industry of a chance stage-manager in the flagrant insecurity of an unprinted prompt-copy.

When Macready retired from the active practise of his profession, George Henry Lewes expressed the hope that the actor would devote his honorable leisure to the preparation of an edition of Shakspere, in which there should be due recognition of the fact that Shakspere was as great as a playwright as he was as a poet. The actor did not accept the invitation of the critic;

and even if he had, we may doubt whether he would have condescended to record all the many traditions of the theater, some
of which he himself devised, while others he inherited from John
Kemble and Edmund Kean, to pass along to Edwin Booth and
Henry Irving. Sometimes a contemporary criticism has recorded for us the name of the actor whose ingenuity was responsible for a striking effect developed out of the unadorned
dialog and yet not discovered by any of his predecessors in the
part; and sometimes the customary business is so old that its
origin must be ascribed to a time whereof the memory of man
runneth not to the contrary.

While it is always interesting to know the name of the performer who first enriched the text with a felicitous accompaniment of pause and emphasis, glance and gesture, what is really
important to remember is that there is no single scene in any one
of the more frequently acted comedies and tragedies which has
not thus been made more pictorial and thereby more dramatic in
the eyes of the actual spectators. Every edition preserves for us
the words uttered by Othello and Iago in the marvellously built
up crescendo when Iago distills the poison of jealousy drop by
drop until Othello writhes in his overwhelming agony. But how
did Iago deliver his corroding insinuations? How did Othello
listen to them? Were they standing or sitting? What was the
arrangement of the room? How was the mounting action intensified by looks and movements? How did the two actors play
into each other's hands to achieve the ultimate peak and summit
to which all that went before had tended irresistibly? These
things we do not find in any existing edition.

It is idle to say that these things are relatively unimportant and
that we have Shakspere's words, which ought to suffice. Shakspere wrote his words specifically for actors, and for the interpretation and embellishment which only actors can give; and his
words demand this interpretation and embellishment before they
surrender their full content or disclose their ultimate potency.
No commentary on Hamlet, of all the countless hundreds that
have been written, would be a more useful aid to a larger understanding of his character than a detailed record of the readings,
the gestures, the business employed in the successive perform-

ances of the part by Burbage and by Betterton, by Garrick and by Kemble, by Macready and by Forrest, by Booth and by Irving. It is not that any one of these renowned actors is necessarily superior in critical acumen to the more intellectual of the commentators; it is that they have been compelled by their professional training to acquire an insight into this character composed specifically for their use—an insight to be attained only in the theater itself and hopelessly unattainable in the library even by the most scholarly or by the most brilliant expositor.

II

Outside of her profession Mrs. Siddons was only an ordinary mortal; and the essay which she wrote on the character of Lady Macbeth is quite negligeable. But inside of her profession she was a genius, gifted with an interpreting imagination by means of which she projected a more commanding and more sinister figure than had ever been suspected to be latent in the relatively few speeches of the comparatively brief part of Lady Macbeth. Mrs. Siddons created the character anew; she made it more dominating than it had ever been before; and in so doing she seems to have carried Shakspere's intentions to a point which he could not have foreseen. When we survey the tragedy as a whole, we perceive that the dramatist spends his main effort on Macbeth himself, on the hero-villain who begins and ends the play, and that the heroine-villian is only an accessory character, marvellously significant, no doubt, but nevertheless subordinate. In writing the words of Macbeth, so Fleeming Jenkin finely suggested, Shakspere "cannot have had present to his mind all the gestures and expressions of Lady Macbeth as she listened," and yet this by-play of Mrs. Siddons "was such that the audience, looking at her, forgot to listen to Macbeth." What Shakspere supplied was a mightily etched outline for the performer of the part to color superbly; and Shakspere is a masterly playwright partly because his plays ever abound in opportunities to be improved by the insight of inspired actors.

Fleeming Jenkin was not relying solely upon the casual discussion of Mrs. Siddon's acting preserved in contemporary criticisms; he was supported by the detailed record of her readings, her intonations, her pauses, her glances, her gestures and her movements made by a competent observer, Professor G. J. Bell, who annotated the text as he followed her performances night after night. And Professor Bell added to this invaluable account of what the great actress did in this great part, a summary of the total impression made by her in the tragedy:—"Of Lady Macbeth there is not a great deal in the play, but the wonderful genius of Mrs. Siddons makes it the whole.... Her turbulent and inhuman strength of spirit does all. She turns Macbeth to her purpose, makes him her mere instrument, guides, directs and inspires the whole plot. Like Macbeth's evil genius she hurries him on in the mad career of ambition and cruelty from which his nature would have shrunk." Possibly Shakspere meant this; certainly he supplied the material for it; but it was the actress who brought out all the hidden possibilities of the character to an extent that the poet could scarcely have anticipated.

Professor Bell declared that when she was impersonating Lady Macbeth, Mrs. Siddons was "not before an audience; her mind wrought up in high conception of her part, her eye never wandering, never for a moment idle, passion and sentiment continually betraying themselves. Her words are the accompaniments of her thoughts, scarcely necessary, you would imagine, to the expression, but highly raising it, and giving the full force of poetical effect." This criticism is completely sustained by his account of her acting in the scene of the assassination of Duncan, a scene unmatched in all dramatic literature for intensity of horror.

This record of Mrs. Siddon's Lady Macbeth is testimony to the truth of one striking passage in the illuminating paper which Fleeming Jenkin prepared to accompany it. The words uttered by any one of Shakspere's chief characters, so the acute critic asserted, "do not by themselves supply the actor with one-hundredth part of the actions he has to perform. Every single word has to be spoken with just intonation and emphasis, while not a single intonation or emphasis is indicated by the printed copy. The actor must find the expression of face, the attitude of body, the action of the limbs, the pauses, the hurries—the life, in fact. There is no logical process by which all these things can be evolved out of the mere words of a part. The actor must go direct to nature and his own heart for the tones and the action by which he is to move his audience; these his author cannot give him, and in creating these, if he be a great actor, his art is supremely great." Here Fleeming Jenkin is putting into other words the almost contemporary assertion of Coquelin that "there are but few masterpieces so perfect that the actor cannot find something to add to them." And all that the supremely great actors can imagine to move an audience, the printed dialog is devoid of; and the mere reader in the library cannot restore it unless he has earlier been a spectator in the theater itself.

III

Just as Regnier's 'Tartuffe des Comédiens' afforded a model for the editing of Molière, so we have in English at least one attempt to supply an edition of a Shaksperian play as it was interpreted by the genius of a great actor. This is E. T. Mason's record of Salvini's Othello, in which we find all that the fortunate spectators of that massive performance need when they become readers and when they endeavor to supply mentally the tones and the gestures with which the Italian actor illuminated the English tragedy. Mr. Mason gave us portraits of the actor costumed for the part; and he supplied descriptions and diagrams of all the stage-sets used by Salvini. He set down the tragedian's readings, his glances and his gestures, and his movements about the stage; and so complete is this record that a lonely student who had never been able to see Othello performed would get from it a fuller disclosure of the essential energy of the tragedy than he could possibly have had before.

It is true that the lonely student might have been aided in the effect to evoke in his mind's eye an imagined performance by a collection and a comparison of contemporary criticisms of actual performances by Edmund Kean, by Macready and by Edwin Booth; and he would find especially helpful Lewes' noble tribute to Salvini's tremendous exhibition of power at the highest point of the wonderfully wrought scene in which Iago unchains the demon of jealousy in Othello. "But the whole house was swept along by the intense and finely graduated culmination of passion in the outburst, 'Villain, be sure you prove' when seizing Iago and shaking him as a lion might shake a wolf, he finishes by flinging him on the ground, raises his foot to trample on the wretch—and then a sudden revulsion of feeling checks the brutality of the act, the *gentleman* masters the *animal*, and with mingled remorse and disgust he stretches forth a hand to raise him up."

Yet eloquent as this passage is, it is not so useful to the lonely student as Mr. Mason's minute account of all that was done in the course of the entire act of which this was the climax. Helpful also are the invaluable notes on his own procedure when acting Othello or Iago contributed by Edwin Booth to the volume on 'Othello' in Furness's Variorum Edition. More than any preceding editor did Furness perceive the importance of considering the actors' specific contribution to an adequate understanding of Shakspere's merits as a playwright; and therefore all the later volumes of the Variorum are enriched by more or less criticism of actual performances, often with indication of readings and of business. Here and there also in the ample volumes of Mr. William Winter's 'Shakspere on the Stage', we find loving record of the manner in which culminating moments were rendered by the foremost Shaksperian actors and actresses of the past half-century. For example, Mr. Winter has preserved for us the interesting fact that it was Adelaide Neilson who first caused Juliet on the balcony to pluck the flowers from her breast and to throw them down to Romeo with an apparently unpremeditated gesture expressive of the ecstasy of her overmastering passion.

Again in Miss Clara Morris's account of her earlier years on the stage she credits herself with the invention of an intensification of the dramatic effect in the final act of 'Othello.' Although she was then only a slip of a girl she was called upon to impersonate the mature Emilia. After the death of Desdemona Emilia gives the alarm, crying aloud,

Help! Help! Oh, help!
The Moor hath killed my mistress! Murder! Murder!

and then the bell tolls a general alarm. The young actress

arranged with the prompter that the bell should sound immediately after her shriek for

Help! Help!

then after this first stroke she raised her voice and cried,

Help! Oh, help!

whereupon the bell rang out again and again. Instantly she resumed her outcry,

The Moor hath killed my mistress!

And then the bell once more tolled the alarm. Finally she shrieked

Murder! Murder!

and the tolling was repeated until Montano and Gratiano and Iago rush in. Miss Morris is pleased to inform us that the result of this novel punctuation of her lines by the brazen tongue of the tocsin was to make her voice seem to combine with the clangor and to soar above it.

It would be pleasant to know whether or not the late William F. Owen should be credited with the devising of the felicitous business which enhanced Falstaff's reception of Prince Hal's exposure of his mendacity in the matter of the men in buckram, when a condensation of the two parts of 'Henry IV' was produced by Robert Taber and Miss Julia Marlowe. After Falstaff has told his tale the Prince and Poins corner him. The scene represented the tavern at Eastcheap with its huge fireplace before which stood a spacious armchair with its back to the audience. After Falstaff had met the Prince's incredulity with abuse, he cried

O for breath to utter!

and, then he sank into the chair, sputtering out his final insults. Whereupon the Prince explained that

We two, saw you four set upon four, and were masters of their wealth. Mark now, how plain a tale shall put you down.

As soon as Falstaff was convinced that his bluff was about to be called, he shrank into the chair and the back of his head was no longer to be seen, so the Prince stated his case to an invisible Falstaff, ending with

What trick? what device? what starting hole cans't thou now find out,
to hide thee from this open and apparent shame?

Then Henry paused for a reply and it was so long in coming,
that Poins backed up the Prince, saying

Come, let's hear, Jack. What trick hast thou now?

Falstaff out of sight of the audience had twisted himself about
in the chair until he was kneeling on it; and he slowly raised his
face above its back—a face wreathed with smiles and ready to
break into triumphant laughter, as at last he was ready with his
retort:

I knew ye—as well as he that made ye! Why, hear ye, my masters; was it
for me to kill the heir apparent? Should I turn upon the true Prince?

Whether this business was Owen's own, or Robert Taber's, or
inherited from Samuel Phelps,[1] it is excellent; and it deserves to
be set down in the margin of the actor's edition of the play. And
there are countless other histrionic accretions which also demand
to be preserved. Valuable as are Winter's and Booth's and
Lewes's descriptions, Bell's record of Mrs. Siddons as Lady
Macbeth and Mason's account of Salvini's Othello, they preserve
for us only a few of the greater moments of a few of the greatest
plays as performed by great actors.

We want more than this; we need to have in black and white the
whole body of stage-tradition. We ought to have all the valuable
readings and all the accessory business set down carefully and
preserved permanently, for if these things are allowed to slip from
the memory of the few who now know them, they can never be
recovered. It may be admitted frankly that some of these traditions are incongruous excrescences, occasionally foolish and
sometimes offensive, handed down thoughtlessly from a time
when the essential quality of Shakspere was less highly appreciated than it is to-day. There is no reason for regret, for instance, that the second Gravedigger in 'Hamlet' no longer delays
the action and disturbs the spirit of Ophelia's burial by stripping off an unexpected sequence of waistcoats to the delight
of the unthinking — a clowning devise which, oddly enough,

[1] Sir Johnston Forbes-Robertson tells me that he does not recall it in Phelps' performance.

is also traditional at the end of Molière's 'Précieuses Ridicules,' where it is not out of place since it is there quite in keeping with the tone of that lively little comedy. And perhaps there would be no loss if Romeo and Mercutio ceased to bewilder Peter when he is delivering the invitation by a succession of ironic salutations, just as Gratiano and Bassanio bewilder Gobbo, — the business being identical in both plays and having no warrant in the text of either.

These may be dismissed as unwarrantable obtrusions to be discarded unhesitatingly; but to admit this is not to discredit the utility of the traditions in general. They are to be received as precious heirlooms, a legacy to the present and to the future, from the finest performers and from the most adroit stage-managers of the past, a store of accumulated devices always to be considered carefully, to be selected from judiciously and to be cast aside only after mature consideration. And, first of all, before any selection can be attempted, these traditions need all of them to be placed on record for what they are worth. Moreover, as the value of a suggestion, if not its validity, is due in part at least to the reputation of its suggester, the record ought (in so far as this is now possible) to register also the name of the originator of every specific piece of business and of every illuminating reading.

IV

John Philip Kemble, for example, although a little austere and chilly as an actor, was a most fertile deviser of points; and it is believed that some of the most striking effects made by Mrs. Siddons were due to the inventiveness of her brother. One of these, and one of the most characteristic, is in the trial scene of 'Henry VIII.' Queen Katharine comes before the King and the two cardinals, Wolsey and Campeius, sitting as judges of the legality of her marriage to Henry; and she begins by an appeal to her husband. When she makes an end, Wolsey, whom she knows for her personal enemy, counters by asserting the integrity and the learning of the judges of the case; and Campeius very courteously suggests that the royal session proceed. Then there follow these two speeches:

Queen.   Lord Cardinal,
          To you I speak.
Wolsey.   Your pleasure, madam.

But there are two cardinals present before her, and Campeius
has just spoken. Why then should Wolsey alone answer when the
Queen says,

Lord Cardinal, to you I speak?

The actress can, of course, suggest a sufficient reason for Wolsey's taking her words to himself by looking at him when she
begins: yet this is barely sufficient, since the two cardinals are
sitting side by side and the Queen is at some little distance.
When Kemble played Wolsey and Mrs. Siddons was Queen
Katharine this is how the brief dialog was managed. At the end
of Campeius' sentence or two, the Queen spoke,

Lord Cardinal,

and then paused, whereupon Campeius rose and moved a little
toward her, evidently believing that she was about to answer
him. As he approached her she turned from him impatiently, so
Professor Bell has recorded, immediately making a sweet but
dignified bow of apology. "Then to Wolsey, turned and looking
from him, with her hand pointing back to him, in a voice of
thunder,

To *you* I speak!

The effect of this outburst is so electric that it has been repeated in the subsequent revivals of 'Henry VIII,' as I can testify
from my memory of Charlotte Cushman's performance, Mod-
jeska's and Ellen Terry's; and in so arranging it Kemble made a
permanent contribution to the staging of Shakspere.

As much cannot be said for an infelicitous invention of Mme.
Sarah-Bernhardt's when she rashly ventured to exhibit herself
as Hamlet. In the interview between Hamlet and the Queen in
which he speaks daggers but uses none, he bids his mother contrast her two husbands:

Look here, upon this picture and on this.

How are those two portraits to be shown to the spectators?
or are they to be shown at all? Henry Irving accepted them as

purely imaginary, seen only in the mind's eye; and so did Edwin
Booth sometimes, although he often preferred to wear a miniature of his father, pendant from his neck so that he might compare this with a miniature of his uncle which his mother wore
suspended also by a chain. Fechter tore the miniature of his
uncle from the Queen's neck after contrasting it with a painting
of his father hanging on the wall. Betterton had two half-length
portraits side by side above the wainscot. Mme. Sarah-Bernhardt employed a pair of full length paintings, framed high up
in the woodwork on the wall facing the Queen as she sat; and
when the young Prince expatiated piously on his father's qualities,
physical and moral, the portrait of the elder Hamlet suddenly
became transparent and through it the spectators beheld the
Ghost—a trivial spectacular trick which immediately distracted
the attention of the spectators.

Irving's suppression of visible portraits was perhaps more in
accord with the spirit of the episode (and of the play as a whole)
than was Booth's occasional use of two miniatures; certainly it
was simpler. And yet Irving was rarely as simple as Booth.
The American tragedian was wont to rely boldly on his mastery
of the art of acting, whereas the British character-actor felt it
advisable to support his impersonation by every possible device
of the stage-manager. Irving may or may not have suspected the
limitations of his accomplishment as an actor, whereas in stage-
management his supremacy over all his contemporaries was
indisputable. He was incessantly fertile and unfailingly dextrous
in the discovery of novel methods for vivifying Shakspere's
dialog. For the scene of Jessica's elopement in the 'Merchant of
Venice' he designed a characteristic Venetian set—a piazzetta
with Shylock's house on the right and with a bridge over the canal
which crosses the stage. Shylock bids Jessica lock herself in; and
then he goes away over the bridge to the supper to which he has
been invited. It is the carnival season; and a merry band of
maskers revels past with light laughter. Then Gratiano comes
on; and a gondola glides up from which Lorenzo steps out. They
hail Jessica, who throws to them out of the window her father's
casket of jewels and money, after which she descends and unlocks
the door, and comes out in boy's apparel, and lets her lover bear

her away in the gondola. Gratiano remains and exchanges a few words with Antonio, who has chanced by. When they have gone, the maskers gaily flash across the bridge once more; and after a little the stage is left empty. Then in the distance we hear the tapping of Shylock's staff, and soon we see him crossing the bridge to stand at last knocking at the door of his now robbed and deserted home. It is only when he has knocked a second time that the curtain slowly falls, leaving us to imagine for ourselves his grief and his rage when he finds out his double misfortune.

Again in the trial-scene, after Shylock is baffled and despoiled, he asks leave to go.

I am not well. Send the deed after me, and I will sign it.

Irving made his exit and there was silence for a little space, suddenly broken by the angry murmurs of the mob outside, hooting at the discomfited usurer. For neither of these effects is there any warrant in Shakspere's text; the first was impossible on the sceneless stage of the Globe theater, and the second was too subtle for the ruder tastes of Tudor audiences; and yet both are perfectly in keeping with the temper and spirit of the play.

It is to be noted, however, that Irving missed a moving dramatic effect in allowing Miss Ellen Terry to declaim the lines on the Quality of Mercy in accord with the customary delivery of that oration, treating it as an eloquent opportunity for triumphant elocution. Miss Ada Rehan adjusted the speech more artistically to the situation; Portia has told Shylock that he must be merciful, and he has scornfully asked,

On what compulsion must I?

Whereupon Portia explains to him the blessings of mercy—and Miss Rehan then spoke the speech as a summons to his better self, addressing herself directly to him, evidently inspired by the hope that her plea might soften his heart and watching eagerly to discover if it did. Thus treated the beautiful appeal intensified the dramatic poignancy of the moment; and thus treated it seems to be more completely in harmony with Shakspere's intent.

Yet there is danger always in spending undue effort in a vain attempt to discover what Shakspere or any other dramatist meant to do, instead of centering our attention upon what he actually did, whatever his intent may have been. It is highly probable, for instance, that Shakspere intended Shylock to be a despicable villain detestable to all spectators; but what Shakspere actually did was to create an accusable human being, arousing our sympathy at the very time when we hold him in horror. Fanny Kemble saw Edmund Kean in 1827, and she has recorded that he "entirely divested Shylock of all poetry or elevation, but invested it with a concentrated ferocity that made one's blood curdle." Quite possibly all that Shakspere intended was this concentrated ferocity, but none the less did he lend poetry and elevation to the sinister character. Kean may have performed Shylock in accord with Shakspere's intent; but Irving and Booth, both of them, preferred to reveal rather the poetry and the elevation with which Shakspere had dowered the character. If Shylock has poetry and elevation, it is because Shakspere gave them to him, even if he knew not what he did; and it is always what the artist actually did, and not merely what he meant to do, which we need to perceive clearly.

Later generations read into a masterpiece of art many a meaning which the author might disclaim and yet which may be contained in it, none the less, because the great artist is great only because he has builded better than he knew, even if he left latent what seem to us patent. A great gulf yawns between us and our Tudor ancestors; and in the centuries that separate us there may have been many changes in taste, in opinion and in prejudice. To the stalwart and stout-stomached Elizabethans Shylock may have appeared as one kind of a creature, while he seems to us a very different being, more human mainly because we ourselves are more humane. Irving's pathetic return of Shylock to his abandoned home would have been hooted by the groundlings of the Globe; and yet it is a pictorial embellishment which serves to bring out the Shylock whom we watch with commingled abhorrence and sympathy, even though Shakspere might himself protest that sympathy should not be wasted on his sordid serio-comic villain.

V

These elucidations and embellishments of the 'Merchant of Venice' should be duly preserved in the actors' edition of Shakspere; and they should be companioned by the equally significant and helpful elucidations and embellishments bestowed on 'Julius Caesar' by the famous Meiningen company. I cherish the memory of their performance of this play at Drury Lane in London when Mark Antony was entrusted to Ludwig Barnay; and I had the privilege of reviving this memory when the German actor repeated the performance at the Thalia in New York a year or two later. Neither in England nor in America were the actors who undertook Brutus and Cassius worthy of comparison with Edwin Booth and Lawrence Barrett; but I have seen no Mark Antony worthy of comparison with Barnay—handsome, graceful, intelligent and a born impersonator of orators. Now, having been a spectator of the Forum scene as the Meininger represented it, when I become a reader I can mentally supply what I do not find in the text that I hold in my hand by the fireside.

Brutus and Cassius come into the Forum accompanied by the mob of plebians. Brutus goes up into the rostrum, and Cassius leads off a part of the crowd that he may speak at the same time as Brutus. The citizens are exultantly on the side of Caesar's assassins; and they are so enthusiastic that they listen rapturously to the logical and frigid oration of Brutus. This pedantic address is interrupted by the arrival of Mark Antony, bearing in Caesar's body on a bier; and Brutus begs his hearers to let him depart that Antony may pay tribute to his dead leader. Brutus, ever deficient in political sagacity, even beseeches them to remain and hear what Antony has to say. When Brutus has gone, Mark Antony is bidden to take the rostrum; and a moment later he begins to speak. Ever since our schoolboy exercises in declamation have we been familiar with the address over Caesar's body; we know it as a piece to be memorized and recited by rote. Not so did Barnay deliver it as he stood there before the hostile throng; he made us believe that he did not know in the least what he was going to say, even if he had clearly in mind the goal to which he hoped to arrive; and as he spoke he conveyed the impression that

he was "making it up as he went along," that his address was
spontaneous, unpremeditated, absolutely impromptu.

Those to whom he was speaking were not only hostile, they
were hopelessly indifferent, broken into little groups, talking over
the speech of Brutus, and caring nothing at all either for the dead
Caesar or the living Antony. Scarce half a score at the foot of
the rostrum were even pretending to listen to him. Therefore
Mark Antony begins by soliciting their attention:

Friends—Romans—countrymen—lend me your *ears*.

And Barnay waited until these words had enticed a group or
two to break off their chatter and to draw nearer to the rostrum.
His praise of Caesar was deprecatory and his praise of Brutus
was not yet ironical. His manner was modest, not to call it
timorous; and it slowly began to win over more and more of
the mob to hear what he had to say. At the end of every sentence,
Barnay paused to let his meaning sink in; and his glance searched
for one little knot of men after another who might be attracted
by the appeal of his voice and his eye. In time the murmur was
vanquished, and the throng slowly compacted itself about the
rostrum, although there were still a few in the fringes of the
crowd who have not been taken captive. Then Mark Antony
broke off suddenly:

> Bear with me,
> My heart is in the coffin there with Caesar.

When he recovered from his exhibition of grief, the plebians
were expectant and almost sympathetic. With the swift instinct
of the orator used to playing with the feelings of the unthinking
masses, Mark Antony appreciated the progress he had made,
and he risked a possibly ironic intonation in his praise of Brutus
and Cassius as honorable men. Then Barnay paused, scrutinizing
intently the attitude of his hearers, as though asking himself
whether he had yet got them up to the proper point where he
could sway them to his will. He decided that he had attained
to this and his manner changed. He was no longer humble, as
became a man speaking only by permission of the conspirators.
He was bold, now, as became an intimate of Caesar. His hand
caught the document hidden in the folds of his toga:

> Here's a parchment, with the seal of Caesar;
> I found it in his closet; 'tis his will.
> Let but the commons hear this testament
> Which—pardon me—I do not mean to read—
> And they would go and kiss dead Caesar's wounds.

When Mark Antony pretended that he did not mean to read the will, Barnary thrust back the parchment into his bosom. He had awakened the curiosity of his listeners and he had aroused their sympathy. He adroitly tested the extent of his conquest over their passions by the frankly ironic suggestion,

> I fear I wrong the honorable men
> Whose daggers have stabbed Caesar.

The outcries of the excited citizens assured him of his victory; and then he yielded to their clamor for the will. Thereafter he held the mob in the hollow of his hand, swaying it to his purpose, sweeping it forward to demand vengeance for Caesar's death. The words poured from him, fiery, burning, heated by his over-mastering emotion, and always, as they tumbled after one another they seemed unstudied, indisputably spontaneous, born of the passion of the moment.

For the reader who has once been a spectator of a masterly performance like this, Mark Antony's address can never again chill itself into a set speech, a piece to be spoken. It cannot but glow and scorch, vitally dramatic, existing not for itself but as a most necessary part of the play, without which the mechanism would not function. In thus elaborating the Forum scene those responsible for the Meiningen performance went far beyond any conceivable intention of the author, since their modern method of presentation could not have been forseen by Shakspere, familiar only with the stage of his own times—a square platform thrust out into the yard, surrounded on three sides by the standing groundlings, cluttered at the edges with gallants seated on their three-penny stools and smoking their long pipes—a platform bare of all scenery and curtained only by long tapestry hanging from the gallery overhead—a platform whereon the Roman Forum could be suggested only by bringing on the rostrum (styled "the pulpit" in the stage-directions as given in the folio edition) and whereon the surging mass of plebians could be represented only by the handful of utility actors who have to utter the remarks of the Citizens, First and Second and Third.

So little could Shakspere foresee the method of the Meininger that there is one line in the text which—if taken literally—would prohibit it. The special point of the Meiningen procedure lies in their skill in bringing out the oratorical mastery whereby Mark Antony slowly wins over a mob which is both uninterested and hostile. Now in the text we read that Antony begins

> You gentle Romans,

whereupon this line follows:

> *All.* Peace, ho! Let us hear him!

So that Shakspere apparently intended all the citizens to begin by giving their individual attention to Mark Antony; at least he caused them to resolve unanimously to listen to him. Yet even if the Meiningen actors here broke the letter of the law, they preserved the spirit of the scene.

VI

In its time Fechter's Hamlet was the cause of a plentiful waste of ink, let loose by the resolute novelty of his performance. Fundamentally Fechter was an emotional rather than an intellectual actor; and what chiefly interested him in the tragedy was not so much the character of Hamlet as the swift succession of striking situations. To him the 'Hamlet' of Shakspere was like the 'Ruy Blas' of Victor Hugo, essentially a melodrama although adorned with exquisite poetry—and there is this much to be said for Fechter's view that we can still catch sight of the supporting skeleton of the coarser tragedy-of-blood which Shakspere endowed with the humanity of a true tragedy. Where English actors had been a little inclined to see an embodiment of philosophic reflection, sicklied o'er with the pale cast of thought, the French actor saw a romantic hero entangled in a complexity of pathetic situations; and what interested him was rather the theatrical effectiveness of these situations than the soul of the hero himself. To Fechter, Hamlet was a picturesque part for the leading man of the Porte Saint Martin; and he naturally treated the play as he would treat any other Porte Saint Martin melodrama, to be made as emotionally effective as might be and to be presented as pictorially as possible.

As Hamlet was a Dane, Fechter presented him a blond, adorning his head with locks not exactly flaxen in tint but rather reddish. (On this point doubt is not possible since the wig that Fechter used to wear as Hamlet is now piously preserved among the other histrionic memorabilia on exhibition in the club-house of The Players in New York.) Himself a sculptor in his youth and always closely associated with artists pictorial and plastic, Fechter was fertile in designing the scenic habiliment of the plays he produced. A large part of the action of 'Hamlet' was made to take place in the main hall of the castle of Elsinore. In this spacious room we saw the performance of the 'Mousetrap' and also the fencing match of the final act. This hall filled the stage; it had broad doors at the back, and above this portal was a gallery with smaller doors at both ends leading off to upper rooms and with curving stairways descending on either side. Most of the exits and entrances were made by means of one or another of these stairways; and Fechter utilized them artfully when the time came for the killing of the King. The throne upon which Claudius sat to behold the fencing was on one side. Kate Field's record of the business, in her biography of Fechter, conforms to my own recollection of it:—

"The moment Hamlet exclaimed

> Ho! let the door be locked.
> Treachery! Seek it out!

"The King exhibited signs of fear; and while Laertes made his terrible confession, the regicide stole to the opposite stairs, shielding himself from Hamlet's observation behind a group of courtiers, who, paralized with horror, failed to remark the action. Laertes no sooner uttered the words

> The King's to blame!

than Hamlet turned suddenly to the throne in search of his victim. Discovering the ruse he rushed up the left hand stairs, to meet the King in the center of the gallery and stabbed him.

.   .   .   As he descended the stairs the potent poison stole upon Hamlet, who, murmuring

The rest is silence!

fell dead upon the corpse of Laertes, thus showing his forgiveness of treachery and remembrance of Ophelia."

VII

Mention has already been made of Miss Ada Rehan's method of delivering the appeal to Shylock's better nature in which she declared the quality of mercy. In default of evidence I cannot say whether her attitude was derived from a tradition which had not been preserved in such other performances of the 'Merchant of Venice' as I have been permitted to see or whether it was assumed for the first time in Augustin Daly's last production of the play. Daly was a producer—to use the term now accepted in the theater—of singular individuality, familiar with accepted traditions, and yet often preferring to discard them in favor of novelties of his devising. On occasion he exhibited a wrongheadedness which was almost perverse in its eccentricity; but far more frequently his overt originality manifested itself in unhackneyed arrangements which set familiar passages in a new light.

Of all his Shaksperian revivals the 'Taming of the Shrew' was perhaps the most completely satisfying in its sumptuous stage-setting and in its intricate stage-management, yet his presentation of 'As You Like It' was a close second. As he was a martinet in the discipline of his company, we may credit to him rather than to the actual actor a new departure in the interpretation of the character of Jaques. In the structure of 'As You Like It' Shakspere closely followed the story of Lodge's 'Rosalynde'; yet he introduced several figures not to be found in this source. One of these is Jaques, who has nothing whatever to do with the plot of the piece, who seems to exist for his own sake, and who is allowed to usurp the attention of the audience for his self-revelatory harangues. I have suggested elsewhere that possibly Jaques was invented for the sole purpose of providing a part for Burbage

—a part rich in elocutionary opportunities. Now, what manner of man is this Jaques, created to disclose himself not by action but only by discourse?

Richard Grant White maintained "that what Jaques meant by melancholy was what we now call cynicism—a sullen, scoffing, snarling spirit." In the view of the American critic, Jaques "was one of those men who believe in nothing good, and who as the reason of their lack of faith in human nature and of hope of human happiness, and their want of charity, tell us that they have seen the world." White declared that in delivering the speech on the seven ages of man, Jaques seizes "the occasion to sneer at the representatives of the whole human race."

For this opinion of Jaques the critic claimed originality for himself, asserting that it was contrary to that usually shown on the stage. Since White first stated it in 1854, it has succeeded in acclimating itself in the theater where Jaques has frequently been presented as an embittered despiser of mankind; in fact, it bids fair to establish itself as the accepted stage-tradition. This reading of the part is attractive to the actor of Jaques, since it increases the wilful perversity of his personality and makes the character stand out in bold relief, his malignity contrasting with the kindliness of the Duke and of his genial companions in the forest.

But is this necessarily the right reading of the part? Is there ever any one interpretation of the more richly rounded characters of Shakspere's plays which we must accept as undeniably the only admissible rendering? In his more ambitious figures Shakspere is not satisfied to give us mere outlines, profiles, silhouettes, to be seen from one angle only; he bestows upon them the rotundity of real life; and we may dispute about them, as we dispute about the characters of our acquaintances and of prominent men in public life. No critic may feel entitled to assert that he has attained to a final decision as to exact character of Hamlet or Shylock or Jaques; and every one of us is justified in defending his own opinion as to these creatures of imagination all compact.

Certainly it was a Jaques very unlike White's that Daly showed us in his revival of 'As You Like It.' Daly held that Jaques was a humorist, recognized as such by all his comrades—a humorist

who affects to be a satirist and who is not to be taken too seriously.
And Jaques himself is quite conscious of this tolerant and amused
attitude of his fellows towards him and that they are always
expecting him to take antagonistic views and are always wondering what he is going to say next, ever ready for his exaggerated
outbreaks and ever ready to laugh with him, even if they are
also laughing at him. As Jaques is aware of their expectation, he
responds to it; he gives them what they are looking for; he
abounds in his own sense; he looses free rein to his wit and to his
whimsical fantasy, certain that his customary hearers will know
that there is no sting to his satire. Such men are not uncommon
nowadays in real life; and in the threatening monotony of our
modern existence they are eagerly welcomed and their over-
emphatic utterances are awaited with smiling expectancy.

It was thus that Daly conceived the character of Jaques and
that he arranged the way in which the other actors should receive the outpourings of the self-conscious humorist. When
Orlando breaks in upon the feast and demands food for Adam,
the Duke bids him go and fetch the faithful old servant. The
interval between Orlando's departure and his return with Adam
must be filled up so that the audience may not be forced to feel
that it has been kept waiting; and Shakspere drafts Jaques for
this service. After Orlando goes, the Duke remarks that

> We are not all alone unhappy.
> This wide and universal theater
> Presents more woful pageants than the scene
> Wherein we play in.

Here Jacques sees his opportunity and declares that

> All the world's a stage,
> And all the men and women merely players.

Then he pauses, to observe whether this meets with approval;
and the others smile back, as if to encourage him to proceed.
Thus heartened by their sympathetic attention he takes up his
parable and evolves the theory of the seven ages of man. He is
not reciting a set speech, prepared in advance; he is extemporiz-
ing, sometimes hesitating for the right word, and always acutely

sensitive to the effect he is producing upon his listeners. Thus delivered the speech is robbed of its bitterness and emptied of its cynicism. And as it falls from the lips of Jaques its hearers exchange glances in recognition of the fact that their humorous friend is in excellent vein, surpassing himself in whimsical exaggeration, even if he ends, as humorists are wont to do, upon a note of melancholy.

When the familiar words are spoken under these conditions they have a freshness which is totally absent if Jaques declaims them as part of a set speech. There is an adverse criticism of the actors concealed in the familiar story of the man about town who complained that 'Hamlet' was "a deuced odd play, you know, it's so full of quotations." In his illuminating address on the 'Illusion of the First Time in Acting,' Mr. William Gillette[1] has dwelt on the danger to which the drama is exposed whenever the actor carelessly reveals himself as knowing by heart the words which the character is supposed to be uttering without premeditation. There is always a temptation for the performer to see in the Seven Ages and the Quality of Mercy, in Hamlet's soliloquy and Mark Antony's appeal, an opportunity for an elocutionary exhibition, perhaps effective enough in itself, yet damaging to the total effect of the play. To turn every one of these speeches into a piece to be spoken may not be fairly described as a stage-tradition; yet the practice is far too prevalent in the acting of Shakspere to-day; and it is probably an inheritance from the past. There would be a stimulus to the adoption of a better method if the actor's edition of Shakspere should record the various devices by which this danger has been averted.

In this paper it has been possible to adduce only a few of the many instances where an unexpected illumination of Shakspere's text has been accomplished by inventive actors and by ingenious stage-managers, who have made explicit what they believed to be implicit in the dialog. Where they found only the seed itself, they have shown the expanding flower potentially contained within it. What they have done for Shakspere they have done for

---

[1] It may be noted that Mr. Gillette's address and the essays of Coquelin and Fleeming Jenkin, from which quotation has been made in this paper, are all reprinted in the Second Series of the Publication of the Dramatic Museum of Columbia University (1915).

Molière and for Sheridan; and this is one reason why the accredited classics of the drama are likely to seem to us, when we see them on the stage, ampler in detail and solider in texture than the plays of our own time, which have not yet been able to profit by the accretions of generation after generation of actors and stage-managers. And a warm welcome awaits the editor who shall employ the most significant of these stage-traditions to vivify the text of his edition of Shakspere.

II

SHAKSPERE IN THE SCHOOLS

By Franklin Thomas Baker
*Professor of the English Language and
Literature in Teachers College*

SHAKSPERE IN THE SCHOOLS

Those of us whose school days are three decades or more away remember that it was in the Fifth and Sixth Readers that we "found" Shakspere. Some of us may have found him in fragments in the 'Beauties of Shakspere,' compiled by the ill-fated Mr. Dodd. Some of us, given to the literary adventure of browsing, may have found him paraphrased but connected in Lamb's 'Tales,' and, if we were hardy pioneers, or suggestible to wise counsel, we may even have read him in some leather-bound edition of 'Shakspere's Complete Works.' If we had imagination, a reasonable amount of linguistic aptitude, and persistence, we may have read a number of the plays, stirred by the poetry and the declamation, sensing dimly the tragedy and the wisdom, though seldom the humor, and feeling that the experience was somehow vaguely doing us good. But this was what the pedagogues now call an "extra-school activity," seldom instigated by any hint given us in school. So far as the schools were concerned, the only literary diet furnished was the school readers; and for the compilers of these useful museums, Shakspere was only a quarry from which to gather specimens for reading aloud.

I have before me, as I write, Swan's 'District School Reader,' printed in Boston, 1846. Its preface, brief and definite, explains that the book is "designed for the highest classes in public and private schools." The reading lessons, "consisting of descriptive, narrative, dramatic and didactic pieces, contain just moral sentiments, and present such varieties of style as are necessary to teach good reading." The rhetoricians might quarrel with this classification, the educator might find the educational aim a little vague, but the moralist must approve the preference given to "just moral sentiments." Our ancestors had no false shame and no tactical reserves about the avowal of their interest in the moral improvement of the young.

The book contains 170 "Lessons," under each of which are given one or more "pieces" to read (aloud, of course); in all a collection of about 300 specimens devoted to clinical uses. The first 72 "Lessons" are, if the note at the head of each is to be trusted, mainly instruction in enunciation, rising by easy stages from drill in the so-called long *ā*, as in f*ā*te, h*ā*te, etc., to such ambitious feats as cu*rb*, cu*rb*'d, cu*rbd'st*, and on up to the heights of da*zzle*, da*zzl*'d, da*zzld'st*. After this conscientious pursuit of the technic of articulate utterance, comes a smaller group of lessons dealing with the grave and serious topic of "Pauses." The impetuous youth is told quite definitely when to "pause": "After the nominative when it consists of more than one word"; "before an adjective when it follows the noun." I feel a twinge of regret at having been born too late to hear this in practice. "Everything is educative," commented one of my colleagues, after hearing a particularly muddled and futile address. Inflection, Emphasis, Quantity, each has a brief quota of lessons devoted to it, and then, from Lesson 95 on, the youth is thrust forth into the open sea of the remaining lessons, with his previous instructions for chart and compass.

The choice of authors for the book is wide, not to say catholic. Among the 112 in the Table of Contents are Hannah More, Prentice, Akenside, Audubon, Congreve, Wordsworth, Milton.

And Shakspere? Yes; and properly enough his entrance is effectively staged, viz., at the apex of the articulatory efforts, Lesson 72, on da*zzled'st*, etc. Here, in company with Thomson, Cowper, Congreve, Campbell and Scott, Shakspere says (through what characters we are not told),

Now my co-mates and brothers in exile,

clear through to his discovery of "good in everything," and the four lines from 'Henry VI' beginning,

What stronger breastplate than a heart untainted

One can hear the younger readers, with who knows what forensic aspirations, looking well to the full values of the palatals and dentals and sibilants as they read

"Finds ton*gues* in trees, boo*ks* in runni*ng* broo*ks*,
Sermo*ns* in sto*nes* and good in everythi*ng*."

Lesson 85 does better: in appearance it is dramatic, not forensic. It contains the whole dialog in which Prince Arthur pleads with Rupert for his eyes.   Let us hope that the poignant suspense of the scene led the readers to forget the admonition at the beginning of the Lesson: "When two questions are connected by the disjunctive *or*, the first usually has the rising, and the second the falling, inflection."   Lesson 86 enjoins that "for the tone of mockery, sarcasm or irony, the circumflex or wave should be used."   Shakspere comes in here for two lines:

> *Queen:* Hamlet, you have your father much offended.
> *Hamlet:* Madame, yoû have my father much offended.

Did the readers wonder who the Queen and Hamlet were, or what they were talking about?   Did the teachers tell them? Lessons 113 to 116, again, are better; two of them, indeed, perilously theatrical.   First, we have the quarrel of Brutus and Cassius entire; then Antony's speech, with the irrelevant mob and the by-play, of course, omitted:—so fine a speech should not be interrupted, except by the conventional "applause and cheers."   Then come Cassius's tempting of Brutus, and Othello's defence before the potent, grave and reverend seigniors of Venice.   Finally, Lesson 137 gives the dialog between Wolsey and Cromwell, containing, as we see, many of the "just moral sentiments" promised in the Preface.

Not one of these extracts is explained by information or comment.   Even the poor satisfaction of knowing the name of the play is disallowed.   The motives and identity of the speakers, the circumstances and significance of the action, remain dark things. The selections are fragments, poetic and declamatory, conveying little hint of their significance as a part of some organized whole; and, we can safely infer, not provocative of interest in the dangerous allurements of the stage.   Indeed, we were not then a theater-going people.   Our instinct for public expression was satisfied mostly by the sermon and the speech.   So it is mainly for forensic ends that there were chosen such Shakspere and other literature as found a place in these old school readers.

Another popular 'Reader,' Sargent's, ten years later, carries these same interests to quite incredible details.   It contains an introduction of 54 pages in small print devoted to the minutiæ of the technic of reading aloud. The literary selections of the book are divided into three classes, "prose, poetry and dialogue," and Shakspere does, at least, get included in this last class. But there is the same indifference to the part of the "dialogues" in working out any unified story. For example, the reader comes upon Adam and Orlando talking. They seem about to take a trip somewhere; where and why the reader is left to glean as he may, nor is he told the name of the play. But he was, let us hope, properly edified by Adam's youthful prudence in not applying hot and rebellious liquors to his blood; for at this date the temperance movement was well under way.

These two samples of the place of Shakspere in schools two generations ago are quite representative, as further examination of the text-books shows. People still believed in the virtue of oratory, still regarded it as an avenue to prominence in public life. They gave little thought to the possibility of achieving an education, either in school or college, through the study of English literature, although cultivated men and women were reading the poets, essayists and novelists of England and America, old and recent. Few of them were theater-goers; we were not yet an urban population—and the stage was looked upon by many intelligent and fairly educated people with grave disapproval. So, with the tradition still unchallenged that Shakspere is the greatest of English poets, he had to be included in the school readers, but represented mainly by the declamatory passages suited to reading aloud and public "recitation." As a playwright he could have no place in the educational scheme.

The second phase of the study of Shakspere in the schools is quite a different thing. It dates back only about thirty years. It is best represented in the school editions of Hudson and Rolfe, if indeed these two editions are not mainly responsible for the movement. Certainly their texts were widely used. Shakspere now appears as a writer of plays, complete units, stories in dramatic form with beginning, middle and end. Striking speeches and spirited dialog are not detached declamatory efforts, but significant parts, high lights, in the scenes that make up the action. The story is mainly a means for the development of character.

The portrayal of character, in contrasts, in its relation to motive and action, in its psychologic insight, is more interesting than the dramatic clash or the spectacular scene. Hamlet is a study in psychology, and the question as to his madness a by-product of this interest. The mind of Brutus is contrasted with those of Cassius and Antony. The harangues of these two are studied for their intellectual bent and rhetorical skill.

But even more important than the psychological interest is the ethical. It was the age, be it remembered, when we were reading George Eliot. Problems such as Hamlet's responsibility to avenge, Macbeth's degree of guilt prior to the opening of the play, and Lady Macbeth's culpability, occupied much time. Was Macbeth a study of a good man led astray by a combination of good fortune, general approbation, malignant witches and a wicked wife? What did the witches symbolize: Macbeth's evil desire objectified, or real maleficent forces of evil such as do exist to the danger of one's soul? Was Brutus to blame, morally, for entering the conspiracy? And is the tragic end of him and his cause a sanction of the law against murder? What was the tragic fault of Othello? Was it credulity or irascibility? or was he punished for a runaway match? And what was Desdemona's guilt? Weakness, or timorous fibbing? And Cordelia? Was she not too proud, too unyielding? Was not her punishment too great? Once in this field of speculation, there was literally no end— and no route. One might wander anywhere, giving himself to any sort of "random provocations" that his ethical bias suggested. In this view Shakspere's plays become a sort of literary "moral science," his characters *exempla*, his stories parables, himself a philosopher and omniscient. I do not exaggerate. I have heard such teaching of Shakspere both in schools and colleges.

This interpretative and speculative study goes back for its origins to various sources: to Coleridge, to Dowden, to Schlegel and Gervinus and numerous other German critics. It flowered in the sentimental inventions of Mrs. Jameson. It attains its maddest pinnacle, perhaps, in the three volumes of comment by Denton J. Snider, an ardent Hegelian of the St. Louis (Missouri) school. For him, Shakspere is a moral and philosophical writer, whose function was to illustrate the Hegelian categories of family, state, etc. In his view, Beatrice is "an unlovely, sarcastic female, who rails at marriage." This kind of study fitted in well with the tendency to be ethically-minded in the presence of literature, and with that heavy seriousness of the school-teacher which has made compulsory education seem to many spirited children a species of premeditated and tyrannous insult. Moreover, it was fatally easy. It required no scholarship; merely a sort of facility in debate and a proclivity to sermonizing. Its elements were only the commonplace ethical experience of daily life.

I should misrepresent the two well-known editors cited above, if I did not add that their editions contained, besides the citations of moral reflections from the critics, a good deal of valuable apparatus. They included notes on the dates of the plays, information as to the various texts, explanations of words and phrases new to the readers, passages from the sources, sure or probable, that Shakspere had used, illustrations (in Rolfe) of Tudor architecture, theatrical and general, and occasionally some great actor's conception of one of the *dramatis personæ*. In fact, considering the interests of contemporary scholarship, they were good editions. I am speaking of what the schools did with Shakspere, and how they used their material, rather than recounting what material they had at hand.

A little later, but still in the same period, arose an interest in the study of the technic of the drama. Some one discovered Freytag. Many teachers fell upon it rapturously, albeit as funeral baked meats; for few of them read the original. But here was something definite, having a fine flavor of analytic scholarship, an opportunity in dialectics, and, like the ethical study, not entailing the burden of scholarship. It became a game to discover where the *crisis* of the hero's fortunes occurred. Was it where Desdemona dropped the handkerchief, or where Emilia picked it up, or where Iago got it from her, or somewhere else? It was thrilling to be able to fix the crisis of 'Julius Caesar' in the middle of the play, almost exactly so by count of lines. It was an exhilarating exercise of ingenuity to fit into the mosaic of a perfect technic such passages as those of the drunken sailors in the 'Tempest,' Hamlet's long interview with the players, the long, resounding declamation of rulers and soldiers (people with the insidious habit of being listened to) and all the rich prolixity of which the Elizabethan dramatists and their audiences seem to have been so fond. Shakspere ever garrulous? Heresy and irreverence. His technic must be proved compact, necessary, perfect; clean, concise, rightly-directed as the cuts of a surgeon's knife. School editions appeared with questions, scores and hundreds of questions, whose answer should explain and justify every turn of the action and even the finer shades of diction: Shakspere was cross-examined by schoolboys through editors on aspects of the dramatist's craft that never entered his mind. Puzzling, indefinite, too, were many of the questions; a favorite one was, "What is the effect of this word (or action)?" A question answerable only by those who knew in advance the particular esthetic or philosophic squint of the questioner. Of course, this study was not all foolish, though a good deal of it was inevitably so. It often led the pupils to see the relations of the parts, the fitness between character and action, the leading up to a fine dramatic effect, and the essential human interest in a scene or play.

At the same time, a good deal of attention was paid to the poetry. The melody of the verse, the beauty and fitness of the imagery, and the suggestiveness of the words were noted. Pupils were encouraged to commit fine passages to memory; and were even shown the recurrence of certain well-known expressions in other literature and in common speech. This was also the period of the development of philological study in the colleges. It was likely to be impressed upon college students that the diction of Shakspere had to be learned thoroughly, perhaps etymologically also. A certain amount of this teaching inevitably filtered into the high schools through the recent college graduates who taught in them. Such exhaustive study of the diction seldom lasted long enough to do much harm; seldom, I fear, long enough to make the high school pupils read their texts with full understanding. For against the impact of too much exact information, most boys and girls are well armored. They can defeat and discourage the most pertinacious pedantry.

On the whole, this second period, though misguided as to some important things, and for the most part missing the essentials, was more good than bad. It did make pupils think, did impress them with respect for the greatness of Shakspere, did leave with them some appreciation of his qualities as a poet.

The schools have recently, within a decade or two, entered upon a new kind of Shaksperian study—the dramaturgic; not, of course, the tracing of Shakspere's development in dramaturgic skill, not studying the development of the drama from its earlier forms up to his time; but the study of his plays as dramas, written to be acted. This interest is directly traceable to three sources: the advanced studies from this point of view made by university professors of English, the interest in various forms of dramatic activity in the schools, both for instruction and recreation, and the large increase in popular knowledge of the theater.

A growing number of the teachers in high schools have not only a college course but at least a year of graduate study. Several states now require the A.M. degree in their appointees. A considerable number of the younger among these teachers have taken graduate courses in dramatic literature where the plays were studied from the dramaturgic point of view, and not merely as to their sources, their parallels and their diction. Naturally, these students tend to present Shakspere as they have come to see him.

The reaction in the schools in favor of reality and against meaningless word-mongering has led, also, to a wide use of dramatic action. In the lower grades simple stories are dramatized in the reading lessons; little plays, sometimes made up by the children, are given; folk-dances and festivals involving dramatic elements are widely popular; and in the high schools there are more ambitious efforts, including the presentation of whole comedies and even complete Shaksperian dramas. In a visit to one famous school I saw two groups of boys spiritedly rehearsing, one group the "rude mechanicals" play in 'A Midsummer Night's Dream,' and another (in Latin) the 'Captives' of Plautus. Many of the better schools have had in recent years, as their main Commencement exercise, a complete out-of-door performance of some Shaksperian play. Their programs have included 'Julius Caesar,' 'Coriolanus,' 'A Midsummer Night's Dream,' 'The Merchant' and others. A number of the larger towns in the

west have come to regard such exercises as a legitimate and
regular part of the high school work; and one at least of these
towns has built a municipal theater largely under the inspiration
and for the occasional accommodation of the high school plays.
So frequent, indeed, are these high school presentations of
Shakspere, that they are assuming the status of an institution.

The relation of all this to our increasing interest in the theater
is obvious. The old prejudice against theater-going is as dead as
the condemnation of novel-reading. What part the moving-
pictures may have had in furthering this general interest in dramatic things, or how far they may now be getting in the way of
the spoken drama, I do not know. But I am sure that they have
helped to dispel any lingering prejudice against entertainments
whose purpose is to tell a story through action. A potent influence in arousing an influence in the drama among the schools
has been the open air performances and the "historic" presentations of Shakspere—that purport to be like the original. Here
was something to catch the "school man." It had a fine scholarly
sound: it would make flexible a conscience that was too stiff towards pleasure in school. So, also, the pageants in celebration of
local history or great historic anniversaries showed how to combine the pleasures of mimicry and pageantry with instruction.

All this has, of course, affected the treatment of Shakspere in
the school-room. Even if the teachers were unchanged, the pupils
would be a little more likely to think of a play as possessing dramatic possibilities.

It is noticeable, particularly on the eve of the tercentenary of
Shakspere, that the interest in the historical background has much
increased. A high school class is not so likely now to be left with
certain generalizations about the glories of the Renascence, the
revival of learning, the development of nationalism in England.
They will probably consider, instead, such matters as the housing,
clothing, work and recreations of the Elizabethan people; the
construction of the theaters, the size, shape and lighting of the
stage, the character, arrangement and behavior of the audiences,
the kinds of plays that were in favor, the significance of allusions
that Shakspere makes to contemporary interests and follies, the
attitude of the Puritans towards the theaters and the restrictions

put upon the actors. In this historical study they will have the help of pictures, and, it is to be hoped, an attractive collection of the books that bring Tudor England before our eyes. They will be told that one must know the meaning of the words to understand the plays, as Shakspere's audiences did, and that this is a matter of no great difficulty if they will use the glossary with their texts. They will discuss motives, situations, suspenses, climaxes, "tragic coils," complication and unraveling of plots, indications of character, with reference to the dramatic interest. They will read aloud a good deal, not as actors but as persons who understand what are the ideas and the emotions an actor would convey. Instead of studying minutely only two or three plays—and these required for college entrance—many schools now read eight or ten.

Of course, I am sketching the aims of the present teaching of Shakspere, not listing its accomplishments. We fall short of our attainments, as we always must when our ideals are high enough.

What are the schools really accomplishing? They don't know exactly; they never do know just how effective their work is in any field; probably they never can. They must rest their self-approbation on a mixture of evidence, conjecture and faith. Certainly pupils won't forget quite all that they have learned—at least, not all of them will. Probably we are right in believing that contact with great poetry and great drama has a civilizing effect; some highly civilized peoples have thought so. The boys of one school who gave a Shaksperian play used to be heard chaffing each other on the athletic field in phrases taken from the play; they were at least increasing their linguistic resources. I am inclined to think the new emphasis upon the historical setting of the plays particularly valuable. We Americans are charged with having too much *contemporaneity*, of living too exclusively in the present. The charge is true; that it is more true of us than of other peoples I am not sure. But I am sure of the principle behind this criticism. A mental outfit that lacks all historic background is thin, flat; its owner accepts his "values" uncritically because he lacks the means of comparison.

Still, uncertainty dogs us. Do we really know what our pupils are getting from their study of Shakspere? Tens of thousands of them, in the past ten years, have read carefully at least the 'Merchant of Venice,' 'Julius Caesar' and 'Macbeth.' These are great touchstones, both as literature and as drama. Has this study made firm a body of good taste large enough to improve the popular reading and to elevate the popular drama? Has it inspired in many the wish to read other plays of Shakspere? I fear the librarians and the dramatic critics would not be enthusiastic in their answers. It is not well to expect too much. Many of these pupils have never seen a Shaksperian play ably presented. Many readers can not, even by earnest effort, construct a full scene in their imaginations. The book and the play that make no tax on the faculties are the line of least resistance that most of us always choose for our recreation, and that all of us sometimes choose. None the less, we shall, I hope, continue to teach Shakspere in the schools for the sake of those who do understand and enjoy. They are, after all, the people most worth our efforts.

III

SOME TEXTUAL NOTES ON 'PERICLES'

By William Peterfield Trent
Professor of English Literature

SOME TEXTUAL NOTES ON 'PERICLES'

The notes that follow are in most cases based on material supplied by me some years since to the 'New Grant White Shakspere.' This material is here utilized with the kind permission of Messrs. Little, Brown & Co., the publishers of the edition just named, and to them I return hearty thanks. Perhaps I ought also to thank my colleague-editors for giving me permission to treat 'Pericles' as in sufficient measure for their purposes a Shaksperian production, without laying on me the obligation of discussing questions of authorship and of determining with mathematical precision those portions of the play for which, in view of the well nigh universal assumption that our chief dramatist could never have written less than superlatively well, he cannot possibly be held responsible. No other preliminary statement seems to be called for, unless it be advisable to say what any one who may examine these comments could gather for himself, to wit, that my bias is toward accepting with as little change as possible the text of what seems to be the first issue of the play, that quarto of the two Henry Gosson printed in 1609, which gives the first stage-direction in a correct form.

I. Pro. 17.
> This Antioch, then, Antiochus the Great.[1]

Q₂ has the comma after *then;* Q₁ has no punctuation. A semicolon seems preferable, as in *Henry Irving.*

I. Pro. 29-30.
> But custom what they did begin
> Was with long use account no sin.

The recent tendency to discard Malone's *By custom* seems justified, but one queries whether, if *But custom* be retained, the

---

[1] The numbering and the text of the line or lines at the head of each note are those of the *Globe* (1893). I have used facsimiles of Q₁Q₂ and F₃, Vol. IX of *Cambridge* (1893) and numerous other helps.

comma of Q_1, Q_2, F_3 after *begin* is not really necessary, the construction being equivalent to "But what they did begin (with shame and hesitation) having become a matter of custom." This construction leads to the further query whether we should not read

> 'Twas with long use account no sin.

The comma after *custom* of F_3 and the *account'd* of $Q_1 Q_2$, and *counted* of F_3, as well as the early comma after *use*, scarcely commend themselves—at least on poetical grounds. But what has the Gower of this play to do with these?

I. i. 8-11.

> At whose conception, till Lucina reign'd,
> Nature this dowry gave, to glad her presence,
> The senate-house of planets all did sit,
> To knit in her their best perfections.

The semicolon after *gave* in $Q_1 Q_2$ seems to have been too rashly discarded. Deighton, though he gives the line in its usual form, suggests that it should stand *Nature rich dowry gave; to glad her presence*, and furnishes a good paraphrase—"at her *conception*, and while she was yet in the womb, Nature endowed her richly; at her *birth*, to give comeliness to her appearance on life's stage, the planets in council combined to invest her with every perfection." There seems to be no necessity to read *rich*, since *this* glances back to ll. 6-7,

> Bring in our daughter, clothed like a bride,
> For the embracements even of Jove himself,

and hence involves the idea of a rich dowry. *Ere* for *till* in l. 8 would seem an improvement, but is no more necessary than in Milton's "wait and think long till they devour thy tender flock."

I. 1.33.

> all thy whole heap must die.

Thy for *the* of $Q_1 Q_2 F_3$ is a distinct improvement from the point of view of the sophisticated reader, but one queries whether it is a necessary change. The *thine eye* of l. 32, makes *the whole heap* mean almost certainly *the whole body of thee*.

I. i. 47-49.

> I'll make my will then, and, as sick men do
> Who know the world, see heaven, but, feeling woe,
> Gripe not at earthly joys as erst they did;

The text of the old copies and the paraphrases and emendations suggested do not seem to help us greatly over the difficulties of this vexed passage. The paraphrase of Malone, "I will act as sick men do; who having had experience of the pleasures of the world, and only a visionary and distant prospect of heaven, *have neglected the latter for the former;* but *at length* feeling themselves decaying, grasp no longer at temporal pleasures, but prepare calmly for futurity," if it represents the thoughts in the dramatist's mind, certainly brings a grave impeachment against his powers of expression, or else gives us reason to admire his extraordinary capacity for succinctness, not to say obscurity. Deighton's proposal of *their* for *see* is much simpler, but leaves the syntax somewhat to seek. The crux of the passage appears to be *but*, for which *by* has been proposed. (Delius, *apud Cambridge.*) Perhaps we come near *a* meaning—not *the* meaning probably—if we substitute *and* for *but* and paraphrase—"and as sick men, who have had experience of the world, do get a glimpse of heaven in their illness, and, feeling woe, gripe not at earthly joys as they once did." Connecting *do* and *see* in this manner is a bit drastic, but surely the passage, from one point of view at least, deserves to have violent hands laid upon it.

I. iii. 26-30.

> Well, I perceive
> I shall not be hang'd now, although I would;
> But since he's gone, the King's seas must please:
> He 'scaped the land, to perish at the sea.
> I'll present myself. Peace to the lords of Tyre!

This is substantially the reading of the old copies, but some editors read *ears it* for *seas*. Q₁Q₂ F₃ print the entire scene as prose, and, while some portions were undoubtedly intended to be blank verse, it is by no means certain that the passage in question may not represent an original speech in prose like Thaliard's opening speech. This would make somewhat more plausible the early suggestion that some words dropped out after *please*. The cadence of *Well—would* suggests prose; that of *He 'scaped——sea* suggests verse. It is by no means clear that here, as in several other passages in this play, we gain much by converting the prose of the quartos into verse, or that in this passage, save in punctuation, the quartos need any emendation. Thaliard might have spoken of the *King's seas* in acknowledgment of Antiochus' great power. It may be added that, if the *hee scap'te* of Q₁ stood for an original *he's scap'd*, the chances that we have a prose cadence in this portion also of the speech are increased. Herford prints the speech as prose.

I. iv. 92-95.

> And these our ships, you happily may think
> Are like the Trojan horse was stuff'd within
> With bloody veins, expecting overthrow,
> Are stored with corn to make your needy bread.

The crux of this passage is *veins*, for which various suggestions have been made, some of them involving a change in *expecting*. For example, Deighton suggests *arms importing*. The passage from Wilkins' novel on which he relies can scarcely be said to lend him much support; but he does show that the misprint of *veins* for *arms* probably occurred in Shirley's 'Love Tricks.' Rolfe (1883), though not bent on adding to the gaiety of his brother editors, printed Collier's *banes* as *bones*, and thought that *expecting overthrow* referred to *you*. Deighton regards this as impossible. It is extremely awkward rather than impossible, and one fails to perceive the necessity of going back so far. The soldiers inside the Trojan horse expected the overthrow of Troy; hence the phrase may be construed with *veins*. And, although *veins* is certainly unusual and suspicious, the horse was undoubtedly stuffed with soldiers bent on *bloody* deeds, and their *veins* were throbbing with *expectation* of the city's *overthrow*. If the poet meant to get all this into a single line, we may well chide him for excessive condensation of his style, but it would seem a bit hazardous to alter the verse by accepting any suggestion made thus far.

II. Pro. 5.

> Be quiet then as men should be,

The comma of Q_1Q_2 F_3 after *then* might well be restored.

II. Pro. 7-8.

> I'll show you those in troubles reign,
> Losing a mite, a mountain gain.

Deighton prints *trouble's* and removes the comma after *reign*. As the lines stand, *those* means *those who*. With Deighton's reading this does not seem to be the case, but we must understand *that* after *you*. Perhaps even if we insert the apostrophe in *troubles* we shall do well still to retain the comma of F_3 after *reign*.

II. Pro. 39-40.

> What shall be next,
> Pardon old Gower,—this longs the text.

The comma after *next* has the support of Q_1Q_2 F_3, but one is tempted to make the dull prolog a little more lively by reading *What shall be next?* The substitution of *that* for *this*, though plausible, is unnecessary. The reading of F_3, *thus long's the Text* is plainly too sophisticated.

II. i. 12.

> What, ho, Pilch!

The early copies have *What, to pelch?* May not the Ms. have read *What's to, Pilch?* i. e., "What's toward?" "What's doing?"

II. i. 56-59.

> Peace be at your labour, honest fishermen.
> *2. Fish.* Honest! good fellow, what's that? If it be a
> day fits you, search out of the calendar, and nobody look after it.

This passage still defies the editors, and justifies the view that all emendation of a prose speech in which a lower-class character indulges his wit is likely to be a losing game for scholars. It is generally held that a line or words containing *day* or *good day*, must have dropped out at the end of Pericles' speech. This is not necessarily so, since the Fisherman, after catching up the word *honest*—with what mental reaction it is hard to say—may, in quite a number of ways, have passed on to thought of the stormy day. "It is not a day for high-flown talk," he may have murmured to himself—not in my academic phraseology—and

then he may have adjured Pericles, on the one hand, to abstract
the day from the calendar, and his companions, on the other,
to omit any inquiry for it.   That *search* is suspicious seems
obvious, but we scarcely need substitute *scratch it* or *steal't*, although the insertion of *it* appears to be plausible.   Deighton's
placing *Hoydey!* before *Peace* in Pericles' address to the fishermen
and his defense of his proposal command some approbation, but
on the whole it seems best to let the passage stand, and to give it
whatever cramped exegesis one can.   The *and* near the close
may, as Deighton suggests, mean *if*.

II.   ii. 14-15.

> 'Tis now your honour, daughter, to explain
> The labour of each knight in his device.

For *to explain* Q_1Q_2 read *to entertaine* and F_3 *to entertain*, the
latter reading being sometimes retained, e. g., by Deighton,
who understands it to mean to "give reception to as they present
themselves."   We need not follow him in his argument that
Thaisa neither *explains* nor *interprets*—cf.   Rolfe and Neilson;
nor need we lay stress on the confirmation he gets for his view
from the old novel.   We may, however, believe that he has given
the real sense of the passage, and may even wonder whether the
original Ms. reading was not *to entrain*, i. e. to put into a train
or sequence, or to bring on as a consequence.   The rarity of the
word—cf. N.E.D.—makes this suggestion almost negligible.

II.   iii. 24-26.

> Contend not, sir; for we are gentlemen
> That neither in our hearts nor outward eyes
> Envy the great nor do the low despise.

This is substantially the reading of F_3.   The reading of Q_1Q_2

> Contend not sir, for we are Gentlemen,
> Haue neither in our hearts, nor outward eyes,
> Enuies the great, nor shall the low despise

suggests that the changes introduced since the early quartos have
been too radical.   The mere substitution of *d* for *s* gives us

> Contend not, sir, for we are gentlemen,
> Have neither in our hearts, nor outward eyes
> Envied the great, nor shall the low despise.

The change to the future seems to make the address to Pericles more dramatically effective.

II. iii. 27-29.

> *Sim.* Sit, sir, sit.
> *Per.* By Jove, I wonder that is king of thoughts,
> These cates resist me, she but thought upon.

The transfer of the lines *By Jove—upon* from Simonides to Pericles and the change of *hee not* Q₁ (*he not* Q₂ F₃) to *she but* seem unnecessary in the light of the old novel; but it appears advisable to accept, with Hudson and Deighton, the change of *he not* to *he but*. It is hardly likely that the dramatist meant to make the much impressed monarch wonder that he could not eat, when he was not thinking of Pericles. The emendation was suggested by Dyce and warmly approved by Elze.

II. iv. 41.

> For honour's cause, forbear your suffrages.

The substitution of *For* and a comma after *cause* for the *Try* and the semicolon of Q₁Q₂F₃ seems scarcely warranted. Helicanus might well have meant to tell the Lords that they ought to endeavor to continue to support honour's cause, or loyalty's, by forbearing for a twelvemonth to give their suffrages to him as their sovereign in place of Pericles. There seems to be no necessity for accepting Steevens' conjecture, *Try honour's course*, or for agreeing with Dyce that the original reading is "nonsense."

III. i. 61.

> Must cast thee, scarcely coffin'd, in the ooze;

Q₁ reads:

> Must cast thee scarcly Coffind, in oare,

and this with the change to *scarcely* is also the reading of Q₂ F₃. The reading *in the ooze*—Malone (Steevens)—is generally accepted, but despite the usual reference to *Tempest* III. iii. 100, it scarcely harmonizes with the picture of the body *Lying with simple shells* (l.65) and one wonders whether the dramatist did not write

> Must cast thee, scarcely coffin'd in, o'erboard.

The dropping of *board* either in the Ms. from which the play was first printed, or by the printer, seems a more likely phenomenon than the substitution of *oare* for *ooze* and the dropping of *the*. The position of the comma before rather than after *in* and the *Where* of line 62 make slightly in favor of Steevens' reading, but only slightly, especially if we close the line with a dash instead of the original comma. It may be remarked that Rolfe's note (1883) on l.64 of this passage

> And humming water must o'erwhelm thy corpse,

with its reference to 'Lycidas', 157, may puzzle readers until they track him to a quotation from Dowden's 'Primer,' which in turn shows that, while the latter scholar had in mind the original form of Milton's line, he did not quite accurately reproduce the line from 'Pericles'. Query—What relation to our own lapses is borne by our insistence upon the lapses of others from accuracy?

III. i. 71-2.

> Sir, we have a chest beneath the hatches, caulked and bitumed ready.

Why not, as in the old copies, print as verse, adding accents of our own?

> Sir, we have a chest beneath the hatches,
> Caulked and bitúmèd, ready.

It may not look so well, but does it not sound better, and is not the rough meter of the lines of Q₁ often more agreeable than the smooth blank-verse the editors contrive to get from the original by adding and dropping words and by a rearrangement of the lines? The appearance of *bitumed* in III. ii. 56 need cause no worry save to those who want to insist on a perfect iambic movement in dramatic verse, and as $Q_1 Q_2$ have *bottomed* and F₃ *bottom'd*, it is by no means certain that we ought to read *bitumed* in the later passage, although that reading seems to have the support of the old novel.

III. ii. 21-22.

> But I much marvel that your lordship, having
> Rich tire about you.

Some take *tire* as furniture, others, as clothes—the latter meaning being supported by the reading of F₃ *rich attire*.   The passage may be merely an expression of surprise that so rich a man as Cerimon is not a sluggard, or it may refer to clothes of a quality which were not usually worn so early in the day.   If the latter be the meaning, the expression is scarcely happy. Possibly the sense of furniture, belongings, may be defended with the explanation that such paraphernalia would deaden the discomfort produced by the storm, and give Cerimon some chance to repose.   In this connection, Steevens' conjecture *Such towers* seems scarcely so wretched as some have thought it.   If there be corruption, which is by no means certain, may we not read *Such tire*, making the phrase equivalent to "working clothes" and connecting it with *pain?*

III.   ii. 77.

That even cracks for woe!

Even has the support of some of the early copies, but why is the *euer* of Q₁ Q₂ Q₃ discarded?   It seems to be the livelier reading.

III.   ii. 90.

The viol once more.

Q₁ Q₂ have *Violl;* F₃ *Viall,* and modern editors are divided as to the proper reading.   Both *vial* and *viol* may be well defended, and no scholar should forego the acquaintance of another because of the stand taken by the latter in the controversy.   If we accept *viol,* we seem to have three orders for music within four lines— apparently a superfluity.   The medicinal restoratives ought to have a chance, even at the expense of Q₁ Q₂.

III.   ii. 93-94.

Nature awakes; a warmth
Breathes out of her.

Q₁ reads

Nature awakes a warmth breath out of her.

Q₂ and F₃ read

Nature awakes a warme breath out of her.

Here it is a pleasure partly to follow and partly to alter the reading of the oldest text, for the reading of the corrected (?) Q₂ and

F₃ is flatly prosaic, and the reading of the modern texts gives us poetry.

III.   iii. 6-7.
> Your shafts of fortune, though they hurt you mortally,
> Yet glance full wanderingly on us.

For *shafts* Q₁ Q₂ F₃ read *shakes;* for *hurt* Q₁ reads *hant,* Q₂ *haunt,* F₃ *hate;* for *wanderingly* all three have *wondringly.* To-day *shafts* and *hurt* are almost universally accepted, and *wanderingly* (or *wand'ringly*) finds nearly as much favor. Deighton, however, accepts Schmidt's plausible *woundingly.* Query—*sund'ringly,* since the meaning seems to be that the shafts sunder the friends. If by any chance the passage was read aloud to the compositor, the change to *wondringly* would be very natural. The use of *though* and *yet* appears to help Schmidt's conjecture, if we read *hurt.* But if Steevens' withdrawn suggestion *hunt* (cf. *hant*) be revived, and *mortally* be construed as equivalent to "with deadly aim," the case for *wand'ringly* or *sund'ringly* is not seriously affected by the conjunctions. The idea in Cleon's mind might well be that, although Pericles was the chief stag aimed at by the hunter, Fortune, nevertheless the glancing shafts sundered the herd.

III.   iii. 12-17.
> My gentle babe Marina, whom,
> For she was born at sea, I have named so, here
> I charge your charity withal, leaving her
> The infant of your care; beseeching you
> To give her princely training, that she may be
> Manner'd as she is born.

Q₁ reads

> My gentle babe *Marina,*
> Whom, for she was borne at sea, I have named so,
> Here I charge your charitie withall; leauing her
> The infant of your care, beseeching you to giue her
> Princely training, that she may be manere'd as she is borne.

Q₂ has the slight change *maner'd;* the changes of F₃ need not occupy us. Would it not be better, going back to verse 7 and making that end with *on us,* to let our lines end at *queen! hither, obey, roar, end* and then to read

> My gentle babe Marina,
> Whom, for she was born at sea—I have named so,
> I charge your charity withal—here leaving her
> The infant of your care; beseeching you
> To give her princely training, that she may be
> Manner'd as she is born.

In the old copies *Here* begins the verse. For a printer to have caught the word with his eye from the beginning of the new clause, and to have carried it to the front of the line is a phenomenon that need excite no wonder. The reading here suggested allows the line *Whom—so* to stand, save for punctuation and spelling, precisely as it does in Q_1.

IV. i. 53.

> My father, as nurse said, did never fear.

For *said* Q_1Q_2 have *ses* and F_3 *saith*, the latter reading being adopted by some editors. As the *nurse* is dead, *said* is literally correct, but the present tense seems more vivid, Marina representing to herself for the moment her faithful old servant as still alive. But why, if we use the present, change *says* to *saith*, since the emendations of the later quartos and the folios are not infallible, and frequently leave something to be desired, e.g., l.20, *like a lasting storm*, where *like* comes from Q_4 Q_5 Q_6 F_3 F_4, Q_1 Q_2 Q_3 reading *a lasting storme*. Some readers might well prefer *as*, the conjecture of the editors of the *Cambridge*, and suggested by my own ear independently.

IV. i. 77-80

> Believe me, la,
> I never kill'd a mouse, nor hurt a fly:
> I trod upon a worm against my will,
> But I wept for it.

Aye, trod (Nicholson) and *Nor trod* (Daniel) are both ingenious conjectures, which commend themselves to some editors. But Marina might very well not have *killed a mouse;* she might never consciously have *hurt a fly;* and she might once have *trod upon a worm* and *wept* for that single involuntary action. One feels, indeed, that Deighton is justified in believing that *But I wept for it* applies to all three actions; it certainly would be made so to apply by any sophisticated writer. But, although the emendations are surely plausible, they seem to be unnecessary.

IV. iv. 19-20.

> So with his steerage shall your thoughts grow on,—
> To fetch his daughter home, who first is gone.

All the early copies read *grone* for *grown on.* Malone's withdrawn conjecture *go on,* although it has been generally neglected, and is incompatible in more ways than one with *gone,* seems to have at least the merit of being what Gower would naturally say. *Grow on* is very suspicious, and one wonders whether the writer, halting meter and infelicity of imagination and phrasing notwithstanding, did not actually intend to say what the old copies make him say—to wit, in modern spelling, *groan,* i.e., labor with such eagerness as to make you groan.

IV. vi. 144-145.

> She makes our profession as it were to stink afore the face of the gods.

All the early copies read *He* for *She.* At first blush the emendation (Rowe) seems a certain one, but it is at least possible that Boult is referring to Lysimachus, having in mind the latter's rough speech beginning *Avaunt, thou damned door-keeper!* The Bawd, not having heard this speech, would naturally continue to denounce Marina.

V. i. 47.

> And make a battery through his deafen'd parts.

Q_1 reads *defend parts,* Q_2 F_3 *defended parts.* Deighton silently reads *deafen'd ports,* possibly a misprint, but a happy one, since *deafen'd parts,* which most editors accept, is, to say the least, not highly poetical. "Ports of hearing" for "ears" is a sufficiently appropriate phrase to warrant, perhaps, the adoption of Steevens' conjecture, *ports.* The *defended* of the early copies after Q_1 is not attractive, but if we retain the *parts* of all the early copies save Q_5 (*part*), why should we not follow Q_1 and read *And make a battery through his défend parts?* This would give us a verse of definite poetical quality.

V. i. 206-210.

> I am Pericles of Tyre: but tell me now
> My drown'd queen's name, as in the rest you said
> Thou hast been godlike perfect,
> The heir of kingdoms and another like
> To Pericles thy father.

Probably the enumeration by *Cambridge* (Note XIX) of the attempts to improve the readings of the early editions ought to check further suggestions. Still it may be remarked that, as Sir Philip Perring seems—practically—to have contended, the passage may stand almost as in Q_1—a little more nearly as in Q_2—and still yield a clear, not unacceptable meaning. Let us read

> I am Pericles of Tyre, but tell me now
> My drown'd queen's name, as in the rest you said.
> Thou hast been godlike perfect, the heir of Kingdoms.
> And another like to Pericles thy father.

The transfer of *my* from the end of the first verse to the beginning of the second needs no defence. The full stop instead of the comma which Q_1 Q_2 F_3 put after *said* seems warranted by the change from *you* to *Thou*, and by the more apostrophic character of the two last lines, the two first, with such a phrase as *tell me now* being more familiar and persuasive. *Thou hast been godlike perfect* may still refer to Marina's remarkable success in making her narrative fit the facts of Pericles' own life, or it may be a less definite encomium. The remaining words really sum up what Marina has said of herself. She has declared herself the daughter of *King Pericles*, and therefore the *heir of Kingdoms*, and she has endured griefs equal to those of Pericles himself.

IV

THE "RESTORATION" OF SHAKSPERE'S PERSONALITY

By William Tenney Brewster

Professor of English and Provost of Barnard College

THE "RESTORATION" OF SHAKSPERE'S PERSONALITY

I

Presumably no one puts down a play of Shakspere's—or any other book for that matter—without some sense of a personality behind the work. The natural exclamation "What rubbish!" that accompanies a perusal of many "best sellers," transfers itself, with variations, to the mind and personality of the author, and the case is dismissed—even if it gets so far as formal sentence. But with Shakspere, evidently, the matter is different; he can not be treated so curtly. He is a supreme writer, and his may easily have been one of the supreme personalities of the world. But of that actual personality we know almost nothing. He has not personality in the sense that Dr. Johnson had it and the Kaiser has it. Now it is Shakspere's quality not to let you cast aside what he has had to say with indifference. Thus, despite the alleged "impersonal" attitude of the dramatist, and our lack of real knowledge, conceptions of his personality spring up in every mind and find expression in varied ways.

It is the more so with Shakspere for the reason that such actual record as we have of his life is not a particularly interesting one. He is presumably a supremely interesting man, but the interest is not palpable; we have to supply it, to transfer it from his works to himself. The record is too scanty to be very engaging: a possible deer-stealing episode, a premature marriage, the shadow of adventures in London, a mysterious "dark lady," a fatal drinking bout with Drayton and Ben Jonson, are about the only moderately specific details which give "tang" to Shakspere's otherwise steadily successful and respectable career— are, in short, about the only "newsy" and "printable" items about the life of the bard. Hence—it always being postulated that Shakspere is a supreme personality—the record must be supplemented by engaging inferences from the Shaksperian tradition or from the plays. Thus it is pleasant to think, with Dowden—the matter being entirely guess-work—that "his mother had not died without having held in her arms a grand-child of her son." ('Shakspere Primer,' p. 27.) She may have had no arms, or have been bed-rid, or have lived in France, or not have been able to endure the squalling child—also guess-work of not so pretty a kind. Thus we delight to feel that his was "the poet's eye, in a fine frenzy rolling," that he himself was oppressed by the idea that

> Life's but a walking shadow, a poor player
> That struts and frets his hour upon the stage
> And then is heard no more: it is a tale
> Told by an idiot, full of sound and fury,
> Signifying nothing.

Thus, going beyond the record and the plays, we like to make pictures and statues of the bard, like the grave upright Shakspere in the Mall, or even like the excessively inspired and scribulous figure of Fitz-Greene Halleck near-by—"biting his cruel pen, beating his tongue for spite." Thus the Shakspere Memorial and the Shakspere Museum at Stratford, displaying spoons and other useful articles, even down to the eighteenth century, which might have been used by Shakspere's great-great-grandchildren, provided he had had any. Thus the homage of George W. Childs to the greatness of the poet, that vitreous mutuality of kindred souls. Thus in all probability the whole Bacon-Shakespere flurry, in order that he might have more personality than the Gods ordinarily allow. Thus this volume which pays tribute to the "immortal bard" by celebrating the anniversary of his personal death.

Now, though everybody feels a personality of some sort, it is only in recent times, comparatively, that the personality has been systematically—I was about to say "scientifically"—reconstructed and restored. There is not a great deal of talk about his personality before the nineteenth century. Indeed, the Ancients, down to the end of the seventeenth century, seem not to have understood the literary possibilities of personality in the contemporary sense. Addison, Fielding, Johnson, and Boswell were perhaps the first to inculcate a habit, a way of looking at people, that has grown mightily in literature and has pretty nearly crowded out other forms. Certainly, as regards Shakspere, the tradition and the record contain almost no hint of the person. Ben Jonson's "I loved the man, and do honor his memory, on this side idolatry, as much as any. He was, indeed, honest, and of an open and free nature," etc., tells us very little in the modern sense of personality, however much it may thrill us when applied to our already drawn picture of the Shakspere of the plays. Fuller is more vivid: "Though his genius was generally jocular and inclining him to festivity, yet he could, when so disposed, be solemn and serious. . . . . Many were the wit-combats betwixt him and Ben Jonson; which two I beheld like a Spanish great galleon and an English man-of-war; Master Jonson (like the former) was built far higher in learning; solid, but slow, in his performances. Shakspere, with the English man-of-war, lesser in bulk, but lighter in sailing, could turn with all tides, tack about, and take advantage of all winds, by the quickness of his wit and invention." But this is far from the modern way; it is at best merely a vivid simile, merely touching on mind and manner. It might, with change of names, be Private James and Major General John. Consider, for a moment, what Boswell would have given us here. Consider, also, how the authors of 'Lost Illusions,' 'Vanity Fair,' 'Anna Karénina,' 'Crime and Punishment,' and the 'Egoist' would have improved on Boswell with regard to variety of method and vividness of portraiture. Consider, again, what lively pictures Shakspere could have made of such interesting figures as Jonson and himself, had he been autobiographically inclined. But that was impossible. Interest in the actual person, even in oneself, as a subject for "copy" and realistic skill were undeveloped in Elizabethan times. There was no journalistic sense. The vivid people are the Hamlets, the Tamburlaines and the Vittorias of the stage, not the Bacons, the Raleighs and the Shaksperes of actual life. If actual, they are vivid chiefly when lampooned and satirized. *Facit indignatio versum;* you do not see a person clearly until you hate him and are prepared to run the risk of libel for your vision.

The necessary skill and interest of an amiable sort were lacking also in those following decades when critics and students no longer had personal acquaintance, but only the works and the record to go by. The warmest praise of the seventeenth century —Dryden's "the man who of all Moderns, and perhaps Ancient Poets, had the largest and most comprehensive soul" touches not the least on the regions of personality as we woo the term, but is a matter of panegyric. It belongs to that state of culture that finds high satisfaction in the utterance of enthusiastic beliefs, or, on its worse side, in the arrangement of men into classes of value. Compare it with the account of Stepan Trofimovitch Verhovensky at the opening of Dostoevsky's the 'Possessed'—or even the analysis of themselves by So and So and So in the current magazines. Nor is there, so far as I am aware, in the eighteenth century much comment on the personal side of Shakspere. Questions of form and art predominate; the endeavor is to settle the real excellence or goodness of an author on more or less rational and canonical principles. The orgy of admiration that struck Shaksperian criticism with Lamb and Coleridge, the "our sweet Shakspere" school founded by these critics and best illustrated by Cowden Clarke, the eager embracing of transcendental German-born ideas regarding the Ego, the Individual, the Personality, initiated the modern restoration movement. The reason is simple (whatever the fact!): the moment a man is elevated on so high a pinnacle as that supplied by Coleridge and Lamb, he becomes all-important. It becomes imperative to ascertain the attributes of the deity; immanence, omniscience, omnipotence, immutability, *et cetera, et cetera*, are postulated. The art of picturing personality meanwhile having made advances, having lost its characteristically satirical quality, the personal side of the great bard becomes an interesting thing to reconstruct. The reconstruction of Shakspere's personality is part and parcel of the general restoral of Shakspere, of his life, of the chronology of his plays, of his texts, of his learning, of his meaning, of his interpretation, and it has on the whole followed, though by no means on all fours—or all hundreds—with these other and perhaps more exact interests.

II

The foregoing analogy of "restoration" is taken from archaeology rather than architecture and art. It suggests not at all
that familiar process by which the dim walls and the dusky
vaulting of some famous cathedral are rendered clean and
glistening, or by which a painting mellow and indiscernable
through age is retouched for the market or for the satisfaction
of its new possessor. The analogy is far more ideal than that.
It is "restoration" in the sense of reconstruction of the plan or
picture of the ruin from a few fragments. We are all familiar with
the process from the pages of Baedeker: "Trajan's Forum;
Restored, after ———," usually some German; for the Germans
take the lead in this as in nearly all other worthy occupations
and efficiencies. The process is akin to the "restoration" of a
prehistoric saurian from a fragment of his tail, of Pithecanthropus
from his skull, of the trail, acts, and person of the criminal from
the quality of his cigar ashes. It is a good and wholesome pursuit, not better or worse than most scholarly occupations,
scientific, literary and linguistic, and it keeps many brains employed and gives much occupation to many worthy men. What
a mercy that the Parthenon and the Roman Forum are not intact!
We could only sit and say, "Oh my!" Were it not for time,
weathering, erosion and bacilli, the world would be æsthetic and
emotional rather than scientific and curious. Think, too, what
good the Germans are storing up for future generations of
scholars; here and everywhere they are provident.

With Shakspere the process is somewhat different. He is not
a basket of potsherds, a Greek torso, a Roman ruin, or a Flemish
town, and he has been only logomachically bombarded by the
Germans. He has, indeed, left a considerable fragment for us to
work upon—his poems and plays. Nor is the method for restor-
ing personality quite the same. With physical restoration, however ideal and inspired, you are completing and piecing out a work
from various fragments; the ground plan is at least partly before
you, and you have other indications as well to go by. That
process is really analogous to the restoration of Shakspere's
text, what he really wrote, or to the piecing together of certain

facts and traditions to form the record of his life. But the restoration of Shakspere's personality is not in the least a process of piecing together of fragments; that is the work of the scholars, thanks to whom we have sound texts and know a great many facts about the bard. The restoration of Shakspere's personality is rather the establishment of something different from and outside of these facts; it is really an act of inference. The record, the plays, the tradition, are, so to speak, an emanation or manifestation; the process is to restore the source of the emanation or manifestation, to see what that *Quelle* or *Ursprung* looks like. Here we begin, obviously, to approach the region of the abstract, of the *Ding an Sich*, that great gift of the Nineteenth Century, of Germany, of Kant and Hegel, to a theretofore groping world. So far as a pure and isolated abstraction we never get, at least in English; and most of the attempts, therefore, to tell in that language what manner of man Shakspere was are interesting rather than fantastic. It is worth while to examine some of them in detail, before passing on to the question of how much can actually be done by way of such rehabilitation. It will be convenient to begin with that enthusiastic group who, with Coleridge, set Shakspere on the pinnacle of the temple. That school, which flourished from, roughly, 1800 to 1850, is quite different from its predecessors, but, on the other hand, takes no such definite views of human personality as have followed in more recent times. Coleridgeans capitalized Personality, and the visible marks of that important human attribute were such things as the open collar and 'Childe Harold' of Byron. You can see it to-day, albeit pale and atrophied, in the magazine portraits of famous contemporary authors.

III

Coleridge is typical of the thinness of that school, whose image of the writer of the plays is very much wanting in what we now know as "red blood." Coleridge is perhaps the most famous English critic of his time, but he "restores" Shakspere much as an earnest theologian — Newman, for example — would reconstruct the Deity. His restoration amounts to little more than the bodily transference of qualities observed in the

drama to the person of the dramatist. For example, speaking of
the 'Tempest,' he characteristically says: "The whole courting
scene, indeed, in the beginning of the third act, between the lovers,
is a masterpiece; and the first dawn of disobedience in the mind
of Miranda to the command of her father is very finely drawn,
so as to seem the working of the Scriptural command *Thou
shalt leave father and mother*, etc. O! with what exquisite purity
this scene is conceived and executed! Shakspere may sometimes
be gross, but I boldly say that he is always moral and modest."
(Notes on the 'Tempest,' p. 69.)[1] The adjectives may obviously
refer to the qualities of the plays, or to the character of the
writer; he puts nothing in his plays that isn't moral and modest,
or he is himself always moral and modest. The quotation is not
quite unambiguous. What is quite clear, however, to anyone
acquainted with the criticism of the time, is that such processes
were continually going on in the mind of Coleridge and his contemporaries. The essence of the process of reconstruction is
this: obviously Shakspere could not have been like all his
characters, like Iago and Desdemona, say, at once; therefore you
generalize the scene or the character into a quality; and this
quality becomes an attribute of the author. That is essentially
the Coleridgean method, so far as reconstruction is concerned.
It is part of what he was pleased to call his "philosophical criticism." The Eighteenth century would have criticised Shakspere
much more canonically and with much less reference to his personality and character.

Again, according to the Coleridgean system, the qualities
of poetry in general become transferred to the personality of the
particular poet. It would be interesting to determine how far
Shakspere was the suggestor to Coleridge of those characteristics
which, becoming a general possession of poets, are then transferred to the personality of that same Shakspere who may have
originated them. Be that as it may, the endowment of the poet
is rich if misty. Thus under the significant heading, "Shakspere, a Poet Generally," Coleridge says that we must admit
"that Shakspere possessed the chief, if not every, requisite of a

[1] The references throughout this section are to the edition of *Lectures on Shakspere* in
Everyman's Library.

poet—deep feeling and exquisite sense of beauty, both as exhibited to the eye in the combinations of form, and to the ear in sweet and appropriate melody." (p. 38) The number of attributes of the generalized poet which the particular Shakspere possesses is too long to name in detail, but it includes fancy and, of course, "imagination, or the power by which one image or feeling is made to modify many others, and by a sort of fusion to force many into one." His judgment was equal to his genius; he was a great philosopher as well as a great poet, the inference being that he possessed the qualities of the "general" philosopher as well as of the "poet generally." Nevertheless, in spite of his common share in the qualities of the poet and the philosopher, "his plays are distinguished from those of all other dramatic poets" by eight characteristics, rather a spiritual than a dramaturgical contribution, though not without some hint of the latter. These matters are, aside from Shakspere's general share in the characteristic of the poet, his net contribution to our spiritual wealth, in that, not existing before, Shakspere created these values. They have little to do immediately with personality, but they serve to show the working of the mind of the critic. The spiritual contribution of the poet displays his character.

In all this attributing and ascertaining of spiritual values, whether purely personal to Shakspere or not, the same thing has happened that happened more flagrantly when Coleridge, in 'Biographia Literaria,' having failed to define poetry abstractly, made a concrete appeal to 'Venus and Adonis.' In that poem he found four qualities—perfect sweetness of versification, remoteness from private interests, the presence of predominant passion, and depth and energy of thought—which forthwith he erected into concomitants of all good poetry whatsoever, and then used to cause 'Venus and Adonis' to elevate itself by its own boot-straps. That is the Coleridgean O: You like and admire; you find reasons for your likings; you erect these reasons into universals; you use these universals to re-establish the fame of your original;—and your "philosophical" circle is complete. You yourself have, however, meanwhile advanced from the regions of mere personal taste to the realm of philosophical delight and truth. The method is based on two things, metaphysics and admiration. As to the first, the critic notes effects, likings, qualities; these become for him attributes or manifestations of the soul behind the semblance. That is the Personality. The process is much like the older psychology, which, from speech and action, reasoned back to the postulation of invisible faculties—memory, judgment, imagination, and many other convenient sources of specific acts.

Of the place of admiration in the system there can be no doubt. It is partly due to the personal feeling of the critic, but partly also to the exigencies of the transcendental method. For one was after verities and was ready to go far to find them. One pursued the good and the true and called it fact. The practical postulate particular to the present subject was that if it was good it was or might be Shakspere's; if bad it couldn't possibly be his. What Coleridge liked was, as has been shown, largely a matter of soul values. Furthermore Shakspere was to be shown as different from and greater than other writers. His soul, mind and personality were defined by being elevated—a crude and vague way of procedure surely. Here are some examples of Coleridge's unseasoned admiration:

> Another excellence of Shakspere, in which no writer equals him, is in the language of nature. So correct is it, that we can see ourselves in every page. The style and manner have also that felicity, that not a sentence can be read, without its being discovered if it is Shaksperian. ('An Introductory Lecture upon Shakspere,' p. 57.)

> To distinguish that which is legitimate in Shakspere from what does not belong to him, we must observe his varied images symbolical of novel truth, thrusting by, and seeming to trip up each other, from an impetuosity of thought producing a flowing meter and seldom closing with the line. In Pericles, a play written fifty years before, but altered by Shakspere, his additions may be recognized to half a line, from the meter, which has the same perfection in the flowing continuity of interchangeable metrical pauses in his earliest plays, as in 'Love's Labour's Lost.' (Ibid.)

Was ever style worse than in the preceding sentence! The substance, where clear, is questionable. Here is some cold critical truth:

> If a drama by Shakspere turned out to be too heavy for popular audiences, the clown might be called in to lighten the representation; and if it appeared

that what was added was not in Shakspere's manner, the conclusion would be
inevitable, that it was not from Shakspere's pen. (The Seventh Lecture, p.
429.)

Here again is sound critical method: referring to a speech
quoted from 'Love's Labour's Lost':

There can be no doubt, indeed, about the propriety of expunging this speech
of Rosaline's; it soils the very page that retains it. (Notes on 'L.L.L.', p. 76.)

Here is a hint at the restoration of Shakspere's public beliefs,
a matter considerably expanded by later restorers:

This play ['Coriolanus'] illustrates the wonderfully philosophic impartiality
of Shakspere's politics. His own country's history furnished him with no
matter but what was too recent to be devoted to patriotism. Besides, he
knew that the instruction of ancient history would seem more dispassionate.
(Notes on 'Cor.', p. 92.)

Obviously Coleridge from a score or more of plausible theories
to account for the subject of the play takes that one which best
pleases him in the game of elevating Shakspere. Here are other
examples of the same sort of false reasoning in a different field:

The speeches of Flavius and Marullus are in blank verse. Wherever regular
meter can be rendered truly imitative of character, passion, or personal rank,
Shakspere seldom, if ever, neglects it. Hence this line should be read:—

> What means't by that? Mend me, thou saucy fellow!

I say regular meter: for even the prose has in the highest and lowest dramatic
personage, a Cobbler or a Hamlet, a rhythm so felicitous and so severally
appropriate as to be a virtual meter. (Notes on 'Julius Caesar,' p. 93.)

That is to say, if you can't elevate Shakspere to your preconceived conceptions by one method, another will suffice. Or
you score a third way, thus:

Caesar's speech:
> She dreamt last night, she saw my *statue*—

No doubt, it should be *statua*, as in the same age they more often pronounced
"heroes" as a trisyllable than dissyllable. A modern tragic poet would have
written—
> Last night she dreamt, that she my statue saw—

But Shakspere never avails himself of the supposed license of transposition
merely for the meter. There is always some logic either of thought or passion
to justify it. (Ibid. p. 95.)

"Statua," says Churton Collins ('Studies in Shakspere', p. 357), "is a conjecture of Malone's and it had no place in the text till 1793."

Or being on the lookout to find excellence you find it:

Oli. What, boy!
Orla. Come, come, elder brother, you are too young in this.
Oli. Wilt thou lay hands on me, villain?
There is a beauty here. The word 'boy' naturally provokes and awakens in Orlando the sense of his manly powers; and with the retort of 'elder brother,' he grasps him with firm hands and makes him feel he is no boy. (Notes on A. Y. L. I., p. 79.)

Here is warm panegyric:

> *Puck.* Now the hungry lion roars,
> And the wolf behowls the moon;
> Whilst the heavy ploughman snores
> All with weary task foredone, etc.

Very Anacreon in perfectness, proportion, grace and spontaneity! So far it is Greek; — but then add, O! what wealth, what wild ranging, and yet what compression and condensation of, English fancy! In truth, there is nothing in Anacreon more perfect than these thirty lines, or half so rich and imaginative. They form a speckless diamond! (Notes on M. N. D., p. 78.)

Instances of bad criticism might be multiplied, but the foregoing will serve to show the nature of the restoral of the Shaksperean personality founded on admiration and on the transference of the quality to the author. It is a pretty crude method, and the results are vague and unscientific. From it you learn little about Shakspere the man; what you learn may be so or may not be so. Such is the main point in the contribution of the great Coleridge to the restoration of this personality.

Almost as interesting as Coleridge's quasi-philosophical-metaphysical efforts to furnish attributes for the dramatic deity, was the contemporary Lamb's vision of the soul of the poet. From a historical, a logical, or a philosophical point of view, the famous essay 'On the Tragedies of Shakspere, Considered with Reference to Their Fitness for Stage Representation' (1811) is probably one of the least satisfactory pieces of criticism ever written; Lamb in his soberer moments could hardly have been unaware of the fact; he is merely brazening out a paradox.

Regarded as sober criticism, however, it errs in that it lays blame where blame does not belong, and because it condemns the plays for the very purpose for which they were written, viz., acting on the stage. Certainly if any one is at fault it is Shakspere and the bad actors, not the good actors and the audiences. But badness in Shakspere would not suit. The paradox and the thesis of the high quality and unique differences of Shakspere are urged with an enthusiasm and plausibility that arouse the partizanship and acclaim of the reader who demands of the critic merely a strong expression of his views. Now Lamb has gone to such a limit in his dream of the poet that he has detached him from all local habitation and name and has made of him a Transfigured Soul whom only the devout see in the silence of the chamber.

Lamb's thesis is that the plays of Shakspere are "less calculated for performance on a stage, than those of almost any other dramatist whatever." This in spite of the historical fact that Shakspere "calculated" his plays for the stage, that they prospered in his own time, and that they have been by all odds the most successful plays in the English language for many scores of years. Lamb's paradox is based on the further paradox that the plays are different not only in degree but also in kind from all other plays. The reason that they cannot be successfully performed is that the real characters of the personages in the plays are essentially transformed by stage representation. The real Shaksperian character is representable only to the inward eye, and though it is obvious that there are hundreds of thousands of inward eyes—even actors have them—Lamb's is the only one whose vision counts enough to enable a definite pronouncement to be made that all attempts to represent the Shaksperian characters as Shakspere intended them to be represented are quite wrong and impossible. Such criticism is

> the very coinage of the brain:
> This bodily creation ecstasy
> Is very cunning in.........

From utterances such as these you infer Lamb's idea of the personality of Shakspere. Lamb does not expound it; but his criticism is obviously based on a vision of the poet, whose soul, even more than Milton's,

was like a star and dwelt apart,

who, if Lamb is correct, presented his thundering conceptions to the groundlings and the "profession" in the interests of his livelihood and fame, but reserved the essence for succeeding generations of readers, *quorum pars maxima fuit agnus.* In like manner, if we are to believe certain erudite critics even of our own day, various authors—Aristotle, Cicero, Plato, Sir T. Elyot, Edmund Spenser, and many others — specifically contemplated us poor moderns. The record of Shakspere's life is obviously of no value, the tradition doesn't help one in ascertaining the personality of the poet. As are the plays, so the man is what you like him to be in the silent chambers of your imagination. If you are keen on personal beauty, you may imagine him with Piccadilly weepers or Burnsides—actual busts, portraits, and Elizabethan fashion plates being of no account in comparison with the radiance of the inward vision. The truth of the matter is that you may imagine Lamb's idea of Shakspere's personality to be about what you like within the regions contemplated by the inward eye. He has really given us no definite picture at any time, and according to his principles you may infer about anything, so long as it is very superior. He is without concern for evidence, is at the farthest remove from those who try to check and substantiate their views by appeal to the facts, and, is, in short, the very best of critics for such readers as wish to have their emotion done for them.

Of the two other great critics of the time, DeQuincey had little more to do than wrangle with the memories of Malone and Steevens over trifling details of the poet's life and to speak at some length of what might be called his intellectual contributions to the world; for example, Shakspere created women as individuals.

Hazlitt was one of the first to treat the characters of Shakspere's plays as if they were real people and to talk about them as human beings rather than as objects whose function was to "strut and fret their hour upon the stage" in accordance with a

set of rules prescribing what they ought to do, or whose diviner
purpose was to illustrate German ethics and metaphysics. Even
the very humane Dryden does not consider Shakspere quite
humanly and his contemporary Rymer's criticism of the dramatist is based on the false assumption that play characters must
act sensibly and consistently as well as according to the principles of Aristotle. Addison would have laid stress on the "just-
ness" and the "propriety" of the sentiments and utterances of
the characters, and if the great Samuel Johnson had admitted
their humanity it would have been to praise or blame it somewhat in a literary way. The point of view illustrated by Hazlitt
has been carried to an extreme by Professor Bradley, who analyzes the tragic characters simply and solely as if they were actual
and as if the drama had really happened. The latter, however,
demands of the characters a good deal more psychology than did
Hazlitt; that is to say, they must, on final analysis, be consistent
wholes and self-contained and complete. With Hazlitt, on the
contrary, merely aspects of the characters are presented, self-
sustaining and consistent aspects, to be sure, but still not the
whole thing. The characters crop up before Hazlitt's vision much
as people crop up in daily life, or in the novels, more than of any
other novelist, of the Russian Dostoevsky. They are not studies;
they appear like real people coming more or less distinctly out of
a mist, growing now dim, now bright, now certain and now
elusive, revealing different aspects of themselves, but though
never inconsistent yet never whole personalities, as Professor
Bradley would fain persuade us to believe with regard to Macbeth, Othello and Hamlet. So Hazlitt's treatment.

It is, therefore, disappointing and perhaps odd that Hazlitt,
whose 'Spirit of the Age' as well as his 'Characters of Shakspere's
Plays' show such keen interest in human beings and an uncommon ability and truth in characterizing them, should have left
only faint hints of his conception of the man Shakspere. It
comes by way of scattering adjectives, from occasional dissent,
much milder and less sweeping than Lamb's, of the rendering
by actors of Shakspere's meaning, and of inferences not unlike,
in some respects, those of Coleridge. Here are two of the longer
passages in which Hazlitt works from the character in the play

to the character of the poet. Of 'Twelfth Night' he says in the
'Characters':

> Shakspere's comedy is of a pastoral and poetical cast. Folly is indigenous
> to the soil, and shoots out with native, happy, unchecked luxuriance. Absurd-
> ity has every encouragement afforded it; and nonsense has room to flourish in.
> Nothing is stunted by the churlish, icy hand of indifference or severity. The
> poet runs riot in a conceit, and idolizes a quibble. His whole object is to turn the
> meanest or rudest objects to a pleasurable account. The relish which he has of
> a pun, or of the quaint humour of a low character, does not interfere with the
> delight with which he describes a beautiful image, or the most refined love.
> (p. 196 [1])

Evidently the kind of play falls in with the character of the
poet. The transfer of the qualities of the play to the personality
of the author is not made formally and philosophically, as with
Coleridge, but one gets the impression of Hazlitt's thinking that
Shakspere was a merry fellow who thoroughly enjoyed his
characters. The second passage is somewhat paradoxical but is
perhaps as thoroughly characteristic of the humanity and
breadth of Hazlitt, of his blessed freedom from metaphysical and
philosophical and canonical obligations, as can be found in his
work:

> Shakspere was in one sense the least moral of all writers; for morality
> (commonly so-called) is made up of antipathies; and his talent consisted in
> sympathy with human nature, in all its shapes, degrees, depressions, and eleva-
> tions. The object of the pedantic moralist is to find out the bad in everything:
> his was to show that there is some soul of goodness in things evil. Even Master
> Barnardine is not left to the mercy of what others think of him; but when he
> comes in, speaks for himself, and pleads his own cause, as well as if counsel had
> been assigned him. In one sense, Shakspere was no moralist at all; in another,
> he was the greatest of all moralists. He was a moralist in the same sense in
> which nature is one. He taught what he had learnt from her. He showed the
> greatest knowledge of humanity with the greatest fellow-feeling for it. ('Char-
> acters of Shakspere's Plays: 'Measure for Measure,' p. 246.)

It is from scattering touches like the foregoing that Hazlitt's
picture of the personality of the poet is made up. There is nothing formal about it, as with Coleridge, nothing so intimate,
"inner-shriney" and sanctified as the vision of Lamb, no set
evaluation as with De Quincey, no formal edifice, as, later, with

----

[1] The references are to the edition of Hazlitt in Everyman's Library.

Professor Dowden, no self-contained character, as with Professor Bradley, no congeries of traits as with Bagehot. Shakspere appears to Hazlitt piecemeal and, even so, as only a moderate number of crumbs. The whole loaf is not there, it cannot well be drawn new baked and fragrant from the oven. The poet is not the same yesterday, to-day and forever, but is a human being who changes his occupations, his interests, and his sympathies from day to day, who shows his readers now one side, now another. Hazlitt refused to invoke transcendental and metaphysical reasons to show off Shakspere. Coleridge, as we have seen, had invoked the impressions that he had of 'Venus and Adonis' to establish the high quality of poetry in general and of 'Venus and Adonis' by inference, not contenting himself with liking the poem as a personal matter, not being willing, also, to rest his case on taste. For this poem and 'Lucrece,' Hazlitt cared not at all:

> It has been the fashion of late to cry up our author's poems as equal to his plays: this is the desperate cant of modern criticism. We would ask, was there the slightest comparison between Shakspere, and either Chaucer or Spenser, as mere poets? Not any. The two poems of Venus and Adonis and of Tarquin and Lucrece appear to us like a couple of ice-houses. They are about as hard, as glittering, and as cold. The author seems all the time to be thinking of his verses, and not of his subject—not of what his characters would feel, but of what he shall say; and as it must happen in all such cases, he always puts into their mouths those things which they would be the last to think of, and which it shews the greatest ingenuity in him to find out. (Ibid. 'Poems and Sonnets,' p. 264)

The Coleridgean criticism put forth its most beautiful and unctuous flower in the essays of the two brother trancendentalists, Carlyle and Emerson. The point of view of Carlyle in 'Heroes and Hero Worship' (1841) concerning the 'Hero as Poet,' and of Emerson in 'Representative Men' (1850) concerning 'Shakspere the Poet' are not dissimilar. Both are in "King Cambyses' [or 'Ercles] vein," though Carlyle naturally wears the larger mask and buskin. The general conception is that of a Truly Poetic Soul sent to dwell among conditions of a less divine sort. There is no object in examining these essays further in detail.

IV

We may now pass to the more modern English restorations. These may be divided conveniently into the attempts to restore the "Man" as concretely as possible, and that more miscellaneous and numerous class of essays and books, which, while generally biographical and critical in character, also attach themselves to what may be called the "Seeing Shakspere's Soul" school. Essays by Bagehot, Leslie Stephen, Goldwin Smith, and Professor A. C. Bradley are the ablest representatives of the first class. Usually short, they confine themselves to statements of those inferences regarding the poet's personal tastes, beliefs and experiences that may be drawn from the record of his life and from his works. They rarely indulge in panegyric or apology, and, descending from the high horse of transcendental abstraction, they attempt to present Shakspere as a human being.

Walter Bagehot's premise ('Shakspere—the Man,' 1853) is that "of no person is there a clearer picture in the popular fancy. You seem to have known Shakspere, to have seen Shakspere, to have been friends with Shakspere." ('Literary Studies,' Vol. I, p. 126). The basis of this impression must, of course, be not from legend or tradition, but "from the sure testimony of his certain works." They were written by a man and not by a "tame steam engine" and they obviously must have expressed the thoughts which he had to express.

Granting this principle—and the minor one that Bagehot himself is no "tame steam engine,"—Shakspere's personality is to Bagehot what that critic sees in him. Briefly, Bagehot's picture is as follows: "Shakspere's works could only be produced by a first-rate imagination working on a first-rate experience." His was not the ready-made mind like Guizot's or William Pitt's, but was one which learned from experience. "If he walked down a street, he knew what was in that street. His mind did not form in early life a classified list of all the objects in the universe and learn no more about the universe ever after. From a certain fine sensibility of nature it is plain that he took a keen interest, not only in the general and coarse outlines of objects, but in their minutest particulars and gentlest gradations."

(p. 129) In this respect he was superior to that great writer of his own caste of mind, Sir Walter Scott. Furthermore, he knew things naturally, incidentally, offhand, not in any "set" way, as did Milton, whose manner is bookish and learned; nor in a laborious, dull way, like Southey, for example. He wrote originally and in an interesting manner because he was one of those few authors who really knew something. His interest was immense and he liked the company of the people he happened to be describing—Dogberry, say, and Shallow. He never hated them or was angry with them. In this respect he was like Sir Walter Scott and unlike the detached and superior and slightly unintelligent Goethe. Shakspere's liking was full of liveliness and high spirits, as could not have been otherwise with the creator of Falstaff; he did not look at things askance, crabbedly, sourly as did Hazlitt. Yet with all this sociability and observation, he united a capacity for solitude and the reflections of a solitary mind; in him was a little latent melancholy. He had a bent for fancies, for April poetry, for believing in small superstitions, which renders him comparable with Keats. Politically, he was evidently a believer in the British constitution and the thirty-nine articles. He disliked the mob, looked with distrust on the middle class and hated revolution, so far as he was capable of hating anything human. So great was his imaginative sympathy that he probably possessed an unparalleled knowledge of women and really got at their mode of feeling. In this respect he was quite a different person from Plato, whose women are part of an institution rather than individual minds. On the other hand, he was not a learned man. Such learning as he had was that of the "natural reader; when a book was dull, he put it down, when it looked fascinating, he took it up, and the consequence is, that he remembered and mastered what he read;" (p. 166); it is doubtful if he could have been induced to read the annotations of his own plays. He was assuredly not dogmatically religious and laid perhaps on the heavenly, less stress than on the worldly side of life, in which he won considerable success.

Bagehot's method of ascertaining the character of Shakspere is something like what is known as "rubbing" in architecture. He, so to speak, places a sheet of transfer paper over all the work of Shakspere and then presents those features which his charcoal has brought into most prominent relief. It is essentially the same method employed by Professor Bradley, though far more brilliantly and sketchily in Bagehot. It is an account of the main impressions that leap into his mind on contemplating the whole of Shakspere.

These impressions are given relief by a characteristic method. Probably no critic uses comparisons and dichotomies so constantly and strikingly as Bagehot. Thus two picture frames are held before the reader, the face of Shakspere pops out of one, that of Guizot, of Pitt, out of the other. The frame is changed; now the counterfeit presentments are those of Shakspere and Milton. Again you are invited to look upon the picture of Shakspere in the frame of original English and then upon the picture of Southey in the frame of closet laboriousness. Bagehot's account of Shakspere becomes, so far as that is possible, a series of moving pictures of the poet, at least of living pictures in different aspects, each with its contrasting portrait, until finally we know pretty well what Bagehot thought Shakspere to be.

Goldwin Smith in 'Shakespeare: The Man' (1899) attempts to find traces of the dramatist's personal character in his dramas. (page 5) His task is quite like that of Bagehot and his findings are not vastly different. For example, Shakspere probably knew something of Latin and Latin poets, had read Rabelais and very likely understood Italian. He was particularly versed in country occupations, had much knowledge of current conventional manners and social customs, had a cultivated taste for music and, though he may have known no law, yet had picked up many legal phrases. He may have travelled, and he certainly had considerable historical knowledge of an inaccurate sort. That he had certain—or rather uncertain—personal experiences of more or less bitterness seems evident from his works, but he was probably personally a temperate man. In politics he was clearly a royalist and a courtier with contempt for the mob. He disliked the demagogue, yet he was full of pity both for men and animals. His estimate of woman was very high, though he probably regarded her as the weaker vessel. He was tolerant and liberal, patriotic and probably a conformist, but we do not know just how religious he was or just how much of a church-goer. Such are the chief points of Goldwin Smith's essay.

It rests, as that of Professor Bradley's rests, on the argument from gratuitousness; that is to say, Shakspere, besides being merely dramatic, besides giving merely what is necessary to the play character, sowed many of his dramas with gratuitous discourses. The classical instance quoted by Goldwin Smith, quoted also by De Quincey and, strange as it may seem, by the skeptical Sidney Lee, is the celebrated injunction of Prospero to Ferdinand, which is by all these writers regarded as somewhat pointedly referring to Shakspere's own matrimonial experience. A little common sense reflection will, however, convince the reader of the absurdity of attaching any special significance to such passages as this, since the situation described and the advice given may be regarded as such common worldly property that no person need have undergone the experience to have given the advice. It, however, illustrates the argument from gratuitousness, and suggests also the necessity of testing this argument in each case as it arises.

The conclusions of Leslie Stephen in 'Studies of a Biographer' (Vol. IV, 1902) are not very different from those of Bagehot, Goldwin Smith and Professor Bradley. A brief summary will suffice. Shakspere probably had a considerable knowledge of field and flower, liked out-of-doors, had religious views of a non-puritan kind, disliked pedants and mobs. By disposition he was probably capable of passion but capable also of firm dealing with himself. The modern chronologies enable one to gain a considerable knowledge of his mental development. Any interpretation of the 'Sonnets,' as of the so-called "dark period," rests very largely upon conjecture; the results, even if true, Stephen wisely adds, were temporary and unimportant. Doubtless Shakspere also could appreciate the gloomy side of life and had himself experienced some of its bitterness. He probably very much believed in keeping one's head, and his own life doubtless exemplified that belief. Some of his characters evidently indicate that he greatly admired energy and sound judgment.

More interesting perhaps than Stephen's specific opinions are the reasons for holding these opinions with which he prefaces his essay. As in the case of other authors—Milton or Scott, Browning, Gibbon, Darwin—the critic feels in his author that literary and personal charm are intermingled. It is unlikely that Shakspere could be the sole exception to the fairly common experience of readers. To be sure, commentators, to an unusual degree, have found in Shakspere different and exclusive qualities and have been impressed by one or another aspect of his genius. That fact may render the interpretation of Shakspere unusually difficult; nevertheless dramatists in general are quite as knowable as other literary men. Though more varied and apparently quite impersonal, he must, like his contemporaries, have had his likes, his dislikes, his ethics, which must be inferred. As a matter of fact, he is thoroughly recognizable, though he is, of course, difficult to define, as is usually the case with complex people. His readers have vivid conceptions of him, though their ideas may not readily be put into language. "A dramatist is no more able than anybody else to bestow upon his characters talents which he himself does not possess." (page 14) Shakspere must, for instance, have had a sense of humor to have shown that quality in his creations. The gist of Stephen's argument is "that what is accepted about the poetry really implies certain conclusions about the man." (page 13) Therefore it is possible for Stephen, like Bagehot, Goldwin Smith, and Professor Bradley, to make more or less correct inferences with regard to the personality of the poet.

Professor Bradley, in an interesting essay, 'Shakspere the Man' ('Oxford Lectures on Poetry,' 1909) goes into the subject more minutely and systematically than the writers whom we have been considering. Like Bagehot, he deems the subject worthy and possible of study and formulation. He dissents sharply from the skeptical position of Sir Sidney Lee: "What I wish to deny is the presupposition which seems to be frequently accepted as an obvious truth. Even if Mr. Lee's view of the 'Sonnets' were indisputably correct, nay, if even, to go much further, the persons and the story in the 'Sonnets' were as purely fictitious as those of 'Twelfth Night,' they might and would still tell us something about the personality of their author. For however free a poet may be from the emotions which he simulates, and however little involved in the conditions which he imagines, he cannot (unless he is a mere copyist) write a hundred and fifty lyrics expressive of those simulated emotions without disclosing something of himself, something of the way in which he in particular *would* feel and behave under imagined conditions. And the same thing holds in principle of the dramas. Is it really conceivable that a man can write some five and thirty dramas, and portray in them an enormous amount and variety of human nature, without betraying any thing whatever of his own disposition and preferences? I do not believe that he could do this, even if he deliberately set himself to the task. The only question is how much of himself he would betray." (p. 313) Employing a very general analogy also, Professor Bradley contends that the impression made by the writings of novelists and poets of whom a good many external particulars are known does, on the whole, square with those known details; therefore the chances are that the impressions derived from the works of Shakspere are true to his actual personality. He is merely dimmer than others in proportion to the greater "universality" of his work. And as a matter of fact all readers get some impression of the personality of the poet, and these impressions agree with each other in the large, as that, for example, Shakspere belongs to the type or class of Fielding and Scott rather than that of Shelley, Wordsworth, or Milton. And again the essays of competent men, not technically Shaksperian scholars but men of high intelligence—Bagehot, Goldwin Smith, and Leslie Stephen—are in substantial accord among themselves, and also with the vaguer impressions of the general reader. Such are the chief reasons for supposing that the personality of the poet may be restored. The rest is a matter of results and methods, of which a few words.

The testimony of Shakspere's contemporaries and the record of his life, though scanty, yield Professor Bradley a decided outline of the personality. More important is the impression given by the writings: "the only question·is how much of himself he would betray." Professor Bradley outlines at considerable length, with far greater detail than can be summarized here, his impressions of the poet's prevailing traits. In disposition, he was modest and unassuming, gentle and sweet-tempered, inclined to like

plain and unassuming people; by no means meek, he could manifest proper spirit and assertiveness, and was even a bit vindictive;
though in class like Scott and Fielding, he was more reflective
than they, but, though often sad, even profoundly melancholy,
he was temperamentally more gay than grave; and so on. In
tastes, he was fond of tranquilizing music, was sensitive to the
beauty of nature—of the sea, the rose, the lily, the lark—was
filled with pity for most animals, but had no use for dogs ("and
then we call him universal!" exclaims Professor Bradley, p. 341);
disliked bloodless people; sympathized with character and personality, but was no partizan or a devotee of causes, however
high and ideal. As to beliefs, he was without political principles,
was rather a pragmatist (Bradley does not use the word) than an
idealist or an extremist. Characteristically, he had special dislike of servility, flattery, pretence, ingratitude, slander and
censoriousness, arrogance, and obsequiousness. He was not
distinctively a religious man, and assuredly no doctrinaire or
sectary or theologian. On the other hand, he was not irreverent,
and had in him a touch of the fatalist, the mystic and "he had a
lively and serious sense of conscience." The most characteristic
play, by and large, a sort of median play, so to speak, is 'As You
Like It'; the most characteristically Shaksperian of the characters is Hamlet. Such are a few of the main points of Professor
Bradley's treatment of a subject which he characterizes as
"endless."

So much for the impressions. It remains to show the method
by which Professor Bradley attempts to demonstrate these impressions, to turn them into objective facts, in short. The method
is based on what might be called preponderance of impression;
the assumption is that constantly recurring thoughts or feelings
are more intimate and personal than the odds and ends of the
mental life. It is closely akin to Goldwin Smith's argument from
gratuitousness. Two examples, the simplest and the most complex, of Professor Bradley's will illustrate the method. Making
allowance for the conventional use of the word "dog" and also for
Shakspere's undoubted liking for the baying of hounds on the
chase, his references to dogs are almost always contemptuous;
his dogs, like the dog of Scripture, are almost always symbols of

unpleasant things. "The things he most loathed in men he found in dogs too."—"To all that he loved most in men he was blind in dogs." (p. 341)

Of this example, acute critics will of course remark that dogs of Shakspere's time may not have merited the affection due to the products of modern British kennels; and that, even so, by reasoning similar to Professor Bradley's, the poet could be proved to have had a Launce-like love for "my dog Crab."

The more complex instance of the method is that of the 'Sonnets' and the 1602-06 period taken in conjunction. The finding is that a good many of the feelings that characterize the 'Sonnets' and the constant recurrence of the subjects of depravity, drunkenness, and sexual corruption, the tone of disgust with which these subjects are treated during this "unhappy period," indicates a strong personal interest, perhaps based on personal experience in these matters. The argument is broadly this: making due allowance for conventions, the 'Sonnets' are original in many ways: there is "no obstacle of any magnitude to our taking the 'Sonnets' as substantially what they purport to be." (p. 332) The tone of the "unhappy period" in the plays is the tone that a man having the personal experience described in the 'Sonnets' might naturally take. That is to say, regarding method, the facts of the 'Sonnets' and the tone of the plays of 1602-1606 are compatible, are, indeed, more than compatible when compared with the tone with which the earlier and the later plays touch on these same matters. On this assumption, Professor Bradley attempts to formulate several impressions of Shakspere and to recast certain actual details of his experience.

The simpler case is merely one of preponderance of impression over the whole of the Shaksperian drama; the more complex instance is of an impression conveyed by the plays of a certain period and their substantiation in the record of another species.

The soundness of Professor Bradley's conclusions will be seen to rest on (1) the soundness of his facts and impressions regarding the plays, and on (2) the soundness of the major contention that preponderant impressions, the drift of opinion, is indicative of personality. One cannot offer quarrel on the first head: the critic's impressions are his impressions, and, furthermore they are the impressions of a critic who knows his Shakspere by heart and knows it with great minuteness and detail. If Professor Bradley says that most of Shakspere's references to dogs are damnatory, that is probably the fact. Furthermore, as in discussing the characters of the plays (in 'Shaksperian Tragedy'), he is careful to find the delicate shades of color and balance and is scrupulous to adjust his impressions to the facts, to accept only that explanation of any of the characters which best squares with all the facts obtainable through observation and analysis. Few critics are more painstaking and competent. If he errs in regard to the value that he sets on his impressions, it is perhaps in failing to take due account of conventions, in an inclination to press the ordinary and the conventional into the significant, to discern tongues in trees, books in running brooks, sermons in stones and Shakspere in everything. Thus the fact is that "the words 'open and free' apply no less eminently to Brutus, Lear, and Timon [than to Othello and Hamlet]. Anthony and Coriolanus are men naturally frank, liberal, and large. Prospero lost his dukedom through his trustfulness. Romeo and Troilus and Orlando, and many slighter characters, are so far of the same type." (p. 324) But several conclusions, if any, are possible—as that these people had to be "open and free" in order to be dupes in a successful play; had Prospero, for example, been canny, he would not have lost his dukedom, and some less practical soul—"another man of the same name," as was said of the authorship of the Homeric poems—would have had to rule Caliban and Ariel. The most that you can say of Professor Bradley's conclusion is that it is as likely as other possible ones: "These affections, passions, and sufferings of free and open natures are Shakspere's favorite [this is really the critical word: in what sense *favorite?*] tragic subject; and his favoritism, surely, goes so far as to constitute a decided peculiarity, not found thus in other tragic poets. Here he painted most, one can not but think, what his own nature was most inclined to feel. But it would rather be melancholy, embitterment, an inactive rage or misanthropy, than any destructive passion; and it would be a further question whether, and how far, he may at any time have experienced what he depicts. I am speaking here only of his disposition." (p. 325.)

It is from this example to be seen that the major contention—that general drift of characterization, preponderant impressions, indicate something definite concerning the personality of the dramatist—is open to doubt. On this point, Lee, as we have seen, is skeptical, but Bradley is hopeful enough to attempt the task of figuring the poet, and he gives the plausible reasons that we have seen for believing that Shakspere "unlocked his heart" not only in the 'Sonnets' but in the dramas as well. This is really the critical problem that calls for a general, scientific and philosophical treatment that it has never yet received. Much is merely a matter of terms. Of that more anon, since it concerns other writers than Professor Bradley. Meanwhile, one may hint with the latter that it is desirable to test the methods on moderns where the impression of personality made by the writings may be checked up by the known facts. Perhaps we might then learn how far, in general, but only in general, we could go, and we might make a beginning of steering the right course in the study of significance. At present, it appears to me, impressions of personality are, as a general rule, by no means so uniform as Professor Bradley would have them to be in order to embellish his major premise. You will find interpretation of the personality behind the 'Doll's House,' for example, ranging between the view, on the one hand, that Ibsen merely nosed about in what was for him a particularly attractive situation, to the view that holds him to have been proclaiming General Truth for which he would have Suffered Martyrdom. The truth is probably that no two authors, that no two works of one author are equally self-revealing. It is gratifying to note, as indeed Stephen remarks, that sounder and sounder methods are being employed for ascertaining what may be rightly believed regarding authors.

V

It will be convenient at this point to say a word or two regarding the incidental restorations of the Shaksperian personality that Professor Bradley makes in his earlier volume, 'Shaksperian Tragedy,'[1] 1904. They belong less to the group of

[1] References are to the second edition, ninth impression, 1914.

essays that we have been considering, than to the class which we have next to consider, but their author determines their place.

These restorals are of the kind that everybody indulges in when he is talking of Shakspere; the poet compels you to utter something about him and his personality. Professor Bradley is chiefly concerned with the substance, the construction, and the characters of the four great tragedies, 'Hamlet,' 'Othello,' 'Lear,' and 'Macbeth.' In all this very interesting inquiry, he is somewhat cumbered with the curse of Coleridge, and is inclined to find reasons for his affections and to discover spiritual or dramatic significance in observed data. So of many of these incidental restorals; they are less reasoned and systematized than those of his own 'Shakspere the Man.' A few examples will suffice; I quote first a general passage:

Hence [i. e. from the fact that, unlike Milton, Pope and Tennyson, Shakspere often wrote carelessly] comes what is perhaps the chief difficulty in interpreting his works. Where his power or art is fully exerted it really does resemble that of nature. It organizes and vitalizes its product from the centre outward to the minutest markings on the surface, so that when you turn upon it the most searching light you can command, when you dissect it and apply to it the test of a microscope, still you find in it nothing formless, general or vague, but everywhere structure, character, individuality. In this his great things, which seem to come whenever they are wanted, have no companions in literature except the few greatest things of Dante; and it is a fatal error to allow his carelessness elsewhere to make one doubt whether here one is not seeking more than can be found. It is very possible to look for subtlety in the wrong places in Shakspere, but in the right places it is not possible to find too much. (p. 77)

The last sentence is the significant one; what are after all, by any uniform test, the "right places" and the "wrong places"?

Here follows an interesting passage, concerning the logic of which one may search one's own heart. If, as is the case with some readers and critics, 'Othello' "occupies a place in our minds a little lower than the other three" great tragedies, it is because of "the comparative confinement of the imaginative atmosphere."

'Othello' has not equally with the other three the power of dilating the imagination by vague suggestions of huge universal powers working in the world of individual fate and passion. It is, in a sense, less 'symbolic.' We seem to be aware in it of a certain limitation, a partial suppression of that element in Shakspere's mind which unites him with the mystical poets and with the great musicians and philosophers. In one or two of his plays, notably in 'Troilus and Cressida,' we are almost painfully conscious of this suppression; we feel an intense intellectual activity but at the same time a certain coldness and hardness, as though some power in his soul, at once the highest and the sweetest, were for a time in abeyance. In other plays, notably in the 'Tempest,' we are constantly aware of the presence of this power; and in such cases we seem to be peculiarly near to Shakspere himself. Now this is so in 'Hamlet' and 'King Lear,' and, in a slighter degree, in 'Macbeth'; but it is much less so in 'Othello.' I do not mean that in 'Othello' the suppression is marked, or that, as in 'Troilus and Cressida,' it strikes us as due to some unpleasant mood; it seems rather to follow simply from the design of a play on a contemporary and wholly mundane subject. Still it makes a difference of the kind I have attempted to indicate, and it leaves an impression that in 'Othello' we are not in contact with the whole of Shakspere. And it is perhaps significant in this respect that the hero himself strikes us as having probably less of the poet's personality in him than many characters far inferior both as dramatic creations and as men." (Ibid. pp. 185-86)

The foregoing bit of restoration rests on the assumption—very common in modern criticism, and perhaps best illustrated by Pater's essay on Wordsworth, as also in another way, by Poe's 'Poetic Principle'—of more intense and less intense moods in the author. The more intense mood is regarded as more significant and personal than the less intense. And lest the critic's own impression of "Intensity" should be over-stressed to the vitiation of the entire finding, careful critics like Pater, and Bradley in the passage quoted, find some general and popular sanction for their selection of the works of the more important mood, as of the 1798-1808 poems of Wordsworth, and the acknowledged supreme tragedies of Shakspere. The further conclusions are open to some logical doubt: logically, for example, we are not more in contact with the whole of Shakspere in 'Hamlet' than in 'Othello'; we are in contact merely with a somewhat different Shakspere. It is only in the whole of Shakspere that we are in contact with the whole of Shakspere! And what, in the name of common sense, is the whole of Shakspere anyway? Is it all the record plus all the writings merely, or is it also all the inferences and abstractions that may be made from these? And, furthermore, what does the allegation tell us of Shakspere's personality? Professor Bradley wrote more reasonably when, somewhat later in 'Shakspere the

Man,' he felt that, on the whole, 'As You Like It,' generally speaking, is possibly the most broadly and inclusively representative of all the plays, though leaving out many Shaksperian characteristics.

Here is an even more direct bit of restoration, which, unfortunately for quotation, is too long to be set forth in all its brilliant subtlety:

> For Dante that which is recorded in the 'Divine Comedy' was the justice and love of God. What did 'King Lear' record for Shakspere? Something, it would seem, very different. This is certainly the most terrible picture that Shakspere painted of the world. In no other of his tragedies does humanity appear more pitiably infirm or more hopelessly bad. (p. 273)

And again,

> Is it not Shakspere's judgment on his kind that we hear in Lear's appeal,
>
> > And thou, all-shaking thunder,
> > Smite flat the thick rotundity o' the world!
> > Crack nature's moulds, all germens spill at once,
> > That make ungrateful man!
>
> and Shakspere's judgment on the worth of existence that we hear in Lear's agonized cry, 'No, no, no, life.' (p. 275)

This view, though common and supported by the admirable authority of the poet Swinburne, does not stand for the total impression:

> Its keynote is surely to be heard neither in the words wrung from Gloster in his anguish, nor in Edgar's words 'the gods are just.' Its final and total result is one in which pity and terror, carried perhaps to the extreme limits of art, are so blended with a sense of law and beauty that we feel at last, not depression and much less despair, but a consciousness of greatness in pain, and of solemnity in the mystery we can not fathom. (p. 279)

I have spoken of 'Shaksperian Tragedy' as if its reconstructions of the personality of the poet were merely incidental. That is true so far as formal rehabilitation goes. In a broader sense, however, Professor Bradley's discussion of the four plays, like the majority of contemporary writing and criticism of Shakspere, where more than merely textual, is based on conceptions of Shakpere's personality and contributes to our image of him. "Our one object," says Professor Bradley in the Introduction (p. 1), "will be what, again in a restricted sense, may be called dramatic appreciation; to increase our understanding and enjoyment of these works as dramas; to learn to apprehend the action and some of the personages of each with a somewhat greater truth and intensity, *so that they may assume in our imaginations a shape a little less unlike the shape they wore in the imagination of their creator.*" The italics are mine: they imply that the reader of 'Shaksperian Tragedy' is to get into Shakspere's mind in the most important detail of it, the detail and aspect that has made him the great celebrity that he is. Professor Bradley tends to make every fact that he has observed in the plays—and there are many of these facts—significant of something in the mind of Shakspere— charged with purpose, philosophy, conviction, reflection, belief. For example, the tragedies of Shakspere answer a conception of life, varying in different plays and doubtless developing, but none the less a general conception differing in many ways, general and particular, from the ideas held by other poets. These distinctions are all intimate, personal, individual, significant, deliberate. Professor Bradley treats Shakspere's characters as if they were real, speaks of them as we speak of actual people, and hence, though they are creations of Shakspere's imagination, he assumes them to be real people in Shakspere's mind and to form for him his real world. That is the fundamental assumption in 'Shaksperian Tragedy.'

Whatever the right hypothesis, in any case the poet reveals himself, but his personality varies of course with the explanation that is offered. Professor Bradley, following the tradition of Coleridge, but with far more learning and acumen, may be said to represent the "high significance" school, as compared with the school of "small significance," represented by Sir Sidney Lee.

VI

The foregoing discussion of the principles and assumptions in 'Shaksperian Tragedy' anticipates many of the remarks that may be made concerning the reasonableness of that very numerous class of books which attempt to present the essence of the whole of Shakespere. 'Shaksperian Tragedy' is assuredly among the most brilliant books in the great modern "Seeing Shakspere" enterprise. It is, however, limited to the four great tragedies. We have now to examine some of the better books of a broader scope. Only a few of these can be treated, and the choice of them is casual, except in so far as they are all based on modern scholarship and the usual tradition which does not attempt to glorify the personality of the poet by crudely borrowing that of another great man. Otherwise the books chosen are representative of no special schools, and if some yield too readily to theory and fancy, the failing, though not uncommon, is special.

One point is notable. In the following books—and probably in others with which I am unacquainted—the writers almost entirely abandon the quest for the personal trait, belief, or preference which was the North Pole of the various essays on the "Man." If it enters it is subordinated to the apparently larger aspects of the Personality which are variously termed Mind, Soul, Character, and Art. Development of the Personality becomes, in the larger books, a principle and object of structure. This is a modern idea. In a more antique form of biography, men did not "develop;" they merely did things, one after another. It is just possible that this modern notion is an incubus which makes us dream of Shakspere in a continually significant way.

Edward Dowden's restoration is perhaps the best known of any in use to-day, and is the approximate basis of much of the teaching of Shakspere's character that is now in vogue. It occurs in two books, the excellent and popular 'Shakspere Primer' (1877) and the more elaborate 'Shakspere, a Critical Study of His Mind and Art.' (1875) Dowden, compared with the Coleridgean restorers, had the advantage of access to the results of contemporary research. Modern chronologies are considerably more accurate than those of Coleridge, and the various tests of rime and meter, as well as the external evidence, have enabled recent critics to assume a fair degree of surety as to the order of the plays. They have also enabled critics to apply to Shakspere that Victorian invention of "early, middle, and late styles."

This is broadly the foundation on which Dowden restores his Shakspere. How far it is original with him I do not know, but since it appears in his books with much of the air of a personal triumph, it may well be his. The main point is its character, which—to consider first the simpler view, that of the 'Primer'— is this. There is a house of four stories, or, better, three stories and a cupola: 'In the Workshop,' 'In the World,' 'Out of the Depths,'' and 'On the Heights,' are the names given them, much as an Elizabethan publican would have named the rooms of his inn. Each of these stories is variously chambered, containing, for example, the rooms labelled 'Early Comedy,' 'Middle Tragedy,' etc. The roof-garden is undivided, containing nothing but 'Romances'; but, on the other hand, one of the rooms on one of the lowest floors is subdivided into the compartments (a) 'Rough and boisterous comedy,' (b) 'Joyous, refined, romantic,' (c) 'Serious, dark, ironical.'

Through this house, from room to room, Shakspere wandered, writing his personality on the walls of each successively. Or to use a closer metaphor, he constructed the house room by room, abandoning the last made for the new, like the chambered nautilus, stretching in his last found home, knowing the old no more, building more stately mansions for his soul, and finally emerging on the roof-garden whence an unlimited prospect of hopeful life—and, presumably, where an abundance of that ale which he drank too copiously in the company of Jonson and Drayton.

This framework method, this series of exhibition rooms for the display of the personality of the poet is evidently different from the methods that we have previously examined, Coleridge's, for example, or Bagehot's. It is interesting and to some degree plausible, but it does not, cannot without much more detail, get very far. It has the inherent vices of the "early, middle, and late style" method or of the "born, lived, drank, and died" formula. Indeed it is really in danger of missing the personality altogether. The poet had no notion of these various rooms; he did not say to himself, "Am I developing properly and to the satisfaction of Professor Dowden? Would it not now be well if I were to enter upon my middle comedy manner, or strike my joyous, refined, romantic note?" He probably did not in 'Henry the Fifth' bid "farewell in trumpet tones to the history of England," to his own knowledge nor did he feel that having, in this play, "presented his ideal of English kinghood," he "could turn aside from history." ('Shakspere Primer,' p. 100 and p. 101) Mr. Masefield, one may note by way of showing the fatuity of this sort of interpretation, makes out Henry V to have been a poor sort, and is as much down on the Helena of 'All's Well' as most critics are keen to praise her as one of Shakspere's ideals of womanhood. Dowden, also, like many modern interpreters, bases his conception of Shakspere's personality on his own guess at the intention of the poet in various plays. This method is very convenient in filling in and giving color to the picture of the poet traversing his Dowden-built house; but the data are probably not wholly facts.

The purpose of 'Shakspere; A Critical Study of His Mind and Art' is considerably more intimate and personal than that of the Primer. It is a very interesting book. "The attempt made in this volume," says Professor Dowden of the first edition, "to connect the study of Shakspere's works with an inquiry after the personality of the writer, and to observe, as far as is possible, in its several stages, the growth of his intellect and character from youth to full maturity, distinguishes the work from the greater number of preceding criticisms of Shakspere." (p. xiii., 3rd ed., N. Y., 1900, throughout) Or again, of the many sides from which the historical plays of Shakspere may be approached, "it is the man we are still seeking to discover—behind his works, behind his opinions, behind his artistic process." (p. 144) The position taken is, on the whole, a very dubious position that Shakspere's chief struggle in life was not with material circumstances, that his chief interest in life was not in people, "but that, by his study of history, Shakspere should have built up his own moral nature, and have fortified himself for the conduct of life, was, we may surmise, to Shakspere the chief outcome of his toil." (p. 145) This point is dwelt upon with iteration and reiteration in Professor Dowden's book. The bard is essentially a puritan-mystic.

The restoration is, of course, difficult. Shakspere is a dramatist, a realist, above all a humorist. His times, and the Elizabethan mind with which he came in contact, were mundane, concrete, vigorous. His own world was, on the one hand, "limited, practical, positive," but there was for him personally another world "opening into two infinites, an infinite of thought and an infinite of passion." (p. 31) In both worlds he grew apace, mastering the material world and retiring a well-to-do and respected burgher; mastering also the other, and in that process conquering a grave and terrible insanity which wrecked other Elizabethans—"the Romeo form and the Hamlet form—abandonment to passion, abandonment to brooding thought—two diseases of youth, each fatal in its own way; two forms of the one supreme crime in Shakspere's eyes, want of fidelity to the fact." (p. 41)

Such is the general course of his life. The detail may be represented under the figure of the pageant; for each of his plays, 'Romeo and Juliet,' say, or 'Lear,' is a pageant of his mind. In them he exhibits his mind as the old guilds used to display their appropriate mysteries. More in detail, his poems 'Venus and Adonis' and 'Lucrece' show how he sat down and carefully studied out subjects that interested him. Four early plays, 'Two Gentlemen of Verona,' 'Love's Labor's Lost,' 'Henry VI' and 'Comedy of Errors' exhibit experiments in different fields and do not stand for his permanent interests, though he wrote them with all the care of early experimentation. 'Romeo and Juliet' was an important interest which, like 'Hamlet,' he held in abeyance for a number of years until sure of himself. Looking over the whole of his life, indeed, one notes several lines of growth, from 'Love's Labor's Lost' to the 'Winter's Tale,' from the 'Comedy of Errors' to 'Midsummer Night's Dream,' from the histories wherein he treated the problem of worldly success to the tragedies wherein he treated the problem of success not material, but spiritual; and thence on to the 'Tempest,' having at last wholly liberated his mind. Resting places occurred, after the histories in 'As You Like It,' and, after the tragedies, in the "Winter's Tale.' His conception of women also grew apace from Margaret of Anjou and Rosaline, through Helena, through the great tragic creations, to Hermione and Miranda and Katharina.

Each class or group of plays had its special significance. The historical plays, "written all over with facts about Shakspere," in some measure show "how Shakspere would endeavor to control, and in what directions he would endeavor to reinforce, his own nature while in pursuit of a practical mastery over events and things." (p. 197) Tragedy was his real interest. He worked long, deliberately and hard over 'Romeo and Juliet' and 'Hamlet,' taking care in the first of these plays not to compete with the brilliance of Marlowe and in the second to vary his tragic model. "When 'Hamlet' was written Shakspere had gained a further stage in his culture of self-control, and. . .he had become not only adult as an author, but had entered upon the full maturity of his manhood." (p. 142) He was, therefore, able to treat of the profoundest spiritual problems of human life in answer, as it were, to the material position of 'Henry V.'

"In the play of 'King Lear' we come into contact with the imagination, the heart, the soul of Shakspere, at a moment when they attained their most powerful and intense vitality." (p. 232) The fact that the first and the second of the Roman plays, 'Julius Caesar' and 'Anthony and Cleopatra' were, unlike the English historical plays, dissociated by a number of years, shows that "the profoundest concerns of the individual soul were now pressing upon the imagination of the poet. Dramas now written upon subjects taken from history became not chronicles but tragedies." (p. 247) The history of Shakspere's laughter plays shows that he went from early comedies, each with a serious attempt of a comparatively limited sort, to great wisdom plays culminating in the 'Tempest,' which closed the long succession of "Shakspere's chief visions of truth." (p. 336) There having risen triumphant over his mental maladies, he emerged radiant and calm like his own Prospero, content to break his magic staff, drown his book and dismiss his airy servants. Such is the essence of Professor Dowden's vision.

It is a very charming moral vision; how one glows to think that Shakspere's heart of hearts and soul of souls was really saintly and a bit ascetic. Unfortunately for its truth, a number of other explanations are possible. In what he says of 'King Lear,' for example, Dowden is obviously arguing from the impression which Lear makes upon him, as upon many other modern readers since Lamb. It seems, to Dowden, to be the most power-

ful and intensely vital of all Shakspere's plays; therefore it was
so to Shakspere, was most significant of his inner life. The fallacy
need hardly be pointed out. It ignores the fact that many other
critics and very likely all Elizabethans were by no means affected
as Dowden had been.

Again, in a more general way, Professor Dowden gives his
beautiful picture of the poet's soul, of his self-development, but
leaves it as a guess unsupported by evidence. When he proceeds
to analyze the plays in detail, his account by no means sub-
stantiates this general picture. One gets the impression that
each of Professor Dowden's chapters, after his general outline, is
broken into two unequal pieces, the first part containing a
sketch of Shakspere's mind during a period, the second the
analysis of the particular plays. Now this latter analysis is
often excellent, but it does not render the preceding picture any
less filmy and transparent; it really does not at all apply to or
illustrate the previously drawn picture of Shakspere's mind.
Such lack of connection is a very common one in books on
Shakspere. Professor Moulton, for example, illustrates a
similar fallacy in his 'Shakspere as a Dramatic Artist' (1885)
when he analyzes in some detail the stories in the 'Merchant of
Venice' and shows their usefulness in that play. He tries to
make them representative of dramatic skill in general, whereas
what he is really doing is but to show the skill of Shakspere in
handling that particular play. In short, plays, like novels, like
events in life, are chiefly specific. Of Dowden's book one gains
the impression that his analysis of the specific plays is a far
truer and sounder affair than the general picture which he so
loosely attempts to derive from them.

Much closer to Shakspere's personality than 'Shakspere as a
Dramatic Artist' is Professor Moulton's 'Shakspere as a Dramatic Thinker' (1912). This book attempts to reconstruct the
moral philosophy of Shakspere from the record of his dramas.
The attempt is based on the analysis, not of the characters, but
of the plots. The characters, of course, have such diverse sentiments that Shakspere could not have entertained them all for
his own. Coleridge, confronted with this same difficulty, got
round it in his characteristic way by the method of qualities and

attributes. The plots, on the other hand, show the working out of Shakspere's ideas, for it is obvious that even though he appropriated a whole story, yet that story must have illustrated some idea which appealed to the poet. The single quotation, like a character, of course, shows nothing. On the other hand, one must not interpret Shakspere in the light of any special ethical theory. A detailed examination of the plots shows, on the contrary, fundamental ideas. Shakspere's handling of the story of the caskets, for example, shows nothing so clearly as his belief in the fact that temperament, training, and character are the determinants of a critical action.

These ideas Professor Moulton classifies as the root ideas— heroism and moral balance, the subject of the first four histories; wrong and retribution, of the later histories; innocence and pathos, in 'Romeo and Juliet'; wrong and restoration, in the 'Winter's Tale' and 'Cymbeline'; the life without and the life within, in 'Henry VIII.' In the second place there is "a world of Shakspere's creation in its moral complexity" wherein he dealt with the inner and outer life applied to Roman subjects, dramatized moral problems, represented life in equilibrium through comedy, and showed in tragedy the disturbance of this equilibrium, and made humor a matter of moral significance. Thirdly, certain moral forces guided Shakspere's genius: personality expressed itself in intrigue and irony; character was shown in momentum and as under the sway of circumstances; the figure of the pendulum represented his conception of the sway of historical events; a supernatural agency ruled, sometimes accidental, sometimes providential, in his moral world.

It is obvious that Professor Moulton, to make out his case for Shakspere, must show that his reading of the facts in Shakspere is correct. Now his reading of the facts at the very opening in his discussion of the character of Henry V, for example, is in direct opposition to Mr. Masefield's reading of these same facts. This does not mean that Mr. Masefield is more right than Professor Moulton. It simply means that further warrant than Mr. Moulton gives for the correct reading of these facts should be supplied. That, of course, is, alas, a great failure in much Shaksperian criticism. Granted your facts are right, the rest

becomes comparatively easy, since Shakspere would not, according to the principles enunciated by Stephen, have used facts
which did not interest him or which he did not understand.
Whether original or not, the facts that he used would probably
be his. But what are the facts? That is, of course, a great
problem in Shaksperian interpretation, and to this problem
Professor Moulton has ventured a solution that is as impression-
istic as that of most modern critics.

An ingenious and interesting restoration of Shakspere is that
of Professor Barrett Wendell ('William Shakspere, a Study of
Elizabethan Literature,' 1894). He essays the very difficult
task of seeing Shakspere, in so far as this is possible at this
distance of time, "as he saw himself." Doubtless Shakspere,
in spite of what Dowden says, did not see himself at all, being,
like most successful and wholesome minded people, concerned
with gaining his living, or getting what he wanted, or amusing
or expressing himself without any great amount of self-consciousness; and, in this human occupation, taking particular care to
live on good terms with his fellows. Professor Wendell's actual
task is different from his announcement. It is the restoration of
Shakspere's personality mainly on its artistic side. 'Midsummer
Night's Dream,' for example, becomes "in Shakspere's development, a first declaration of artistic consciousness." (p. 108)
Or again "To understand 'Julius Caesar,' in short, we must appreciate that when Shakspere read Plutarch, the narrative awakened
in him a definite state of feeling; this state of feeling, as well as
the facts which awakened it, he was bound as an artist to express." (p. 242) The author's object is throughout to feel
Shakspere's artistic rather than personal development. Professor Wendell is, therefore, skeptical as to the personal significance of much of Shakspere's work.

Something like Coleridge, however, Professor Wendell is
inclined, from the data presented by Shakspere's works, to
generalize regarding the typical mind which must have shed
these exhalations; for example: "Without other evidence than
is as yet before us, we cannot assert that Shakspere thought, or
believed, or cared for this ideal or that; nor yet that to have
known in imagination what he has expressed he must personally

have experienced certain circumstances, good or evil. We can assert, however, that he could hardly have expressed these things without at least three qualifications: first, a sympathetic understanding of such great historic movement as is finally phrased in 'Henry IV' and 'Henry V'; secondly, a sympathetic sharing of such romantic feeling as underlies both the single tragedy of this period and all the comedies; and thirdly, a sympathetic understanding of how a charming, idealized woman can fascinate and enchain an adoring, romantic lover. All of which, while lastingly true, is not spiritually profound." (pp. 215-216)

Even so, one may know something about personal traits of Shakspere in addition to the general character of his mind. This is particularly true of the 'Sonnets,' which show certain "leading personal traits" of Shakspere. They "alter any conception of Shakspere's individuality which might spring from the plays. . . . . . Even though they tell nothing of the facts of Shakspere's life, the 'Sonnets' imply very much concerning the inner truth of it." (p. 236) Professor Wendell, indeed, in common with us all—for who can help such an accident?—falls under Shakspere's spell in a human way.

Thus the record of Shakspere's life and his plays enable one to restore something of an artistic personality, which, however, rests upon a very human foundation. "Throughout Shakspere's career his imagination, for all its power, was concentrated on matters of detail. He created a greater number and variety of living characters than any other writer in modern literature. He made innumerable final phrases. Ever and again, by patient and repeated experiment with familiar motives, he combined old materials in constantly fresh and lastingly beautiful artistic effects. To a degree hardly paralleled, however, he was free from vagaries. Throughout his career, one may almost say, what he really and constantly did was this: instead of soaring into the clouds or the ether, he looked calmly about him, took account of what material was at hand, and with the utmost possible economy of invention decided what might be done with it and disposed of it accordingly. Among imaginative artists he is unique for practical prudence." (p. 422)

In general, Professor Wendell's interpretation is based upon the four group system most successfully popularized by Dowden. Shakspere successively enters these chambers of apprenticeship, experience, suffering, and tranquility. Here, for instance, is the summary of his third period; a curious classifier can detect in it a quasi-archaeological division—'Much Ado' and the 'Sonnets' being the first subdivision, 'Macbeth' and kindred plays, the second, 'Timon' and 'Pericles,' the third. One is reminded of Early, Middle and Late Minoan, 1, 2, 3:

During the third period of his artistic career—from 1600 to 1608—we found again this superb fusion of his own peculiar creative power and his own strong sense of fact. During this period, however, we found something far more significant than the merely artistic impulse which had preceded. Up to this time his plays had expressed nothing deeper than the touch of irony which underlies 'Much Ado About Nothing.' Now, in place of the old versatility first of experiment and then of concentration, we found a constant, crescent expression of such emotion as should come only from profound spiritual experience. He began to use his thoroughly mastered vehicle for the dramatic expression of such motives as we had seen to underlie his wonderfully finished 'Sonnets'. In these motives we observed first a profound and increasing sense of irony, of fate, of the helplessness of human beings in the midst of their crushing environment. Then came, with endless variations, a profound sense of the evil which must always spring from the mysterious fact of sex. Finally, perhaps as a result of these two causes, came a state of mind so over-wrought that, had it not been balanced by his supreme artistic sanity, it might almost have lapsed into madness. At the height of this period, when he produced his four great tragedies, his imagination was working with its fiercest power, and his sense of fact meanwhile controlled it with ultimate firmness.

One by one, the profound traits of this period began to disappear. With 'Macbeth' we saw the end of the morbid excitement of mind; with 'Anthony and Cleopatra' we bade farewell to the evil of woman; with 'Coriolanus,' where at length eccentricity or humor began to replace inevitable character, came the last complete expression of despairing irony. In other words, the power of his imagination, perhaps exhausted by the very intensity of its exercise, began to weaken under the pressure of a crushing sense of fact.

In 'Timon' and 'Pericles' we found a moment of artistic transition. The spontaneous power was gone. All that remained of the old Shakspere was the marvellous command of language, palpable even in his earliest work, and crescent with him to the end. (pp. 417-418)

It is very doubtful if Shakspere "saw himself" in any such way as this. Had he done so he would probably have been a supreme egoist as well as a supreme poet. Probably Professor Wendell means that he may have lived through the periods without recognizing them.

In his critical discussion of these matters, Professor Wendell makes use of a number of interesting methods of sharpening his definition of Shakspere. Most constant is a method of differences, perhaps best illustrated in the discussion (pp. 57 ff) of the difference in effect between Marlowe's 'Hero and Leander' and Shakspere's 'Venus and Adonis' and the causes, rhetorical and intellectual, by which these differences are produced. This method is used to define various plays.

Another method might be called that of the transference of the common or abstract quality to the individual—let us term it the argument from abstraction. Having abstracted the qualities of the poet or poetry, you souse the particular poet in as many of them as he, or the fancy, will stand. It is in Coleridge's way, though Professor Wendell happens to deal with artistic rather than philosophical material and is far from pushing it to the extremes of the transcendentalist. For example, speaking of the creation of Falstaff, Professor Wendell says:

> Imagine it to be as true of Falstaff as it is of the smaller creatures whose growth we may still watch in detail. Intended for a burlesque Puritan, the fat knight begins to speak and move of his own accord. By an inevitable process of spontaneous growth, he gathers about himself a new, fictitious world, more real if anything than the historical world amid which it is placed. As must constantly be the case, in short, with the work of artists whose creative imagination is fully alive, the conception outgrows its origin; it develops not into a conventional type, but into an individual character of unique vitality. Long before Falstaff was himself, Oldcastle and Puritanism must have been forgotten; until at last, with complete truth as well as manners, Shakspere could write that 'Oldcastle died a martyr, and this is not the man.' (pp. 171-172)

It is not at all unlikely that in such reasoning as this, Shakspere himself has furnished the stuff out of which the generalization regarding artistic consciousness is made, only to have it return upon his head in the shape of appreciation.

A third method, one better adapted to the ascertaining of specific facts than personal traits, might be called a method of harmony of expression. We have seen it used by Professor Bradley in his argument for the reality of the 'Sonnets.' Here is a good instance of the method furnished by Professor Wendell; "Had Shakspere actually undergone such an experience of folly and shame as Tyler conjectures, these poems would fitly express it." (p. 225) The method also works by comparison of one piece with another. "Here, finally, while there is no direct self-revelation, the frequent analogies to the moods expressed in the 'Sonnets' go far to make you feel that the mood of 'Measure for Measure' is unstudied, spontaneous, sincere." (p. 264)

An uncommonly interesting and illuminating restoration of Shakspere is that by Sir Walter Raleigh in the 'English Men of Letters.' ('Shakspere,' 1907) The principles on which it rests are probably among the soundest that we have examined. It is not a record of tradition, of gossip, of event, of personal trait, but a picture of that more important part of him, his mind. That mind is revealed chiefly in the poet's work. Essentially, "Shakspere was a man, and a writer: there was no escape for him; when he wrote, it was himself that he related to paper, his own mind that he revealed." (p. 5) And again, "If we desire to know how he wore his hat, or what were his idiosyncrasies of speech, it is chiefly because we feel that these things might be of value as signs and indications. But a lifetime of such observations and inferences could not tell us one-tenth part of what he has himself revealed to us by the more potent and expressive way of language." (p. 6) The common argument that he was a dramatist and as a dramatist was merely feigning in the various situations and characters which he represents, does not hold. We may not, however, from these works construct the particular details of his life. Doubtless his vast knowledge of humanity resulted from his experience, yet the exact detail of that experience, so far as it is a particular and personal thing, cannot be ascertained. The results we see in his knowledge of character and his generalizations about life, but we cannot restore the exact source of the suggestion. Again we are likely to demand in him a character in some exact sense, some preconceived sense which he had not. "His character was not all of a piece, neat and harmonious and symmetrical." (p. 15) "The truth is that Shakspere by revealing his whole mind to us, has given us just cause to complain that his mind is not small enough to be comprehended with ease." (p. 17) He was "that rarest of all things, a whole man." (p. 19)

Sir Walter Raleigh's task is, therefore, to reconstruct Shakspere's mind at work—"functionally and vitally" as is said in the elaborate pedagogics of to-day, though neither the poet nor Raleigh would ever use such a phrase. The book is a picture of a mind acting on the education and the experience of its possessor and on the customs and institutions among which he lived. These were of Elizabethan England, and the poet's actual experience of them was probably not unusual or untypical. Other men may have lived in the same scenes, may have made many of the same motions in life. The essential point is what Shakspere did with this material; the book is an interpretation of Shakspere's mind in terms of his time and in terms of his material. Mr. Bernard Shaw in the 'Dark Lady of the Sonnets' "presents" Shakspere as a connoisseur of fine phrases picked up from casual acquaintances, chiefly women. The same point of view, with far more scholarly knowledge and poetic insight is Sir Walter Raleigh's. The late Churton Collins, in 'Studies in Shakspere' (1904), has, like many other critics, discussed the matter of indebtedness in many of its details and with great learning. But Raleigh emphasizes the more important point— how a not unusual knowledge and experience were remade in the mind of the poet.

Thus it is probable that Shakspere while at Stratford gained that information of nature which is so vivid in his work. On the other hand, in many of his references to animals he is merely following common tradition, "taking words as he finds them, and refusing to impoverish the language of abuse by a forlorn protest on behalf of the goose, the ass, the ape, the dog, or the cat." (p. 36) So the history and traditions of his early life, the incidents of his reading, the stories which he heard, were worked into his plays and there vivified. The people and the events of city life which he has described are presumably what he saw in London. "Books served him in two ways; as a mine and as a school: he lifted from them the tales that he rehandled, and he learned from them some part of his dramatic method." (p. 63) His reading, which was fairly extensive, he used like personal experiences for the material of his plays, always heightening the poetry. Plutarch probably moved him more than other writers. "He gathered much of the floating debris of popular literature" and embodied it in his work. "In the 'Sonnets' Shakspere gave expression to his own thoughts and feeling, shaping the stuff of his experience with the laws of poetic art, to the ends of poetic beauty." (p. 94) In the theater, on the other hand, especially when he first came to London, he conformed pretty closely to the fashion and usages of the time. It was only as he grew older that he made experiments of his own. Many of his plays are clearly written for what material he had, for the actors in his company, for his audience and for the sake of a story that would go. He knew thoroughly well how to put a play on and what would succeed. Taking over the old apparatus, he produced those events which we call "Shaksperian" as well as plenty of stuff in a lower vein.

This is the skeleton of Sir Walter Raleigh's book. The charming detail he who would may read, is advised to read; for it is in the author's peculiar treatment of these common motifs that his notion of Shakspere's essential personality lies. The present summary must obviously be vague, though the complete picture is brilliant. Raleigh shows the reader the picture of these flaming peaks, touched with the fire of genius, lifting themselves out of the ordinary landscape—which is itself drawn with uncommon knowledge. Or, if you prefer, he plays a beautiful Shaksperian air to an Elizabethan accompaniment. These figures will have to serve as an illustration of the method which Raleigh uses.

It is curious, however, to what different conclusions identical facts may lead different critics without any apparent reason. Professor Wendell, for example, deems 'Cymbeline,' the 'Winter's Tale' and the 'Tempest' a last desperate struggle of the poet against "the crushing sense of fact which was fatally closing in not only on him but on the school of literature to which he belongs" ('William Shakspere,' p. 419) and against the competition of younger men. They give you the impression of being his last gasp. Of these same plays Sir Walter Raleigh, however, says that Shakspere "was at the top of his profession and was no longer forced to adapt himself to the narrower conventions of the stage. He might write what he liked, and he made full use of his hard-earned liberty." (p. 210)

This last quotation contains a not uncommon conclusion, but Raleigh does not err in pushing it to another extreme, wherein Shakspere, being at last wholly at liberty, could express his real self more completely than in less significant plays. (See, for example, L. A. Sherman: 'What is Shakspere?' 1901.) The present book, on the contrary, is based on extensive knowledge of Elizabethan literature and Elizabethan life. It is, of course, always possible that any restoration of Shakspere, like some of those that we have already examined, is a picture quite as much as a fact. Still, when all is said and done, there is in Raleigh's book not only an uncommonly good background of Elizabethan England, but a wholesome absence of any attempt to make Shakspere a specific moralist, or any other special kind of man, or to pry into the particularities of his life. It is probably the soundest in principle and in fact of the books of the class that are under consideration—these books wherein the critic, not confining himself chiefly—as does Sir Sidney Lee, for example, in his 'Life of William Shakspere'—to the facts of record and history, tries also to make of the poet a person as well as a series of events, to picture him "in his habit as he lived."

One further example of these larger pictures of Shakspere will suffice—a treatment of the subject sufficiently original. Sir Walter Raleigh, in the book which we have been considering, says that "the poets, and but few others, have approached him from the right point of view, with the requisite ease and sincerity." (p. 3) Mr. John Masefield being, since Coleridge and Emerson, about the only self-confessed and publically acknowledged poet who has tried panoramic Shaksperian criticism, it is perhaps well to examine some of his contentions in 'William Shakspere' (1911). Mr. Masefield doubtless has the insight and the vision, but being poetically bereft of arguments and reasons, his interesting book is a bundle of some 40,000 words of quick, nervous and occasionally crabbed assertions done into sentences averaging not more than twelve or fifteen words in length. "That the 'Sonnets'," says Mr. Masefield in an un-

commonly long sentence, "are now widely read while the plays
are seldom acted, is another proof that this age cares more for
what was perishing and personal in Shakspere than for that
which went winging on, in the great light, surveying the eternal
in man." (p. 247) This sentence, which occurs toward the end
of Mr. Masefield's book, states his purpose.

Now that "which went winging on" in Shakspere is for Mr.
Masefield a fairly uniform and steady moral problem of profound
significance. Humor has no part in it. The following sentence
is typical. "In this play of 'Othello' the ideas are those that
inspire nearly all the plays, that life seeks to preserve a balance,
and that obsessions, which upset the balance, betray life to
evil." (p. 181) Or again, "Like most Shaksperian tragedy,
'Macbeth' is the tragedy of a man betrayed by an obsession.
Caesar is betrayed by an obsession of the desire of glory, Anthony
by passion, Tarquin by lust, Wolsey by worldly greed,
Coriolanus and Timon by their nobleness, Angelo by his right-
eousness, Hamlet by his wisdom." (p. 196) 'Lear' "is an
excessive image of all that was most constant in Shakspere's
mind. Being an excessive image, it contains matter nowhere
else given." (p. 190)

The plays, then, show continuity of thought, but each has
its special moral significance. In 'Much Ado About Nothing,'
for instance, "Shakspere writes of the power of report, of the
thing overheard, to alter human destiny." (p. 134) 'Twelfth
Night' "presents images of self-deception, or delusional senti-
mentality, by means of a romantic fable and a vigorous fable."
(p. 139) In 'All's Well That Ends Well,' he "treats of the
removal of an obsession by making plain to the obsessed, by
pitiless judicial logic, the ugliness of the treachery it causes."
(p. 145) 'Hamlet' is "a tragedy of a man and an action continually baffled by wisdom." (p. 158) In 'Measure for Measure' he "seems to have brooded on the fact that the common
prudential virtues are sometimes due, not to virtue, but to some
starvation of the nature." (p. 175) These instances are typical
of the way in which Shakspere, according to Mr. Masefield,
even also in the early light comedies, embodies in all his plays
some profound reflection upon life.

Mr. Masefield's particular findings that ensue from these problems are, as one might expect, often highly individual and unusual. To him the much admired Helena in 'All's Well That Ends Well' is detestable. "Helena has been praised as one of the noblest of Shakspere's women. Shakspere saw her more clearly than any man who has ever lived. He saw her as a women who practises a borrowed art, not for art's sake, nor for charity, but, woman fashion, for a selfish end. He saw her put a man into a position of ignominy quite unbearable, and then plot with other women to keep him in that position. Lastly, he saw her beloved all the time by the conventionally minded of both sexes." (p. 147)   Henry the Fifth, esteemed by Ruskin to be Shakspere's one substantial hero, is to Mr. Masefield a disloyal and treacherous ruffian. "Katharina is vexed and plagued by forced submission to a father who cannot see her merit, and by jealousy of a gentle, useless sister. She, who is entirely honest, sees the brainless Bianca, whom no amount of schooling will make even passably honest, preferred before her. Lastly, she is humbled into the state of submissive wifely falsehood by a boor who cares only for his own will, her flesh, and her money. In a page and half of melancholy claptrap broken Katharina endeavours to persuade us that

> Such duty as the subject owes the prince,
> Even such a woman oweth to her husband."
> (p. 108)

In such judgments Mr. Masefield is quite the antipode of, say, Professor Bradley, who dissects and analyzes, argues and reasons, while you wait. Mr. Masefield takes the poetic short cut and clips the corners of his arguments—therein possibly following the so-called "late" or "final" style of the bard of Avon.

Here follows an interesting paragraph of Mr. Masefield's in which more than elsewhere he touches on the development of Shakspere's personality rather than on the significance of his plays. It is one of the many ways which critics have had of saying that Shakspere was different in the 'Merry Wives of Windsor' from what he was in the following play, 'As You Like

It.' But if 'As You Like It' had happened to precede the 'Merry Wives'—and the chronology is not definitive—then of course other conclusions and interpretations would be in order; the best way of mending the broken head of a generalization is surely to get a new one.

It is possible that when this play ['Merry Wives'] was written Shakspere had thoughts of consecrating himself to the writing of purely English plays. There are signs that he had reached a point of achievement that is always a critical point to imaginative men. He had reached the point at which the personality is exhausted. He had worked out his natural instincts, the life known to him, his predilections, his reading. He had found a channel in which his thoughts could express themselves. Writing was no longer so pleasant to him as it had been. He had done an incredible amount of work in a few years. The personality was worn to a husk. It may be that a very little would have kept him on this side of the line, writing imitations of what he had already done. He was at the critical moment which separates the contemplative from the visionary, the good from the excellent, the great from the supreme. All writers, according to their power, come to this point. Very few have the fortune to get beyond it. Shakspere's mind stood still for a moment, in this play and in the play that followed, before it went on triumphant to the supreme plays. (p. 127)

VII

The list of restorations could be indefinitely increased, but enough has been said to indicate the saner and more interesting examples of the enterprise. That enterprise is, as we have seen, largely modern. Shakspere as a personality was hardly thought of before the beginning of the nineteenth century. Then, rather suddenly, emerged the notion of High Personality somewhat abstracted from particular human concerns. Latterly there have been many attempts to make the poet more interesting in a variety of less sublime ways: to show him as a human being with beliefs and experiences, to show how his mind and art developed, to portray him as a man of his times with some outstanding qualities of high order. Portraits have been painted, grave and gay; the poet has been identified with many of his characters; he has unlocked his heart in copious aphorisms and recounted his experience in his sonnets; he has suffered from the *Weltschmerz*, the *Zeitgeist*, and other Teutonic perils.

Fertility of method has not been lacking. Naturally, impressionism has played a large part in determining the facts on which the inferences regarding the personality rest. Personal interpretations of certain sentiments and characters in the plays have perhaps been the greatest determinant in the various portraits of the bard. That is the Lamb stage. A little less crude, perhaps a trifle more logical, but still not very satisfactory, as a method, is Coleridge's way of endowing the personality of the poet with the generalized qualities of his class and of his characters. Later methods, with more fact to go on, have also been closer and more productive. The salient saying, the preponderant impression, the gratuitous speech, have been used to determine the more personal tastes of the poet and even to reconstruct his particular experience. On the other hand, differences—of the poet from other poets, of one play from another—have been tellingly used to define the quality of Shakspere's mind and the exact state of his development. One might, indeed, create from these books quite a system of personality logic, similar to Mill's system, for establishing correct inductions concerning the personalities of Shakspere and other human beings. Every part of his plays and poems—the plots, the characters, the references, the versification, even—has been made to yield its quota of inference to the great work of reconstruction.

The essays and books that we have latterly considered are probably among the most temperate of the treatises which, going beyond the historical fact and the logical inferences therefrom, essay the more difficult task of interpretation. The short essays on the Man strike one as the soundest; taken together, they represent a fairly uniform and continuous impression; the independence and ability of the critics lend weight to this view; as a composite the picture may be pretty much trusted. The longer books, which attempt the more difficult task of assaying the soul of Shakspere, differ considerably among themselves and are by no means equally convincing. Perhaps all that one can do is to take the treatment, as of a doctor, that suits one best— with some regard for logic and likelihood—or, throwing them all aside like harmless nostrums, to drink only the pure waters of the Avon.

VIII

Interesting as all the foregoing efforts have been it is doubtful if many have succeeded in their tacit aim—to make Shakspere, apart from the special manifestation of his works, a supremely interesting person.   The reason lies both in the vagueness and, possibly, in the futility of the quest.

The terms "man," "individuality," and "personality," common to this subject are, of course, used very loosely. All, like the terms "life and letters," "life and work" indicate disjunctions. "Man," for example, is commonly used to mean something apart from such emanations of the man as his "works," his business, and many other matters that partake of the world about; for the essential point in "man" appears to be the *in-* and *e-*, but not the *ex-*, *ternal*. "Individual" implies distinction from other generally like objects, and is used to connote differences. "Personality" is even vaguer and more uncertain in meaning:—persons are opposed to things; personality is what counts; his personality is agreeable or unattractive—in these and other like phrases there is often implied the existence of some quintessential of interest behind appearance, act, and word. This existence is established much in the same way as the functions of the mind—memory, reason, judgment, and the rest— by a generalization of certain classes of specific acts and a reasoning back to their alleged source. But "personality" is obviously vaguer than these generalizations of an earlier psychology.

What happens, however, in life with regard to these entities that we call "personalities" is that our impression of them is more or less constantly changing. "I thought I knew my Adrian," or "After all, I didn't really know my Adrian," the narrator in Mr. Locke's 'Jaffery' is constantly saying, stupidly enough but with quite human truth. Nor do different people regard the same personality as a uniform thing, except when it developes character or reputation. The reason is simple enough. We know people only through their appearance, their words, and their acts, directly by our own experience, or indirectly through what other people report. If a person is interesting at all, if he isn't merely commonplace, on the one hand, or frozen solid with character and reputation on the other, he can never appear twice alike to one person or the same to different people. Now the philosophical question is this: Is a man's personality the sum of all that he says and does and appears, or is it something behind these words and acts which "informs" them with interest? In neither case is it possible for any one person to arrive at the full view of the personality of another. In the case of the books and essays that we have been considering it is evident that Hazlitt, Bagehot, Smith, Stephen, Bradley (in 'Shakspere the Man') and Raleigh incline to the former view; whereas Coleridge, Lamb, Dowden, Wendell, Moulton, Masefield and Bradley (in 'Shaksperean Tragedy') entertain something like the latter—with variations, however, from very much abstracted views of Personality as something eternal in which the Gifted Individual has a share, to reasonably sensible generalizations from evidence.

Personality is therefore vital and the quest for it a shifting occupation, impossible to be put on any thoroughly scientific basis. We do not use the word definitely enough to hope for any uniform result, simply because we do not know what we mean by the thing. To ascertain it is probably more difficult in the case of men long dead, for the reason that the data of personality are often few and indistinct. Dr. Johnson and Napoleon are sometimes said to be the first people of whom we know anything "personal." With Shakspere, the data consist of a few recorded facts of no great interest; an indifferent bust and some fairly crude portraits; and, above all a hundred thousand odd lines of verse and prose, usually thought to be more pregnant with poetry and sublimity than any equal or proportionate amount from any other single brain. Perhaps the nearest one can get to a definition of the personality of the poet is to say that it is the total impression made by this data of the mind that produced it—of the man who did it, in short. That is, on the whole, the view of the later critics, whose restorations, in this aspect of the case, become merely tentative essays.

From what has been said it would follow that the only way at all approximating scientific treatment would be a sort of composite picture of the many different impressions that Shaks-

pere has made on thousands of readers in the three hundred years
of his increasing vogue. Provided such opinions could be got
at, even if one per cent. of these impressions had been recorded,
it would be a huge task to count the noses, weigh the results, and
bury copies of the resulting monographs in various libraries.
As a matter of fact, our picture has actually grown informally,
of course, in much the way indicated—by a series of accretions
and of sloughings-off. Thus succeeding critics have built on
Dryden's "largest and most comprehensive mind." Thus the
Rymer view of 'Othello' has atrophied. Thus Lamb, Coleridge,
Hazlitt, and others are accepted, modified, resurrected in the
contemporary pictures. Thus further discoveries, further
arguments, new methods, elicit new data for the alteration of
the picture. The writer of any new book on the subject (as
Bradley in 'Shaksperian Tragedy') is usually candid enough to
acknowledge in this respect his debt to his predecessors.

These individual impressions are themselves, of course, subject to logical check, of the kind that we have been examining.
Therein perhaps lies the chief value of any excursus on the recreation of the personality of the poet. What was with Dryden
scarcely more than an exclamation, and with Coleridge a crude
transfer of general functions or an *O Altitudo*, and with Lamb a
prayer in his closet and an *auto-da-fe* in public, assumed with
Bagehot something of an economical and psychological inquiry
and with Bradley and others a deliberate application of likelihood and probabilities. The method of preponderant interests is
one that carries far in advance of the critics of a hundred years
earlier, and, as we have seen, yields more definite results than
the unsystematic talk of the school of Coleridge, with its lover-
like deductions from the major premise that the lady is perfect.
Assuredly the better critics of to-day are far sounder in fact and
logic than the most brilliant of their predecessors a hundred
years earlier.

IX

But even if one's method of ascertaining the facts and of
drawing correct inferences from them were perfect, there would
still remain the possibility that the quest for Shakspere's per-

sonality would be futile. We all concede his supreme importance
and his hold over the imaginations of mankind. It seems as if
he ought to have been a supremely interesting person. Well, so he
was in one sense, but not necessarily so in another. All reconstructions of his personality assume, I take it, a restoration
of the man, or his mind, or his soul, or his art as he was when
alive. The very essence of such restoration of the "man" pre-
supposes a live man and not a museum mummy. He could not
have pursued his art when dead. Since these vital activities
ceased three hundred years ago—however much his soul went
"winging on"—any restoration is very much indeed concerned
with him as he appeared between April, 1564, and the corresponding month of 1616, during the first year or two of which time
he was

> Mewling and puking in the nurse's arms,

and hence not a specimen of High Personality at all. Doubtless
his mind as we see it in his plays and the development of his art
were all that the saner critics of later generations have found
them to be. Still, as a man, as a personality, the important
question is what he was as a live man, in other words, how he
appeared to his contemporaries, what he did and said among them.

If this contention is sound, we are at once thrown back upon
record and tradition and upon such inferences as may be properly
made not only from his works, but also from other knowledge of
Elizabethan literature and life. From this point of view, the
inferences of Coleridge and the visions of Lamb are practically
valueless, and only the essays on the "Man" that we have been
considering together with such lives as Sir Sidney Lee's and Sir
Walter Raleigh's are at all illuminating. From the record we
know that he was "gentle," that he was successful, that he probably got on well with his contemporaries, and several other
commendable things; by inference we learn, correctly enough,
certain of his beliefs, which we may be reasonably sure he did
not urge in his personal dealings with his fellows. Beyond this
and a few other matters it is impossible to go in refurbishing
his habit as he lived. But the record and the inferences do not
indicate a supremely interesting personality.

We may speculate further on the likelihood suggested in the preceding sentence. Doubtless he is the supreme poet, but from that it does not follow that he was a particularly interesting man or that his personality was more important than that of hundreds of his contemporaries. One of his critics very wisely remarks something to the effect that children would not have interrupted their play when he passed. His capacity, noted by several critics, for pensive melancholy and for brooding would not tend of themselves to make him attractive; on the other hand, his gayety and high spirits must usually have been an asset, as human nature goes. There are many chances, of course, that a man so supremely gifted with words and ideas would have been a very interesting companion, especially when relaxed, as in the celebrated colloquy with Drayton and Ben Jonson. But we know that he was usually prudent. Like many men, he may have saved himself for his plays. Nothing is commoner than the personal dullness of celebrated men, except the austerity and gloom in their own households of genial and popular public characters. The wit says with some truth:

> H. is the humorist dumb;
> Why sits he so silent and glum?
>   He's revolving some gay
>   Impromptu to say,
> When the opportune moment shall come.

We are all familiar with the phenomenon at dinners. But in spite of that we swallow the fallacy that there is some connection between the works of the great man and his personal impressiveness. There must be thousands of men—like Carlyle, for example—of high public reputation whose works some people admire but who would be "gey ill to live with."

Let us go a step further in suggesting the human chances. Whatever personal experience Shakspere may have had, whatever beliefs he may have held, were probably not extraordinary among his contemporaries. Others may have stolen deer, or married prematurely, or had intrigues with dark ladies, or risen to be prosperous burghers, and had nothing come of it all by way of egregious interest. It is quite possible that even on the humorous side of life or in its deeper tragedies, a thousand other men may have laughed and pondered and wept quite as much. The chances are that in the course of fifty years many men, even among our contemporaries, may see a good many Dogberrys and Pistols, Desdemonas and Kents; but most people do not have the incentive to write them down, and only one, Shakspere himself, has had the literary skill to make them eternally interesting. His mind and his literary skill are what count, as Sir Walter Raleigh justly remarks. Abstract his published works and what reasonable proof is there that he was an extraordinary personality? It is possible, indeed, that to his contemporaries he would have been much more entertaining, since he might not have saved his best for his plays. All this is, of course, conjecture; for he did write the plays, they were not destroyed, they cannot be abstracted. The plays are undoubtedly the thing; but they, like the record, by no means demonstrate the poet to have been a supremely interesting personality when alive. Personally, one is under no compulsion to find any of the restorations of Shakspere a supremely engaging picture, except for the fact that they are about Shakspere, of whom nothing may be said in vain.

V

'A MIDSUMMER NIGHT'S DREAM' ON THE NEW YORK STAGE

By George Clinton Densmore Odell
Professor of English

'A MIDSUMMER NIGHT'S DREAM' ON
THE NEW YORK STAGE

Certain interesting facts impress the student of the acting-history of Shakspere's fairy play:

1. From the closing of the theaters in 1642 until Mme. Vestris's revival in 1840, 'A Midsummer Night's Dream,' as its author left it, was never seen on the stage. It suffered utter neglect or, if produced, was transmuted into something new and strange, a droll, a mock opera, an operatic comedy—never once in all these two hundred years did it appear as the dream of Shakspere himself. I make this statement in spite of the entry in Pepys's Diary under date of September 29, 1662: "To the King's Theater, where we saw 'Midsummer Night's Dream,' which I had never seen before, nor shall ever again, for it is the most insipid ridiculous play that ever I saw in my life." I have no fear that a representation bounded in the past by the drolls, and in the near future—to the north-north-west, as it were—by Dryden and Davenant's perversion of the 'Tempest,' was likely to be very close to the spirit or even the text of our play. Aside from this testimony of Pepys, we are on firm ground. The droll, the 'Merry Conceited Humors of Bottom the Weaver,' published in quarto in 1661, and included in the first part of Kirkman's 'Wits or Sport upon Sport' in 1672, is composed of the fairy episodes and the low comedy scenes of the original; the quartet of lovers is eliminated. The 'Fairy Queen,' a spectacular affair, with music by Purcell, was acted at the Theater Royal, in 1692, to the delight of the town but the depletion of the treasury of the house. Its extra-Shaksperian matter is large in quantity. In 1716, Richard Leveridge, a bass singer, derived from our comedy a "comick" masque called 'Pyramus and Thisbe,' performed at the theater in Lincoln's Inn Fields. It is really nothing but a burlesque on popular Italian opera, as, for instance, where Crotchet asks whether the lion is to sing and Semibreve answers, "Never

wonder at that, for we that have studied the Italian opera may do anything in this kind." 'Pyramus and Thisbe', a mock opera, set to music by J. F. Lampe and produced at Covent Garden in 1745, was obviously an effort of like character. But now fashion changed; the hard-handed men disappeared altogether. and Garrick featured the poetic elements in the 'Fairies,' brought out in 1755 at Drury Lane, with Italian singers in the parts of Lysander and Hermia. Twenty-seven songs were in the offering, and, as Genest says, " 'A Midsummer Night's Dream' turned into an opera and assisted by two foreigners must have been a blessed exhibition, and highly to the credit of Garrick, who talked so much of his zeal for Shakspere." The confection was enjoyed nine times in the course of the season. On the contrary, a similar attempt in 1763 was withdrawn after one performance at the same theater. This was Garrick's alteration in five acts, with the original dialog curtailed and with thirty-three songs included; Shakspere's title was retained. Garrick, who had started on a long continental tour, left the production in charge of George Colman, the elder; according to a quaint note by the editor of the Garrick correspondence (1831), "it was brought out, and the audience, like the characters, at one time were all asleep." Colman reduced the affair to a two-act afterpiece, called 'A Fairy Tale'—a mere hodge-podge of the fairy episodes and the rehearsal of the mock-play—and three nights later (November 26th) it concluded a bill whose chief attraction was 'The Jealous Wife.' It was acted again on May 23, 1764, for the benefit of the fairy actors, when Miss Hopkins, as fairy page, spoke an epilog by Colman.

Concerning these various Garrick-Colman versions subsequent editors have made many confusing statements; the facts are as detailed above. In light of the evidence we can understand Colman's remark that he was "little more than god-father" to the 'Fairy Tale,' and "the alterations should have been subscribed Anon." Both of the 1763 renderings were printed, perhaps to be sold in the theater, as librettos to-day are sold in opera-houses; otherwise why print such failures? 'A Fairy Tale' was acted, again under the management of Colman, at the Haymarket in 1777; once more it was printed. In both performances of this

trifle (I shall ask you to remember), the part of Oberon was played
by a woman, Puck by a boy.   In 1755, "Master" Reinholt had
played the King of Fairyland.   The year 1777 is the last in which
any sort of 'Midsummer Night's Dream' is found on London
programs, and this fact justifies Frederick J. Reynolds's note in
the preface to his 1816 acting edition that the comedy had not
been seen on the stage for fifty years; the farce produced in
Birmingham in 1798 escaped his inturned London eyes.   His
revival at Covent Garden in 1816 followed the tradition from the
preceding century of making the 'Dream' an opera, though
enough of Shakspere was restored to warrant Reynolds's boast
that he had brought the work back to the stage.   This rendering,
of which I shall speak later, had music by Bishop, and was in its
way a notable affair.   So far as I can discover, the above is the
starved history of the play in London until in 1840 Mme. Vestris,
probably inspired by similar experiments in Germany, enacted
something like the original at Covent Garden, with songs indeed,
but to Shakspere's words.

2.   Whenever managers have tired of the easy and the conventional, they have eagerly turned toward the mounting of this
play.   Its aggregation of difficulties in scenery, attire and mechanical trickery—starting in 1692, with a transformation scene,
and dances by monkeys as well as "Chineses," with disappearing
bridges and swans turning into fairies—has tempted all to accomplish the best the theater can do.   Like Robin Goodfellow, it
has led them up and down, up and down, to glory or the
grave.

3.   It is quite apparent that most of the New York revivals
of the comedy were inspired directly by successes with it in London just a short time before.   This will be clear in the discussion
which follows.

I.   At the Park Theater, 1826 and 1841

The first performance in America of something resembling
Shakspere's comedy was thus quietly advertised in the *Times*
newspaper:

PARK THEATER

MRS. HILSON'S BENEFIT

THIS EVENING, NOVEMBER 8, 1826, WILL BE PRESENTED FOR THE
FIRST TIME IN AMERICA THE OPERATIC COMEDY OF A

MIDSUMMER NIGHT'S DREAM

Mortals—Theseus, Mr. Lee; Egeus, Mr. Foot; Lysander, Mr. Woodhull;
Demetrius, Mr. Denman; Snout, the Tinker, Mr. Placide; Starveling, the
Tailor, Mr. Nexsen; Bottom, the Weaver, Mr. Hilson; Hyppolita (*sic*), Mrs.
Stickney; Hermia, Mrs. Hackett; Helena, Mrs. Brundage; *Immortals*—
Oberon, Mr. Richings; Titania, Mrs. Sharpe; Puck, or Robin Goodfellow, Mrs.
Hilson.

"after which," the announcement goes on to promise, "the petit
comedy of 'Maid or Wife, or the Deceiver Deceived,' and the
melo-drama of the 'Lady of the Rock,'" a liberal evening's entertainment; but, as the announcement reads further that "performances in future will commence at one quarter before seven
o'clock" and as any one could presumably depart at will, a good
time was no doubt had by all.

I should like to remark that this is perhaps the first time since
1826 that so much of the original cast has been printed. Ireland,
whose invaluable 'Records of the New York Stage' have since
been invariably quoted, confesses that he had but a "mutilăted
copy of the bill" for the occasion, and could furnish only an incomplete distribution of the chief parts. The allotment of the
characters of Theseus, Bottom, Snout, Oberon, Puck, Titania,
Hyppolita (*sic*) and Hermia is all he reports; I suspect his "muti-
lated bill" may have been an advertisement in an old newspaper,
for these are the only parts and actors advertised in some of the
papers of the time—the New York *Evening Post* of November
3rd, for instance. Whatever the service may be worth, I would
claim the distinction of having saved the rest from oblivion; they
will live now just as long as my article lives!

A second thought suggested by a search in old news files concerns itself with the extreme lack of excitement that attended this
occasion, which seems to us, ninety years later, so highly interesting. The first performance of a Shaksperian play in America!

think what our Sunday supplement would make of such an event! But in 1826, it was just as if you offered the stolid householders who were theater-goers, a large comfortable cabbage; evidently much blood of Holland still coursed imperturbably through their veins. There was no preliminary notice except what the theater paid for in advertising columns, and the following constitute the entire after-glow of criticism, so far as I can discover it in old periodicals.

The *Evening Post* of Friday, November 10, 1826, thus chronicles its experiences at Mrs. Hilson's benefit:

Midsummer Night's Dream. This play of Shakspere's, transformed by modern ingenuity into a comic opera, but not so transformed as wholly to lose the beauty and humor of the original, was performed last evening at the Park Theater. The more serious parts of it went off heavily enough, and would have been hardly endurable, but for the singing. The whole fairy machinery is too light, changing and ethereal for actors of flesh and blood, and the clumsy contrivances of the stage. Richings is a stout, heavy, fairy king and Mrs. Sharpe a substantial fairy queen. Richings has much improved lately, but he should not mangle Shakspere as he does. For instance, where Shakspere says

        At a fair vestal, throned by the west,

Mr. Richings should not say

        At a vestal throned by the west.

And where Shakspere says

        Yet marked I where the bolt of Cupid fell:
        It fell upon a little western flower,
        Before milk-white, now purple with Love's wound;

Mr. Richings should not change the last word in these lines to *wounds*, for this simple reason, that it makes nonsense of the passage.

The comic parts of the piece which form a large proportion of it went off quite well and the audience were exceedingly delighted. Those who were inclined to laugh, indulged themselves without scruple, because the wit was Shakspere's; those who were not, sometimes found themselves compelled to it, and we saw many a grave face wrinkling with laughter in spite of itself. Hilson made an excellent Nick Bottom, but it is a pity that he should let the audience see him put his hand behind him to pull the string that moved his asses (*sic*) ears.

The Truth Teller, a weekly, is even less informing in its notice of November 11th:

Park Theater. Shakspere's operatic comedy of A Midsummer Night's Dream was presented for the first time in America to a crowded and respectable audience, on Thursday evening, with music, dances, etc., incidental to the piece, being for the benefit of Mrs. Hilson. Of the performance little need be said (*sic*) than the characters were ably cast; Mr. Hilson as *Bottom* and Mr. Placide as *Snout*, played as well as they play anything; that is, they never fail to make the most of their characters, to the great amusement of the audience. The piece met with a brilliant reception, and affords a rich treat to the lovers of comedy.

These are the records, and difficult enough it is to reconstruct from them the actual performances in the fashionable old Park Theater so far down town, with its lamp-light, its inartistic furnishings, its provincial air. The play was repeated on November 24th, but not again before the close of the year, and perhaps for the entire season. What was it like? I do not know, but I hazard the guess that it was founded on the version used at Covent Garden in 1816, and still accessible in the copy printed in the same year "for John Miller, 25, Bow Street, Covent Garden." This is the peccant thing so contemptuously treated by Genest. Obviously, there was some little effort to live up to the opportunity offered. The earlier advertisement in the *Evening Post*, referred to above, stresses the fact (1) that the play—"an operatic comedy—is to be presented for the first time in America"; (2) "as performed in London with unbounded applause"; and (3) "with music, dancing, and various scenic displays, incidental to the piece." All this seems to point with a considerable degree of probability to the Covent Garden "hit" of ten years before; Genest records no performance thereafter in any of the theaters-royal.

And what was that 1816 'Midsummer Night's Dream'? Well, a Shaksperian of this day will shudder with disgust, as did Genest and Hazlitt, at the mere recital of the violence done to the work of the gentle bard. The "opera" is divided into three acts of three, five and four scenes, respectively. The stage directions, as printed, call for such effects as "A Grand Doric Colonnade appertaining to Duke Theseus' Palace"; "a Wood. Moonlight"; "Another part of the Wood. Titania's Bower, decorated with flowers. In the center, the Duke's Oak." Incidental to the second set instanced above there was: "A March. *Enter, in procession,* OBERON, *King of the Fairies, at one wing, with his*

Train, and the Queen at another, with hers. TITANIA *is in a Car.—*
OBERON in another Car." At the end of the play was performed
a grand pageant, commemorative of the triumphs of Theseus.
Evidently the Londoners in 1816 were treated to some considerable spectacle; how much did the New Yorkers of 1826 get?

But the greatest liberties were taken with the text. I shall cite
the most notable. (1) The entire scene with *Helena* is omitted
in Act I, making it rather difficult for the audience to know how
Demetrius has come (in Act II) into the knowledge of the proposed flight of Lysander and Hermia. Against this excision
Hazlitt and Genest both inveigh. (2) Much of the dialog of
the four lovers is mercilessly curtailed throughout the play.
(3) The scene of the acting of 'Pyramus and Thisbe' is transferred
to the wood, Theseus and Philostrate observing from behind a
tree.

This transposition is effected, in order to allow at the end of the
play of the grand pageant of Theseus' triumphs. Shakspere's
final scene with the fairies is omitted. All these changes were
made necessary by the great number of musical numbers inter-
spersed wherever possible. These are by Bishop, Arne and Smith.
All the opportunities for singing offered by Shakspere are seized
upon; but everywhere we get gems like this, sung by Demetrius
just as he flies Helena to hide in the brake:

> Recall the minutes that are fled,
>   Forbid fleet time to move;
> To new life wake the sleeping dead,
>   But ne'er recall my love.
>
> Forbid the stormy waves to roar,
>   The playful winds to rove,
> Revive the sun at midnight hour,
>   But ne'er recall my love.

And while at the close Theseus, with the rest, modestly reviews
his own deeds, Hermia sings, having been royally bidden thereto
by these interpolated lines:

> Hark, they approach!
> My hardy veterans!

My grave companions in the toils of war!—
And since ourselves, we boast not of the pow'r
To welcome them in aught, save the plain
Rough language of a soldier,
Hermia, stand forth, and with thy dulcet tones,
Give, give to all, harmonious greeting.

Hermia, apparently nothing loth, warbles a martial lay by Bishop, beginning (after recitative),

Now Pleasure's voice be heard around!
And sweetly lute and lyre resound!

From two bones, construct the monster. When timid students quote Hazlitt as saying that he preferred Shakspere in the library to Shakspere on the stage, let them remember that it was of this very performance of "A Midsummer Night's Dream" that he was writing. His evidence is worth just what that fact implies. Other comedies of the great dramatist were treated in exactly the same way.

And what was the performance in New York like, in 1826? From the data arrayed above, can you not guess? It was doubtless a feeble attempt to reproduce what, for the thing it attempted, was very well done in London ten years before. One thing I bid you note; Oberon was played by a man, as in 1816 at Covent Garden; the part was not so played again in this city till 1906, at the Astor Theater. Mme. Vestris's Oberon, in 1840, apparently set the fashion of female Fairy Kings for all that length of time.

This fashion was followed in the performance which opened the season at the Park Theater in New York, August 30, 1841. Perhaps the most amusing, if not the most interesting document connected with that revival is to be found in the issue of the semi-weekly *American*, under date of August 31st:

The Park Theater opened last night to a very full, and, in part, a somewhat disorderly house. More than once were the performers interfered with by the interruption of the upper tiers. This should be prevented for the future. The Midsummer Night's Dream was produced in a handsome style, and, barring a few exceptions, with effect. A repetition of the piece will render the performers more familiar with their parts.

The review ends with an account of a fight between Moonshine's dog ("an ugly-looking bull") and the Lion, at which part of the audience was manifestly delighted, and tried to encourage the row. And that was dramatic criticism in this city in 1841! and for the second revival in America of one of the great Shaksperian comedies! The *Herald* of the same date is more flowery, without being more informing:

PARK THEATER. Long before the curtain drew up, last night, there were symptoms of a very full, if not a very fashionable audience. After the national airs had been performed by the orchestra, and duly honored by the house, that rare conceit, 'A Midsummer Night's Dream,' was introduced to the American stage. This play, abounding as it does with the most poetical imagery and overflowing with the most subtle wit, is yet deficient in that essential for dramatic success—interest to keep the audience alive. In the closet, the devotees of the bard of Avon pore over its beauties, and revel in the glorious poetry of its author; but on the stage it is quite another affair, and we saw numbers almost ready to yawn, who would have been ashamed to confess themselves insensible to its merits as a poem.

Of the performers we have but little room to speak now. They all did their best for their several parts, and were received with a fervor of applause which speaks well for the future popularity of the management. . . . There was about $1100 in the house.

The play ran only one week, yet, according to Ireland, it was produced with great care; the *Herald*, of August 30th (the day of the performance), announced that the cast includes some old favorites, as well as new candidates for public favor, and "great expense, we are told, has been lavished on the getting up by the manager." The actors "featured" by the directorate in preliminary notices were Mrs. Knight (Puck), Mr. W. H. Williams (Bottom), and Miss Cushman (Oberon). This seems, to later fancy, an astonishing rôle in which to find Charlotte Cushman; her fame, however, was then in the making. Other well-known players (well-known in later days, at least) were William Wheatley (Lysander), C. W. Clarke (Demetrius), Susan Cushman (Helena), Mary Taylor (Titania). The comedy, according to Ireland, did not prove attractive. "Mrs. Knight was too substantial in appearance for the frolicsome sprite, a part that would have suited Miss Taylor perfectly, although the management had not penetration enough to know it."

Curiously enough, we can discover less about this production than about that of fifteen years before at the same theater.

The above data are all I could collect. But from Macready's
'Reminiscences' we learn that the directors of the Park were in
the habit of crossing annually to London in search of novelties,
especially in actors. Now the season before, 1840-1841, Mme.
Vestris had played in this piece fifty-nine times at Covent Garden;
she reproduced it at the opening of the season in 1841. What
could be more natural than the assumption that Simpson, then in
sole charge, saw the Vestris performance and decided to imitate
it on the stage of the New York house? The fact that Oberon
was given to a woman confirms this guess to a considerable degree.
It was put on "with new music [Mendelssohn's?], scenery and
machinery." No doubt, the American mounting lagged far
behind, but let us hope that the play at least was Shakspere's
and not something like Reynolds's. The critic of the *Sunday
Courier*, reviewing, in 1854, the Burton revival, says, justifying
his use of the term "unacted,"

> We use the term 'unacted', because this comedy has never been performed
> before entire, according to the text of Shakspere, and only occasionally in any
> shape. It was produced at the Park Theater a good many years since, under
> the supervision of Mr. Barry, in something approximating to a complete form,
> but was got up in haste and without any labored attempt at scenic display or
> strictness and splendor of costume, and fell completely lifeless.

It will, at any rate, furnish food for conjecture to examine the
scenic version of Mme. Vestris's 'Dream,' as printed in Volume 28
of Lacy's 'Acting Plays':

Act I, Sc. 1. Hall in the Palace of Theseus—with a view of Athens.
        Sc. 2. Room in Quince's Cottage.

Act II, Sc. 1. Moonlight landscape—High sloping bank, 3 E. R.—Small
                made-out bank against it. do. R. C. up stage. do. 4 E. L.—
                flowery bank, 4 E. L., fire-flies, etc.
        Sc. 2. The previous scene works off gradually and discovery (*sic*)
                another part of the wood.

Act III, Sc. 1. Moonlight—transparent wood—platform colored and rising
                 ground, crossing from the back, R. Water piece joining it and
                 running off L.—(In the course of this scene occurs the stage
                 direction: The moon sinks very gradually; the rays disappear
                 from tops of the trees; daylight continues to increase until the
                 lights are full on).

Act IV, Sc. 1.   The Wood.—Titania's bower—sloping bank, 3 E. R., with
                   Slote and concealed bower.
          Sc. 2.   Room in Quince's house.
          Sc. 3.   The transparent Wood, as in Act III, Sc. 1, which changes to
                   sunlight.

Act V.   Hall of statues, with raised stage in the centre hung R. the
                   back with curtains. Couch R. and two Grecian stools—two
                   do. chairs, L.   .   .   .   Change to another part of the Pal-
                   ace—staircases, R. and L.—raised stage to form a staircase and
                   platform centre—smaller staircases lead from the platform to
                   side stairs—gallery running along the back from R. to L.—
                   Parisian lanterns of various colored paper for all the fairies.

This last effect was designed by J. R. Planché, who also made
the acting version.

I have gone into this description at such length because, in
view of the scantiness of early records, I believed it would be of
real interest. I cannot think New York had anything like such
magnificence, but obviously our manager hoped for something of
the same success. After a week, however, the play was shelved
for another thirteen years or more.

Meantime, of Mme. Vestris's revival we can repeat (1) that it
brought back to the stage Shakspere himself; (2) that it set the
fashion of assigning Oberon to a female performer, though this
had prevailed to some extent, as we have seen, in the eighteenth
century; (3) that it introduced the habit of the panorama or
sliding scene (see above, "The previous scene works off gradually," etc.); (4) that it was the first to use some, at least, of Mendelssohn's music; and, (5) that it made the production of 'A Midsummer Night's Dream' the desire of every great manager of the
future.

II. At Burton's and the Broadway, March, 1854

No event in our mid-century theatrical history is more interesting than the double production of 'A Midsummer Night's
Dream' brought about by managerial rivalry in 1854. I have no
doubt that it was inspired by the success of Samuel Phelps at
Sadler's Wells, in 1853, but I have been forced to give up my
original suspicion that either of these or any of the revivals in
New York except that of 1867 employed scenery imported from

an English rendering of the drama. At Burton's and the Broadway we have assurance that the painting was by the artists connected with the theaters involved. It is extraordinary that a play acted but twice before in the city should thus emerge simultaneously at two houses. W. E. Burton, at that time perhaps the most popular of New York comedians had, at his theater, one of the best companies of actors in the English-speaking world; old comedies and new were presented on his stage with incomparable art. He was turning more and more to Shakspere, and had given or was shortly to give memorable performances of 'Twelfth Night,' the 'Winter's Tale,' and the 'Tempest.' One might say that this revival was his, by right of service; besides he was a thorough Shaksperian scholar. But the Broadway Theater, near Anthony Street, was a house of no settled policy; it was a huge affair, seating, we are told, about 4,000 people, and had been built as a speculation. It was never a success, and obviously the performance of our comedy about to be discussed was purely a commercial inspiration. Nevertheless, it was beautifully done, and rather eclipsed, scenically, the production in Burton's small, more intimate theater.

One thought impresses as we look about for records of these rival attractions; the newspapers were now awake, and advertisements and criticisms throw ample light on the methods of staging. The press, as well as the theater, had made enormous strides in the years between 1841 and 1854; it is little short of marvellous. Let me illustrate by placing in parallel columns the announcements of the competing establishments:

The advertisement for Burton's, *The Daily Tribune*, Feb. 3, 1854

Produced from original Text, with but few curtailments, and graced for the first time on any stage with

MENDELSSOHN'S MUSIC!

ENTIRELY NEW SCENERY, of the most beautiful description, painted by Mr. Heilge. Gorgeous new costumes by Mr. Keyser and assistants. The

The advertisement for the Broadway, *The Daily Tribune*, Feb. 6, 1854

The whole of Mendelssohn's beautiful vocal and instrumental music. The scenic illustrations entirely new, painted by Mr. Heister and his assistants; the costumes by Mrs. Wallis; the decorations, banners and appointments by Mr. Wallis; the machinery by Mr. John Furze; the ballet produced under the direction of Mlle. Leader; the music

Classical Dresses are from the first authorities—The Fairy Habiliments, Decorations and Accessories are of the very best and richest construction. Extensive machinery by Mr. William Foudray and assistants. Costly Properties by Mr. T. Cross. The Fairy Dances and Groupings, arranged by Mons. Frederic, Ballet Master. The Comedy produced under the immediate direction of Mr. Burton, materially assisted by Mr. J. Moore, Stage Director.

arranged and adapted by Mr. Jo. Mayer, produced under the direction of Mr. Roberts.

The casts at the two houses have always been thus opposingly grouped in subsequent records, and I follow the invariable custom in so doing. Unlike the Park Theater cast of 1841, these two are worth repeating almost in full:

	Burton's	*Broadway*
Theseus	Charles Fisher	F. B. Conway
Lysander	George Jordan	Lanergan
Demetrius	J. Norton	Grosvenor
Bottom	Wm. E. Burton	William Davidge
Quince	T. Johnston	Howard
Flute	George Barrett	Whiting
Puck	Master C. Parsloe	Little Viola Crocker
Oberon	Miss E. Raymond	Mme. Ponisi
Titania	Mrs. Burton	Mrs. Abbott
Hippolyta	Miss J. Cooke	Mrs. Warren
Hermia	Miss Lottie Hough	Mrs. Nagle
Helena	Mrs. Buckland	Miss A. Gougenheim
	(Kate Horn)	

Ireland, in speaking of the performance at the Broadway, remarks, "it had already been produced (though not with quite equal magnificance) at Burton's." Col. T. Alston Brown, in his 'History of the New York Stage' agrees: "The play," he says (vol. i, 397), "at Burton's ran until March 6, and at the Broadway until March 11. In effectiveness of stage setting, and in the costuming, the comedy had an infinitely more brilliant showing here than at Burton's; in the acting, there was little left for critical cavil in the performance at either house."

Actual contemporary criticism gives the same impression. The New York *Tribune*, February 4, 1854, became enthusiastic over Burton's spectacle: "The representation of the Midsummer Night's Dream at Burton's Theater last night may be signalized as one of the best representations, in regard to stage effects and appointments, if not the best, that we have yet had in this city. The theater itself is a miniature affair and the stage incompetent as to depth and breadth for the right setting-forth of the dainty imaginations of the great poet; but viewing it not as a great but as a neat affair, the whole is deserving of emphatic approval." The *Herald* of February 8, however, shows the superiority scenically, of the other production: "The dancing and spectacle were as good as such things usually are when Leader leads the way. The scenery, by Mr. Heister, has certainly never been excelled in this city. Loud bursts of genuine applause greeted the panorama with which the first act ended; and for our part we will add that we doubt whether a more perfect triumph in the way of decorations is ever achieved at any of the theaters of Europe. To see that panorama...is well worth a visit to the Broadway."

For this one production it is possible to rehabilitate the spectacle and set it before imaginative eyes. In the invaluable collection of prompt-books bequeathed to the New York Public Library by the late George Becks is the acting-copy of this very Broadway revival, with elaborate descriptions of the scenes. The version used was in three acts, as against Burton's in five; it is still published in French's 'Standard Drama.' Now in the Becks collection is another prompt copy, with unusually detailed manuscript accounts of the way the scenery was manipulated; this copy has the autograph "J. B. Wright, 1854." A Mr. Wright was a member of the Broadway company at this time; J. B. Wright was a well-known Boston stage-manager. Probably the two Wrights are the same. Thomas Barry staged the piece here; a few months later he is manager of the new Boston Theater, and J. B. Wright is his assistant. So convinced am I that both these prompt-books refer to the same revival, that I shall run together the two sets of directions, indicating the source of each.

Scene by scene the Wright acting version corresponds to French's. I am moved to set all this before my readers, since it is the only thing of the sort to which we can have access, and because it will show our fathers' idea of a beautiful spectacular treatment of Shakspere's play. Unless otherwise indicated, the directions are from the first of the two prompt-copies cited above. Over against it I will place the synopsis of scenery at Burton's, quoted from a pamphlet published by Burton himself during the run of the play at the theater, and giving cast, arrangement of scenes and numerous selections from the reviews in the daily press. The latter are eulogistic, though discriminating in tone. For the opportunity to examine this pamphlet and for the use of programs of other productions of the play I am indebted to Mr. Charles H. Burnham, so long of Wallack's Theater.

BURTON'S THEATER

Act I

SCENE 1. The stage represents the courtyard of the Palace of Theseus, King of Athens, as seen through the arch of entrance. Statues of the household gods are observable in the various avenues; and in the back view may be seen the principal buildings of the Acropolis or the Upper City, and the Hill of Mars. Theseus, a Grecian hero, who flourished 1235 B. C., having conquered the Amazons, is about to marry their Queen. He is accompanied by his warriors, attired in the correct costume of old Greece, as pictured by Willemin in his Costumes des Peuples de l'Antiquité. Hippolyta and her attendant Amazons are dressed from their presentations in Pinelli, Piranesi and the Etruscan vases. Theseus instructs Philostrate, his master of Revels, to direct the order of his marriage fête. Egeus, an Athenian noble and father of Hermia, presents himself with his

THE BROADWAY THEATER

Act I

SCENE 1. A hall of state in the Palace of Theseus. Huge columns, supporting a massive arch, through which is seen a portion of the City of Athens leading to the left; on the right a portion of the bay. A landing place beyond the archway, with marble steps leading to the stage in front.

Music. As the curtain rises, Athenian soldiers with their officers enter from the W. E. R., and form on each side of the stage, to receive the Duke. A galley then approaches from W. E. R., and lands C., containing Theseus, Hippolyta, Philostrate, Ladies, Lords, and attendants. The Duke, etc., land and advance to the front.

SCENE 2. A room in a cottage at Athens.

SCENE 3. A romantic landscape through which is seen a stream of water (By moonlight). A bush in C.

daughter and her lovers. The Athenians are dressed in the rich tunics given on the authority of Hope in his Ancient Costume, with the cothurnus or buskin, and Attic fillet on the head. The ladies wear the long sleeveless tunic, the caladiris or stola, with the rich and varied peplum over the bust, and the crepida sandal.

SCENE 2. The House of the Athenian Artisans—a plain room in the severe simplicity of the earliest Doric, built of wood and stone, and opening to the suburbs of the Catapolis or Lower City. The workingmen of old Greece are dressed in the usual short tunic of coarse material, with, in some instances, the dipthera, or under-jacket, made of leather.

ACT II

SCENE 1. Puck, the Hobgoblin, is here dressed as a lower order of fairy —"a lob of spirits"—a shrewd and knavish sprite — whose shape and making betray his name at once to the other mythological beings. Puck in all other versions of this piece, has been, and still is, represented by a pretty piece of femininity in ringlets and muslin skirts. It is for the public to judge which is the Shaksperian truth.

Oberon, the King of Fairyland, is represented as the miniature model of a Grecian warrior, an appearance assumed in compliment to his "buskined mistress and his warrior love, the bouncing Amazon."

The "lovely boy, stolen from an Indian King," never before placed on the stage, although undoubtedly intended to be personated, is costumed from an ancient print, and is believed, both in beauty and apparel, to be

A troop of fairies are discovered grouped. A fairy touches the bush with her wand, and Puck comes out; the bush disappears through the stage.

At the end of the scene:

(As Puck exits L. H., Oberon waves on a singing fairy.)

Duet

"I know a bank."

(The music continues. The fairy exits. R. 2 E. Oberon gets in the car, drawn by swans. A Panorama.)

(In the prompt-book of G. Becks, with the name of J. B. Wright, New York, 1854, this panorama seems to be described.)

Duet: Bishop's Music

Oberon and the Second Fairy (who enters from 2 E. R. H.). Same time a Dolphin car enters from 3 E. R. drawn by dolphins. End of duet. Fairy goes off R. Oberon goes to car. Music. Footlights full down. Gas full down.

PANORAMA OF FAIRYLAND now passes from L. to R., during which moon becomes visible back of gauze flats of panorama. When the Fairyland has disappeared, a beautiful Illuminated Fairy drop is discovered the full extent of the stage, with gauze waters, and tone in with those in front. Fairy children on working trucks in the water. Raise straight wood Border in 3 G., with groove, and now exhibit arch sky from 3 G. to illuminated drop. Border lights now full on. Wings now darkened. 12 Fairies now trip on, R. & L. 2 E., waving their wands, and form worthy the love of the Fairy Queen.

The Satyrs, or Fauns of the Wood, were never before introduced in this comedy, but, as a part of Fairy Mythology, have a right to participate in all Sylvan Frolics. They are costumed from Rubens' celebrated picture of the Bacchanals.

The substitution of graceful and intelligent children as Fairies in immediate attendance on Titania, is certainly preferable to the heavy heeled, six-footed, broad-shouldered conventionalities which the generality of managers insist upon forcing on the public as fairy gossamer and miniature etherealities.

The Athenian lovers enter in this scene in a change of attire. The men wear the petasus or Thessalian hat, with the chlamys or travelling cloak, as depicted in the figures in the frieze of the Parthenon. See Elgin Marbles.

SCENE 2. An open glade, about a mile from the City, with a view of the Great Temple of Theseus.

In this scene, the Fairy Queen is sung to sleep by the Elfin Court— "Ye spotted Snakes"—a beautiful solo and quartette, as arranged by Mendelssohn.

The Fairy Sentinel mentioned by Shakspere, was never embodied on the stage until now.

ACT III

SCENE 1. The Duke's Oak, and Titania's Bower, with rehearsal of the Artisans.

The mischievous Puck gives Bottom, the Weaver, an Ass's Head for daring to profane the sleeping place of the Fairy Queen.

Tableau thus

```
  ×   × ×        × ×    ×
   ×   ×             ×   ×
  Fairy Children in
  gauze waters
  ×  × × Oberon in car  ×   ×
×  ×
×  ×  × ×                   ×   ×
×                                × ×
   × ×      × ×
```

End of Act

We return to the first prompt-book:

ACT II

SCENE 1. A Moonlight Wood. The moon shines brightly. A bank R. 2 E.; another R. 3 E.; another L. 2 E.; also R. 3 E. A mossy bank at the back. A large tree, R. The branches and foliage spread completely over the stage, which forms a fairy bower.

Music. The whole troop of fairies discovered in groups. They dance, after which enter Titania and her train.

At the end of the act:

(The mist clears away. The scene becomes light, a troop of fairies enter and group. Three fairies are seen, ascending in a car surrounded by flying fairies. Demetrius, Helena, Lysander, and Hermia, Tableau.)

ACT III

SCENE 1. As the curtain rises, the fairies are seen dancing and grouping. Enter Titania, conducting Bottom, followed by Oberon unseen. Titania waves her wand, and a Bank of Roses ascends through the stage, C. During this scene, the day is breaking and sun rising.

Titania, influenced by the Magic Flower, falls in love with the Transformed Clown, and causes her subjects to do him homage.

Scene 2. The Dark Wood.

In this curious scene of cross-purposes, the Athenian lovers are sadly perplexed by the merry mischief-maker, Puck.

Act IV

A Reverse View of the Vale of Attica, looking from Athens.

Fairy Ballet (nightly encored) and the Disenchantment of Titania by Oberon.

The sweet music of the Elfin tribe and the dancing Fauns are now, for the first time, placed upon the stage. Sunrise. A wonderful scenic effect— supposed to take place at the termination of the Midsummer Night.

The mist rises from the valleys and the God of Day rises in powerful splendor.

Scene 2. The Carpenter's House as before.

Act V

Scene 1. A Port in Ancient Greece.

Theseus, said to have been one of the Argonauts, has the reputation of having taught the art of shipbuilding to the Greeks, and a view of the assemblage of his war-vessels in the Phalaron, the oldest Athenian port, is therefore not considered out of place.

Scene 2. The Grand Hall in the Temple of Theseus, with stage erected for the performance of the lamentable comedy of Pyramus and Thisbe.

Scene 2. Athens. A room in Quince's House.

Scene 3. Athens. A lofty room, hung behind with curtains, in the Palace of Theseus.

Music. Wedding March.

For the acting of the Play by the artisans: Curtain rises and discovers a stage in the Gardens of the Duke.

At the end of the Act, after the departure of the Mortals, the stage becomes dark. Oberon and Titania rise through stage. During the last speech of Puck, four rows of gauzes rise through the stage, and when they are well on, the scene behind is struck up. The gauzes now work up and discover a fairy bower, with a large revolving sun in the center.

(The J. B. Wright prompt-book describes this: A cloud opens and a Working Sun. Within it, First Fairy. After it opens, Titania, Oberon, and four Fairy Children get on platform of sun, which is masked by clouds. Then the sun moves down to 1 G. 8 Fairies are discovered with garlands. They move with the Sun. The fairies that were in front, when change takes place, pirouette in and out, with principal dancers in C. Continue till Grand Tableau is formed for curtain. The chorus remain firm 1. E. R. H. Red Fire in sun, and on R. & L. H. Final.

For the costumes in this production, let us quote from the edition of the play in French's Standard Drama: Theseus. Flesh-colored arms and legs—white skirt trimmed with silver —rich jewelled belt—richly embroidered Grecian drapery of crimson— sandals of gold tissue—rich fillet.

The manager of Burton's Theater claims, as original, the whole arrangement of this scene—including the rendering of the comedy before Theseus.

A Fairy Transformation—the King and Queen with their suites, attend, to bless the House and Marriage of Theseus to Hippolyta.

The Fairies carry illuminated flowers, the Satyrs bear torches of variegated Greek fire, and the curtain falls on

A BEAUTIFUL CLASSIC TABLEAU.

LYSANDER. Flesh-colored arms and legs—white spangled shirt—light blue robe bound with black, and richly spangled—sandals—rich sword and belt.

HIPPOLYTA. Richly embroidered dress—long train robe of crimson, trimmed and flowered with silver—jewelled tiara—sandals of gold-tissue.

HERMIA. White dress trimmed with pink and silver—pink robe—pink sandals—waist belt.

OBERON. Flesh arms and legs—white shirt richly spangled—blue gauze drapery, spangled—jewelled head-dress.

PUCK. Flesh arms and legs—white muslin skirt, trimmed with silver—silver head-dress—gauze and silver wings.

This is undoubtedly what they tried to do at these theaters in 1854: how like you the picture? a bit too much red fire at the Broadway? a bit tawdry? But very wonderful it must have seemed to its mid-century audiences, and, as I have said, it was probably the most elaborate Shaksperian staging up to that time attempted in this city. Since the two theaters mentioned in this section thus pitted forces against each other, why should not we, taking the hint from them, end by placing side by side two literary estimates made by famous theater-goers of that day? At least the connection will show that each production had its following of enthusiastic youth:

Says W. L. Keese, in his 'Life of Burton':

A Midsummer Night's Dream was produced at Burton's in 1854, and the manager played *Bottom*. We well remember with what delight the play was received, and what a marked sensation was created by the scenery and stage effect. The public won-

And Laurence Hutton, in 'Plays and Players', New York, 1875:

Mr. Burton was anxious to match his reputation with that of Mr. Davidge as Bottom. . . . In our humble estimation, however, the presentation of the part of Bottom by Mr. Davidge has had no equal before or since. . . . Public interest

dered how so much could be presented on so small a stage. . . . The fairy element was made a beautiful feature, and the spirit of poetry brooded over the whole production. The unanimity of the press in its encomiums was remarkable. . . .

As we think of it now, it seems to us that Burton's idea of Bottom was the true one. . . . We remember his acting in the scene where the artisans meet—how striking it was in sustained individuality, and how finely exemplified was the potential vanity of Bottom—He was capital, too, in the scene of the rehearsal, and of his translation. . . . What pleased us greatly was the vein of engaging raillery which ran through his delivery of the speeches to the fairies, Cobweb, Peas-Blossom and Mustard-Seed. It goes without saying, that as *Pyramus* in the tragedy, Burton created unbounded amusement. . . .

was now excited and full houses the result. At the Broadway the entertainment was well worthy its popularity and success.

We have seen lately in print articles on the splendor of theatrical representations of the present, that ignore the magnificence of the scenic effects of other days, but we have had on our stage nothing more gorgeous in late years than the setting of the "Midsummer Night's Dream" at the Broadway. . . . Particularly fine, as we remember it, was the panorama of fairyland, done by the "compounding of flats" and the artistic adjustment of lights. George Heister, the scenic artist of the Broadway, may have been wanting in some of the improvements and inventions of modern stage craft, but his taste was then . . . artistic and correct in its judgment of effects. . . . The piece as a whole is recalled by old theatre-goers as one of those bright particular productions where master, art, artist, and public were in perfect accord. . . . William Davidge . . . alone of the present school haš fully comprehended the part (of Bottom).

To a reader familiar with mid-century methods of production, it will be apparent that these two simultaneous revivals were unique in our history; probably no play had ever before in this city been so carefully and so sumptuously mounted. If I were to weigh evidence, I should guess that Burton gave the more scholarly, and Marshall of the Broadway the more spectacular presentation. The men of the cast at Burton's were far better than those at the Broadway; but the pulchritude of the ladies at the latter theater quite eclipsed that of the *routinières* of Burton's company. Adelaide Gougenheim and Mrs. Nagle, the Helena and Hermia at the Broadway, were two of the most beautiful actresses of their time; Mme. Ponisi, the Oberon, was for years the only Lady Macbeth (Charlotte Cushman excepted) that New York would hear of. It is to be observed that now, for the first time in America, Puck, in both these productions, is played by a child, by a boy at Burton's, at the Broadway, by la Petite Viola (later briefly on the stage as Viola Crocker—a sister of two famed actresses, Mrs. F. B. Conway and Mrs. D. P. Bowers). Little Viola by her beauty and cleverness made quite the hit of the piece. It will be seen, then, that in every way extreme care had been exercised in each theater; I feel justified in repeating that the twin production marked an epoch in New York staging. Every new Shaksperian revival (apart from the hack repertory) had to model itself satisfactorily to the memories of those who had passed excitedly from Burton's to the Broadway in 1854, taking sides and arguing, no doubt to the swelling of the box-office receipts.

III. At Laura Keene's Theater, 1859

Time swung full circle, and another New York manager, five years later, pursued the same will-o'-the-wisp to artistic and possibly financial success. Laura Keene was now in possession of the second most popular and fashionable theater in New York, Wallack's being the first. Burton during this same season finally retired from the management of the playhouse which had for so long ministered to the pleasure of New Yorkers. Miss Keene evidently wished to signalize her accession to the highest rank by a performance of more than usual brilliancy. She was just finishing the phenomenal run of 140 nights which 'Our American Cousin,' with Jefferson and Sothern, had piled up to the credit of her management and her treasury, and during the last weeks of this course she had turned with great zest to preparations for the Shaksperian play. Shaksperian revivals were in the air; Wallack, on December 9, 1858, had remounted the 'Merchant of Venice' at great expense and with a cast that reads well even to-day. It was on view for thirty-three nights, and at the Broadway (soon to be demolished to make room for business houses) 'Antony and Cleopatra' was brought out for twenty-four nights with great splendor and with much attention to historical accuracy.

Laura Keene, then, struck the "psychological moment" when, on the 18th of April, 1859, she used all the resources of her establishment on 'A Midsummer Night's Dream.' Her company was then very strong, and she had at her disposal, for the lovers, Sothern, who had just made himself famous as Dundreary, Milnes Levick, Sara Stevens and Ada Clifton; W. R. Blake for Nick Bottom, and C. W. Couldock and Mary Wells for Theseus and Hippolyta. Oberon was played by Marian Macarthy, mentioned here to show the continuance of the tradition that since Mme. Vestris had given the character of the King of the Fairies to a woman; Miss Keene herself appeared as Puck, a part which Joseph Jefferson flatly refused. The assigning of this sprite to an adult female was a reversion, as we see, to an earlier practice. Miss Keene spent a great deal of money on scenery and properties, and was at great pains in both to secure accuracy to Grecian models.

There is no question that Charles Kean's elaborate production at the London Princess, in 1856, inspired the lady whose name sounds so like, and looks so different. In the preface to her acting edition, published by Samuel French and Son, in 1863, she acknowledges indebtedness to Mr. H.—of Harvard College for valuable assistance on the subject of Greek, and more particularly, Athenian antiquities; also to Mr. W.—(probably Richard Grant White) for elucidation of obsolete and ambiguous phrases in the play; and to Mr. Genio C. Scott for advice on the subject of costume, "he having kindly supplied me many designs from his sketches taken during his antiquarian searches at or near the scene of events represented." But to Charles Kean she extends thanks for his acting edition of the play . . . . . "and I should have availed myself more of his scholarly labors had I not desired to blend with the poetry of Shakspere the music of Mendelssohn."

A comparison of the acting version of Charles Kean and Miss Keene will reveal what the latter implies by the reservation in her last sentence; she is referring merely to heroic curtailment of the text. Helena's last speech in Act I, Scene I, for instance, is gone; almost all of the great poetical passages between Oberon and Puck have suffered the same fate; and no more is left of the scenes between the four lovers in the wood than will serve for making clear the plot. This is buying Mendelssohn's music at a very high price indeed; and, furthermore, the sacrifice was not necessary. Using all of the Mendelssohn music, the Broadway production, though it ran the play together in three acts, "cut" very little of Shakspere's text. This, then, is what Miss Keene meant by saying she could not employ all of Charles Kean's scholarly labors on the acting edition; but as far as arrangement of scenes is concerned, she certainly availed herself of those labors to the full. A comparison of the two versions will convince of this. Mr. William Winter asserts that Miss Keene's version was made by Richard Grant White; I hate to think he would hew away so much of his own beloved bard.

Miss Keene stretched the capabilities of advertising to publish her wares. Full columns of matter appeared for some days in several papers, and from them we can get an almost complete picture of what the production was like. So unique, not to say amusing is her scenario, and so informing for the purposes of my essay, that I venture to reproduce it verbatim; it is almost like seeing the actual show:

Synopsis of Scenery and Incidents
ACT FIRST

Scene 1. A Terrace adjoining the Palace of Theseus, with Athens in the distance, by Sunrise.

Theseus and Hippolyta—The approaching nuptials and their appropriate festivities—A discordant element—Paternal complaints—Love at cross-purposes—Cupid bewitched—Ancient punishment of refractory daughters—The convent or the tomb—An unloved fair one—Contemplated flight from Athens—Misplaced confidences.

Scene 2. Workshop of Quince, the Carpenter.

Amateur theatricals—An insight as to how plays are cast—"One man plays many parts," or would if he could, i. e.—Bottom, who, unlike most people, not satisfied with the best part in the play, evinces a desire to monopolize all the characters.

ACT SECOND

Scene 1. A Shady Grove.

Meeting of Puck and the Singing Fairy—Immortals, like the denizens of earth, fond of gossiping and scandal—Puck's vagaries and tricks upon travellers—Grand entree of Oberon, Titania and suite—Fairy jealousies and domestic inquietude—Mutual recriminations—The love charm—Puck in quest of it—The lovers again—A woman scorned—Apollo flies Daphne—Puck's return with the charm.

GRAND PANORAMIC

CHANGE TO TITANIA'S BOWER

and

THE NYMPH OF THE FOUNTAIN

Fairy revelries—The incantation—Application of the love philter—Titania bewitched—Lovers caught napping—Puck's trick—Love in a maze—Affection transferred—The players again—The tragedy discussed—Manifold devices to prevent the audience taking fright—An explanatory prologue decided upon —A new character—Puck at work during rehearsal.

SUDDEN TRANSFORMATION OF BOTTOM

Fright of his colleagues—Titania's awakening—She is infatuated with the Assinine (sic) Animal.

FLIGHT OF THE FAIRIES
BEARING BOTTOM TO TITANIA'S BOWER

ACT THIRD

Puck relates to Oberon the tale of his prank upon Bottom—Oberon discovers Puck's error—The wrong lover bewitched—The sprites in conquest of Helena.

GO, I GO; LOOK, HOW I GO.
PUCK'S FLIGHT

Incantation, Puck's return; The lovers; Love's rivalry; an incipient love affair of honor; Puck becomes a mediator; By his agency, the stage becomes enveloped in an

IMPENETRABLE MIST

A would-be sanguinary game of Bo-peep; The lovers asleep; Puck's charm; An anomaly.

A PALM TREE GROWING FROM THE EARTH

and covered with

GARLANDS OF FLOWERS,

terminating with

A FAMILY MAY-POLE DANCE

ACT FOURTH

Scene 1. The Mists of Morning by Sunlight, which are gradually dispelled by

THE RISING SUN

Bottom entertained by Titania; Bottom in the land of dreams; Oberon and Puck; Incantation; Titania awake to a sense of her position.

THE MORNING LARK
DISSOLVING OF THE FAIRY COURT

Bottom relieved of his head-dress—His surprise at his dream—The sleepers discovered by Theseus and his train—The awakening—The Duke's pardon—Love rewarded.

Scene 2. Workshop of Quince, the Carpenter.
A play well-nigh marred—The leading man missing—A discussion—Appearance of Bottom—General happiness—The play accepted.

ACT FIFTH

Scene 1. The Palace of Theseus.
The wedding festivities—A choice of amusements.

THE COMICAL TRAGEDY
PYRAMUS AND THISBE

enacted by Messrs. Bottom, Quince, Snug, Flute, Snout and Starveling, for the delectation of Theseus and Hippolyta—Midnight—Dispersement of the guests—Appearance of Puck—The stage becomes enveloped in clouds.

GRAND SCENIC CHANGE TO
OBERON'S BOWER IN
FAIRY-LAND
AND MAGNIFICENT TABLEAU

A chorus of critical approval brought delight to her ambitious and daring soul. The New York *Times*, of April 22nd, after a learned disquisition on the impossibility of knowing anything of architecture or costume in the time of Theseus, says of Miss Keene: "But when she passes with Shakspere from the bondage of fact into the freedom of fancy, she gives the rein to her imagination of fairy scenes and supernatural skies. She has, in a word, combined more of the legitimate and effective Shaksperian spectacle than have ever before been brought into the service of the American stage....Take it for all in all, the scenery of the play at this theater is more varied, more striking....than any person familiar with our usual stage resources could have expected it would be.....The fairy landscapes, in particular, shift, fade, and change with a kaleidoscopic charm worthy of all praise. What, for instance, has New York seen more ample, more seducing, more exquisitely suffused with the soul of the summer moonlight than the scene in which Titania holds her court beneath the spreading forest trees?"

The *Daily News* follows suit: "The scenery and mechanical effects are most wonderful.... The transitions of light and shade, from the beautiful to the grotesque, are so rapid, that one sits in actual bewilderment." The *Tribune* of April 19th is even more specific. "As an exhibition of scenery, costume, mechanical effects and general display, it has never been equalled in this country......The most critical eye can detect but few faults. The panorama in the second act, the fairy grouping and transformations in the third....are most creditable to the management."

The play ran until May 28th, assuredly a good showing for those days. Mr. William Winter, however, states that the production was a failure. As a matter of fact, though the cast contained excellent names, I doubt if it was wholly good. Blake, admirable actor as he was, was not suited to the part of Bottom. The *Tribune*, of the date above, sums it up thus: "Much curiosity and great expectations were felt to see Mr. Blake's performance of Bottom, and that artist can afford to have it candidly stated that he was exceedingly bad in the part." If you read between the lines, you receive a similar impression from the *Times* review: "Mr. Blake is a clever Nick Bottom and delivers his part as it is set down with a rare abstinence from gags or superfluous grotesque interpolations" (i. e., there is nothing much to say about his impersonation.) Even Miss Keene herself gets from this paper only "Miss Keene's Puck is a sprightly, mocking conception, but aerial, subtle, and full of the true legendary spirit." Pretty noncommittal?

What interests me in "reading up" the production, is the continuance in it of the traditional woman-Oberon, the "panorama" and the grand "transformation" scene at the end; and the reversion to an adult female Puck. There seems no doubt that this same mature sprite was whisked through the air on wires or by other means at the words, "I go, I go, Look how I go!"

The fearsome accuracy of Laura Keene's properties and costumes may be gauged by her description of costumes prefixed to her acting edition of 'A Midsummer Night's Dream.' Lysander, for instance, wears a white chiton embroidered with blue; cloth pallium, richly embroidered with gold; fleshings and red cothurni. Hippolyta first appears as an Amazon, copied from a Greek vase: armor of red and gold, red sandals, leopard skin, cap and spear. In the last act she wears a white chiton and chlamys, armilia, zona of gold and jewels, necklace of gold and jewels, wreath on head.

As a matter of fact, I seem, thanks to the manageress' extravagant advertising, and to my knowledge of what her people could do, to visualize this particular revival of our comedy with a great deal of clearness. I believe the scenery was unusually fine for its day and generation, with just a little of garishness and absurdity in its "palm-trees with garlands of flowers" and its last transformation. The acting was unquestionably lacking in poetry, but all in all New York could be proud of the production, as one representing much artistic endeavor. Poetry, in fact, was never found to a high degree, except possibly in Burton's, in any production of this piece until it was put there by Augustin Daly in 1888. But many of his actors were the best that New York ever saw in the parts they portrayed. Laura Keene's at least has won its place in theatrical history.

IV. The Olympic in 1867; the Grand Opera House in 1873

These performances are linked by the participation in each of G. L. Fox, the famous Humpty-Dumpty, as Bottom, and by the fact that the first was given in a theater controlled by relatives-in-law of Augustin Daly, while the second was wrought by Daly himself. The first was one of the very few revivals of the comedy that swelled the coffers of the theater to a noticeable degree; it ran one hundred nights to enormous business. The second limped to the grave in three weeks in the dread year of the fearful panic. In spite of this difference, the likeness is increased by the fact that both were extravagantly and beautifully mounted. The final resemblance is found in the fact that neither was acted to any extent by actors capable of elucidating the text. There was more scenery than poetry. Neither performance is remembered or recorded as were those of Burton, the Broadway Theater, Laura

Keene and Augustin Daly (of 1888). There was something hit or miss about the performances in both cases, and by a subtle irony one happened to hit and the other happened to miss. "You never can tell in this business."

The Olympic Theater production was made on the same stage as Laura Keene's. This lady had gone the way of all popular institutions in this fickle city; she had lost her health, her public and her theater, which was now called the Olympic. It was really under the management of John Duff (Augustin Daly's father-in-law), though his name did not appear on the bills. That honor was reserved for another son-in-law, the scene-painter, James E. Hayes, responsible for some of the splendors of the revival about to be considered. According to Mr. William Winter, Joseph Jefferson supervised this important production; he also brought with him from London, during the preceding summer, Telbin's magnificent panorama of Fairyland used in the second act. Jefferson finished at this house his first great engage-ment (since his return) in 'Rip Van Winkle,' just before the 'Dream' came forth; his sister Cornelia played Titania. These are the facts; but it is hard to see exactly why Jefferson was interested in the venture. Mr. Winter also states that the version used was Charles Kean's.

The cast was not strong. G. L. Fox, one of the funniest of all stage entertainers, had not the imagination to body forth the asinine, conceited weaver; Fanny Stockton, the Oberon, was a mere novice, though a novice with a fine singing voice. William Davidge, an excellent actor, now played Quince, not Bottom, as at the Broadway, and Owen Marlowe was Flute. Puck was given to a child, little Willie Young. The rest of the cast is composed of forgotten names, and met but little praise in its own day. The *Herald* thought Fox a bit vulgar and smacking of the Bowery, from which he had recently come. The casting of Oberon and Puck, it will be noted, was according to the more generally accept-able usage. Laura Keene's Puck found no mature followers for many years. But something caught the popular fancy; in all probability it was the spectacle. This was the day of the 'Black Crook' at Niblo's Garden, and wonderful transformation scenes, marching Amazons, crowds of dancers, were the accepted order.

On the wave of this craze for something wonderful to see, Shakspere's poetry floated to a success such as it has had only once again in this town.

Four scene painters (including Telbin, who painted the much-discussed panorama) were engaged on getting up this particular show. In 1867, the newspapers were so modern that we can with perfect ease learn from them how the results appealed to contemporaries. The scenes were arranged as follows:

ACT I, Scene 1. Grecian Colonnade in the Palace of Theseus. Triumphant entree of Theseus and Hippolyta. Scene 2. The Carpenter Shop.

ACT II, Scene 1. A Wood. Puck, Peas-blossom and Cobweb. Song by Peas-blossom, "Over Hill, Over Dale." The King and Queen of the Fairies. The Athenian Lovers. Duet: "I Know a Bank," by Oberon and Peas-blossom. Song: "Ye Spotted Snakes." Beautiful Magical Transformation to Titania's Bower.

ACT III, Scene 1. A Wood. Song: "Where the Bee Sucks." Ascension of Puck on a Brilliant Serpent, entwined around a Globe of Pearl.

ACT IV, Scene 1. Titania's Bower. Fairy Group. Scene 2. The Carpenter's Shop. Scene 3. A Fairy Lake. Voyage of Oberon. Grand Panorama.

ACT V, Scene 1. Theatre in the Temple of Theseus. The Play. Mendelssohn's Wedding March. Scene 2. The Clouds. Finale: "We Will Sing and Bless this Place."

GRAND TRANSFORMATION SCENE

In three Beautiful Changes. The Golden Vineyard of Aurora, Fairy Land, the Valley of Ferns, the Temples of Arcadia, with groups of Winged Fairies upon Rising Pedestals. Gorgeous Culminating Effect.

Says the *Herald* of November 26th: "The panorama of the voyage of Oberon combines in itself all the elements of a charming poem passing before us in the constantly changing beauties of the earth and sky, land and sea, light and shade; and the closing and crowning tableau and illumination are unquestionably one of the most brilliant, graceful, tasteful and exquisitely beautiful combinations of pretty things ever produced on the stage during the present generation." The writer in the *Tribune* (was it the youthful William Winter?) becomes poetic in enthusiasm: "The final scene was really the most dazzling that we have ever seen upon the stage....The combinations of color were admirable.....The eye drank in its beauty, intoxicated with odor and color and music and poetic suggestion. A little further back, the spectator must have been conscious of a kindred effect in gazing on Telbin's beautiful panorama of Athens. This is one of the few perfect stage pictures that we can recall. It is introduced to illustrate the return of the lovers and the strayed revellers from the woods to the city of Athens. It is brief, but it is packed with meaning. .....Another striking scene is that which closes the third act, where Puck appears, standing upon a golden globe which is surrounded by a glittering serpent.....One fine point succeeds another, until the mind is completely overwhelmed with a sense of magnificent richness."

And how like you *this* picture, gentlemen? Is it not, at least, pleasing to read these panegyrical notices? It is clear that most of the encomiums were bestowed on setting and scenery, but even at that disproportionate rate it is well to have Shakspere's lines in the public ear for over a hundred performances. Let us hope that the liberties taken with the text were not commensurate with what is indicated by the assigning of the lines of the First and Second Fairies to Peas-blossom and Cobweb, in the scenario quoted above. It may be noted that in May, 1867, Mrs. Conway produced the 'Dream' at her Park Theater in Brooklyn, herself acting Oberon. Were both performances inspired by Charles Calvert's at Manchester in 1865? Calvert's fame was growing fast, and Jefferson, we know, was on the spot. Shortly after, the 'Dream' was played at Selwyn's Theater, Boston.

In 1873, Augustin Daly had too many irons in the fire, and it was, besides, one of the worst years, financially, on record. His little Fifth Avenue Theater had burned down on New Year's Day, and while the new one was building at Broadway and 28th Street, his excellent stock-company was "on the road"; he was managing that great handsome barn, the Grand Opera House, at Eighth Avenue and 23rd Street, as a first-class theater, and he still had a finger in the affairs of the Olympic, a theater which never seemed to know when it was dead. At the Grand Opera House, on August 19th, he opened, with his usual grandiloquent flourish, with our elusive fairy-comedy, painted exquisitely by George Heister, who had performed the same service for it at the Broadway in 1854. The announcement of settings follows, and in many respects is strangely reminiscent of that of Burton, quoted previously. There is something rather mysterious about all this.

THE SCENE IS LAID IN ATHENS AND A WOOD NEAR ATHENS

ACT I, Scene 1. The stage represents the Palace of Theseus as seen through the arch of entrance (by HEISTER); statues of the Household Gods are seen in the various avenues; and in the back view may be seen the Acropolis, or the upper city. Theseus, a Grecian hero, who flourished 1235 years B. C., having conquered the Amazons, is about to marry their Queen. He is accompanied by his warriors. Queen Hippolyta and her attendant warriors follow. Theseus instructs Philostrate, his Master of the Revels, to direct the order of his Marriage Fete, after which Egeus, an Athenian Noble, and father of Hermia, presents himself before Theseus with a complaint of his daughter and her two lovers. Scene 2. (By LA HARPE.) The house of the Athenian artisans—a plain room in the severe simplicity of the earliest Doric, built of wood and stone, and opening to the suburbs of the Catopolis or Lower City.

ACT II, Scene 1. View of a Fairy Wood near Athens (by HEISTER). PUCK, the Hobgoblin, OBERON, the King of Fairyland, The "LOVELY BOY, stolen from an Indian King." The SATYRS or Fairies of the Wood and TITANIA are here introduced. In this scene the FAIRY enters his Dolphin bark to pursue Titania, is sung to sleep by his elfish attendants—a beautiful Quartette in which the famous GOLDEN QUARTETTE of California, in the dress of Satyrs, take part. The panorama which terminates this act is also by Mr. GEO. HEISTER.

ACT III, Scene 1. The DUKE'S OAK and TITANIA'S BOWER (by HEISTER) with the Rehearsal of the Artisan's Play. In this scene the mischievous Puck gives Bottom the Weaver an Ass's head, for daring to profane the sleeping-place of the Fairy Queen. TITANIA, influenced by the Magic Flower, falls in love with the transformed Clown, and causes her subjects to do him homage. In this, a curious scene of cross-purposes is developed, caused by Fairy Magic, in which the Athenian Lovers are sadly perplexed by the merry mischief-maker, PUCK. In this act will be introduced an original series of Dances and Groupings by a

BALLET OF FIFTY CHILDREN, UNDER THE DIRECTION OF MME. KATHIE LANNER

ACT IV, Scene 1. The House of the Artisans. Scene 2. The Grand Hall in the Palace of Theseus, with stage erected for the performance of— Pyramus and Thisbe (by HEISTER). A Fairy transformation. The king and Queen with their suites attend, to bless the House and Marriage of THESEUS to HIPPOLYTA, and the Curtain falls on a BEAUTIFUL FAIRY TABLEAU AND TRANSFORMATION, BY MR. CHAS. W. WITHAM.

I may remark that, besides Mr. Fox, the best artists involved
were Nina Varian (Helena), D. H. Harkins (Lysander), Charles
Leclercq (Flute), Annie Kemp Bowler (Oberon) and Little Fay
Templeton (Puck).   The reader can now see for himself that
traditional casting of Oberon and Puck occurred.   Since this performance enjoyed so short a life, I believe one contemporary
criticism will suffice for its merits.

> Mr. G. L. Fox's personation of Bottom—a familiar one—is first in order.
> It is, as may be imagined, a highly entertaining effort.   Mr. Fox is not a great
> comedian, for we are not aware that he has ever elaborated a character; but
> he has a keen appreciation of humor; the most comical and expressive face
> looking upon American audiences, and vast experience.   .   .   .   It is impos-
> sible not to laugh heartily over the speeches of the weaver as one glances at
> them in the book, and they are twice as droll when they are delivered, with a
> countenance and an attire provocative of the wildest mirth, but with an
> imperturbable gravity, by the performer we write of.   .   .   .
> Of the pageants, the children's ballet, occurring in the third act, was most
> conspicuous.   The fifty children   .   .   .   present some very pretty group-
> ings.   .   .   .   The scenery is superb.   Every set is not only grateful to the
> eye, but extremely artistic.   A deliciously cool wood in the second act from
> the brush of Mr. Heister, and a fine panorama unrolled soon after, were greeted
> with loud applause.

This is the tribute of the *Times*, on August 20th.

V.   At Daly's Theater, 1888

By the time of the great revival we are about to discuss, certain
conventions had incrusted themselves upon the methods of presenting 'A Midsummer Night's Dream' on the stage.   A consideration of the documents I have already adduced will show
(1) that every manager had tried in Acts I and V to reproduce the
costumes and architecture of what he conceived to be the classic
age of Pericles; (2) that he had let loose his fancy in stage trickery, as in the flight of Puck through the air, in the magical appearance of Puck from an opening flower or mushroom, and in the
surprising apparition of "palm-trees wreathed with flowers"
or other supernatural phenomena of that sort; and (3) that he had
taken upon himself to present a panorama of moving scenery,
descriptive of the journey of Oberon from one part of the forest
to another (as in the Broadway Theatre, in 1854), or of the return

of the lovers and Theseus to Athens (as, according to the critic of the *Tribune*, at the Olympic in 1867). More important was the almost invariable rule in the assignment of the parts of Oberon and Puck. Evidently no one ever thought of breaking the tradition of female Oberons or of childish Pucks. Yet what woman ever satisfied in the one, or what child ever could do more than pipe and whistle the wonderful verses of the sprite?

All these conventions were, however, carried on by Augustin Daly, when, on January 31, 1888, he added this work to the repertory of his famous theater. He was now the acknowledged leader of the American stage; Lester Wallack was an old man and had not kept abreast of the times. At the end of the preceding season he had given up the famous company which had been in existence since 1852. Daly's beautiful theater, his magnificent company, led by James Lewis, Miss Rehan, Mrs. Gilbert, Mr. John Drew, Mr. Otis Skinner and Charles Fisher, and the exquisitely artistic effect of the house from foyer to stage exactly satisfied the cultivated theater-goers of that day. He had inaugurated the policy of reviving at least one classic comedy annually, and had already put to his credit 'She Would and She Wouldn't,' the 'Country Girl,' the 'Recruiting Officer,' the 'Merry Wives of Windsor,' and the 'Taming of the Shrew.' The last named had run about 125 nights during the previous year, and had placed Ada Rehan at the head of American comedy actresses. 'A Midsummer Night's Dream,' then, merely continued a line of notable successes. It remained on view till April 7th, and was acted at intervals during the seasons that followed, once at the Grand Opera House (1896) by a "second" company.

The play was revived with scenery by Henry E. Hoyt, who painted much for the Metropolitan Opera House, and who had become celebrated on Broadway as the designer of the famous pink ball-room scene in 'Erminie.' Readers who remember that confection need not fear for Daly; the scenes of Shakspere's fairyland were most imaginatively treated in this best of all 'Dreams.' Well do I remember the architectural beauty of the opening picture of the Palace of Theseus, the lofty Corinthian columns, with their Grecian paintings of dull red hue for about one-third their height, the rich, sombre curtains pulled back to show an inner room of equal beauty, cut in two by another pair of graceful pillars, and the door in the extreme rear, opened, and giving by its vista an effect of almost unlimited spaciousness; in fact, for such a production the great depth of the stage of Daly's Theater was a priceless asset. The chief woodland scene was equally lovely in its way. Tall trees formed the middle distance, approached by slopes of rich growth and with an occasional tall flower of luxuriant bloom; and all the background was a sylvan stream of exquisite beauty, its rocky banks shaded by great trees, in whose dimly outlined forms the imagination loved to lose itself. A more beautiful picture has seldom been revealed to an audience; the lighting was perfect. A very remarkable effect was brought about by the mists that gradually rolled in and veiled this scene, and by the glimmering of fire-flies through the mists; it was really enchanting, and very new at that time. Such wonders were possible only in this revival, the first since the invention of electric light. When Mme. Vestris desired some such effect, she was compelled to use Parisian lanterns of various colored paper! At Daly's, the panorama of the return to Athens I did not so much care for; I could not help feeling that the scenery was really moving, while the characters were stationary in the barge. But the effect was much talked of.

Probably the play had never been better acted, in all its parts. The performances of Theseus (Joseph Holland), Demetrius (John Drew), Lysander (Otis Skinner), Egeus (Charles Fisher), Helena (Ada Rehan), Hermia (Virginia Dreher), "Envy could not but call fair." They were all excellent, but the poetical, exquisite Helena of Ada Rehan stands out most in memory; somehow, when thinking of this actress, I recall most often the picture she presented as the wronged, suffering maiden, standing alone and comfortless amid the splendors of Theseus' palace. That Bottom the Weaver did not fit the personality of James Lewis annoyed many critics of the time. In a brisk, lively, dapper way, Lewis was one of the funniest of comedians; but tradition assigns the part to a large, heavy, oily personality, for which Lewis could not qualify. We may say that he thoroughly succeeded in conveying an idea of the colossal conceit of the character and in amusing his audience; in the acting of the tragedy he was extraordinarily funny as Pyramus, and received able support from William Gilbert as Thisbe. The Oberon (Miss Alice Hood) was a well-trained amateur, but Miss Effie Shannon was a charming Titania. Puck was played by a clever child, Bijou Fernandez; the best you could say for her was that she was "cute." Probably no child could have done better. And certainly she was a very pretty sight when whisked away through the air in a floral car, to put a girdle round the earth in forty minutes. She appeared first from an opening mushroom. It was not, however, the excellence of individual performances that told in this particular revival; it was the wonderful balance, the exquisite proportion of the whole. And the poetry has never been more beautifully spoken. It was music to the ear.

It may be said that in this production all the resources of the theater were brought to bear to create a perfect illusion; the imagination resigned itself and dreamed its dream and found it fair. Across the years the vision still seems sweet, and in history Daly's performance of the play will rank as that in which the elements were so justly mixed that Shakspere himself might have been satisfied with the result.

To continue my habit in discussing the successive productions of the play, I will add Daly's very succinct account of the scenes:

Act I. The Palace of Theseus.
Act II, Scene 1. The Workshop of Quince. Scene 2. A Wood near Athens.
Act III. The same by Moonlight.
Act IV, Scene 1. Titania's Bower. Scene 2. The Wood at Sunrise.
    In this act a panoramic illusion of the passage of the barge of Theseus to Athens.
Act V. The Outer Court of the Palace of Theseus.

The version used by Daly was very close to the original. According to Mr. Dithmar, of the *Times*, February 1, 1888, some "cuts" (but slight) were made in Act I, and somewhat longer (about thirty lines) in the first fairy scene; the events are transposed in Act II, to bring the episodes of the lovers together, and end with the revels of Titania and her train; slight transpositions occur in Act IV to allow of the passing of the barge of Theseus among the islets of Greece; and in Act IV, Demetrius (played by the leading man!) reads to Theseus the list of entertainments provided. The version was printed by Mr. Daly with an introduction by Mr. William Winter (from whose work I have already quoted in the progress of this essay).

A second review of the performance appeared in the New York *Times*, on February 5, 1888. I should like to end by quoting a large part of this excellent article:

> The loveliness of the scenic pictures is not to be denied. The Grecian architecture in the views of the palace; the vast and antique wood through which in the moonlight a 'maze of light and life and motion is woven'; the passage of the royal barge among the islets to the stone and marble city with stately Mount Hymettus rising in the distance; the falling mists; the revels of the fairies by the fireflies' light; the visions of dreamland revealed as the estrayed lovers sleep on their soft couches in the forest; the rising of the young moon, 'like to a silver bow' . . . as Titania rests and piqued Oberon places his spell upon her—all these enchant the eye and justly convey a sense of the mystery and beauty of the subject. The dresses are tasteful and accurate in the true sense of that word, as applied to the appointment of a play. . . .
> But all these things are mere accessories, and subordinate to the acting. . . . The performance is spectacular only so far as it was absolutely necessary to make it so. . . . The artistic success of the production of 'A Midsummer Night's Dream' at Daly's Theatre is due to the fact that the actors of the play have mastered its meaning, and communicate it, in their own graceful manner, unhampered by musty theatrical conditions, with fidelity to the poet.

VI. Later Performances of the Play

A pendant to Daly's production was furnished on October 28, 1889, when J. W. Albaugh of Chicago brought out at the Star Theater his travelling company, which had had success in his own town and on the road, in a revival evidently designed to rival Daly's. It was an error of judgment; he had not the resources at his command, and he treated the work more or less as a comic opera, engaging three Casino favorites for the principal fairy parts. Henry E. Hoyt painted the scenery, as he had done for Daly, but apparently with less felicitous result. His panorama, this time, showed the journey of Oberon and Titania from the wood near Athens to Fairyland. The spectacular effects were probably very pretty in an easy, unimaginative way. I refer to this performance (which ran only two weeks) with great pleasure, because of the opportunity it offers me to bring forward the following delightful caustic criticism from the *New York Herald* of October 30th.   Obviously Chicago had come to New York and was not going back with a bag-full of scalps.

STAR THEATER.   *Bottom's Dream*, a spectacular pantomime in five acts, re-arranged from *A Midsummer Night's Dream*, by William Shakspere, with songs and dance music by JONES, BONES, BISHOP and Dr. FELIX MENDELSSOHN.

I have taken the liberty of slightly altering the title of the play presented at the Star last night, because, as the weaver himself explains, 'it hath no bottom.'   It is only fair, too, that Messrs. Jones, Bones, and the other gentlemen, who did so much to make the piece a success, should be restored the prominence due them.   Dr. Felix Mendelssohn was literally "not in it."

Not that such a trifle mattered to the audience which filled the bright little theater.   As a belated neighbor of mine remarked when he plumped down on his seat, 'Bother the music.'

'A Midsummer Night's Dream,' in its new Chicago dress, is very different from the work we are accustomed to see played under that name.   Very different from the Daly edition or the versions familiar to London and Berlin audiences.   Nor can I say that Mr. Jones (or Bishop himself) quite atoned for the omission of Mendelssohn music—the music which made its composer famous in a day.   .   .   .

Viewing the play from the operatic standpoint, the Chicago management has wisely paid great attention to his vocalists.   Several, especially the Oberon, Titania, and the Singing Fairy, boast excellent voices, and all are pretty.   Miss Post has a tendency to take things tragically, however, like several other members of the company.   The daintiest fairy of them all is Hattie Harvey, the Puck, who looked and mimed her part to perfection.   It would be useless to quarrel with her for her hornpipes and shadow dances, and worse than useless, for they were clearly what the audience wanted.

In the purely human parts of the play, some relief was found by sticklers for orthodoxy.   Miss Seligman and Miss Alvord made charming rivals as Hermia and Helena, though they ranted.   The Lysander was weak and the Demetrius heavy.   As Bottom, Mr. Lyons overtopped them easily.   So excellent a low comedian would have carried the house with him, without recourse to the practicable asses' (*sic*) ears which took the public by storm last night.

I cannot rhapsodize over Mr. Hoyt's scenery.   The costumes haunt me. O those rag-doll fairies! and those pink and red 'harmonies'!

Fourteen years later (October 26, 1903), the New Amsterdam Theater was thrown open by Klaw and Erlanger with a revival of this same piece, presented on the usual grand spectacular scale, and for the first time without a panorama.   Mr. N. C.

Goodwin was starred as Bottom, but the cast beside was more than usually good. White Whittlesey was Lysander; William Farnum, Demetrius; Florence Rockwell, Hermia; and Ida Conquest, Helena; a very good quartet of lovers. Edmund D. Lyons, who was Bottom in 1889, was now Quince, and William Sampson, long of Daly's, was Snout. The Oberon, the Titania and the Puck have never been heard of since, but they were really not bad. The only unsatisfactory performers were one or two of the artisans, who were simply incomprehensible in their fooling.

The play was given in four acts and six scenes. The first act had three scenes: (a) exterior of Theseus' palace; (b) Quince's house; (c) a wood near Athens. The second act was a woodland glade; the third, Titania's bower, the fourth, the interior of the palace. The scenery was really beautiful and presented in a radiancy of light. A festival procession of Dionysus in Act IV is among the most dazzling things I have seen on the stage. But with all this the production failed of public approval. In that hectic day Shakspere had but slight chance in the theater; comic opera and frivolity had won the field. The critics were hard on Mr. Goodwin's performance of Bottom, which indeed showed no great gift of poetic or comic insight; but this was not the cause of the failure. Almost any Shaksperian play would have met the same fate just then.

The really memorable thing about the production was the music, arranged, mostly from Mendelssohn, by Mr. Victor Herbert; the sense of hearing was almost wearied with the burden of sweet sound. Choruses, beautifully garbed and grouped, rendered the best of Mendelssohn, until it seemed that the play was swallowed up in the waves of melody. It was almost too much. The sense of hearing was soothed, while the eyes were enraptured by the radiancy of light in which the mortals threaded the mazes of the palace or by the soft green effulgence in which the fairies fleetly footed it under the forest boughs. There is no doubt that Shakspere was buried under the beauties of the setting.

Let me give just one bit of contemporary criticism from the *Times* of October 27th:

The stage was thronged with fairies beautiful in face and figure; beautiful in the richness and daintiness of their costumes; with diminutive sprites and

elves of all sorts. Fairies soared through the air. Puck made a most brilliant entrance from the upper regions with skill and effect. Electric bulbs
twinkled in endless profusion among the flowers, and the woodland glade and
Titania's bower were symphonies of soft light and subdued color. The ass's
head became Bottom as though he had been born to it and was full of all
asinine graces and expressiveness as to eyes, ears and mouth. There was, in
fact, an unceasing showing of the things that mechanical skill could accomplish. . . .

The music is one of the most delightful features of the performance. Mendelssohn . . . wrote the overture to the play when he was a boy of
eighteen. . . . Seventeen years later, he composed twelve pieces of
entr'acte and incidental music for the stage representation of the play at the
desire of the King of Prussia. . . . Mr. Herbert found many places
where music could be further employed. He has filled these places entirely
in the spirit of Mendelssohn by arrangements of his music admirably chosen.

The production lived only three weeks.

The last revival in the old style of spectacular pretentiousness
occurred on September 21, 1906, once more for the formal opening of a since popular playhouse—the Astor. On this occasion
Miss Annie Russell attempted to do what Miss Keene could not
do in 1859, make a woman Puck seem reasonable and convincing.
Miss Russell's production was not so beautiful or elaborate as
Mr. Goodwin's; my memory tells me it was darker and simpler
and less distinguished. The acting was almost wholly mediocre.
Most of the performers were then unknown and have ever since
remained in a safe and sane obscurity. John Bunny was a rotund,
jolly Bottom, without much idea of what the character was about,
but comic withal, and liked by the groundlings from the neigh-
boring hotels. He won by sheer force of his fat, humorous personality. Miss Russell's Puck was a very interesting study, full
of nimbleness, animation and sprightly laughter. It was made up
as a hairy creature with pointed ears and dressed in furs and
slashed rags, that were meant to flutter and suggest the volatility
of the character. The cloak opened out like a bat's wings. The
agile grace of the performance stamped itself permanently on my
memory. I cannot say that it has merged into my conception of
Shakspere's Puck, but in itself it was a pleasing thing. For the
rest, the production was hardly worth while, except as Shaksperian revivals are always worth while. It added nothing to
what Daly and Goodwin had done, and after four weeks it went

its way to the limbo of disappointed desires. The one thing to note is that Oberon was, for the first time since 1826, played by a man, Mr. James Young, who made the fairy monarch a rather effeminate person but still male. This had been done also at the London Adelphi the year before (November 25, 1905) in Oscar Asche's production. Mr. Walter Hampden then played the part of Oberon, giving him somewhat more than six feet of good American manhood.

Let me leave Miss Russell's production with this composite photograph from the New York *Times*, October 22, 1906:

> A lovely spectacle, some beautiful music, vivacious acting, and not a little rollicking fun. . . . Splendid pictures rich in color. . . . Rich grouping of figure and costume and plenty of pageantry. . . . Colored lights bob up in flowers when Puck kisses them, an owl hoots and blinks his eyes, and a whole troupe of little elves and fairies, very well trained in the antics of fairyland . . . play leap frog, tumble down hill and indulge in a most bewitching cooing that gets as near the soughing of night-winds in the trees as any one could wish. But still no dream feeling. It may well be doubted whether Phelps or any one else ever managed it.

I may end by saying that Miss Russell's arrangement of scenes is almost identical with Mr. Goodwin's: Act I, Scene 1. A portico of the palace of Theseus. Scene 2. A room in Quince's house. Scene 3. A wood near Athens. Acts II-III. A Wood. Act IV. An apartment in the palace of Theseus. Neither version provided for the second scene in Quince's house; the coming back of the transformed weaver must have been effected in the palace scene, a time-saving device not without dramatic incongruity.

These were the last efforts in New York to present the play in the time-honored manner, with greater and greater attention to display and opulent beauty. Perhaps the method was dying from inability to advance farther. But we know that in the last few years a great endeavor has been made to simplify stage-setting, especially in works of this nature. Youngsters of all nationalities, from Reinhardt and Gordon Craig to the managers of the Washington Square Players, have been striving to make outline and mass take the place of solid properties, and light and shade do all the work in furnishing a scene. Suggestiveness has banished realism from the world of art, and such productions as Daly's or Goodwin's 'Midsummer Night's Dream,' with their wealth of detail, are called very old-fashioned, vain and shorn of true poetic delight. It is with extreme caution, now, that we admit we like what we like, for fear some Puck of a Gordon Craig may cry boo! at us from the shadows. Hence we are singularly fortunate in being able to close our account of 'A Midsummer Night's Dream' on the New York stage with the record of a performance thoroughly modern and provocative of just that heated discussion which the modest lovers of the simple so ardently crave.

On February 16, 1915, Mr. Granville Barker presented at Wallack's Theater his London production of Shakspere's play. It had had considerable vogue the year before in the British capital, and it was deemed worth while, by those anxious about the state of our theater, to bring it over here. Much curiosity was aroused in advance, and the performance was given on Saturday afternoons for some weeks of Mr. Barker's engagement. Let it be said that it represented the last cry in the new stage decoration.

"Decoration" is the word; "scenery" is now a term to be eyed with suspicion. Mr. Barker divided his play into three parts; the first dealing with the "mortals"—Theseus and his court, Quince and the other hard-handed men; the second running together without break the fairy episodes and the affairs of the perplexed lovers, as well as the transformation of Bottom; the third showing all the characters again in the palace of Theseus. The stage was built out far into the auditorium, and the huge apron thus formed was used as a place for posing actors in effective groups; the part behind the proscenium was used for whatever "decoration" was required. The fairy scene was built up to a round mound in the middle of the stage, and covered with bright green velvet carpet. Just above the mound was suspended a large terra-cotta wreath of flowers that would have been the envy of a German pastry cook, and from it depended a veil of white gauze, lighted within by vari-colored electric bulbs, hanging at irregular lengths. At the back and sides of the stage fluttered curtains of chintz or silk, designed to suggest forest branches. Like forest branches they waved vigorously in the breeze, so that one felt disposed to ask some one to shut the windows of heaven in order that the trees might not blow out so violently into Titania's bower (the gauze canopy aforesaid). The scene of Theseus' palace in the last act, however, was a very solidly-built affair, with steps and many heavy columns of black and silver, and with a door at the back letting in much red light. It was evidently quite Egyptian in its mass and design. The other changes of scene were indicated by curtains that waved, to the loss of all illusion. The first, Theseus' palace, was of white silk, with conventional gold design. The Quince curtains were of salmon pink silk, with steel-blue masses supposed to represent the roofs of the city. There was another curtain of electric blue, heavily spangled with silver stars and moon. This was all supposed to be very much more artistic than the kind of thing Augustin Daly aimed at, and far more suggestive. It was thought to be full of illusion. Of course, it was not. Any one who has imagination can get the poetic illusion by seeing these things acted on a bare stage or on a stage hung with curtains or with just a conventional unchanged setting, such as Mr. Ben Greet has used. No human being, however, can be expected to be anything but worried and annoyed by pink silk curtains that are supposed to be the roofs of houses, or green silk curtains that are supposed to be forest trees; especially when they blow and stream out in the gales of the stage. Curtains that are not supposed to be anything, yes! but curtains that are supposed to be some particular thing and look like——No! a thousand times no!

Perhaps no feature of this "show" awakened more discussion than Mr. Barker's fairies. From head to foot they were differentiated by a coat of bronze paint, that made them look precisely like something you might buy to set up in the corner of the parlor; their dresses exactly corresponded. These fairies clanked as they walked. Viewed just as decoration, without regard to time, place or sense, they were very pretty; groups of them were novel and interesting. Their dancing under and around Titania's gauze bower was really a pleasing sight. By the aid of their bronze you could tell at a glance whether any person in the play was a fairy or a mortal, and as Mr. Barker evidently had no faith in Shakspere or the imagination of the audience, this was an advantage. Let it be admitted, then, that in his way he solved the problem of making the fairies seem different. He also gave the part of Oberon and Puck to men, for which I thank him; I hope the silly custom of the nineteenth century, in this regard, has been broken forever.

With the time-saving device of the curtains Mr. Barker was able to give the play entire. The verse was delivered at a rapid pace. None of it was spoken well, and Puck and Titania (at least on the opening night) were practically unintelligible. But their makeup was artistic! And when one grew weary of trying to understand what Puck was saying, he could find solace in wondering why the sprite was not gilded like the other fairies but made to look like a toy Loge in the 'Rheingold,' flaring, flaming hair and all. I hope this is not indicative of what will happen when stage setting ceases to be scenery and becomes only decoration.

This is the last of our play on the regular stage. It has, of course, been acted by schools and colleges in outdoor performances; at Riverdale School, May 24, 1909, for instance, and by Barnard undergraduates on May 31, 1912. In the '90's, a company of actors under E. D. Lyons acted it once in Madison Square Garden, with a few shrubs for scenery. Ben Greet's company gave a performance on April 22, 1911, at Carnegie Hall, without scenery, and with Mr. George Vivian as Puck (the first man-Puck in New York, I believe). These performances, so far as I can discover, close the record.

I end as I began, by saying that on this particular play of Shakspere's the managers have lavished their utmost endeavors, and have almost invariably reaped a high artistic reward. The crescendo of praise went steadily forward to the time of Daly's production. Those since have lacked the scholarship the earlier managers could apply; Burton and Daly at least were great students of the drama and of Shakspere in particular. What I have tried to do is to give the reader of this essay as clear as possible an idea of how each of the great productions was made, to set it, so to speak, anew before his eyes. If I have succeeded, he will see that there came to be a definite tradition in connection with these representations, and that generally that manager did the play best who did it last. In most cases the "feeling" of the poet himself was partially lost; only in the versions of Burton and Daly (his later one of course) does it seem to have been conserved. But all the productions up to and including this of Daly are milestones in our theatrical history; by them we literally count progress toward the best the theater can accomplish.

VI

SHAKSPERE AS A DEBTOR

By Ashley Horace Thorndike
Professor of English

SHAKSPERE AS A DEBTOR

Criticism during the past twenty-five years has had a good deal to say about Shakspere's literary indebtedness. This has been in part a reaction against the Romanticist criticism of the nineteenth century which was inclined to regard creative genius as a miracle, not to be explained by natural causes and quite superior to the influence of its surroundings. The thirty-seven plays of Shakspere were worshipped and studied for their revelation of his personality or of his philosophy. Shaksperian criticism, indeed, has been one of the last fields of human activity to feel the force of the modern scientific frame of mind, and to approach its idol from a historical rather than a religious point of view. But once started on the matching of causes and effects, it has been resolute in its efforts to find how and why these thirty-seven plays came into being. If the romanticists were forever announcing how much we owe to their creator, the historical critics have become equally insistent on how much he owed to others. Each one of the plays has been analyzed as to its sources, borrowings, and relations; and the discoveries of indebtedness have now accumulated to a total that in the eyes of some of the discoverers seems likely to impair his long-established credit.

On an anniversary, then, when the world is called upon for another of those ever-recurring appraisals of the value of Shakspere's plays, it may be worth while to consider certain old bills against him, some of which have only recently been presented for payment. These accounts must be scrutinized a little closely. Of what are they composed? By what methods are they reckoned? To what do they total? If valid, do they appreciably diminish his estate?

There has never been any doubt that Shakspere borrowed his plots. The stories of most of the plays were already in print in prose narratives and many had been used by other dramatists before he chose them. The search for these sources has in recent years been carried so far that his stories have been found in forms which he could not have seen; and the few plays for which sources have not been discovered have been provided with hypothetical Italian novelle or imaginary lost dramas. But the efforts of such far-flung investigations were not needed to demonstrate that the material of his plots came very largely from English and Italian fiction and from the histories of Holinshed and Plutarch. In this respect his practice was that of the great majority of Elizabethan dramatists, especially of those writing before 1600. The mere fact of a borrowed plot has indeed very little to do with the issue of a dramatist's originality, which is better indicated by the way he treated his material. Even then, it is difficult to find any common divisor for measurement. In one sense, no one of the earlier dramatists treated his materials with greater originality than Lyly. He took an incident of a few lines from Ovid and developed it into a five-act play. But, having made one or two plays and thus secured a formula, henceforth he followed his formula. He failed to bring a widening range of experience into his plays, and they do not show much progress or variety. Ben Jonson, to take an opposing instance, based his Roman tragedies on an elaborate and pedantic search of available sources, and did not hesitate to copy long passages word for word; yet his 'Sejanus,' with whatever faults, has the merit of a striking originality.

Shakspere's treatment of sources is extremely varied. In the case of Holinshed and Plutarch where there is an abundance of detail, he usually adds little new incident; and in the case of Plutarch where the characterization is full and the narrative often essentially dramatic, he makes surprisingly few changes in detail. In the case of an Italian novella, where the narrative is compressed, he may alter the incidents, add important persons, and fill out a plot that has only slight resemblances to the original. Yet, to make the extent of the difference between his play and its source the measure of his dramatic originality would be to ignore many other matters of selection and treatment. Take, for example, four plays, all based in different ways on preceding narratives. In the 'Merchant of Venice' the two stories were old and probably had already been united in a play. In 'Othello' the Italian story is transformed to such a degree that it is almost unrecognizable. In 'Twelfth Night' the direct indebtedness to any source is slight, but the motives, situations, and types of character were familiar and had been used before by Shakspere. He was, so to speak, following his own formula. In the 'Tempest' no source has been discovered, and if one was used, it amounts to little in the play, which was undoubtedly very much of a novelty on the Elizabethan stage. But the elements from which Shakspere drew his suggestions are traceable in many directions from the Court Masques to the narratives of a notable shipwreck. The selection and treatment of material vary greatly in these four plays, but the dramatic originality displayed is about as great in one as in the others. Certainly no one else has produced anything like any one of them.

It is absurd to state the Elizabethan problem of translating prose narrative into drama in the terms of a similar problem to-day. The task of turning a novel into a play might be accomplished to-day by any craftsman with a deftness then unknown because our theatrical technic is fairly fixed and much advertised. The earlier Elizabethans had to devise their technic as well as fill out the materials of their stories. They had the entire range of secular story in classical, medieval, and modern literature waiting to be put on the stage, and they had a public hungry for story. Their situation was not unlike that of the moving picture theater of to-day. It has an immense number of stories, it is buying up all the old novels and plays, and it has a public hungry for stories in this new scenic form, and it has an uncertain and experimental technic. We are all waiting to see whether it can attract the ingenuity and imagination that will suit its material to its means. A similar situation, in fact, always recurs with a new theatrical development. Twenty-five years ago some were hopeful that the vogue of the vaudeville show would result in a dramatic and literary achievement of a high order, but they have been disappointed. Early in the nineteenth century the melodrama offered an opportunity for a fresh technic that might win poetry again to the theater. In France this was brought about in the plays of Victor Hugo, but in England no one succeeded in utilizing the theatrical opportunity. In the Elizabethan drama, however, theatrical means both crude and novel were rapidly adapted to the service of literature. Many stories that had already found some place in literature were translated from narrative into drama that pleased the public and yet added new interpretation of human motives or a new poetic expression. Technic developed but not at the expense of imaginative power. It was in this work of translation that Shakspere was engaged. When his source already possessed the merits of great literature as in Plutarch, he had the tact to rest well content with his material. But the fact that the significant changes from Plutarch are slight does not lessen the originality of the dramatic and poetic achievement which carried over the story of 'Julius Caesar' to an illiterate London audience and to all posterity.

In spite of this translation, the Elizabethan drama in its total effect produces little sense of an imitation of preceding literature. Ben Jonson, who prided himself on inventing his plots, shows perhaps the largest subservience to literary and scholarly tradition, yet he could produce a play as aboundingly original as 'Bartholomew Fair.' His friend Chapman also had both learning and reading, but they affect only slightly the character of his plays. Heywood, who had read enormously and busied himself with many compilations as well as with two hundred plays, might have written many of the two hundred without any knowledge of books. Shakspere, who perhaps had read less extensively and thoroughly than any of these men, certainly does not betray in his plays the attitude of a bookish man. Like his contemporaries, he took his stories from books in order to make them alive on the stage. In this common effort the dramatists naturally used common means. They made over their borrowed stories in similar ways. With all the variety of life presented, motives, situations, and types of character show marked similarities. Types of drama developed, and in the busy traffic of the stage, success was always followed by imitation. Every dramatist owed a good deal to his fellows. In considering Shakspere's indebtedness, it is therefore important to discover to what extent he made plays like those of other men.

His indebtedness to contemporary dramatists is naturally most apparent in his early plays. He came to London a dozen years

after the first permanent theaters were built, at a time when a
number of clever university men were carrying literature to the
public via the stage. After a few years of lively experimentation,
success had given its approval to certain situations, characters,
and methods. A few types of drama, as Marlowe's tragedy and
Lyly's comedy, had become definitely established. Shakspere,
like every other young dramatist, was influenced by the work of
these poets and by the types of play that had proved popular.
'Titus Andronicus' and the 'First Part of Henry VI' are so much
in the prevailing fashions that, in spite of the ascriptions of the
early editions, they have been thought unworthy of Shakspere.
But the most persevering scholarship has been unable to determine whether each play was written by three or four of the well
known dramatists of the day, or by some one imitating their
methods and styles. The subsequent parts of 'Henry VI' and
'Richard III' are clearly under Marlowe's influence, and depart
in no large degree from the models that he had set. If 'Richard
III' is superior to any of Marlowe's plays in a permanent dramatic
interest, it accomplishes this by bettering, not by departing from
his instruction. 'King John,' as possibly 'Titus Andronicus,' is a
very vigorous and complete rewriting of an old play whose
scenario it retains. In comedy, 'Love's Labour's Lost' follows the
methods of Lyly, and the 'Two Gentlemen of Verona' owes not a
little both to Lyly and to the romantic comedies of Greene,
though in these plays Shakspere shows a greater individuality
than in his early histories. In the 'Comedy of Errors' he attains a
greater mastery of dramatic technic than in these other early
plays, because he has the benefit of the well-tried Plautian model
already used by a number of his contemporaries.

These nine plays, in poetry, characterization, and stage effectiveness, are at many points superior to those of his contemporaries, and give signs of an increasing power and individuality.
But they were not revolutionary in the sense that Marlowe's were,
or even Lyly's. They occupied five or six years of Shakspere's
life, and by the time they were completed he was thirty. If like
Marlowe he had died at that age, he could not be counted the
greatest of Elizabethan dramatists. He had achieved no marked

eminence over his contemporaries and had made no large departure from their methods.

For a long time criticism has been aware of the imitative nature
of this apprentice period, although only within recent years have
the extent and explicitness of his indebtedness been generally
recognized. Even now its implications have not been fully emphasized. Such apprentice work is common in all fields of literature, and perhaps most necessary in the drama, and almost in-
escapable in a period of theatrical change and experiment. Yet
we must note that it seems to have been more prolonged in the
case of Shakspere than with most of his fellow dramatists. He
evidently did not take the stage by storm as did Marlowe, and he
required somewhat longer to arrive at his full power than did
Jonson or Fletcher. A young man's poetic ambition and devotion to literature are shown by his poems. His early dramas
indicate rather the poet learning the trade of playwright. Apparently he did not come to the stage with a message or with a
grist of new ideas, or with a determination to display his originality. For a young man he seems to have been unusually alive to
the opportunities of his theater and patiently appreciative of the
methods of his predecessors.

With a widening experience of men and affairs and a rapidly
developing power of expression, other qualities soon became manifest in his plays, but they continue to reflect this keen attachment
to the affairs of the theater. This attachment was encouraged
not merely by the growing profits of a successful profession, but
also by the keen rivalry of brain and fancy among his fellows.
The popular success of the drama was causing the building of
new playhouses and an extraordinary activity in producing new
plays. The one company of which records have been preserved
produced about twenty new plays annually from 1594 to 1598;
and the four or five other companies may have done as well.
Men of talent in increasing numbers were attracted to dramatic
writing. Of the many occupations that assumed a new importance in this era of change, none offered opportunities and incentives with a more lavish hand than did the theater. No
dramatist could neglect the lessons and examples which were
afforded by its rapid and varied development; and anyone who

kept familiar with its multiform reflection of the age had little time and perhaps little need of other stimulus for his art or for his wisdom.

If it is affirmed that throughout the plays of his maturity, Shakspere is always attentive to his audience and his actors and often making use of the practices of contemporary dramatists, it must be admitted that the nature of his indebtedness is very different from that of the time of his apprenticeship. With a growing consciousness of his own powers, he borrows more from himself and less from others, and he is sure to give to whatever he takes a new value and beauty. In order to illustrate the nature and extent of this concealed indebtedness, it will be necessary to examine a few cases in some detail. For this purpose, I shall venture to return to several investigations of my own, published some fifteen years ago,[1] which may serve to define the ways in which Shakspere continued to make use of the work of other men.

Two of the cases are not of much importance in themselves but serve very well to indicate his general attitude toward contemporary drama. 'As You Like It,' certainly acted in 1599-1600, is based on Lodge's pastoral novel 'Rosalynde' but to this it adds the forest scenes of the Duke and his outlaws. The facts that two Robin Hood plays by Munday and Chettle, the 'Death' and the 'Downfall of Robert, Earl of Huntingdon,' had been produced by the chief rival company in 1598 and secured enough success for presentation at court, lead to the inference that they suggested to Shakspere the introduction of a Robin Hood element in 'As You You Like It.' The indebtedness goes little beyond the mere suggestion. Working over a pastoral novel and not unmindful of preceding pastoral plays, he was quick to take the hint that the idyllic life of the greenwood, which other men were trying to present, could be used as a fitting background for Rosalind, Orlando and Jaques. Of course, he did not have to go to Munday and Chettle for Robin Hood, but it is characteristic of Shakspere's methods that the direct stimulus came from a con-

[1] *As You Like It and Robin Hood Plays, Journal Eng. and Germ. Phil.,* 1902.
Influence of the Court Masques on the Drama, Publ. Mod. Lang. Assn., 1900.
The Relations of Hamlet to Contemporary Revenge Plays, Publ. Mod. Lang. Assn., 1902.
The Influence of Beaumont and Fletcher on Shakspere. 1901.

temporary play. And it is significant that in the theatrical means of presenting this outlaw life his play has striking similarities to its rivals by the Admiral's men.

The second case is the use in the 'Tempest' of suggestions from the Court Masques. These sumptuous spectacles had gained a definite form and, for some years before the 'Tempest' (1610), had been performed at the Court of James I with lavish expenditure. In their dances, decorations, music, and costumes, contemporary dramatists frequently found something that could be adapted or imitated for the public stage; but only in two plays of about the same date is there a well defined effort to combine the masque and the regular drama into a distinctive and novel dramatic entertainment, in the 'Four Plays in One' of Beaumont and Fletcher and the 'Tempest' of Shakspere. Ben Jonson, chief writer of librettos for the Court Masques, believed in keeping the two forms separate, and Shakspere's effort at combination brought forth his well-known gird at "those that beget tales, tempests and such like drolleries" and his refusal "to mix his head with other men's heels." Whether his criticism had some effect or the public stage found rivalry with the expensive court spectacles impossible, there seem to have been no later attempts at integrating the masque and tragi-comedy. The masque proper is used by Shakspere in the fourth act with its descents of the goddesses and the graceful dance of nymphs and reapers. The anti-masques or grotesque dances, just then novelties at the court, appear in the 'Strange Shapes' of Act III, Scene 3 and the 'divers spirits in shape of dogs and hounds' in Act IV, Scene 1. Ariel, Prospero, and even Caliban are also proper figures for a court show. Shakspere's beautiful romance must have appeared to him as a stage-spectacle and in it he made effective use of the construction, pageantry and devices of the Court Masque. Trifling though this borrowing may seem in comparison with the total effect of the play, it indicates again how closely he watched the contemporary theater and how ready he was to heed its novelties and fashions.

In the third case the borrowing is more important of itself and more far-reaching in its suggestions as to Shakspere's methods. His 'Hamlet' in its final form appeared in 1604 and was probably completed shortly before this, although the pirated quarto of 1603 may represent an earlier version. In both versions he was revising or remaking a 'Hamlet' written a dozen years before, probably by Thomas Kyd. As this early 'Hamlet' is lost we can not tell how much Shakspere owed to it. But this 'Hamlet' was only one of a considerable number of tragedies dealing with the story of the revenge of a son for a father, and having many common characteristics. The direct ancestor of the group seems to have been Kyd's 'Spanish Tragedy,' acted about 1587 and maintaining a great popularity for many years. This told the story of a father's vengeance for a murdered son, and the old 'Hamlet' was apparently a companion piece to it. Blood-revenge was a common tragic theme, but the story of a hesitating avenger, directed by a ghost, and opposing tricks to tricks, proved especially successful on the stage, and seized on the imaginations of many poets besides Shakspere. A year or two before his first version of 'Hamlet,' Marston's 'Antonio's Revenge' carried on the Kydian tradition; and at the very time that Shakspere was rewriting the old 'Hamlet,' Ben Jonson prepared additions to the 'Spanish Tragedy' for the rival Lord Admiral's company. By the time of the appearance of the final 'Hamlet,' the revenge of a son for a father had been presented with new variations in two other plays, Chettle's 'Hoffman' and Tourneur's 'Atheist's Tragedy.' The later development of a species now established followed the initiative of Marston and Tourneur rather than that of Shakspere.

Shakspere's 'Hamlet' then appears not merely the revision of an old play but one taking advantage of a special type of play, and in many respects conforming to the type. It offered little that was new in the material of the plot. The main elements of the action and many of the incidents reappear in many plays. The main motive is blood-revenge, usually directed by a ghost but delayed by a hesitating avenger. Only in one of the plays mentioned, 'Hoffman,' does the son go directly about his task, but in this case he is impeded by a love-affair. In the other plays the avenger is over-burdened by the weight of responsibility, asks for further proof, questions fate, and postpones action. Insanity, real or feigned, often occurs, and there are parallels to the mad Ophelia as well as to the mocking Hamlet. The wife, daughter, or betrothed of the victim is wooed by the villain, and in the later plays this illicit passion occupies a large place. Trickery opposes trickery, and in all the plays the action progresses through assassination and suicide to a final slaughter of many of the dramatis personae.

The indebtedness of Shakspere's 'Hamlet' extends beyond the leading dramatic motives to details of the stage situations and business. A play within the play, an appearance of the ghost to the watch, an interview of the ghost with his wife and son, a refusal of an opportunity to kill the villain, a murder of an innocent intruder, a mad girl singing snatches of songs, grave-yard scenes—all these had received dramatic development in other revenge tragedies. Embassies, poisonings, duels and drinking scenes were, of course, common material. And such minor bits of stage business as the voice of the ghost in the cellarage, the swearing on the sword hilt, the entry reading a book, the midnight clock, and the playing with death-heads, had appeared in other stage-versions of the revenge of a son for a father.

Amid the tumultuous action that such scenes suggest, there was, however, ample time given for reflection and self-examination, usually expressed in soliloquies that wrestle with the problems of fate, suicide, and injustice. These soliloquies often aid in defining the character of the protagonist and in focussing upon him the interest and sympathy of the audience. Already in the early 'Spanish Tragedy' he has the traits that appear more highly developed in the later plays. Moody and meditative, he is ever oppressed by the burden of responsibility which the duty of revenge has thrust upon him and wavers between avowals of vengeance and doubting introspection. When he finally frees himself from his distraction and forces his resolution to the sticking point, he goes about his task with elaborate dissimulation and trickery, and also with irony. It was this irony, distraction, and introspection that Jonson eloquently elaborated in his additions to the old play. There is in fact hardly a trait in Shakspere's 'Hamlet' which cannot in some measure be paralleled in the other revenge plays. Some details, as the refusal to kill the King for a bad reason, the murder of Polonius, the frenzied desire to drink hot blood, and the childish trickery of the voyage to England manifestly belong to the old story or to the stage type, and were preserved by Shakspere at the risk of inconsistency in characterization.

The borrowing, however, was not merely of plot or of stage situations and characters but of the imaginative motives that have given the play its abiding appeal. Inferior as are their plays to Shakspere, it is manifest that Marston, Jonson, and Tourneur aimed at a close study of character and the presentation of a philosophy of life. Along with the violence and spectacle of the external conflict between hero and villain, their plays were devised to exhibit also the internal struggle of souls at war with their own selves. The melancholy avenger of the stage who finds the time out of joint had become for others than Shakspere a symbol of the incompatibilities and accidents that result in the torture and waste of spirit in life's tragedy.

The play thus illustrates more fully perhaps than any other the extent and variety of Shakspere's borrowings from his colleagues of the theater. The success of 'Hamlet' was not that of an innovation in technic or ideas but that of a consummate adaptation of a type of play that others had fostered. Not primarily from Greece or Rome or philosophy, but from the plays and playwrights of the London stage, came the matter for its plot and persons and the stimulus for its poetry and wisdom. Yet, if we are asked to measure this debt in terms of the final value of the play, the answer must again be in comparison with a rival play. Manifestly the debt of 'Hamlet' to its predecessors cannot be much larger than that of any of the other later revenge plays. Marston, Tourneur, Webster and the others had the same materials and incentives to draw upon as did Shakspere. The value of his own contribution must be measured in terms of the superiority of his 'Hamlet' to any of their plays.

The fourth case presents an indebtedness insusceptible of absolute proof but affecting some of the larger aspects of Shakspere's art. A few years before his retirement, two young dramatists, Beaumont and Fletcher, after a few experiments won a series of extraordinary successes by plays written in collaboration. For the preceding decade the theaters had been given over largely to tragedy and to realistic and satiric comedy, and the plays of Beaumont and Fletcher produced a revival of romance. Moreover, their romances, though using, of course, material common in earlier romantic comedy, created a peculiar kind of romantic tragedies and tragicomedies destined to exercise a predominant influence on the theater for the next thirty years. Novel in plots and introducing new material and a new technic, these plays seemed to their contemporaries hardly less triumphant as poems than as plays. New contrasts of tragic and idyllic incidents, sensational conflicts of lust and sentiment, love and honor, unexpected dénouements, a constant use in structure of the alternation of suspense and surprise, a cast of stock characters not carefully individualized but running the gamut of many emotions—these are some of the elements of a formula, to which their flexible and lucid verse gave freshness and verisimilitude.

Shakspere, after some seven or eight years devoted mainly to tragedies, seems to have been attracted by the success of these new romances. The result was 'Cymbeline,' to the historical material of which he appears to have added romantic situations and persons after the fashion that Beaumont and Fletcher had just made popular in their tragicomedy 'Philaster.' There are certain marked similarities between these two plays that indicate some direct imitation, but the exact date of neither is known. We do know, however, that they were both acted by the same company, and not many months apart, during the years 1608-1610. 'Philaster,' one of the earlier products of the collaboration of Beaumont and Fletcher, was one of their most immediate and lasting successes; and none of their plays is more characteristic of their methods and temperaments. It owes much undoubtedly to preceding Elizabethan drama, something certainly to 'Hamlet', but it was to a marked degree a novel and epoch-making play. Like Marlowe's 'Tamburlaine' in 1587 and Jonson's 'Every Man in His Humour,' in 1598, it introduced a virtually new species of drama, and set a long enduring fashion. There are few romantic tragicomedies of later years that do not owe a manifest debt to it and its companion plays. With those circumstances in mind, it seems to me highly probable that Shakspere was again, as so often in his career, the borrower and adapter, and that his change from tragedy to tragicomedy, marked by 'Cymbeline,' may be credited to an initiative received from the younger dramatists.

If this view is accepted, there is left little ground for those to stand on who attribute Shakspere's changes of theme and method to the effects of his personal experience, resulting in periods of spiritual depression and exaltation. His whole career rather becomes mapped out in accord with the changes and movement of the drama of his time. The arguments on which my hypothesis rests need not be rehearsed; but during the fifteen years since they were first presented, the increased attention paid to details of the Elizabethan drama and the resulting recognition of the importance and distinctness of Fletcher's contribution have worked, I think it may be said, toward a greater tolerance if not acceptance of my contentions. They have been opposed by many, and by no one with more generous appreciation then by the late Professor Dowden, against some of whose theories my attacks had been perhaps too sharply directed. At the basis of his and most other criticism there lies the fear that the admission of so much indebtedness by Shakspere to his contemporaries must diminish our admiration for the work of his genius. I have been often accused of seeking to detract from his fame, but really it is not I, but my critics who by their very timidity for his reputation, betray a lack of faith in its stability. This fear is particularly manifest in the general unwillingness to yield anything of the 'Winter's Tale' and the 'Tempest' to Beaumont and Fletcher. Even if they must lose 'Cymbeline,' they refuse to sacrifice these masterpieces. But my own contention never suggested that the influence of the younger men on these plays was of a sort to lessen the greatness of Shakspere's achievement.

Certainly the 'Winter's Tale' and the 'Tempest' offer no such resemblances to any of Beaumont and Fletcher's romances as does 'Cymbeline.' Shakspere is no longer in an imitative or adaptive mood. Having in 'Cymbeline' followed a new lead, he now knows his way and marks out new paths of his own. The indebtedness is no longer either specific or pervasive. What is borrowed is the general characteristics of the type, already used in 'Cymbeline,' and now varied and transformed with fresh invention. In the 'Winter's Tale,' for example, the sentimental love story, the involved plot, the contrast of tragic and idyllic elements, the rapidly shifting situations, the loose and parenthetical style, the borrowing from court masques, the elaborate and surprising dénouement, the idealized characters—these are some of the traits which link the play with the Beaumont and Fletcher tragicomedy. But the adoption of a formula or a fashion does not make a play. The development of the idyl in the fourth act, for instance, is Shakspere's own variation and at once distinctive and admirable.

This may indicate the process which seems to me always found in Shakspere's borrowing. He took the kind of plays which were succeeding and was quick to make use of ideas or motives as well as of themes or incidents. But his invention responded to these suggestions and, having once secured its starting point, often departed very far from the indicated course. If 'Cymbeline' is an example of only partially successful experimentation with new methods, the 'Winter's Tale,' and still more the 'Tempest' seem to me triumphant and unguided excursions of his own in the new field. At the close of his career he had turned from historical tragedies to romantic tragicomedies, not primarily because of any personal experience, but because two young dramatists were succeeding in that field. He accepted their invitation to enter the new territory but he quickly made it his own. At his best this is what he always accomplishes. In 'Julius Caesar' the closeness to Plutarch is undeniable, the wonder is that with such slight changes he could make so effective and veracious a tragedy. In 'Hamlet' his indebtedness to current drama is large and detailed, but the marvel is that he could make a play so much greater than those of his contemporaries who were working with the same dramatic material. In the 'Winter's Tale' and the 'Tempest' we may admit their obligations to Beaumont and Fletcher, and still admire the daring of Shakspere's invention and the freshness of his humor and fancy.

I have ventured to dwell on my essays rather than on many other investigations in this field, because they furnish me with the easiest means of illustrating the extent and character of Shakspere's indebtedness to contemporary dramatists, and also because they seem to me to suggest certain limits beyond which indebtedness cannot be charged against him. There are, indeed, many other cases where a careful study of contemporary literature and drama have shown that he was to a considerable extent following and adapting. Sir Sidney Lee's extensive study of contemporary sonnets has indicated that in the lyrical as well as the dramatic poems, there are conventional and imitative elements. The comedies 'All's Well' and 'Measure for Measure,' which exhibit striking differences from preceding romantic comedies, may, I think, be brought into connection with the sudden vogue of contemporary comedies dealing with similarly casuistical problems of sex and giving similar presentation to the seamy side of city life. Almost every one of the plays has been related in some way to contemporary practice. Further, in the study of particular classes of situation, types of character, and even stylistic peculiarities, Shakspere's work has been in many particulars closely related to that of his associates. What do these debts amount to in comparison with the total effect of the completed play? To no more, in my opinion, than in the cases of 'Hamlet' and the 'Tempest.'

If, however, these attributions of indebtedness do not diminish our sense of Shakspere's achievement, they may very likely render less acceptable some of the adulations piled up by a century of appreciation and interpretation. Studies of indebtedness from a historical point of view are manifestly serviceable as a basis for interpretation and appreciative criticism. Before interpreting a character in the terms of the dramatist's or the critic's personality, it is essential to know how much the character has in common with other representatives of the stage-type. Before praising a situation or a phrase as an indication of the greatest genius, it is desirable to know whether it was borrowed from an obscure writer. Historical criticism of Shakspere has, indeed, been largely employed in counteracting some of the over subtleties and refinements of appreciative criticism. No one has done this more vigorously than Professor E. E. Stoll in a series of acute essays[1] in which he has analyzed some of the best known characters, Shylock, Iago, Hamlet and Falstaff. It is surely an aid to a right interpretation to examine these creations from a strictly Elizabethan point of view. But it must also be said

---

[1] *Falstaff, Mod. Phil.*, Oct., 1914; *Shylock, Journal Gem. Phil.*, April, 1911; *Criminals in Shaksperian and in Science, Mod. Phil.*, July, 1912; *Anachronism in Shakspere Criticism*, April, 1910; *Hamlet and Iago, Kittredge Anniversary Papers*, 1913.

that the most searching array of parallels or the most convincing proof of borrowing still leaves a larger portion of the final
effect of character, style, or play unaccounted for. The final
work is Shakspere's, and even when you can prove just what
he borrowed, you can not always subtract it. In the creative
process it has undergone a transformation, and it cannot be
taken away. If the romanticist has tended to exalt and mag-
nify the individual's contribution in art, the historical critic may
easily run into the danger of underestimating its value.

The case of Falstaff is notable. Romanticist criticism virtually
began with Morgann's well-known essay which undertook the
kind of elaborate interpretation of character of which we have had
so much in the century and a half since. Falstaff then had been
for many generations the delight of the stage and the closet, but
Morgann felt that he had never been fully appreciated. Indeed,
his own appreciation of the fat knight was the result of his finding
much in the character not obvious to most readers, and the result
of his research was the paradox that Falstaff was no coward.
Since then, the romanticists, as Professor Stoll's essay reminds us,
have delighted to dwell on this or that neglected trait, or to discover a new subtlety until it now only remains for some twentieth
century critic to prove that Falstaff was not really fat. But now
comes Professor Stoll and, by comparison with other plays,
shows that in many respects Falstaff was a coward, a braggart, a
butt, and a stage-type. Does this suggest that he is little more?

The *miles gloriosus* of Latin comedy is not a very interesting
person, but he provided a fertile type for Renaissance drama.
Braggart soldiers were doubtless frequent enough in fact, and
they made active and effective parts for comedians. There are
innumerable buffoons and braggarts with little wit or individuality to relieve their baseness, but in several cases these stage-
parts became distinct and individual persons as in Bascilisco of
'Soliman and Perseda' and Ben Jonson's Bobadill. Like any
dramatist, Shakspere took suggestions for both his Pistol and Falstaff from the stage-type. In the case of Falstaff he brought together characteristics, incidents, stage-tricks, phrases, and kept
adding to them until in mere number of traits there was a character far surpassing other comic parts. This varied accumulation

Shakspere did not develop with the kind of unity demanded by either classicist or realist. Falstaff is not as consistent a person as Jonson's Bobadill, nor is he merely the amplification of a few prominent traits like Dickens's Pecksniff or Micawber, nor is he as carefully explained as George Eliot's Tito. He cannot be reduced to fact or formula or moral. He is conglomerate, heterogeneous, full of inconsistencies, and transcending life. We all know persons who remind us of Falstaff, who have some of his vices and a touch of his wit, but we know of no one really like him, no one with his extent and variety. "Falstaff," writes Professor Stoll, "is simple as his author and his times." The truth of the comparison involved in this statement is beyond question, but for the adjective I should prefer to substitute complex. The complexity of Shakspere's characters was, I think, due to his times as well as to his own personality. Perhaps men's motives were simpler then than now, but it can hardly be questioned that their actions were less conventional, more inconsistent, more strikingly individual. One does not need to recall Benvenuto Cellini, the life of almost any Elizabethan worthy exhibits conflicts of turpitude and nobility, vice and wit, as unblushingly displayed as Falstaff's own. Something of this Elizabethan exposure of many-sided individuality enters into Shakspere's characterization, and may help to account for its reality along with a lack of unity.

Now it is precisely in the inconsistencies and incongruities that the Romanticist critics have found their assurances of individuality. The critics of the classical school and to some extent those of the present day prefer to stress the main and typical elements of the characterization. Falstaff was a coward, say the latter; but he did and said things that made him something quite different, say the former. One may agree that the romanticists carried too far their search for the hiding places of individuality, without having much sympathy for an effort to reduce Shakspere's characters to simplicity by pointing out that the main elements in one of his persons were the common properties of a current stage-type. That merely marks the beginning of his creative work, a process of vitalizing in which the extension and variation of trait played almost as large a part as the unifying power of his marvellous gift of phrase. The other stage cowards were mostly still-born. Falstaff is alive after three hundred years, mainly because he was not true to type.

After all, historical criticism is only incidentally occupied in correcting and fortifying an appreciative interpretation of literature. It is mainly concerned not in teaching us to love Shakspere or another, to approve of one method of characterization or another, but rather in recording how books came to be written and how the imagination has done its literary work. The study of such borrowings and adaptations as I have examined has its chief interest as illustrating the processes of literature in the making.

Enough has perhaps been said to indicate that Shakspere's indebtedness is manifestly not a matter of addition and subtraction, of debit and credit. Rather, it raises the whole question of literary creation. Every writer draws upon a host of suggestions and incentives that may come from reading, observation, or intercourse and conversation. It is the unending task of the literary imagination to change and transform such suggestions into something different from what has been written before. But not even the greatest literature escapes the processes of borrowing and imitation. With most modern writers the world of books exercises an overpowering influence. How rarely is there a dramatist who, like Ibsen, carries out large and effective innovations. How rarely is there a novel which is not a good deal like other recent novels. In poetry, a style so individual and influential as that of Keats was formed on the careful and continued study of Shakspere, Spenser, Dryden, Milton, and his own contemporaries. Our most original modern writers get certain theories or obsessions, which remain nearly fixed and in conformity with which they frame their impressions; so Wordsworth, Shelley, Browning, and Ibsen. But it is usually not necessary to hunt far in order to find where these obsessions and theories came from.

Shakspere's dramas owe comparatively little to the world of books, though he used his reading to advantage and his style was, like that of Keats, formed on a study and imitation of others. He was a dramatist, and unquestionably a statement of his debts shows that his interests were centered on the theater. To some degree, the range and character of his creative work were limited by the necessities and demands of this theater. His audiences were heterogeneous and wide-awake, but they had little culture or decorum. His stage afforded opportunity rather than the proper restrictions for dramatic art. His actors required parts suited to their powers and similar to those they were used to. Throughout his career he was very attentive to the work of his fellow dramatists, and was ever getting suggestions from acted plays.

It is not therefore necessary to regard him or his fellows as mere stage-carpenters. The Elizabethan drama, of which his plays were a part, unfolds to its student an extraordinary imaginative activity. From Marlowe and Lyly on, there was an extremely rapid and multifarious development, in which imitation was ever giving way to new initiative. Shakspere's associates were not only actors and playwrights, but a group of clever men engaged in translating both the world of books and the life about them into poetry. During the period of Shakspere's authorship, London probably often saw one hundred new plays in a single year. These plays dealing with an enormous range of material were written in a small city for a few theaters by a group of men closely associated in rivalry and emulation. Among them were men of great and diverse knowledge and talent, as Chapman, Jonson, Dekker, Marlowe, Webster, and Fletcher. It would be difficult to find in any other period or place so much that was stimulating to the imagination of a dramatist.

In all this activity, Shakspere does not stand out as an innovator and path breaker, as, for example, do Marlowe and Jonson. Neither does he appear as an imitator bound to the established traditions, as do Massinger and Shirley. If he began by frank imitation of current forms, he soon made them his own and, for the seven years after Marlowe's death, won unquestioned pre-eminence as the leading dramatist of the leading company, and as the creator of the most popular as well as the most original plays in the fields of romantic comedy and English history. When, about 1600, the fashion set hard toward realistic and satiric drama, he was little affected by it, but kept his own way, producing the great series of tragedies. Amid the rivalry of the brilliant group which gives primacy in English literature to the first decade of the seventeenth century, he maintained his leadership whether on the public stage, at court, or in the Mermaid tavern. Other men followed his successes as he followed theirs. What he availed himself of in stage-business, situation, type of character, motive, technic, or verse was open to all. If he was quick to catch at suggestion, he was also quick to improve and transform.

A study of his indebtedness places him back in his own age and theater, with his contemporaries and fellows. He does not appear as a prophet or reformer, a philosopher with a system, or an egoist bent on writing himself into his plays. He appears borrowing freely from what was a common fund, or in other words, as a dramatist using freely whatever could be learned from a stage that was crowded with stimulating experiments. In making over stories for this stage he does not seem to have been much aided or hindered by fixed theories of life or rules of art. He did not crowd his mind with the great literature of antiquity, and he did not travel far with the science, philosophy, and theology of his own day. He lacked the advantages of a knowledge of scientific evolution and of twentieth century dramaturgy. But, while he was keen to stage opportunities, he was also alive to the imaginative realization of all the possibilities and implications of story or character. Humanity and Poetry had made their home in the London theater before Shakspere came thither from Stratford, and he took them for his masters.

As a result of a study of his relations to his contemporaries, Shakspere's creative processes may appear more like those of other men and less miraculous than they seemed to Coleridge, and less the accident of headstrong genius than they seemed to Dr. Johnson. If such study tends to give more credit to his time and environment and less to individual peculiarity, it conforms with our modern habit of explaining things. But it does not alter the meaning or beauty of his plays; and it need not detract from our admiration of that amazing imagination which made so much out of the world he knew. The student who brings new debts to account may well join with Coleridge and Johnson in echoing that exclamation of amazement with which Dryden celebrated the fiftieth anniversary of the death of "the man who of all Moderns, and perhaps Ancient Poets, had the largest and most comprehensive soul."

VII

THE LOVE-STORY
IN 'TROILUS AND CRESSIDA'

By William Witherle Lawrence

Professor of English

THE LOVE-STORY IN 'TROILUS AND CRESSIDA'

I consider 'Macbeth' Shakspere's best acting play; it shows the greatest understanding of the stage. But would you learn to know his unfettered spirit, read 'Troilus and Cressida.'

GOETHE: *Conversations with Eckermann.*

Coleridge, in commenting upon 'Troilus and Cressida,' remarked that he scarcely knew what to say of it, and that "there is no one of Shakspere's plays harder to characterize." His view has been shared by the ablest modern critics. Even the great tragedies, with all their psychological subtlety, have proved far less perplexing. Perhaps we are at the present time a little nearer to a satisfactory solution of the difficulties of this play than we were a hundred years ago, but we are still far from having plucked out the heart of its mystery. The superb poetry and imaginative reach of many of its passages, which appealed so strongly to Goethe, make failure to understand it as a whole doubly annoying. Barrett Wendell has summed up the feeling of many critics of later days by concluding, "A puzzle we found 'Troilus and Cressida,'.....and a puzzle we must leave it; our best comment must be guess-work." But is it possible to say nothing more definite than this?

The chief difficulty lies in explaining the repellent treatment of the main theme, in which Cressida is made the most sensual of loose women, while Pandarus is drawn with savage cynicism, and of the secondary plot, or enveloping action, which gives disagreeable pictures of the warriors contending about windy Troy, particularly of those in the Greek camp. The atmosphere of the piece is unhealthy; immorality, cowardice, rancor and boasting are always in the air. Much noble verse is stained with a pessimism hard to reconcile with the essential sanity of most of the plays. Neither love nor adventure seems glorious.

"Can Shakspere's view of things have been the same as Thersites'?" asks Dowden. Many critics would reply in a qualified affirmative. Bradley is cautious about the matter, but he notes that "a spirit of bitterness and contempt seems to pervade an intellectual atmosphere of an intense but hard clearness," and conjectures that "the comparative confinement of the imaginative atmosphere .   .   .   ." is "due to some unpleasant mood." Brandes goes much further: " 'Troilus and Cressida' is the outcome of the disillusionment, suspicion, and bitterness of ripe manhood," the result of Shakspere's own personal sufferings and of disgust at contemporary laxity in morals. Dowden adopted a somewhat similar view, calling 'Troilus and Cressida' "the comedy of disillusion," and styling the period of Shakspere's life at which it was written "In the Depths." This general explanation of the disagreeable features of the play has gained wide currency. 'Measure for Measure' and 'All's Well that Ends Well' may have been written at about the same time as 'Troilus and Cressida,' the great tragedies following shortly after. It has frequently been assumed, then, that at this time the poet was pouring out the bitterness of heart which arises from bitterness of experience.[1]

This view is open to serious objections, as critics have already pointed out. We do not know with certainty when 'All's Well' and 'Measure for Measure' were written, and the dating of 'Troilus and Cressida' is almost as difficult as its interpretation. The theory is, moreover, contradicted by the evidence of misfortune in the poet's life when he was writing the most sparkling and joyous of comedies, and by the testimony of the servants of the sister arts, who have frequently undergone severe affliction without revealing it in their works. Beethoven composed some of his sunniest music in blindness and misfortune, and 'The Magic Flute,' compact of happy melody, was written under distressing circumstances a short time before Mozart's death. Conversely, works of tragic gloom have often been produced amid happy surroundings. So, while the shadow upon 'Troilus and Cressida' is dark indeed, we cannot safely

[1] For the opinions just quoted, see Coleridge, *Lectures and Notes on Shakspere and other English Poets*, London, 1890, p. 306; Wendell, *William Shakspere*, N. Y., 1901, p. 277; Dowden, *Shakspere, His Mind and Art*, N. Y., 1881; A. C. Bradley, *Shaksperean Tragedy*, London, 1905, pp. 186, 275; and Brandes, *William Shakspere, A Critical Study*, N. Y., 1898, Vol. II; also his preface to the Brandes Shakspere volume of *Troilus and Cressida*.

assume a period of personal misfortune as an explanation for this.

Nor is it convincing to suppose, as others have done, that Shakspere's quarrels with contemporary dramatists led him to vent his animosity through the medium of this play. Fleay and George Wyndham thought it to be a savage satire on Marston and Jonson, and Furnivall, Gollancz and Boas have conjectured that much in the treatment of the story and of the Greek heroes, in particular, was due to dislike of Chapman, "in all probability the rival poet who ousted Shakspere from his patron's favor." How little either of these views accords with the evidence has been convincingly shown in the elaborate study by Small.[1] At most, there may be a touch of satire on Jonson in the figure of Ajax. But this affords no explanation for the prevailing tone of the play. It seems, indeed, inherently improbable that Shakspere should have altered the whole character of his piece for the sake of indulging so ill-tempered and petty a revenge.

Equally unsatisfactory is the theory of Ulrici that the play is a satire on the ideals of Greek antiquity as reflected in the Homeric poems, or the view recently championed afresh by Boas, that Shakspere, in the intrigue of Troilus and Cressida, was holding up to ridicule the ideals of chivalry, that he saw in the story "the materials for a merciless satire of the high-flown ideal of love, fostered by the medieval cycle of romance, whence the tale had sprung. The absolute devotion of a gallant to his mistress, which this form of literature had glorified, is transformed into the delirious passion of a youth for a mere wanton." It appears highly doubtful if, in a piece designed for the public stage, Shakspere was chiefly influenced by a desire to ridicule classical ideas, or the exaggerated love-conventions of the chivalric period, or even of his own day. This was not his habit; satire is incidental in his plays, lurking in details, but it is never the moving cause of the whole action. Proof of such satirical intent is difficult; the rapturous utterances of Troilus cited by Boas are no more exaggerated than those of Othello or Romeo. Nor is it more convincing to suppose that Shakspere wrote the play in order to pour

---

[1] R. A. Small, *The Stage Quarrel between Ben Jonson and the so-called Poetasters*, Breslau, 1899.

out his righteous wrath upon the scandals of the times of King James or the closing days of the reign of Elizabeth. He was no preacher; there is a "moral" to be found in his work, as there is in every sincere reproduction of human life, but he does not shout it at us. From all that we can learn, he wrote primarily to amuse and interest his public, not to play the moralist or the satirist. Since we have no means of knowing absolutely what was in his mind, we cannot disprove, any more than we can prove, satirical intent. But I think it may be shown that what appears to be irony is largely due to other causes.[1]

Structurally, the play falls into two well-marked divisions: the love-story, in which Cressida, Troilus, Pandarus and Diomedes are the main figures, and the background of debate and contest about Troy, in which the protagonists are the Greek and Trojan heroes familiar to us all. These two actions Shakspere drew from different sources. For the love-story he was chiefly dependent upon Chaucer's 'Troilus and Criseyde,' for the rest, in all probability, upon Caxton's 'Recuyell of the Histories of Troye,' aided by Chapman's translation of the 'Iliad.' He could not, of course, have drawn the intrigue of Cressida from Caxton, since it is there related in great brevity, Pandarus not even being mentioned, nor could he have drawn it from Homer, since it does not appear there at all. Conversely, Chaucer's poem is little concerned with the doings of the Greek and Trojan heroes, and hence could have afforded little suggestion for the secondary action. Shakspere was uniting, then, two different streams of tradition.

His use of Caxton goes far to explain why the contending warriors, particularly the Greeks, who appear in Homer as radiant and almost god-like beings, are so unsympathetically portrayed. The medieval versions of the Troy-story were quite lacking in the serenity and classic elevation of Homer, and they exalted the Trojans at the expense of the Greeks, in deference to the old notion that the sovereigns of Western Europe were descended from Æneas, the Trojan, through his great-grandson Brutus. As might be expected, Shakspere reflects the spirit of Caxton's

[1] For the theory of Ulrici, see the *Shakspere-Jahrbuch*, Vol. IX (1874), p. 39; for that of Boas, *Shakspere and his Predecessors*, New York, 1905, p. 373.

version. This has been urged with much force by Tatlock, who has further contended that "an examination of other Elizabethan versions of the Troy-story modifies the impression of bitterness which Shakspere's 'Troilus' makes on a modern, and shows that the play was probably less original than it has been considered." And Griffin, in a careful study of the un-Homeric elements in the medieval story of Troy, points out that "the altered English representation" is not due to "a deliberate desire on the part of the English poets to accommodate the Homeric representation to some aesthetic or moral purpose of their own, such as the wish to oppose the essentially sensuous and immoral standards of antiquity to the more exalted ethics of Christian Europe," but that "it is to be ascribed to a pre-existing, traditional conception of the Trojan War, which Chaucer and Shakspere felt bound to respect and obey........The English poets, so far from having any ulterior moral or artistic purpose to serve, based their poems throughout upon the traditional conception of the Trojan War as found in the works of their medieval predecessors and as still current in their own day."[1] So the delineation of the Greek heroes is in great measure to be explained as the perpetuation of a tradition rather than as the result of Shakspere's personal attitude towards the story.

How does the case stand with the main plot? How is the repellent treatment of the Troilus-Cressida intrigue to be explained? Here we touch the very heart of the whole problem. For it is after all this intrigue which forms the chief interest in the play, however large the subsidiary material may loom up behind it. Obviously, the whole conception is quite different from that in Chaucer's pages. So different is it that Deighton, in a recent study of the play, after querying why Shakspere has presented, in contrast to Chaucer's modest and reserved heroine, "a character who at her best betrays the manners and morals of a grisette, at her worst can boast little more refinement and purity than Doll Tearsheet herself," reverts to the theory of "a pessimistic frame of mind" on the part of the playwright, and conjectures "that

---

[1] For Tatlock's views, see preface to the *Tudor Shakspere* edition of the play; also abstract of a paper read at the meeting of the Modern Language Association of America in New York, December, 1914. (*Publications* of the Association, Vol. XXIII, No. I, p. xiv.) For Griffin's argument, see *Journal of English and Germanic Philology*, Vol. VII (1907), pp. 32-52.

his insight showed him how ill-suited for dramatic treatment was the view conceived or accepted by Chaucer; how impossible the reconcilement between the Cressida of the clear dawn and the Cressida of the murky sunset." But he thinks Shakspere may have used other sources. "The absence of any other known source—play, poem, or romance—dealing with the story in a cynical spirit does not seem conclusive."[1] We may fairly take his statement as reflecting the indecisions which assail those who at the present day attempt to interpret the character of Shakspere's heroine. But no one of his suggestions really strikes the root of the matter. "A pessimistic frame of mind" may partly explain the portrayal of Cressida, but this is, I believe, quite secondary to other causes. There seems to be no reason why a master of psychology like Shakspere could not have made the character of Cressida vivid and convincing in a poetic drama, along the lines laid down by Chaucer, if the same thing had already been accomplished in a narrative poem. The striking dramatic qualities of Chaucer's 'Troilus and Criseyde' have been emphasized by the late Professor Price, who conceived the action of the whole poem as a sequence of fifty scenes.[2] Finally, there seems no occasion, as we shall see, to assume that Shakspere worked from a source or sources now lost.

The main cause for the degradation of Cressida and of Pandarus and indeed of the whole love-story seems rather to lie in the changed attitude of Shakspere's day towards the tale itself, and towards the conception of love upon which Chaucer's whole fabric rests. In remodelling the medieval story for his own day, Shakspere was constrained, if he kept its main outlines—which he was obliged to do because of their familiarity to Elizabethan audiences—to present the character of Cressida in a highly unfavorable light. We can understand his depiction of Cressida only by observing the changes from medieval tradition which the love-story had undergone since the fourteenth century. The social conventions which had in the beginning determined the character of the heroine had been forgotten, and the degradation of her

---

[1] K. Deighton, Introduction to the *Arden Shakspere* volume of *Troilus and Cressida*, London, 1906.

[2] *Publications of the Modern Language Association of America*, Vol. XI, pp. 307-322. (1896.)

character inevitably followed, as time went on—a degradation hastened by the very popularity of the story, since popular tradition paid small heed to the subtleties of courtly observance. Shakspere was obliged to follow the traditions of his own day; he was writing not for the fourteenth century, but for the seventeenth.

Obvious as this point seems, it has been constantly overlooked. Certainly the chief authorities neglect it surprisingly. Small, in the monograph already referred to, notes that "Shakspere modifies the character of Cressida to accord with the traditional notion that she was fickle and light from the beginning." But the matter can hardly be disposed of so summarily. Analysis of the character of Cressida from Boccacio to Shakspere requires— and repays—careful study. The same may be said of the delineation of Pandarus, which has been widely misunderstood. Much has already been done, of course, to make clearer the character of Chaucer's heroine, and to establish Chaucer's exact dependence upon his sources. But far less has been written about the later development of the tale. The present essay aims to suggest the successive alterations in the portrayal of Cressida and of Pandarus, and to consider these alterations in connection with accompanying changes in social conventions. The subtler issues demand treatment more detailed than can be given here; but the broader lines of development may be sketched in, and their significance suggested. The writer hopes to be forgiven if, in his endeavor to make the situation perfectly clear, he repeats information which the reader finds superfluous.

It is scarcely necessary to observe that the story of Troilus and Cressida is entirely the creation of the Middle Ages; that it grew up about the tale of Troy like the ivy about the oak, attached somewhat loosely to the trunk to which it clung. Developed mainly out of hints in late Latin accounts of the Trojan War, it was first created, so far as we can determine, by Benoit de Sainte More, in his 'Roman de Troie,' written in the second half of the twelfth century. About a hundred years later, Guido delle Colonne put the story into Latin prose, abridging Benoit in many places. Guido found many imitators, among them Lydgate, and Caxton, whose 'Recuyell of the Histories of Troye' was, as we have seen, probably the main source of Shakspere's enveloping plot. The love-story of Troilus, though considerably developed by Benoit, was secondary and episodic; its full development really began with Boccaccio, whose 'Filostrato' was the first version to subordinate the Trojan war, making it merely a background for the history of the lovers. Here for the first time 'Pandaro' appears as a character in the love-intrigue. Benoit had dwelt chiefly upon the relations of the heroine and Diomede; Boccaccio greatly elaborated the love-affair with Troilus. Young has shown that much in the poem is imitated from Boccaccio's own earlier 'Filocolo,' a version of the well-known medieval tale of 'Floris and Blanchefleur.'[1]

In order to comprehend Boccaccio's poem, it is of the first importance to gain a clear idea of the circumstances under which it was written, and the society which it portrays. This is quite as essential as attention to sources. For it is at once a picture of the life of Boccaccio's own country and day, and a mirror of the author's own experiences in love. No one, of course, expects historical accuracy in medieval narrative. In the 'Filostrato' the manners of the city of Troy are modelled upon those of Naples in the fourteenth century. The poem was inspired, as Boccaccio himself tells us, by his love for the beautiful Maria d'Aquino, or "Fiammetta," the illegitimate daughter of King Robert of Jerusalem and the Two Sicilies. It was apparently written at the time of Boccaccio's most ardent devotion to her; he was striving to soften her heart by depicting the sufferings of Troilus. His efforts were successful. Fiammetta granted him her love, but, after a while, cast him off for another. The essential thing to note is that this affair was not inconsistent with the social standards of the Italy of that day. Maria d'Aquino was married, but she had many lovers, an arrangement sanctioned, if kept discreetly concealed, by the love-conventions of the later Middle Ages. It is probable that the character of "Griseida" as she appears in Boccaccio's pages—a compound of charm, weakness, voluptuousness, inconstancy, and calculation—is a veracious picture of Fiammetta. Troilo is little more than the hand-

---

[1] Karl Young, *The Origin and Development of the Story of Troilus and Criseyde. Chaucer Society*, 1908, for the issue of 1904.

some, ardent lover. Far more interesting is Pandaro, a gay young Italian courtier, and a cousin of Griseida. Out of friendship for Troilo, he uses his good offices to bring the lovers together. These people are all frankly sensual, but they proceed with a certain respect for good form, like obviously hungry guests at a dinner-party, who are restrained by a proper regard for social usages from devouring their food too eagerly. The whole poem, while artificial in much of its effect to the modern reader, is made vivid and realistic by the truthfulness of its character-drawing, and, no doubt, by the real emotion which underlies it.

With Chaucer, the tale takes on a new significance. Boccaccio wrote a graceful story of courtly intrigue; Chaucer produced a masterpiece of subtle psychological analysis. 'Troilus and Criseyde' is written in elaborate stanzaic form, since at that time verse was the common medium for romantic narrative; but had Chaucer lived three or four centuries later, he would have cast it in prose, as Richardson did 'Clarissa Harlowe,' and Hawthorne the 'Scarlet Letter.' For it is with such works as these, by virtue of its analysis of character, that Chaucer's poem belongs. It is based upon Boccaccio, with some details from Benoit and Guido. The chief interest lies in the transformation of Pandaro and Griseida. Troilus is much like the Troilo of Boccaccio; his character changes little from age to age. Pandarus becomes a humorous man of the world, much older than Troilus, and the uncle of the heroine. It is Criseyde upon whom Chaucer's subtlest art is lavished. So complex does her character become that critics have differed widely in their estimates of it. But she is certainly sympathetically treated by the poet. The view that would make of her "a scheming adventuress" is, as Kittredge remarks, "so patently erroneous as to need no refutation." The same critic, after a remarkably penetrating analysis, sums up her character as follows: "As Cressida is at the beginning, such is she to the end; amorous, gentle, affectionate, and charming altogether, but fatally impressionable and yielding. Her strength of will is no match for her inconstant heart.........Cressida is not a simple character, like the elemental Griseida of Boccaccio; but her inconsistencies are those of human nature."[1] In Chaucer's pages,

[1] G. L. Kittredge, *Chaucer and his Poetry*, Cambridge, 1915, p. 135.

the chief emphasis is upon the development of her love-affair with Troilus; the later part of the story is much more briefly told.

An understanding of the character of Criseyde as conceived by Chaucer is impossible without an understanding of the social conventions of the time, since it is in terms of these conventions that the whole action of the poem is interpreted. To us Criseyde might, at the first glance, appear like the wanton heroine of a novel by Maupassant or Bourget, but not as a wanton did she present herself to Chaucer. Nothing could be more uncritical than to judge the motivation of the poem by modern ethical standards.

The medieval system of courtly love, which had grown up under the influence of social conditions in Provence during the twelfth century and earlier, and had received its most elaborate form in the lyrics of the Troubadours and the romances of Crestien de Troyes, was still in vogue, in somewhat modified form, in the fourteenth century. Chaucer was quite as much under its spell as Boccaccio, feeling its influence very directly in the French verse with which he was so familiar. At the court of Edward the Third, where all things elegant were French or Italian, a brave show of chivalric splendor was kept up against the muttering storm of social and political upheaval—a kind of troubled purple autumn of the foliage which had bloomed so brilliantly in a long-past spring. Every English courtier was familiar with the code of courtly love; it would indeed have hardly been possible for an English poet of Chaucer's day to tell a romantic love-story without interpreting the adventures of his well-born heroes and heroines in accordance with its laws. We may use the term "laws" with no reservations. The correct procedure in love had long since been codified and reduced to rule, quite in the fashion of legal or theological doctrine. Courtly love was not, according to modern conceptions, moral; the lady was usually a married woman, and the granting of the last favors to the lover was not held to be reprehensible, but on the contrary entirely proper. Secrecy was of the utmost importance; one of the greatest sins against love was inability to conceal an intrigue, as the charming story of the Chatelaine de Vergi reminds us. Honor was compromised not through performance but through detection. The lady must not be too easily won; her favor was to be gained by a display of extravagant suffering, often bringing the wretched lover close to death itself. Theoretically, the lady stooped to pity rather than to love; she was the idol and the man the abject worshipper. Love was frequently interpreted in terms of religious devotion in a universe ruled by Cupid and Venus, or in terms of feudal obligation, in which the lady exercised control over her vassal and "servant," the lover. When once love had been granted—and this was no mere form of words—the greatest of sins was inconstancy, on the part of either man or woman. Machaut's pretty poem, the 'Judgment of the King of Bohemia,' proclaims that it is better that the beloved one be dead than faithless.

Chaucer's whole story is built up on this system of love-conventions. His characters are no more Trojan than Boccaccio's; they might have lived at the court of Marie de Champagne or of Edward the Third. The poet announces himself at the beginning as the servant of all lovers, and dedicates his work to them. Troilus is at first a scoffer at Love; he is punished by being smitten by Cupid with passion for Criseyde. After the approved fashion, he reveals his passion to no one, but betakes himself to his chamber and suffers atrociously in secret. His close friend, Pandarus, at length persuades him to violate this secrecy, and tell him of his woes. Thereupon the good-natured, whimsical uncle of Criseyde, genuinely moved by the distress of Troilus, volunteers to aid him in his desires. Only after much urging by Pandarus is Criseyde brought to confess a liking for Troilus. Long she holds off, with well-assumed indifference. Finally, at the close of a banquet, she is persuaded to speak with the wretched lover, ill in his chamber. She accords him her love—as a sister. So matters go on for awhile. At last, Pandarus invites Criseyde and others to a supper-party, and in consequence of a violent storm, she spends the night at her uncle's house. Again through the intervention of Pandarus, she is led to accord to Troilus the last favors. The lovers now enjoy a brief season of ideal happiness. Then comes an exchange of prisoners, and Criseyde leaves Troy as Antenor enters. She promises to return in ten days, but meets with no success in her attempts to persuade her father Calchas

to let her do so. Meanwhile, the handsome and valiant Diomede
has been making ardent love to her. At length she yields to him,
though bitterly condemning her own unfaithfulness to Troilus.
Her former lover is ultimately slain by Achilles.

It has repeatedly been urged, and must again be emphasized,
that according to the conventions of the code of love, Criseyde
committed no sin in giving herself to Troilus. Modern ethical
views are totally out of place here; the surrender of the lady,
after a due season of coldness, was held to be right and proper.
There is much talk of "honor" in the poem, but we must be careful not to understand this in the modern sense of "chastity."
Criseyde's "honor" will be stained if she is discovered, but not
if she engages in a well-concealed intrigue. Her discretion and
solicitous care for her reputation are constantly emphasized.
It is in such concealment that "honor" consists. In the present
case, this very observance of secrecy forces Troilus to let Criseyde
go to the Greek camp, since if he attempted to keep her, their
intrigue might be discovered, and her "honor" would be
smirched. Troilus cannot at first reconcile himself. Full "of
anguish and of grisly drede," he seeks to find a plan

> First, *how to save hir honour*, and what weye
> He mighte best theschaunge of hir withstonde. (IV, st. 23)

Love constrains him to keep her, but Reason tells him that if
he does their love might become generally known. So, acting in
strictest accord with the conventions, he lets her go. His lady is
not equally punctilious. The supreme sin against decorum is
Criseyde's; she is faithless to Troilus. Here Chaucer's sympathetic portrayal of his heroine is put to a severe strain. He can
only say that he will not condemn her; he pities her weakness.
He also suggests the influence of Fate—the love of Troilus and
Criseyde, like that of Romeo and Juliet, is "star-crossed."

But what of Troilus? What does he get for his faithful service
to the God of Love? The answer is—disillusion, a broken heart,
and death. The further answer is that Cupid is not the deity for
men to serve; they should rather put their trust in the Christian
God, who will treat no man falsely.

> —sin he best to love is, and most meke,
> What nedeth feyned loves for to seke? (V, st. 264)

In short, then, the story, in Chaucer's hands, is an attempt to analyze love on the basis of traditional conventions, which leads to the decision that these conventions break down as a rule of life. The situation is much the same as if a theologian were to interpret the facts of human existence in accordance with a preconceived system, having assumed for the purposes of the experiment that the system is sound, and were to find out at the end that it breaks down in its application completely.

It is important to determine just how far Pandarus is culpable in this affair. His part in the intrigue has been much misunderstood by modern critics, many of whom have allowed themselves to be influenced unduly by later ethical standards. It is essential that his conduct be viewed, like Criseyde's, from the point of view of the artificial conventions of the fourteenth century. This is equally true whether we consider the poem of Boccaccio or that of Chaucer. The intervention of Pandarus springs, of course, from his friendship for Troilus, and we might, if it were necessary, defend him by appealing to the medieval notion that in fulfilling the duties of friendship one may commit a crime, as Amile sacrificed his children to heal the leprosy of his friend Amis. The fault of Pandarus, however, according to the conventions of courtly love, is one not of morals but of manners. If we judge the episode in which he figures from this point of view, and agree that Criseyde acted properly in yielding to Troilus, we ought, apparently, not to condemn her uncle for his furtherance of the intrigue. But in theory the love-affair admitted of the intervention of no third person; it had to be perfectly secret, the affair of the lover and the lady alone. Procurers were common enough in those days, but they were supposed to have no part in courtly amours, carried out according to the approved system. They were unsavory persons, with whom no gentleman could allow himself to be confused. It is this confusion that Pandarus fears. As an experienced man of the world, he knows the ardor of Troilus and the responsiveness of his niece, and the consequent danger of an episode of headstrong passion, conforming in no satisfactory manner to convention, and likely to become an open scandal. Then Cressida's "honor" will suffer, and Pandarus will suffer too, as the one who persuaded her, and led her into public disgrace.

Such an event would place him upon the level of a common procurer, acting for money—him, a gentleman, and the uncle of Criseyde! We must remember that, according to medieval ideas, a man of the upper classes must never lower himself by an act suggestive of the doings of the lower classes. It was a terrible disgrace for Lancelot to ride in a cart,

> Honiz est chevaliers an terre
> Puis qu'il a esté an charrete—[1]

though he did not hesitate at an illicit relationship with the wife of his sovereign.

The position of Pandarus is elaborately set forth in his conversation with Troilus in Book III. "For thy sake," he says to Troilus, "I have become a go-between, and made my niece, who has thus far been free from errors of conduct,[2] trust thy chivalrous action (gentilesse). But I call God to witness I did it with no desire for gain (coveityse), but only for thy love. So keep her out of scandal, for no one knows that she ever did amiss. Woe is me, who am the cause of all this, to think that she is my niece, and I am her uncle, and a traitor to her! Were it known that I had persuaded my niece to this, all the world would say that I was guilty of the worst treachery. So take every precaution to keep this secret"—and he urges secrecy in the next eight stanzas. Troilus reassures him, emphasizing the difference between "bauderye" and "servyse"—that is, between unregulated passion and love ruled by convention, and finally offering to gain for Pandarus the love of any of his own sisters.

> And, that thou knowe I thenke noght ne wene
> That this servyse a shame be or Iape,
> I have my faire suster Polixene,
> Cassandre, Eleyne, or any of the frape;
> Be she never so faire or wel y-shape,
> Tel me, which thou wilt of everichone,
> To han for thyn, and lat me thanne allone.[3]

In other words, Troilus is confident that Pandarus would never act as a vulgar procurer, that his action is dictated by friendship

---

[1] Chrestien de Troyes, *Lancelot*, 490-1.

[2] "of vyces clene" (III, 257). The common meaning of "vyce" in Chaucer is "fault," "error" (cf. Skeat, *Glossary*), not "vice," which gives a different implication to the passage.

[3] III, 407-413.

and compassion, and that he would act only in accordance with convention. So confident is Troilus of this that he feels it would be quite safe for Pandarus to engage in an intrigue with one of the Trojan princesses, and not to bring her into scandal.

It was, then, one of the absurdities of the code of love that a love-affair like that of Troilus and Cressida, if revealed, would be held disgraceful, and that the person who brought the lovers together would have no excuse in the eyes of the world. In theory, the mere fact that Pandarus knew of the affair at all was to be regretted. Hence the unwillingness of Troilus in the beginning to tell him the name of his lady. And Pandarus, in running the risk of detection, and putting himself in the place of a go-between, has endangered his honor. He has no regret for his conduct, however, after the intrigue has been carried to a successful climax; on the contrary, he is glad of his part in it, in so far as it gave Troilus happiness, though he bitterly condemns the faithlessness of his niece. In judging of the character of Pandarus, then, we must remember the inconsistencies of the laws of love, and how much "honor" depended upon good form, upon due observance of the rules of the game of love, and upon concealment and discretion. Again, in Chaucer as in Boccaccio, Criseyde is no green girl, without experience of the world. She has been a wife and is now a widow; and she knows perfectly well what she is about in allowing the pursuit to continue, as the poem very clearly states.[1] While Pandarus has a duty in protecting her from scandal, as he would any kinswoman, he is not at all in the position of a father or husband, responsible for assaults upon the heart of a maiden ignorant of the facts of life.[2]

The passages which have just been cited are based very closely upon the 'Filostrato.' [3] Indeed, Chaucer's whole conception of the responsibility of Pandarus can be understood only by reading

[1] Book III, stanza 173.

[2] The character of Pandarus in Chaucer deserves a more detailed study than space permits here. The complexity of his character and of Cressida's, and the inconsistencies in the code of courtly love and the working ethics of the end of the fourteenth century, make the analysis peculiarly delicate and difficult. What has been said above will serve to indicate some lines of departure in a conception of the part played by Pandarus which differs somewhat from the usual view.

[3] See W. M. Rossetti, Chaucer's *Troilus and Criseyde compared with Boccaccio's "Filostrato"*; London. *Chaucer Society*, 1873. A somewhat more detailed comparison than Rossetti's is much to be desired.

Boccaccio. The Italian poem is built up on the same foundation of love-conventions. In his 'Proemio' Boccaccio speaks of himself as one who has been in the service of Love from his youth, and has pondered subtle questions of courtly observance. In the Neapolitan society in which he moved, moral issues, as we understand them, were far less likely to interfere with the rules of the game of love than in the less sensuous and more sturdy English nature. So there is no repudiation of love at the end of Boccaccio's poem, but young people are exhorted to pray to love that Troilus may rest in peace, and to take care that they do not fall victims to fickle women, and die for it, but rather choose ladies who are noble and constant. Pandaro is no saint in Boccaccio's pages, but he is a distinctly sympathetic character, who has had to bear a most undeserved amount of abuse from modern critics and moralists. This has been elaborately pointed out by Savj-Lopez, who cites many instances to prove that the obliging friend is no stranger in the romances.[1] The knight Claris loves the sister of his friend Laris. The lady is already married, the wife of the king. Laris, discovering by accident his friend's passion, reproaches him for concealing it from him, and promises his assistance in furthering the amour with his married sister.

> "Claris," says he, "little have you loved me,
> In that you have concealed this from me.
> For this, truly, I shall not hate you,
> Rather will I advance your interests
> With my sister, be well assured of it!
> Don't concern yourself about it any longer,
> But anticipate enjoyment!
> For I expect to win to this
> My sister (I don't see why I should not say so!)
> So that you may have her at your pleasure."[2]

Savj-Lopez rightly insists that the sympathetic portrayal of Pandaro was made possible by the conditions of the time at which Boccaccio lived and wrote. "Only an imagination filled with the medieval spirit, and inspired by courtly models, could conceive as noble the character of Pandaro; only a time in which Love

---

[1] *Romania*, Vol. XXVII (1898), pp. 442-479.

[2] *The Romance of Claris and Laris*, ed. Alton, Tübingen, 1884, ll. 3970-3979. See also Young *Origin and Development of the Story of Troilus and Criseyde*, p. 46.

was held to be the highest aim in life, the best means of moral elevation, could represent the go-between under the garb of a real hero." This holds true of Chaucer's work as well, if we make due allowances for the changes in the English version. The most notable alteration, perhaps, is in the greater age and added worldly experience of Pandarus. There is much about his figure that suggests Chaucer himself—the Chaucer of the 'Envoy to Scogan.' But that little rhymed jest conveys only a suggestion of one side of Pandarus; it is perhaps more just to apply to him the happy phrase which Kittredge uses of Chaucer himself— "a sympathetic ironist."

With the fifteenth century, the degradation of the story begins. As the elaborate conventions of love ceased to have any meaning in real life, and were employed rather as literary devices, the poems of Boccaccio and Chaucer were misunderstood, and the actions of the characters interpreted in the light of newer social ideals, different from those of the century preceding. This is manifest in Italy; Æneas Silvius Piccolomini (Pope Pius II) introduced Pandarus into his Latin romance 'De duobus amantibus,' in no flattering light.[1] Æneas Silvius was of course far from the point of view of Boccaccio; medieval conventions of love were alien to the point of view of this humanist writing a lubricious tale. In Britain the Chaucerian story received a new coloring through 'The Testament of Cresseid' of Robert Henryson. This is a particularly interesting poem, because it indicates the feeling in regard to Cressida in the latter part of the fifteenth century, because it illustrates changes in the conventions of love as applied to poetry, and because it had great influence upon later conceptions of the story—more especially upon Shakspere's. It was long attributed to Chaucer, and issued in collections of his works.

Henryson tells us that "to cut the winter nicht" he was reading Chaucer's 'Troilus,' after which he took "an uther quair," in which he found the fatal destiny and wretched end of Cressida. The chances are wholly that Henryson invented his story, the "uther quair," as Skeat notes, is a literary device, no more.

[1] See Savj-Lopez, p. 470: "Chi vorrebbe confondere quest' ignobile mercante d'onore con l'amico di Troilo?" See also Voigt, *Enea Silvio de' Piccolomini*, Berlin, 1856, Vol. II, pp. 298 ff.

According to this alleged authority, Cressida was deserted by
Diomedes, who loved another woman.

> Than desolait sho walkit up and doun,
> And, sum men sayis, into the court commoun.

So, it is hinted, the gentle and erring lady of Chaucer has degen-
erated into a harlot. Henryson protests that he wishes to excuse
her, and blames Fortune for her troubles. According to his
version of the story, Cressida in her despair curses Venus and
Cupid. Then in a dream she sees the gods in assembly, and Cupid
demanding vengeance for her blasphemy. This is granted;
Saturn strikes Cressida with leprosy. Troilus, in the meantime,
has been active in the war, and returns to the city in triumph.
As he passes, he looks at the leper sitting with cup and clapper
by the roadside, and seeing something in her face that reminds
him of his faithless lady, throws her a purse. Cressida makes her
"testament," and dies of a broken heart. In conclusion, the
the author points the moral for "worthy wemen"—they are not
to "ming their luf with fals deceptioun.[1]

It is important to observe that Henryson constructed his poem
on the basis of love-allegory. But the old system was breaking
down, and modern ethical ideas were creeping in. The medieval
notion that Cressida's fickleness is the supreme sin against Love
is mingled with the reprobation of the woman who gives herself
to more than one man. Society no longer countenanced even a
secret intrigue like that with Troilus. Under these circumstances,
the degradation of Cressida was inevitable. Gregory Smith notes
that Henryson's didactic habit "points to a declension in the
spiritual force of allegory. It remains as a poetical form, but it is
becoming no longer self-sustaining as a *motif*—as the mystical
expression of the love-fervors of the Middle Ages." Gregory
Smith strangely misconceives the situation, however, when he
says that Cresseid "prays" to Venus and Cupid. She curses
them, and for this and for her "leving unclene and lecherous" is
smitten with disease. Beneath the thin mask of allegory, it is
easy to see that this account of Cresseid's punishment was due

---

[1] For the *Testament of Cresseid* see Skeat, *Chaucerian and other Pieces*, Oxford, 1897, pp. 326-
346.

partly to the feeling that poetic justice should be done for her faithlessness to Troilus. Of this there is nothing in Chaucer's account. How far the general changes in the story in the attitude towards the heroine are due to Henryson himself, and how far to popular tradition, it would be hard to say. Perhaps to each in about equal measure.[1]

It must not be forgotten that 'Troilus and Criseyde' was by far the most popular work of Chaucer in the fifteenth and sixteenth centuries—far more so than the 'Canterbury Tales.'[2] The vogue of the story was by no means confined to the upper classes. Sir Walter Raleigh calls it "incomparably the most popular love-story of the earlier sixteenth century." The changes in the delineation of its characters which we have just been noting were naturally much hastened by this popularity. The common people, who even in the Middle Ages had had their gibes at courtly conventions, had now even less power to understand them, or desire to reverence them. They liked good stories, but they interpreted them according to their own views of life—the subtleties of courtly allegory were not for them. In the sixteenth century they summed up Cressida in a short and ugly word. But she fared little better at the hands of the bookish. Skelton, in his 'Book of Philip Sparrow,' probably written in the opening years of the sixteenth century, is severe both on Cressida and Pandarus.

> She was much to blame,
> Disparaged is her fame
> And blemished is her name,
> In manner half with shame.
>
> . . . .
>
> Pandara that went betweene
> Hath won nothyng, I ween,
> But light for somer green.
> Yet for a special laud
> His name is Troyllous baud,
> Of that name he is sure
> Whiles the world shal dure.

---

[1] For Gregory Smith's criticism see *The Transition Period*, New York, 1900, p. 45; *Cambridge History of English Literature*, 1908, Vol. II, p. 282.

[2] Spurgeon, *Chaucer devant la critique*, Paris, 1911, pp. 111 ff.

By the time of Elizabeth, the degradation of Cressida and Pandarus was complete. Whetstone, in his 'Rocke of Regard' (1576) makes Cressida sum up her own character by implication:

> You ramping gyrles, which rage with wanton lust,
> Behold in me the bitter bloumes of change.

The poetic collections, like the 'Gorgious Gallery of Gallant Inventions' or the 'Paradyse of Dainty Devices,' are full of references to the deceit of Cressida,

> Whom Leprosy painted
> And penury tainted.

The influence of Henryson was evidently strong—one thinks of Shakspere's reference to "the lazar kite of Cressid's kind" in 'Henry V.' Almost never is the story mentioned without a slur on the heroine.[1] Pandarus suffers the same fate. Lyndsay in 'The Testament of the Papyngo,' classed "pandaris" with "pykthankis, custronis (scullions) and clatteraris," and showed that a new word had been adopted into the English language. "E.K.," in the Epistle prefixed to the 'Shepherd's Calendar,' refers to the Pandarus of "the old famous Poet Chaucer," and speaks of "his bawdy brocage" (i. e., brokerage, pandering). There are also various interesting passages in Shakspere's earlier plays; not the least of which is that in which Ancient Pistol and Corporal Nym express their view of Pandarus. Neither of these worthies, certainly, is an over-squeamish person morally. Falstaff proposes to use them in his attempt on the virtue of the Merry Wives.

> *Falstaff*........Go bear thou this letter to Mistress Page; and thou this to Mistress Ford: we will thrive, lads, we will thrive.
> *Pistol.* Shall I Sir Pandarus of Troy become,
>   And by my side wear steel? then, Lucifer take all!
> *Nym.* I will run no base humour . . . . . . I will keep the haviour of reputation. (Act I, Sc. 3.)

Not even "the ranging Cressid," as Peele calls her, fared worse than Pandarus at the hands of the Elizabethans.

The old conventions of love-allegory were kept, of course, but in altered form; the didactic tendency which has already been

---

[1] There is an exception in Tottel's *Miscellany* (1557) ed. Arber, p. 192; *A Comparison of his* [i. e. the poet's] *love with the faithful and painful love of Troylus to Cresida.*

noted in Henryson warped them still further, and they were much affected by the development of later ethical conceptions. These changes can best be realized by comparing the "machinery" of the 'Faerie Queene' with that of a twelfth or thirteenth century metrical romance. Roger Ascham, speaking for the severer moralists, called the love of the earlier romances "bold bawdry," and branded the greatest lovers of medieval story as "those who commit foulest adulteries by subtlest shiftes." The people of Elizabeth's court liked to play at chivalry, but they were very far from understanding or accepting the system of such a court as that of Marie de Champagne or even of Edward the Third. They were no more moral, perhaps, but the conventions prescribing what was moral and what was not had become altered. There is a far greater amount of truth in Sidney's comment on Chaucer than we sometimes realize: "Chaucer undoubtedly did excellently in his 'Troilus and Cressida,' of whom truly I know not whether to mervaile more, either that he in that mistie time could see so clearly, or that we, in this clear age, walke so stumblingly after him." The Elizabethans read their Troilus story as Chaucer had set it down, and they felt its power and mastery, but they rarely, if ever, saw in it more than the tale of a dissolute woman, a broken-hearted lover, and an unprincipled procurer.

With such a tradition as this confronting him, how could Shakspere make the heroine of Chaucer's poem a sympathetic character? The story was too familiar to alter; its very popularity had stereotyped it. It is safe to say that the Elizabethans would have jeered at a pure and noble Cressida, just as the pit of an English theatre to-day would jeer at a self-sacrificing and high-principled Guy Fawkes. It is true that in the seventeenth century Dryden ventured the experiment of redeeming the character of Cressida in his dramatic version of the story, but conditions in Restoration days were vastly different from those at the opening years of the sixteenth century. The theater was far less close to the people as a whole, and the tale of Troilus and Cressida had lost something of the popularity which it had formerly enjoyed. Moreover, it was not Shakspere's habit to alter the main outlines of the older stories which he recast for the stage; he strove, while keeping them in general as they were, to make them more plausible by truthfulness of characterization, by peopling the stage with real men and women, who could, by their very natural-ness, make absurd acts seem convincing. Even if he had desired to do so, Shakspere could no more have whitewashed Cressida than he could have whitewashed Richard the Third, who was historically far from being the monster of Elizabethan tradition. He could not alter the well-known incidents of Cressida's career any more than he could have made Richard repent, and die in the odor of sanctity. Tradition determined his work, both in the representation of events and in their motivation. How impossible it would have been for him to introduce into his play the ideals of courtly love which underlie Chaucer's poem, even if he had understood them, may be realized by reflecting that according to those ideals it would have been proper for Cassio to make advances to Desdemona, for Emilia to encourage them, and ultimately, provided strict secrecy was observed, for Desdemona to grant Cassio her love, as far as he desired. The social ethics of the Elizabethan stage were of a very different sort. Not even in his treatment of Cleopatra does Shakspere attempt to justify wantonness—he strikes the key-note of the play in the opening lines, in which the *raisonneur* Enobarbus informs us that Antony's love is dotage on a gipsy's lust, that the triple captain of the earth is become a strumpet's fool. Cleopatra's vicious instincts are unsparingly revealed, but with her extraordinary fascination

> vilest things become themselves in her,
> That the holy priests bless her when she is riggish.

This fascination, and her commanding position as a great queen, surrounded by the dazzling luxury of the Alexandrian court, and loved by the greatest soldier of his day, blind us to the coarseness of her nature and the sensuality of her intrigues. But Cleopatra was never a by-word for a loose and faithless woman, like Cres-sida. Sir Thomas North speaks of her "courteous nature" and her "noble mind and courage." The difference between the treatment of her by Shakspere and Chaucer is amusing; to Chau-cer she is one of the Saints of Cupid, the first of the procession in the 'Legend of Good Women.' How complete was the change in the sixteenth century from Chaucerian ideals may further be seen by observing Shakspere's treatment of Helen, whose relations with Paris are of much significance in judging those of Troilus and Cressida. Chaucer intended Helen, too, for one of Cupid's saints, a female martyr to love, but Shakspere etches her portrait in these biting words:

> For every false drop in her bawdy veins
> A Grecian's life hath sunk; for every scruple
> Of her contaminated carrion weight
> A Trojan hath been slain.

Noteworthy, too, is Hector's speech, in which he defends the laws of morality:

> If Helen then be wife to Sparta's king,
> As it is known she is, these moral laws
> Of nature and of nation speak aloud
> To have her back return'd: thus to persist
> In doing wrong extenuates not wrong,
> But makes it much more heavy.

There was no place in Elizabethan ethics for adultery.

Attempts to find the explanation of Shakspere's conception of Cressida in definite sources other than Chaucer are bound to be unconvincing, then, because the temper of the play is in large measure accounted for by the literary and popular tradition of the time, and by its altered ethical ideals. It is almost absurd to attribute to Greene's 'Euphues his Censure to Philautus' the determining influence in fixing the atmosphere of Shakspere's play, as Herford has done. "Shakspere . . . . . . found in this pallid copy of the Trojan legend, this familiar (though not vulgar) travesty of the most heroic of classical romances, the suggestion of a story fit to serve as basis for his own drama of hollow heroines and shallow love."[1] A reading of Greene's stilted dialog, which serves as a framework for equally stilted stories, and which contains little suggestion of the events of Shakspere's play, either in the main or the minor plot, is sufficient to reveal the weakness of Herford's theory. We have already seen that the heroic glamor which modern scholarship throws

---

[1] *Publications of the New Shakspere Society*, Series I, Part VI, p. 190. London, 1887.

about Homer was far from being shared by the Elizabethans, that medieval tradition was often severe upon these celebrated chieftains, particularly those on the Greek side. We know that the actions of these warriors, when viewed in the light of cold common sense, appear in many respects the reverse of heroic. The verdict of the age of Elizabeth was somewhat like that pronounced by an American critic, Henry Cabot Lodge, who finds that cowardice and meanness and self-glorification are prominent characteristics of such men as Achilles and Agamemnon. "In a word," says Lodge, "the Homeric poems describe to us the doings of certain primitive tribes who were cruel and treacherous, subtle and cunning, liars and braggarts, and, withal, not over brave, although fighting was their principal business in life, and courage should have been their conspicuous and redeeming quality."[1] Robert Greene was no innovator in treating the people of the Trojan War in a half-cynical spirit; this spirit was in the air. And when we add to this the degradation of the story of Troilus and Cressida, we see that it was natural enough for Shakspere to produce a play with all the cynicism of Jules Lemaître's 'La Bonne Hélène,' though without its humor. We may perhaps add to this the popularity of plays introducing brothel-scenes and women of doubtful character, which is noticeable after 1600. There was, at all events, no shrinking from Hogarthian realism in the midst of a romantic story, as certain scenes in 'Pericles,' which are perhaps from another hand than Shakspere's, sufficiently attest.

Tradition, then, determined the character of Shakspere's work, making it virtually impossible for him to write a play in which the warriors should appear wholly heroic, or in which Cressida and Pandarus should be sympathetically treated. The main theme was unpleasant, and Shakspere made little attempt to gloss it over. The shadows were deepened by his unknown collaborator, to whom, "it is practically certain,"[2] the closing scenes are due. This writer chose, as the ending of the play, a foul address to the pimps and bawds in the playhouse, spoken by the wretched "broker-lackey" Pandarus. To this depth had one of the finest

---

[1] *Certain Accepted Heroes and Other Essays*, New York, 1897, p. 21.
[2] Neilson, *Cambridge Shakspere*, p. 260.

of medieval love-stories been reduced. The age of Elizabeth clearly believed that the most fitting epilog to the story of the faithless Cressida, the foolishly romantic Troilus, and the elderly lecher Pandarus was one which should leave the audience in the atmosphere of a Vienna without an Isabella, of a Mytilene without a Marina.

NOTE: To the more important articles dealing with the Troy-story in Shakspere's day should be added one by J. S. P. Tatlock, published after the present essay was sent to the printer—*The Siege of Troy in Elizabethan Literature*, especially in Shakspere and Heywood; *Publications of the Modern Language Association of America*, Vol. XXIII, No. 4 (1915), pp. 673-770.

VIII

'ROMEO AND JULIET'

By JOHN ERSKINE
Professor of English

ROMEO AND JULIET

I

Even before Shakspere increased its beauty and widened its appeal, the tragedy of Romeo and Juliet was, if not a classic, at least a popular story. The cruder versions of it suggested some resemblance to the best ancient and medieval love-legends—for example, to the story of Hero and Leander, of Pyramus and Thisbe, of Tristram and Iseult, perhaps also of Troilus and Cressida; and in the continual re-handling of the theme by French and Italian paraphrasers and translators, these reminiscences of long remembered tales developed into unmistakable symptoms of immortality. Shakspere was dealing, therefore, with far richer material made ready to his hand when he meditated on Brooke's poem, or on other accounts of Romeo and Juliet, than when he studied Holinshed's record of Macbeth or Cinthio's dark tale of the Moor. Yet in no other version than Shakspere's did this love-story enjoy a much larger audience, or appeal to a much later time, than that which read it first. Every known form of it, from Masuccio to Brooke, contained some passing note, some temporary emphasis, which clearly enough, as we can see now, narrowed and shortened its fame.

If it is curious that a tale of such vitality should have waited so long for an adequate rendering, it is still more extraordinary that in order to transfigure it into a world poem Shakspere should have made so few and such simple changes. In one sense, of course, his changes and additions were large and momentous, for at a stroke he expressed adequately for the race what it had long tried in vain to say. But in another sense the changes were slight. In fact, 'Romeo and Juliet' illustrates better than some of his greater dramas the essentially corrective quality in Shakspere's genius—the gift for setting an old story right, for adjusting it to the criticism of facts, rather than for contriving novelties and surprises. It might be argued that this play, though in subject less complex and in many ways less profound, is a happier instance than even 'Hamlet' of his genius for revising the labored inventions of other men into an obvious immortality; for Hamlet, even when clarified in Shakspere's imagination, remains still a special case, arousing and baffling our curiosity, whereas the two lovers, as he drew them, illustrate a universal experience in a manner which, with all differences of time and of language, is still universally understood.

That a love-story already acceptable to the Continent in various forms for various reasons should be transmuted by English genius into a world poem, must seem extraordinary even when the genius happens to show itself in a Shakspere. The English temper has often revised a well-known legend in order to accommodate it to English ideals, but the process has rarely seemed to the whole of Europe an improvement. Tennyson, for example, remolded the Arthurian cycle into an adequate rendering of English taste in the mid-century, yet the Continent then, and most of us now, would not prefer his Arthur, his Lancelot or his Guinevere to the characters so named in medieval romance. Chaucer, indeed, departed frequently from his sources to get a finer poetic justice, as when he rearranged certain details in the 'Reve's Tale,' to save his audience from pitying the miller's daughter. Walter Scott, also, had a kind of cosmopolitan breeding which exercised itself usually in such tactfulness as all readers would approve, though the absence of it would have offended, perhaps, only the British public. But neither Scott nor Chaucer gave Europe a story of great passion, unless the 'Bride of Lammermoor' be called such, and even this legend is a romance of sentiment rather than of passion. 'Romeo and Juliet,' however, takes its place easily with the story of Helen and Paris, of Lancelot and Guinevere, of Tristram and Iseult, of Abelard and Heloise. When we are praising Shakspere, we observe that the scene is not really in Verona, nor are the lovers in any special sense Italian; we sometimes forget, however, that the scene is also not in London, nor are the lovers in any limited sense English. This universality could hardly be claimed for all the plays. To write discerningly of 'Macbeth,' as Maeterlinck has done, or of 'Lear' or 'Hamlet,' implies in a European critic some special sympathy with the English genius, but to understand 'Romeo and Juliet' is the common gift of lovers.

It is natural to ask by what changes, however slight, was the story made to fit a universal experience. It is natural to ask also whether something besides Shakspere's genius did not contribute to the remarkable result; for if his genius alone had accomplished it, why is not 'Hamlet' or 'Lear' as germane to the Latin taste as 'Romeo and Juliet,' or why is not 'Romeo and Juliet' less intelligible to the northern mood? As he tells the story, it is far more simple than in the earlier versions; for this difference his dramatic instinct may entirely account. But the story is also far more innocent, and the characters are more pure; and this difference makes of the play an essentially new drama, in spite of its far-descended plot, for the innocence of the lovers appeals to certain emotions which the Italian or French Romeo and Juliet could hardly have aroused, and the appeal to these emotions has proved as effective in Italy and France as in England and Germany. To put the whole matter in a phrase, the story before Shakspere touched it was a tragedy which befell two young lovers; he made it the tragedy of young love.

II

We may see more clearly the direction in which Shakspere simplified his plot if we first observe the contradiction which appears in all the great tragedies of love. Hero and heroine are doomed to love at the cost of whatever sacrifice, yet in circumstances which forbid their loving. Out of much experience of what is typical in passion, the race has chosen to remember chiefly that where the union of hearts seems most imperative, the barriers to it seem insurmountable.

If the form of this encounter between passion and its obstacles varies from story to story, we should expect as much, to parallel the changing definitions of love and of fate. The love of Paris and Helen was ascribed to the victorious goddess on Ida; the wrath of the other goddesses forbade their happiness. To be sure, Helen was married already, and so was Paris, but as Homer tells the story the vows of wedlock were no great obstacle; it was the rising tide of Greek destiny, rather than the revenge of Menelaus, which overtook the lovers. Tristram and Iseult were bound by a tangible obligation, in the magic draught; and to the men who made the story Iseult's marriage with King Mark seemed, without further interference from the gods, sufficient obstacle to her love for Tristram. Youth and beauty, in an age that could conceive of no causes more constraining, kindled in Abelard and Heloise, in Lancelot and Guinevere, in Paolo and Francesca, the flame that will not be denied; the obstacle in each case was a vow of religion or of wedlock, an obligation of friendship or of kinship. So in Romeo and Juliet the fated love meets the fatal barriers, though time has altered the terms of the paradox. Something more than youth and beauty or the fury of passion drew them to their doom. Before Shakspere told the story, men had learned a spiritual fineness in love; Dante and Petrarch, devoted to the memory of dead women, had conferred on the human passion a mood and a ritual that raised it to the dignity of a religion, so that after them any well nurtured lover, even in the midst of the Renaissance delight in the body, would hold as the best part of his ideal the marriage of true minds. In this harmony of soul Romeo and Juliet recognized their destiny. They loved at first sight, as we say; and though the philosopher rightly reminds us now that in times when women were rarely seen and ordinarily not to be spoken to, people fell in love at first sight since they must fall in love somehow, yet the poet made something universal of that circumstance—with true lovers there seems to be no wooing, for they are mated ere they are born. The feud also, which was to defeat Romeo and Juliet with implacable hate, had been prepared for them before their birth. Their destiny was one passion, the obstacle to it was another.

This constant opposing of desire and disappointment in the great love-stories has inevitably suggested some relation between them, some migration of history or myth such as scholarship delights to trace. It is because of this conflict in all the stories that 'Romeo and Juliet' has been thought to show kinship with some of them—with the legend of Pyramus and Thisbe, for example, or of Hero and Leander, or of Tristram and Iseult. In all four instances, the lovers are separated; in each, the woman, finding the man dead or dying, kills herself. Yet the resemblances among the convincing tragedies of love probably spring from the disposition of love itself. It is not necessary to suppose that Shakspere studied these old tales, or even glanced hastily at them, as we have done, to recall the motions and attitudes of human passion; from experience and from observation he would know that to believe their passion authentic and obligatory is always the way of man and maid, whether they explain their persuasion of fate by the will of a goddess, or by the working of a magic draught, or by a blessed recognition between affianced souls. That this world is not a hospitable place in which to realize the destinies of the heart, is naturally the second conviction of impatient love; the particular fate that speaks distinctly to lovers, society around them is always slow to hear. When the moral sense was crude, the highhanded suitor might well locate this social inhospitality in the protests of the lady's discarded husband, or in earlier and frankly buccaneering times he might assume an angry goddess, or several of them, to explain the husband's unreasonable sensitiveness. But ages nobler and more refined have discovered the world's unreadiness for love in the reluctance of unacquainted families to rush into each other's arms, even to the third and fourth cousin, with that abandon of enthusiasm which lovers think fitting. This coldness of the families Shakspere raised to the tragic menace of an ancient feud.

An ancient hatred, a destined love—upon this irreconcilable conflict the poet focuses all the distracted interests of the story he inherited, and this concentration brings about his simplicity. To fill the tragedy with meaning for all young lovers, he had only to emphasize the estrangement of Romeo and Juliet from their environment; he therefore rearranged his material so as to bring out clearly three contrasts—the contrast of love with hate, of youth with age, of courtesy with vulgarity. The contrast with hate has often been analyzed, and it needs but a brief summary here. It shows itself in the old quarrel of the houses, so old that no one remembers how it began. The servants of the families fight in the streets till they become a public nuisance, yet the quarrel with them is mechanical. With Tybalt, however, it is quite conscious; the feud is stored up in him as pure venom, hate incarnate. As though to explain him, Shakspere makes the Capulets the quarrelsome family, whose hot temper and wilfulness center in this one unpleasant character. Juliet's sorrow for him is no deeper than kinship demands, and that her parents should think her to be grieving over his death is explicable only by their exaggerated clan loyalty. Yet though Shakspere clarifies the story by distinguishing between the temper of the families, he is too observing to set up an absolute or mechanical difference; he allows the Capulets, even Tybalt, a better self, a melting mood. To be sure, whether it is a servant or Tybalt himself, it is always a Capulet who begins the fight, whereas the Montagues, at least Romeo and Benvolio, are consistently for peace. Yet we too easily overlook the instances when the impulsive Capulets take a generous course. The one glimpse we have of the gentler Tybalt is, unfortunately for him, where few readers find it—in a silence. When he comes upon Romeo and challenges him to fight, angry because the Montague had dared to come uninvited to the Capulet banquet, the newly-married husband asks for his friendship instead of his hate, and Tybalt drops the quarrel. If Mercutio had not misunderstood Romeo's motive, and had not then provoked Tybalt on his own account, there might have been a chance of reconciliation. Tybalt's kindly moment, it should be noted, seems to be an invention of Shakspere's, one of his simple but important changes. In Brooke's poem Tybalt did not see Romeo at the banquet, and therefore had no cause to be angry with him, but challenged him merely for the sake of fighting, whereupon Romeo promptly slew him in self-defence. Shakspere specifies also that it was old Capulet who first confessed himself wrong and asked forgiveness at the grave of his child. Yet with all these shadings of character, the poet manages to concentrate every degree of malevolence in an almost visible cloud of death, which shadows the story from beginning to end, and which is felt quite naturally in the dark metaphors of the dialog. 'My only love sprung from my only hate,' says Juliet, when she learns who Romeo is. 'Where be these enemies?' asks the Prince ironically at the end of the play, when the two fathers look down at their dead children.

The estrangement of the children from their parents, which is suggested in the contrast between love and hate, is indicated sharply in the contrast between youth and age. The lovers are young, and in the story as Shakspere tells it only the young can sympathize with them. It is probably far-fetched to think, with some readers, that the poet deliberately sounded the theme of youth in his metaphors, as he had sounded the theme of hate; it was probably in order to express Romeo's character rather than his own comment that he often gave the youthful lover a presentiment of evil, a sense of approaching death, which would seem but the humor of love melancholy did not the event give it tragic force. 'The game was ne'er so fair, and I am done,' he says, moping not for Juliet but for Rosaline. It is probably due to the exigencies of the plot rather than to any purpose of symbolism that the poet lays so many scenes at dawn or in the morning hours. We first hear of the sentimental Romeo as haunting the woods at dawn. It is in the morning that the first fight occurs. Romeo seeks Friar Laurence in his cell at dawn; at dawn he leaves Juliet, who is then told she must marry Paris; at dawn she is found apparently dead; at dawn she and Romeo and Paris are found in the tomb. Yet if these many sunrises are implicit in the story, it is otherwise clear that Shakspere knew the dramatic importance of the youth of the lovers. 'Wert thou as young as I,' says Romeo to Friar Laurence, 'then mightst thou speak.' Shakspere takes obvious pains to emphasize Juliet's youth by making her but fourteen years old, two years younger than she had been in earlier versions of the story; and he does more than name her years—he removes from her character every suggestion of experience with the world.

This morning-glamor in hero and heroine is set off by the age of their parents, age that has forgotten what love and youth are like. So violent has Shakspere made the contrast, that the tale seems to be of grandparents and grandchildren. 'Old Montague,' as Capulet calls him, cannot guess what ails Romeo, nor can Lady Montague, although the malady is too obvious to younger eyes for Benvolio not to hit it in his first question. Neither parent has the son's confidence. Yet here again, as in the other contrast, Shakspere makes his general point clearer by distinguishing

between the families. If the Montagues do not understand their
son, at least they show for him a tender solicitude, which the
Capulets never felt for Juliet. Lady Montague in particular
loves deeply and fatally, as we should expect, if to love comes by
inheritance. When she hears the details of the first street-fight,
her involuntary exclamation is full of concern for Romeo's safety;
and when he was exiled, her grief killed her. She died on the same
night, Shakspere tells us, perhaps at the same moment, as her son.
If age had separated her from the world of his desires and his
sufferings, she yet bore him a disinterested love, and neither she
nor her husband hoped or planned save for his happiness. It is
hard to say as much for the Capulets; their affection was worldly,
and they were as aggressive in their worldliness as in their feud.
Shakspere makes Juliet's father so old that his best virtue is the
patriarchal one of hospitality, and his wrath is petulant and
senile. When he loses his temper, his wife reminds him none too
politely that he had better call for a crutch than for a sword.
We wonder if Juliet is not the child of a second marriage, for in
his affectionate mood he says the earth has swallowed all his hopes
but her, yet later in his wrath at her refusal to wed Paris he
exclaims

> Wife, we scarce thought us blest
> That God had lent us but this only child;
> But now I see this one is one too much,
> And that we have a curse in having her.

Did Lady Capulet, for mere social position, marry without love
a man far older than herself? Certainly she is the least attractive
person in the story, with fewer qualities to admire than even Tybalt. By her own account she is young, though we suspect she
exaggerates her youth when trying to persuade Juliet to an early
marriage; but whatever her years, her heart is more withered than
her husband's. He at least had the impulse to spare his daughter's childhood for a time, and he urged Paris to win her affection,
saying with unconscious irony

> My will to her consent is but a part;
> An she agree, within her scope of choice
> Lies my consent.

The sequel shows, of course, that the old man never dreamt of
her loving any one of whom he did not approve. But though he
failed to carry out his generous sentiment, he was capable of
feeling it, whereas his wife was thoroughly selfish. Few women
in Shakspere have so hard a heart. She speaks casually, and hope-
fully, of a plan to poison Romeo. When she sees the lovers dead
in the tomb, she says not a single word of regret for them, but in
her conventional moralizing she reveals her egotism:

> O me! This sight of death is as a bell
> That warns my old age to a sepulchre.

As though to emphasize these master themes, these contrasts of
love with hate, of youth with age, Shakspere announces them together in one consecutive passage, in the scene of Capulet's
feast. It is always unsafe to ascribe to deliberate intention in
Shakspere what may be only a coincidence, and it is not necessary
to suppose that here the poet is conscious of all the irony in his
lines; but those lines would hardly have been written had he not
imagined the story as in essence a conflict between love and its
inhospitable environment, between the immediateness of youth
and the forgetfulness of old age. Juliet's father, who represents
Age, welcomes another Capulet to the feast, asks how long it is
since they two were 'in a mask,' and is astounded to find it is
thirty years; in other words, the dancing days of Juliet's father
ended some sixteen years before she was born. Then follows the
impassioned speech of Romeo, who in the double contrast represents Youth and Love; he has caught sight of Juliet, and his
heart is lost. At once Tybalt speaks, the pursuing Hate—

> This, by his voice, should be a Montague.
> Fetch me my rapier, boy.

The inhospitality of environment has the effect of setting
Romeo and Juliet off by themselves, in a kind of loneliness. At
first we meet them in their proper society, surrounded with
friends and relatives; but as the story proceeds they are estranged
from their world. It is this common estrangement that makes
them appeal to us as one character, as devoted to a single tragic
fate. In a world such as theirs, of which the strongest principle

is family pride, to become strange to one's own people is disaster
enough, whether or not other sufferings follow. Even if they had
escaped successfully to Mantua, or to any place under heaven,
their fate, so wrenched from its order, would have been tragic;
so that it even seems a kind of saving from total wreck that, if
they must die, they should die in the ancestral tomb, with the
reconciled living and the unreconciled dead about them. Yet
until that moment the effect of the story is to isolate them. They
had each found a sharer of their confidence in place of the dis-
qualified parents, but the course of the story robs each of this
comfort also. Romeo's adviser is Friar Laurence, who as ghostly
father serves partly to represent the church, but also, as a philosophical dreamer, more particularly to set up a contrast with the
impetuous and unconsidering lover. The good man's way of
solving life is to meditate upon it; his great antidote is patience—
patience for young love, patience for Tybalt's insults, patience
for exile. This spiritual panacea had yielded its fascination while
Rosaline was the adored; to brood and speculate upon his passion
and her coldness had been not unpleasant to Romeo then. In the
new love for Juliet, he at first pursued his habit of consulting
Friar Laurence; perhaps some share in the Friar's pious wish for
reconciliation, as well as his own happy impulse of the moment,
prompted him in the attempt to pacify Tybalt. But for the swift
entanglement of real passion the Friar's gentle theory cannot
serve. When he offers it as a salve for banishment, Romeo re-
nounces the remedy with forgivable vehemence—

> Hang up philosophy!
> Unless philosophy can make a Juliet,
> Displant a town, reverse a Prince's doom,
> It helps not, it prevails not: talk no more.

The Friar naturally does not perceive that his old influence is
gone; he girds him to the familiar argument of patience. 'Let
me dispute with thee of thy estate,' he says. But Romeo sees
clearly at last the disqualifications of the priestly comfort.

> Thou canst not speak of that thou didst not feel:
> Wert thou as young as I, Juliet thy love,
> An hour but married, Tybalt murdered,
> Doting like me, and like me banished,

> Then mightst thou speak, then mightst thou tear thy hair,
> And fall upon the ground, as I do now,
> Taking the measure of an unmade grave.

To be sure, Romeo leaves the Friar's cell comforted, but Shakspere explains the comfort by the timely arrival of the nurse with a summons and a token, the ring from his bride, not by the Friar's somewhat chop-logic philosophy. 'O, what learning is!' exclaims the nurse. In older versions it was Romeo who was persuaded by the learning, but Shakspere sent him away for the last time from the holy man, thinking only of his approaching visit to Juliet. After all, it is for this world rather than for the next that he sought Friar Laurence's guidance, and in this world the Friar is not expert. When the lover hears that his bride is dead, he makes his own preparations for the next world.

That Juliet should have confided in the nurse is natural, since the nurse alone of the household loved her. It is perhaps too easy, in view of the old woman's short-comings, to forget her affection for Juliet. When Capulet in his fury lays his insulting curse on his daughter, only the nurse braves him—

> God in heaven bless her!
> You are to blame, my lord, to rate her so.

Yet her loyalty is not single; however privileged, she is still the servant and messenger of the house. She enters the love story with words less sinister but no less ominous than Tybalt's call for his sword. Juliet and Romeo have just met, and their fate is sealed; 'Madam, your mother craves a word with you,' says the nurse. Between the mother and the daughter she would be loyal to the daughter, according to her lights, but the situation is too difficult. She has, moreover, a radical failing which in time destroys Juliet's confidence in her; she represents that third contrast which Shakspere's audience would feel more acutely perhaps than we do—she is too vulgar to understand love. She illustrates inversely, as it were, the troubadour doctrine which Dante among others bequeathed to the Renaissance, that love is identical with gentleness of heart. Her heart was warm but not gentle; the coarseness of its fibre is shown by the anecdotes she inflicts upon her mistress, and—most fatally—in the sort of advice she gives to Juliet. So long as that advice concerns Romeo, Juliet nobly misunderstands it, and takes the counsel of physical passion to be only a rude phrasing of her own pure desires; but when the nurse urges her to marry Paris, on the ground that a living husband is better than the dead or as good as dead, Juliet perceives that they talk different languages, and she confides in the nurse no more. 'Speakst thou from thy heart?' she asks.

Nurse	And from my soul too; Or else beshrew them both.
Jul.	Amen!
Nurse	What?
Jul.	Well, thou hast comforted me marvellous much. Go in, and tell my lady I am gone, Having displeased my father, to Laurence' cell, To make confession and to be absolved.
Nurse	Marry, I will; and this is wisely done.
	(Exit)
Jul.	Ancient damnation! O most wicked fiend! Is it more sin to wish me thus forsworn, Or to dispraise my lord with that same tongue Which she hath praised him with above compare So many thousand times? Go, counsellor; Thou and my bosom henceforth shall be twain.

The change that Shakspere here made in Brooke's account has the effect of stressing vulgarity in the nurse, rather than immorality. In the passage just quoted, Juliet is angry with the old woman for advising her to consider Romeo a dead man, as legally he is, and to marry Paris. In Brooke's poem the nurse advised Juliet to marry Paris and at the same time encourage Romeo's love, if ever he should return, so that she might be provided with both a husband and a paramour.

III

These contrasts between love and hate, youth and age, gentleness and vulgarity, which serve to remove Romeo and Juliet from their environment, Shakspere found almost ready in his material; he had but to clarify and emphasize them. But by rearranging certain episodes in the older story, he managed to isolate the lovers further, in a more subtle way—he cut them off from their own past, as he had estranged them from their surroundings, and by so doing he increased the feeling that a single experience, a single moment of fate, draws them together. Each had had in some sense an earlier love affair. Romeo had been infatuated with Rosaline, the pale lady with the dark eyes. If men fall in love first with love itself, and afterwards with a woman, the desire for Rosaline was but the illusion of an immature heart, like Duke Orsino's sentiment for Olivia in 'Twelfth Night.' Instead of making his way into his lady's presence, as by Viola's success it appears he might easily have done, the Duke called for music to feed the sensation of being in love; so Romeo revels in his feelings, consults the Friar rather more than Rosaline, and makes a point of sharing his melancholy with all his friends. It was this behavior, if we may expand the Friar's hint, which persuaded Rosaline that she ought to reject his suit; she knew well that his love 'did read by rote and could not spell.' Perhaps she loved him; the Friar, who knew her best, did not think it improbable that Romeo should win her. Perhaps she would not take advantage of a sentimental boy who did not yet know his own mind; we should then understand why, when she refused him, she vowed never to marry. Whatever her motives, she is the most interesting of those unseen, hardly portrayed characters which Shakspere frequently sketched in his early plays; we compare her with Viola's imaginary sister, who never told her love, or with Katharine's sister, in 'Love's Labour's Lost,' who died of a broken heart. But Rosaline, though unseen, is far from an imaginary person. Her influence is perceptible, and in many unexpected ways she lights up Romeo's character for us. For example, she was related to the Capulets—she was a cousin of Juliet's. Was Romeo predisposed by his romantic temperament to fall in love with one of the hostile house?

It was long ago observed that as soon as he met Juliet he became another man, less sentimental, more mature. He certainly became a man of action, decisive, daring, and resolute, and his character was ennobled by love, yet he was but one man after all, and if he appears to change, it is only because the altered circumstances give us another view of him. It has been said, for example,

that in his second love he ceases to be talkative, and no longer
advertises his passion. Perhaps this new secrecy is somewhat due
to the fact that his life now depends on it. But it is not clear that
he ceases to be talkative; certainly he was always a trifler with
words. Moreover, a careful reading of this play, even without
other acquaintance with literary fashions in Elizabeth's reign,
would show that the young Shakspere saw nothing amiss in
elaborate wordplay. The wordplay of Romeo or of Juliet is
not in Shakspere's eyes a fault, nor does the habit disappear as
the story proceeds. The modern reader is perplexed by Romeo's
puns as he grieves for Rosaline:

Rom.	Give me a torch: I am not for this ambling;
	Being but heavy, I will bear the light.
Mercutio	Nay, gentle Romeo, we must have you dance.
Rom.	Not I, believe me: you have dancing shoes
	With nimble soles: I have a soul of lead
	So stakes me to the ground I cannot move.
Mercutio	You are a lover; borrow Cupid's wings,
	And soar with them above a common bound.
Rom.	I am too sore enpierced with his shaft
	To soar with his light feathers, and so bound,
	I cannot bound a pitch above dull woe.

But the reader will be no less perplexed when Romeo in the same
manner grieves over his banishment from Juliet:

> More honorable state, more courtship lives
> In carrion-flies than Romeo: they may seize
> On the white wonder of dear Juliet's hand
> And steal immortal blessings from her lips,
> Who, even in pure and vestal modesty,
> Still blush, as thinking their own kisses sin;
> But Romeo may not; he is banished:
> Flies may do this, but I from this must fly.

And when the nurse enters, the impatient lover asks, 'What says
my *conceal'd* lady to our *cancell'd* love?' These comparisons show,
not that he was less noble after he met Juliet, but that even in
his sentimental days—so Shakspere is at pains to have us understand—he was noble and lovable. Benvolio and Mercutio were
devoted to him. Even the ferocious Tybalt would have been

appeased by his courtesy, if Mercutio's reckless tongue had not spoiled all. Old Capulet testifies to his reputation even among enemies—

> He bears him like a portly gentleman,
> And, to say truth, Verona brags of him
> To be a virtuous and well-governed youth.

And obviously he must have spent his time in other occupations besides love-dreaming; his life-passion finds him a man of accomplishments, the best swordsman in the play, for example, better than Mercutio or Paris or even Tybalt.

The change that really transfigures Romeo is the terrible sincerity that overtakes him. All that he had said or been or done in unconscious trifling, fate now remembers against him in earnest, and brings to pass. 'I'll be a candle holder and look on,' he had said cheerfully enough when Rosaline declined his suit, with other hints that happiness in love is not for him. But life takes him at his word, the imagined tragedy comes true, the sentimental words become fatal. Our perception that he is caught between the passion and the obstacle, that he knows the reality and is doomed, turns our attention from the trivial to the heroic in him. We cannot even tease him for over-confidence in his first love. He had gone to the Capulet ball, at Benvolio's challenge, to prove that no woman more beautiful than Rosaline would be there. 'Thou canst not teach me to forget,' he had sworn, yet within twenty-four hours he was saying—

> With Rosaline, my ghostly father? No;
> I have forgot the name, and that name's woe.

In a play of another key such boasting would not pass without remark; a Benedick or a Beatrice, so caught, must stand teasing. But here the sincerity is too deep. Careless words are overlooked in the tragic shadow, or are left for fate to comment on.

It is easy for the reader to think kindly of Rosaline, whom Romeo forgot, but hard not to bear some ill-will to Paris, whose wooing of Juliet precipitated the tragedy. Our interest in the fortunes of the newly wedded lovers makes us forget that Paris was no interloper. In the earlier versions he did present himself after the marriage and the separation of the lovers, but Shakspere

makes him ask for Juliet's hand and receive the promise of it
before Juliet had ever seen Romeo. The fact that he sought
Capulet's permission as a preliminary to wooing the girl, does not
indicate that he was less ardent than Romeo; had it not been for
the feud, Romeo might well have followed the same course. Paris
certainly appears to lack his rival's capacity for expression; we
expect no torrent of ecstasy or of grief from his lips. Yet if
reticence has been observed in Romeo as one of the maturing
effects of true love, surely Paris deserves credit for the virtue
from the first. His secret visit to Juliet's tomb shows that he
was not devoid of sentiment. Indeed, it is singular that our pity
should go out to Romeo and Juliet, and not to Paris, for he was
in the truest sense a victim of love. We even forget that Juliet
had accepted him, in words that parallel Romeo's boast to be
true to Rosaline. Old Capulet was at least not inconsistent,
though he first stipulated that Juliet should choose her husband,
and afterwards compelled her to the marriage; he was angry
because she seemed ready to break the family word. In form, at
least, the choice of a husband had been left to her; 'Can you like
of Paris' love?' her mother had asked; and Juliet had answered—

> I'll look to like, if looking liking move:
> But no more deep will I endart mine eye
> Than your consent gives strength to make it fly.

To be sure, this answer is to her mother; Paris had no direct
promise from her. Yet her words with him in Friar Laurence's
cell would certainly convince a lover, eager to be convinced, that
he at last knows her will, and that she is preparing to marry
him. There is no rational explanation of the fate of Paris, any
more than of the fate of Rosaline; those critics mislead us who
would find some flaw in the character or conduct of either, as
proof of their unfitness for the love of Juliet or Romeo. No
Renaissance poet would have thought of love as a kind of reward
of merit. By standards of ordinary obligation both Rosaline
and Paris suffer harsh treatment; the poet, however, needed no
other reason for their fate than the evidence of his own eyes that
the contagion of love obeys no human logic, and cannot be foreseen.

If the will of love is without caprice, and yet no logic of ordinary deserts will account for it, so in the world of hate in which he sets this love the poet admits no accident, though the cause be not always evident in the effect. It is hard to sympathize with those readers who feel that Romeo and Juliet came to their end by an accident, and that therefore the story lacks the high truth of art. To what particular accident shall we attribute the end? To Friar John's failure to reach Romeo? To Friar Laurence's delay in reaching the tomb? To the fact that Capulet put the wedding forward by a day? We might consider other chances, but it is unnecessary in a story that breathes the very atmosphere of casualty. To solve a plot by coincidence may ordinarily be poor art, but not in those departments of life where coincidence is inevitable. In tales of war or polar exploration, shall we call it accident if the hero is shot in battle or frozen in the ice-fields? The feud of Capulet and Montague prepares us for any catastrophe. The killing of Mercutio and Tybalt is unforeseen, but not accidental; had they not died then, they would have been killed the next day, or the day after. The manner and the time of the death of Romeo and Juliet can similarly be reckoned inevitable; their unsupported love fell in a gross tide of hate; the unavoidable doom enveloped them. Shakspere seems to have taken the disaster for granted, so much so that he laid no great emphasis on the particular incidents that brought it about. His only care was to show that just as the lovers were estranged from their families and from their environment by their contrast with age, hatred and vulgarity, so in the quality of their love they were set apart, consecrated in some special fate which almost excludes from our sympathy the significant figures of Paris and Rosaline. In this treatment of his material, Shakspere's art, one must think, was his complete understanding of young love; this isolation, this elevation, this dedication of soul, is what romantic youth everywhere recognizes as the spiritual symptom of a noble passion.

IV

In Shakspere's simplification of his plot, he took it for granted, as we have just said, that his characters should have no escape.

But a plot which allows hero and heroine no escape will interest us less in their conduct than in their feelings; for this reason the tragic love-stories, as we have described them, are naturally lyrical. They offer us sorrow or joy for its own sake; they give us the flavor of life in a noble and intense moment. Single passages of 'Romeo and Juliet' are famed for lyrical beauty, but we sometimes forget that the whole play, though written for the stage, is a lyric. As we read or see it, we live entirely in our emotions, and know what it is to be caught between the irresistible passion and the immovable obstacle. Did not our emotions occupy us fully, such a story would be baffling in the extreme; if we looked for that harvesting of the past which is the essence of drama, we might perceive it in the death of Mercutio or Tybalt, and in the banishment of Romeo, but not in the love story, which is the principal theme. The love between Romeo and Juliet is the result of no past here revealed, nor is it in the logic of Juliet's heredity that she should be capable of love at all. Nor can we find in the story a prospect of destiny, the epic prospect; nor, if we adopted the old definition of epic which made it exhibit the will of the gods, can we make much of a divine will which contradicts itself. But it is significant that such questions are far from us while we read or see the play. In the presence of this tragedy we simply feel.

The feelings the play inspires in us indicate the innocence into which Shakspere transposed the story, and it is probably this innocence of feeling, more than the simplification of the plot, which made the play universal. The changes in the plot are important chiefly because they bring out new lights, new values, in the portrait of hero and heroine. In Brooke's poem Juliet was sophisticated, a 'wily wench,' who knew how to deceive her mother, and who after her marriage and Romeo's banishment encouraged Paris to make love to her. Her mother trusted neither her nor the nurse, but set another servant to watch them. In Brooke, Juliet is experienced and calculating; she knows all the symptoms of falling in love, so that she can diagnose her case, and provides herself with a reason for marrying Romeo if he can be got to propose—the hope that their union may end the feud. Shakspere assigns this good wish to the Friar, and takes from

Juliet her craft and her experience, so that she becomes innocent and pure, almost fragile:

> So light a foot
> Will ne'er wear out the everlasting flint.

By betrothing her to Paris before she has even met Romeo, at a stroke the poet refines her character and converts Paris into a tragic victim. Shakspere also reduces her age, as we saw, from sixteen years to fourteen, just as a previous version reduced it to fourteen from sixteen; to increase the pathos by making her younger was perhaps a natural tendency. In Brooke's poem and in other accounts of the story, Romeo too was less fine. He went to the Capulet feast, for example, not in defiance of his friend's advice to fall in love with another beauty, but actually in the hope of finding a substitute for his obdurate mistress; Shakspere made him an uncalculating lover, with delicacy of speech and manners. Perhaps inspired with Protestant overzeal, Brooke had hinted that Friar Laurence's retired cell, where Romeo and Juliet were married, had served the ghostly father in his youth for amorous adventures of his own; Shakspere imagined the Friar as noble and sincere. He also brought out, as we saw, the contrast between the age of the parents and the youth of the lovers; he brought out the contrast of the Friar's philosophy with Romeo's passion, of the nurse's vulgarity with Juliet's refinement; he gave the tone of destiny to the feud by introducing Tybalt early, at the moment when Romeo sees Juliet; he developed in Mercutio that gaiety which now reinforces in the story the atmosphere of youth, just as he increased the suddenness with which the lovers realized their passion, making them fall in love actually at first sight; and by crowding the action of the story into days instead of months, he set the whole tragedy in the abrupt, volcanic atmosphere of youthful romance.

These changes contribute to a wonderful purity of character and conduct—all the more wonderful since the play exhibits, along with its spiritual innocence, such a natural frankness towards the physical basis of love as a close study of the text makes even startling. Would Juliet be so specific in her thoughts? If so, what constitutes the immense gulf between her nature and that of the nurse? The difference is that Romeo and Juliet, speaking frankly of the body, think always of the soul; recognizing intuitively, as the philosopher says, that life 'is animal in its origin,' they feel as instinctively that it is 'spiritual in its possible fruits.' So they keep the beauty of this world before our eyes, and ideal values in our thoughts—and to no other love-story can such praise be wholly given. But perhaps Shakspere ought not to have all the credit for this idealization. Perhaps we should not leave out of account those noble heroines who had fascinated the English imagination just before he wrote or just at the same moment—Surrey's rather dim but exquisite Geraldine, Sidney's Stella, Spenser's Una and Florimel, and the heroines of Greene's novels and plays. If they did not influence Shakspere, does not their fame indicate a public admiration for the ideal they illustrated? At least it was in the direction of this ideal that Shakspere remolded his story, and the chief impression his lovers still make is of an impassioned innocence. This fact answers our original question, why 'Romeo and Juliet' should to-day enjoy an immortality so general wherever English poetry is known. The sense of the dignity of life and the sympathy with human wrongs, to which time has accustomed mankind, have brought as an inevitable corollary a certain lukewarmness toward all ancient love-legends save this. Meanness and trickery now obscure the beauty of Helen, of Cleopatra, of Iseult, of Guinevere, and of their lovers; to them we do not look for modern ideals of youth. Heloise and Abelard are indeed young, but vows surreptitiously broken stain their memory. Of all the tragedies dear to the Renaissance, this alone of Romeo and Juliet became thoroughly accommodated to English ideals, and in the process, fitted to express the dream that young love now has of itself everywhere.

IX

THE QUESTION OF SHAKSPERE'S PRONUNCIATION

By Harry Morgan Ayres

Assistant Professor of English

THE QUESTION OF SHAKSPERE'S PRONUNCIATION

The question how we know that Shakspere or Chaucer, or more often Cæsar and Cicero, pronounced "that way" is one that comes early to the student of language. And his inquiries meet only too often, one fears, with a very indefinite response from the teacher or the book that he catechizes. Always the question is "how we know," as if, of course, we *did* know. Seldom is there question of what sort of knowledge is possible on this head; and of what we have, how much is reasonably certain and how was it found out; again, where there is uncertainty, what is the nature of the uncertainty? Such questions would be more to the point.

To the first of them—what sort of knowledge is possible concerning the sounds of a language which may not be heard with the ear or analyzed by means of instruments—an answer demands some appreciation of the principles of phonetics. If, however, the student turns for light from the bald, dogmatic assertions at the beginning of his reader or grammar ("*a* as in *artistic*, *ē* as in *they*" and so on) to the works of the phoneticians, he does not always find these as helpful as might be. They bristle with a terminology that bewilders, and engage in subtleties of discrimination which fatigue him. Then, if he has a quick ear, he notices that the speech he hears every day varies amazingly from individual to individual. How could one be sure, he asks, of these *nuances* in the speech of the past, which even in our own are so bafflingly varied and shifting? In the result, it may be, he says to himself, "I no more believe in the subtle dogmatism of the phonetician than I do in the crude dogmatism of the first page of my 'reader.' "

For such a state of mind the student is not wholly to blame. The meager page or two devoted to pronunciation in current manuals of Chaucer and Anglo-Saxon, or the classical languages, is far more crude in its comparisons and dogmatic in its assertions than is necessary; something more might be done, even thcugh the method must always be somewhat roughly and readily adapted to practical ends. And phonetics, itself, it must be admitted, has an embarrassing richness of terms, frequently for a very simple thing. Beneath this luxuriance it is not inexcusable that even the inquiring student should miss what it is that the phonetician is trying to do.

The phonetician knows, of course, that the refinements of phonetic description are infinite because sounds themselves are really infinite. Even in the most detailed and careful work approximation and convention are to some extent inevitable. It would be impossible to record the infinity of little personal variations, due to minute raisings and lowerings, advancings or retractions of the tongue, the configuration of the teeth, the position of the velum, the control of the nasal air chamber, the quantity of breath and rapidity of utterance, cadence, pitch, stress; all these things and more which result in no two of us talking quite alike. But just as for the speech-organs of any individual certain complex positions become habitual, the ear also tends to classify sounds in types and to refer all sounds which approach this type to that particular sound which the habitual position of the individual's speech-organs has led him to regard as typical. Thus there might be said to be an *e*-type of sound.[1] There is an infinite number of slight variations of this sound which the naïve ear would unhesitatingly refer to this type. The phonetician can distinguish and describe some half dozen, perhaps more, of these variations; but even he has to stop somewhere. In dealing with sounds of past ages, then, and to some extent with living sounds, the phonetician is dealing with these types. He does not imagine that he is producing the precise cadences of Shakspere or Chaucer; he cannot reproduce precisely and completely the speech of his

---

[1] It is hoped that there are embodied in the text hints sufficient to make clear to the non-phonetic reader the symbols employed. If he will give the vowels their "continental" values, such as he ascribes to them in German or Italian or the "Roman" pronunciation of Latin, moderating as much as possible the diphthongal character which long vowel sounds assume in English, he will be safe enough. The symbol [ɛ] may be given the sound in *there*, [ə] as in the final vowel of *sofa*, [ɔ] as in *law*. A dot after the vowel [e·] indicates length. [χ] represents the German or Scottish *ch*-sound. Remember also that what we call "long *i*" in English is really a diphthong composed of an *a*-sound plus an *i*-sound, just as the vowel of *house* is made up of something like *a* plus something like *u*.

best friend; but he does try to attain to a sound which Shakspere and Chaucer would accept and refer, let us say, to the *e*-type and not to the *i*-type or something else; a sound which Shakspere, say, would understand and not regard as hopelessly barbarous, even though it were not precisely his own.   The phonetician would, in short, hope to be on the *e* target, even though he might not hit what a given individual would choose to regard as a bull's-eye.

Even within the type distinctions can sometimes be made. Chaucer has two sorts of $\bar{e}$ which, though he complained of the scarcity of rime in English, he is careful not to rime together. The two types have different ancestry and yield different results in Early Modern English.   Therefore they must have been different to Chaucer, and somewhat strikingly different, or he would not have avoided riming them.   Two easily distinguishable types of *e* are the "closed *e*" of the French *fée* and the "open *e*" of *fête*.   While it cannot be asserted that Chaucer's vowels were identical with these French vowels—they might have been relatively higher or lower to a very slight degree—yet a differentiation similar to that of the French is the only one Chaucer could have made.   So we may speak of his "open e" and his "closed e," terms intended to be inclusive of those phenomena which some phoneticians describe as "slackness" and "tenseness."   Further, of the two *e*-types one of them, certainly in the early part of the sixteenth century, has passed definitely up into the *i*-type, whereas the other remains an *e*-type, of what sort we cannot now be perfectly sure, until well into the seventeenth century, in some cases and regularly in some dialects to the present day.   And of the two types it must have been the higher, that is the "close *e*," which moved up first, so that we may pronounce Chaucer's *medes* (rewards) as [meˑdɪs] and his *medes* (meadows) as [mɛˑdɪs] with some confidence that he would understand the distinction as intended.   Precisely the same line of reasoning may be applied to his two types of $\bar{o}$ in *to* (toe), phonetically [tɔˑ], riming approximately with our modern *law*, and *to* (too), [toˑ], a fair rime for the American pronunciation of *go*.   In Greek similar processes of reasoning establish the difference (apart from quantity) between the open η and the close ε, the close o and the open ω, whereas in Latin the corresponding vowels were open when short and when long, close.

For Shakspere so nice a distinction cannot often be made. He has his $\bar{e}$-type (representative of the old "open e") and his $\bar{o}$-type (the representative of old open $\bar{o}$). But was the sixteenth century sound open or close, or in a state of transition from open to close? One may entertain an hypothesis, but genuine evidence on a point so fine as this there can scarcely be; comparisons made by contemporary grammarians between English and foreign sounds are in cases of this sort too crude to be of much help. Were the vowels slightly diphthongic, as in Modern English? Again a point too fine to be discernible at this distance, though one may defend an hypothesis. One can only deal with a type; and if one could be projected into an Elizabethan environment, there would be no surprise to hear, then as now, variations within the type. This type, then, the phonetician would choose with full knowledge that there streams from it, in one or both directions, a fringe of closely related sounds, one of which, rather than the sound habitually assigned to the symbol by the phonetician himself or his reader, may have been the commonest sound, or that of the particular individual or group under discussion; and all of these variations may have been, and in all probability were, heard, at one time or another, among one group of speakers or another, during Shakspere's lifetime. If, then, the phonetic symbol is by hypothesis somewhat flexible, it is only because the linguistic facts for which it stands are themselves flexible and refuse to be perfectly contained in any formula however elaborate.

All this means simply that should we presume in Shakspere's presence to pronounce *meat* and *sea* with the somewhat open and barely noticeable American diphthong in *bait* and *way*, and *bone* and *go* likewise with their American diphthongs, he would, we may believe, regard the pronunciation as perfectly natural. He would unhesitatingly, we may suppose, refer them to his own types though these may have been less noticeably or not at all diphthongal. Within the limitations and in the sense described above, this may be said to be "known." And in the same sense, the Elizabethan value of the vowels in *hit* and *met* may be regarded as having been the same as our own. Again, in *deem*,

Middle English "close *ē*" had gone up to an *ī*-type, and in *doom*, "close *ō*" had gone up to an *ū*-type, for which our modern American vowels will do as well as anything that could be devised. They would hardly arouse a stare, certainly not a gasp from any Elizabethan Quintilian.

In just this sense it is known that the late sixteenth century representative of Middle English *ī* and *ū* were diphthongs, the first elements of each a mid vowel gliding up to an *ī* and an *ū*-type, respectively. They may have been, as contemporary authorities describe them, [ei] and [ou]; but it is also quite possible that the first element of the diphthongs had already in the sixteenth century begun to move, with some speakers at least, toward the mixed [ə], the sound of the final vowel of *sofa*. This position we know it clearly reached by the middle of the seventeenth century. What is certain is that the man who pronounced *time* and *down* as [teim] and [doun], with a long or half-long second element, would have remarked nothing outlandish in the man who pronounced them [təim] and [dəun], but either of these men would have regarded the older [ti·m] and [du·n] or the usual American diphthong [taim] and [daun] as something quite alien to them.

This, then, may be said to be known, just as it is known that in the sixteenth century and for some time after, the *k* and *g* were still heard in *known* and *gnat*, or that the *l* was sounded in *would*, *should*, *could*, and not in *fault*, *realm* and not always in *soldier*. But sometimes our knowledge is of a negative, though not necessarily less interesting character. It is, for example, certain that *due* and *knew* were alike as to vowel sounds, and equally certain that they differed in this respect from *few* and *dew*. Again, it is certain that whatever values Shakspere attached to the vowels of *made* and *maid*, they were not the same value. It is certain that in these respects his language differed from that of to-day. What precisely his sounds may have been, offers a field for inquiry; the possibilities are fairly restricted and there is evidence which admits of hypotheses more or less convincing, even if it does not lead to certainty.

With so much indication of what sort of knowledge may be had, a glance is in order at the body of evidence on which the preceding recital rests. Here are reckoned puns, rimes, meter, spellings, and authorities: grammarians, that is, and writers on orthoëpy of the sixteenth and seventeenth centuries.

Ellis, whose work on "Early English Pronunciation" first placed the subject on a solid basis, examined Shakspere's puns without any very striking results. It is not surprising, for puns are not bound to be perfect, especially for the Elizabethans, who liked a verbal echo without feeling obliged to try to laugh at it. But occasionally they can be made to yield some information. Of the two pronunciations of the word *one*, the older, which survives in the modern *alone, atone, only*, and the new dialectic form with prosthetic *w*, which was not universally recognized till the end of the seventeenth century, can there be any doubt which Shakspere intended his actor to utter in the following colloquy?

> *Speed.*   Sir, your Gloue.
> *Valen.*   Not mine: my Gloues are *on*.
> *Speed.*   Why then this may be yours: for this is but *one*.
>
> ('Two Gentlemen of Verona,' II, i. 1)

And what is to be made of this:

> *Pro.*   But what said she?
> *Sp.*   I.
> *Pro.*   Nod-I, why that's noddy.
>
> (*Ibid*, I, i. 119.)

unless Speed's nodding assent ("ay") was spoken with the same diphthong as that represented by the final *y* of *noddy* [nodei]? That native words in -*y* were thus pronounced is amply confirmed by the testimony of rimes and the authorities.

Shakspere's rimes, particularly in his poems, have been examined in detail by Viëtor. The most interesting results are negative. It is Shakspere's refusal to rime words like *new* with *few, care* with *fair, leap* with *sleep* that makes us sure that for him they were not good rimes. No other consideration could have induced him to forego these common rimes in a language which is notoriously deficient in that commodity. Occasionally he allows himself a bad rime and of the first group there is (as I interpret Viëtor's material) one such; of the second, three; and of the third, four, and of these several are dissyllabic rimes in which imperfect vowel correspondence is less striking. Suppose a few have been missed; in any equal bulk of modern poetry, where, of course, they would be perfect, such rimes would be counted by the score.

Positive inferences from rime must always reckon with the possibility that the rime is a bad one, though the Elizabethan poets are, on the whole, less than modern poets given to traditional rimes, because there is so much less tradition behind them, and to "eye-rimes" because their verses were more than in modern days directed to the ear. Some cases are fairly above suspicion. If Shakspere rimes *friend: end*, and *head: bed*, it is a fair inference that in these words he had the modern short vowel, and did not say [fri·nd] and [he·d] as some of his contemporaries undoubtedly did. *Rome* riming with *doom* and *groom* and two puns on *room* ('Julius Caesar,' I. ii. 156, and 'King John,' III. i. 180) suggest his preference for this well-known but now old-fashioned pronunciation of the word. The pun on *Rome* and *roam*, in '1 Henry VI,' III. i. 51, may not be Shakspere's, in the first instance, but it is no worse than many that are. The rimes *orator: publisher: singular* ('Lucrece,' 30) shed some light on the vexed question of unstressed vowels, and strongly suggest that though the "docti" then, as now, may sometimes have pretended to make a distinction, these words commonly ended, then, as now, on the obscure vowel [ə]. Frequent rimes of the type *go: grow* show that the original diphthong of the latter word was not very different from the original simple vowel of the former, while the apparent avoidance of rimes like *stone: known* indicates that before the nasal the diphthong was still marked. Rimes like *light: white* show that in the former word the spirant [χ], still to be heard in Scottish, was for Shakspere scarcely audible, if at all. Rimes like *first: curst* are frequent enough to suggest that the two vowels had already fallen together before *r* in the mixed type [ə], but *erst* and its like do not rime freely with these words and presumably had a different vowel. No one would care to argue a modern poet's pronunciation from his rimes, but for older poets, used with care and checked by other evidence, they teach us a good deal.

The evidence from meter does not give help with respect to sounds. It establishes many differences in stress between Shakspere's words and ours—*charácter, triúmph, revénue, dividable, pérspective*. It shows, too, that he felt at liberty to say "enterance" and "Henery" and to make four syllables of *affection, confusion*, and of *venturous* two. Shakspere, it thus appears, had many common Elizabethan contractions, like *i'th'* for *in the, be't* for *be it, on's* for *on his, twentith* for *twentieth*, which are no longer current, but when the Folio prints "to take your instant leaue a' 'th king" ('All's Well,' II. iv. 49) it indicates what is still the normal utterance. Metrically, in spite of some Middle Englishisms like "whalë's bone" ('Love's Labour's Lost', v. ii. 332) and the sounded *-ed*, Shakspere is Modern English and as such can be read, as Chaucer cannot, with entire satisfaction.

The evidence from spelling bears on general Elizabethan conditions rather than on the pronunciation of the individual, Shakspere. There is no possibility that the spellings of Quartos and Folios, even though we make the large assumption that they were set up from his manuscripts, accurately reflect Shakspere's personal practice; the Elizabethan compositor was too ready to accommodate a mere matter of spelling to the exigencies of the "stick." Such Folio spellings, however, as *ortagriphie, hether* (hither), *togither, divell, then* (than), *bile* (boil, ulcer), *fadom* (fathom), *filom* (film), *foorth* (forth), *affoord, boson* (boatswain), *berrord* (bear-herd or bear-ward) *handkercher, shrow* (shrew), *venter* (venture), and *conster* (construe) are all indicative of pronunciations which there is no reason to suppose Shakspere would repudiate. Those contemporaries of his who spelled the name *Shakspere* or *Shaxper* were, on every analogy, trying to express a pronunciation, a perfect rime for which would lie somewhere between American "cock-spur" and "back-spur." Spellings alone, however, do not prove much; taken in conjunction with other evidence they may be significant.

The most important use to which the evidence afforded by spellings has recently been put is in the question of chronology. The direction of change from the Middle English vowels to the Modern is fairly clear, but how far at a given moment had a given vowel proceeded on its line of march? Obviously such changes will be in existence some time before they can be recognized and described by a grammarian or orthoëpist. Long before that, it is argued, they will appear in letters, memoranda, or manuscripts of any sort written by people who were either uneducated or for whom spelling was less than now a fixed tradition. Thus, if one writes *l i g h t* nothing is proved with regard to pronunciation, for the spelling is purely traditional. But if one writes *white* as *w h i g h t*, it is clear that for such a person the spirant [χ] no longer exists, and *-ite* and *-ight* are for him interchangeable symbols for the same sound-complex. Proceeding from an unquestioned case like this to the more delicate problem of vowel *nuances*, it is argued that, if *make* is found in the fifteenth century spelled *meke*, *ā* must have already become a front vowel; a spelling *reword* shows that *a* was already rounded after the labial; a spelling *groin* for older *grine* would not have been hit upon unless [i·] and [oi] had already fallen together in some such sound as [əi]. By the application of such reasoning the origin of many modern pronunciations may be carried pretty far back into Middle English times. The very nature of this evidence calls for great care in its use, and Zachrisson, who has recently employed it most systematically and ingeniously, is careful. But it is not easy to feel that we have sufficiently grasped the psychology of bad spelling to be perfectly sure of our results here; and, from the nature of the evidence, the argument usually rests on a very few examples.

When all is said, it is the authorities who furnish the most interesting evidence concerning bygone speech. There are many of them and they represent all sorts of aims and abilities. Trying to express themselves in a science which had as yet no adequate body of facts or terminology, they contrive often to utter some very dark oracles. Everything they say has to be interpreted with due reference to the whole context. Different as they are among themselves, they fall roughly into two main groups, English authorities and French. The most important writers on English orthography and orthoëpy stand at the beginning and at the end of Shakspere's lifetime. In 1568, Sir Thomas Smith, statesman and scholar, published his little treatise 'De Recta et Emendata Linguae Anglicae Scriptione Dialogus,' for English a pioneer work. The phonetic alphabet which he devises is a good one, but his explanations are often not clear enough to render certain the values he attached to the vowels. He is a good deal influenced by classical writers, but he has scattering observations on dialectical forms which seem first-hand and acute. The appearance of this book encouraged John Hart, who was Chester Herald, to put forth his long pondered 'Orthographie' (1569). Hart's hostility to traditional spelling which is "without any regard vnto the seuerall parts of the voice" is uncompromising. He is a skilful analyser of sounds and in his phonetic transcripts tries his best to represent them. Occasionally, as in the case of the *ai* diphthong, which he writes *e*, he fails to make himself clear. But we are indebted to him for much information; that *p* and *t*, for instance, were exploded with a good deal of breath, as they are still in British, especially Irish speech, leading him to write *pipe, p-heip;* he also tells us that *of, is, as, this* were affected as to voice by the character of the following sound, as *this salt,* but *thiz way.* Hart is a witness of great importance. Both he and Smith have left other writings which contribute something.

Hart is blamed in the 'Logonomia Anglica' (1619, 1621) of Alexander Gill, for not sticking closer to traditional spelling, to which Gill in his transcriptions pays more deference. Gill was master of St. Paul's School, and he is probably in some cases recommending a hyper-correct pronunciation; the pronunciations he makes fun of—*fictitiæ Mopsarum*—are usually very instructive. The extent of his illustrative material adds to the value of the book. Two books appeared during Shakspere's youth, one of which, William Bullokar's 'Booke at Large for the Amendment of Orthographie' (1580), attempts to do something for English spelling by means of diacritical marks instead of new symbols; and the other, the 'Elementarie' of Richard Mulcaster (1582), whom Gill succeeded at St. Paul's, undertakes a defense of traditional English spelling. The former has thus far been the source of more confusion than real help; the latter has some valuable asides.

After the work of Gill, who was born in the same year as Shakspere, come Charles Butler's 'English Grammar' (1633), Ben Jonson's 'English Grammar' (1640), Simon Daines's 'Orthoepia Anglicana' (1640), and John Wallis's 'Grammatica Linguæ Anglicanæ' (1653), where some of the diphthongs are first correctly analyzed into their modern components. For the late seventeenth century the chief authorities are Cooper (1685) and Jones (1701). Of works published before Shakspere's time, Palsgrave's "Lesclarcissement de la Langue Francoyse' (1530) and Salesbury's 'Dictionary in Englyshe & Welshe' (1547) are the most important.

It was to Salesbury that Ellis owed the clue by means of which he traced the labyrinth of English sounds. In the course of this study he relied principally on the English authorities. Latterly the French grammarians have been more carefully studied. Among these may be named Jacques Bellot, whose 'Maistre d'Escole Anglois' (1580) was re-edited in 1625 for the benefit of the courtiers who came over with Queen Henrietta Maria; Claude de Sainliens (Holyband he called himself in England), whose 'French Schoolemaister' appeared in 1573 and 'French Littleton,' it seems probable, in 1576; and Peter Erondelle, whose 'French Garden' came out in 1605. Of the later French authorities, Mason (1622), Mauger (1652), Festeau (1667) and Miège (1688) are the most important. Florio's comparisons between English and Italian sounds in his 'New World of Words' (1611) are valuable.

Many of these works, it may be interesting to add, are now accessible in reprints by various foreign scholars. Of those which are not, there is a splendid copy of Hart in the library of Mr. W. A. White of this city, and another in that of Mr. George Plimpton. Mr. Plimpton also has Mulcaster, Florio, and Wallis, and a great deal more; Mr. White, among much else, has the re-edited Bellot, Holyband, and Erondelle. To both of these gentlemen I am deeply obliged for their generous permission to examine these and other volumes. The works of two men, Delamothe and Hodges, which Zachrisson found useful, I have not yet succeeded in running down in this country.

After such a review, necessarily incomplete, of the sources of evidence and some of the results obtained from them, it only remains to hint at some of our ignorances. These are of two kinds: uncertainty concerning the Elizabethan average of utterance, as to back or front, diphthong or monophthong; and uncertainty as to which of two pronunciations known to be at his disposal Shakspere actually adopted. Perhaps it is not possible to keep the two categories entirely separate. The first may be illustrated in this way. Fifty years ago Ellis gave as Shakspere's pronunciation of *due, make,* and *fair* as [dy·], [ma·k], [fair],: that is, he attributed to the first French *u,* to the second Italian *a,* to the last a real diphthong (a + i) as in *fire.* An attempt to-day to represent Shakspere's pronunciation would write instead [diu] [mæ·k] [fæir], all of them very much nearer the modern sounds; with the exception of the second, identical, indeed, with pronunciations which may still be heard in America.

This change has come about by reason of the greater weight attached to the statements of the French grammarians and a clearer recognition that some of the descriptions of the English authorities are dictated by theoretical standards of correctness or due to imperfect analysis. In the case of *due, knew, rude,* it was long held and still is by most scholars that two distinct types of pronunciation existed, but I am persuaded by the arguments of Jespersen and Zachrisson and my own reading of the sources that this is not the case. There is really no evidence that the French *u*- sound was heard in Elizabethan English, except perhaps in some French words in the mouths of those who spoke French correctly. Those Englishmen who thought the French and English sounds identical were merely misled, as many Englishmen have been since, or satisfied with a rough approximation. The French writers are careful to say that the sounds are not the same.

There is doubt about *ă,* though a good case can be made out for its continuance into the seventeenth century as a back vowel; after *w,* as in *war, wash,* it was probably still unrounded. Virtually, all the evidence, except Hart's who may have been old-fashioned in this respect, points to the fronting of *ā,* and it cannot have gone much higher than [æ·], the vowel of *hand* slightly prolonged, or it would have tended to become confused with [e·] in *sea.* Besides, the vowel of *care* differed from that of *fair,* and it is doubtful if the mere presence of an up-glide to [i] in the latter word would make sufficient difference to induce Shakspere to forego riming them. It is quite possible that the first element of the diphthong of *ai* was a little higher, say [ɛi]. It would not

be surprising if the first element of the diphthong had been
raised a little in the direction of the second. The Latin diphthong
æ went through precisely the same stages of development. The
French authorities, it is true, do not describe this sound as a
diphthong at all, but the slow diphthongs are hard to detect,
and the grammarians' method does not encourage them to refine
too far.

With regard to the sound of *au* Ellis's judgment is
probably right. On the strength of his interpretation of the
earliest authorities he at first ascribes to Shakspere the diphthongal pronunciation [au] as in *how*, in *all*, *saw*, but later, influenced chiefly by Gill, he ascribed to Shakspere the present
sound [ɔ·]. Still, there always remains the possibility of a diphthong [ou] especially before *l* or when final, though nothing that
the orthoëpists say is above suspicion of having been suggested
by the spelling or by a real'misunderstanding of the structure of
the sound. Equations between this sound and continental *ā*
sounds cannot be taken as proving that there was unrounding
or underrounding in English; the authorities may here, as so
often, have been making a comparison between the two types
which, without being identical, stood nearest to each other.
But again the possibility of underrounding must be reckoned
with; it is frequently present in Modern English.

Formerly this sound—and we now come to some nice points
of divided usage—was heard not only in *walk* and *salt*, but in
shall (when emphatic), the last syllable of *several*, in *calf*, *half*,
balm, *calm*, and from what the pedant Holofernes says about the
"rackers of orthography"who call calf, *cauf* and half, *hauf*
('Love's Labour's Lost',V. i. 21) there is little room for doubt that
this was what Shakspere regarded as the normal pronunciation.
But in words like *vaunt*, *haunch*, where modern usage is divided,
we cannot be sure of his vowel; the chances favor [a].

There is an old division of usage presented by the words containing the modern diphthong *oi*, a relic of which survives in the
vernacular pronunciations *j'ist* (joist) and *h'ist* (hoist), and in
Pope's well-known rimes like *line: join*. Two types of pronunciation existed in the Elizabethan period, and the early authorities
drew up lists of words, in which *boil* and others have the diphthong

[ui] and *joy* and others a diphthong [oi]. But there is by no means perfect agreement in these lists, and their later history shows many perplexing crossings. Shakspere's rimes hardly justify conclusions, for the rimes may be slightly imperfect. Folio spellings like *bile* and *byle* for *boil* (ulcer) and the rime in 'Venus and Adonis,' 1115, *groin: swine,* suggest that in these two words, which originally did not belong here at all but had Middle English *ī*, Shakspere retained the representative of the old sound.

In the case of *ŭ*, as in *buck, come,* usage was only beginning to be divided in Shakspere's day. Such evidence as there is suggests that the modern unrounded sound was not widely used and was regarded as a vulgarism. But Shakspere, of course, may have used it instead of the traditional vowel which is preserved in *pull.* His frequent rimes like *come: doom, some: tomb* point, however, in the other direction. Words like *flood* and *blood* vacillated between [u·] and [u], just as *room* and *roof* do to-day; perhaps for rime he felt free to take his choice.

Perplexities, due to vacillation between *o-* and *u*-sounds, are presented by *word, world, among,* though in many words like *afford, mourn,* we can be sure that Elizabethan English usually had [u·]. Much of this trouble is caused by the *r*, the precise quality of which is not to be determined. It was not trilled so much as in contemporary French; probably it was a markedly retracted or inverted sound, with one or two vibrations of the tip of the tongue at most. Before this sound the treatment of *ĕ* vacillated, as the surviving doublets *Clark* and *clerk, hearth* (with [a·] and [ə·]), *parson* and *person* show. *Heart* from Middle English *herte,* was already established with [a], and we may suspect that Shakspere found a perfect rime for it in the verbs *desert* and *convert.* But how did he regard *marchant* and *parlous (perilous)* and *arrant (errand)* and *hard (heard),* which remained good pronunciations long after his day? It is Dogberry who says *desartless* and Costard who calls "guerdon," *gardon;* but perhaps here Shakspere was anticipating the modern humorist who writes "wuz" and "mister," as if that was not what people generally say.

The most striking and best established of the differences between Shakspere's sounds and our own is his careful distinction

between Middle English "open *e*" (for him [e·]) and Middle
English "close *e*" (for him [i·]). "Spake the speech," began
Hamlet in his address to the players. But this distinction brings
in its train a question of divided usage. As is well known, a small
group of Middle English words, containing an *ē* of various origins,
rime, in a careful poet like Chaucer, sometimes on the open, sometimes on the close sound. This vacillation persisted into the
seventeenth century, and is reflected both in occasional statements of the orthoëpists and in the hesitation of the spelling between *ea* and *ee*. This situation opened the way for further confusion, and presently another small group of words in which
original "close *e*" stood before *r* begin to be sounded [e·] instead
of [i·], and still other words went through the reverse process.
So there is doubt whether Shakspere pronounced *hear, weary,
dear* and *spear, tear* (noun) and *ear* with the vowel of *bear* or that
of *beer*. But he rimes them with undoubted [e·] words and the
spellings point the same way. It is clear that whichever vowel
he used he would not be surprised to hear the other; and that he
should not be surprised were he confronted with them is the
highest success we could hope for any attempted reconstructions
of his speech.

X

JULIUS CAESAR

By Algernon de Vivier Tassin
Assistant Professor of English

JULIUS CAESAR

I

A noted English critic in one of his many books upon English literature speaks of "the sort of person who prefers 'Julius Caesar' to any other play of Shakspere's." The characterization seems intended to indicate that such a person lacks imaginative perception and poetic appreciation. It is true that elsewhere Shakspere exhibits greater imaginative and poetic powers, but on the other hand, they many times occur merely as splendid outbursts in chaotic or unreasonable stories. The distinctive contribution of drama is not to afford a framework for dazzling gems of poetry, imagination, or social philosophy, but rather to tell by means of the speech and behavior of believable people a striking story of life. So considered, the play of Julius Caesar— which by persons looking chiefly for the former commodities has been regarded as something of a Cinderella—has claims to stand foremost among the sisterhood.

II

It has frequently been pointed out that the play is faulty in construction, that it falls into two parts—the murder of Caesar and its revenge. But the structure is by no means so loose as some have maintained. Merely calling the play 'Brutus' would not only shake it all into shape but into a shape more compact than that of any other tragedy of Shakspere's except Othello. And Professor Barrett Wendell has called attention to the fact that Shakspere the manager knew well enough that in doing so he would throw away a considerable commercial asset—where one of his audience had heard the name of Brutus, a hundred knew who Caesar was. That he intended Brutus to be regarded as the actual hero is obvious as early as the second scene of the first act. Instead of following Caesar to the games and beholding the superlatively picturesque and dramatic scene of the enforced refusal of the crown (a scene which must have required much self-restraint on Shakspere's part to forego), we get the effect of Casca's narration of it upon the two principal characters of the future conspiracy. Moreover, all the sympathetic side scenes, those apart from the main dramatic action, concern Brutus and are largely invented by Shakspere; and no dramatist so persistently builds the sympathy of his audience for anyone but his hero. Yet though Brutus is the actual and visible hero, it is not at all far-fetched to say, as has been said, that the spiritual hero is the "great daemon" of Caesar. And this interpretation Shakspere himself urges frequently by the mouth of his actual hero. At the inauguration of the conspiracy Brutus cries with passionate earnestness, "We all stand up against the spirit of Caesar"; over the body of the other chief conspirator, he exclaims, "O, Julius Caesar, thou art mighty yet! Thy spirit walks abroad and turns our swords in our own proper entrails!"; and his last words, "Caesar, now be still," are a cry to that spirit. Then, as if to clinch the matter, Shakspere makes one of his most concrete changes from Plutarch. There the apparition is the evil spirit of Brutus himself and is not identified with Caesar at all.

But whether faulty or not, the structure of the play represents no plot-work on Shakspere's part since it comes directly from the biographer. The Life of Caesar jumps at once from his death to the death of the men who assassinated him, in its most imagination-moving passage. Plutarch, casting most of his lives in dramatic form, has particularly done so in the case of Caesar, points out his modern translator, Mr. George Long. "He begins by representing him as resisting the tyrant Sulla when others yielded, and then making his way through a long series of events to the supreme power, which he had no sooner attained than he lost it. But his fortune survived him, and the faithless men, his murderers, most of whom owed to him their lives or their fortunes, were pursued by the avenging daemon till they were all hunted down." Dramas of retribution were very popular with the moralizing Elizabethan stage, all the more so since the retribution offered further opportunity for interesting violence. The structure which Plutarch suggested would fall pat with the leading contemporary stage fashion, the murder-and-revenge play. 'Richard III' had been a retribution play with a series of Nemeses in quite the style of the Life of Caesar, and Shakspere's next tragedy is more directly of the type in which the ghost of the man murdered, before the play begins or at its beginning, incites to revenge and accomplishes it through his agent at last. Hamlet, indeed, resounds with echoes of Julius Caesar; and in it Shakspere more than once, whether with artistic or commercial intentions or both, deliberately advertises his previous work.

Retribution is the laughter of fate. The tragic irony in which the play is steeped, not only of destiny but of casual circumstance, is written large and with repeated comments by Plutarch. The dramatist is forced rather to give up the greater part of it than to invent any of his own. Plutarch told him that Brutus the idealist died of his idealism, and that Cassius the practical died of his practicality. To him, the gods seemed to decree that Pompey should be avenged by the death of Caesar; and all the little happenings which might have frustrated that result were by apparent trivialities rendered abortive. Likewise the gods had decreed that Caesar's death should be avenged on his murderers, not only in punishment but to solidify the state under Octavius, in spite of many happenings that should have brought success to their cause. He says of the first battle: "And Brutus thought that he was completely victorious as Cassius thought that he was defeated. And this was the only thing that ruined their cause, that Brutus did not aid Cassius because he thought he was victorious, and that Cassius did not wait for Brutus because he thought that he had perished."

But though no one could arise from the reading of Plutarch without being strongly, and perhaps chiefly, impressed by the irony of circumstance therein recorded, in the play the two most powerful instances are of Shakspere's invention. One is where the two men who alone can warn Caesar of his doom get in each other's way. The other is the third plebeian's acclamation of Brutus after his speech against tyranny, "Let him be Caesar!" These four words sum up the futility of the democratic movement for which Brutus had killed his friend and staked his life. The people of Rome, as the system made inevitable, cared nothing for liberty but only that they should have rendered unto them the things that were Caesar's to bestow.

Not only its structure, then, but its enveloping atmosphere of irony Shakspere got from Plutarch.

III

Heroes of the grand style have always complacently announced their virtues and certainly not less in the Elizabethan age than in other classic periods; nevertheless if Shakspere admired Brutus entirely and desired us to do so, he has made some odd slips and failed to accomplish his purpose. Furthermore, he has seemingly been at greater pains here than in any other play to retain or recapture sympathy for his hero by humanizing and tender minor episodes of his own invention. The two items taken together call for a detailed examination of the Plutarch material, to verify the suspicion they create that he did not intend the portrait of Brutus to be the idealization which has been so generally assumed.

The little that Brutus is allowed to say in the First Act, which Cassius dominates, is but a condensation of Plutarch's opening description of him. His only long speech follows the style of his apothegmatic brevity of which Plutarch gives examples.

It is not until the second act that Shakspere by departing from Plutarch—either in alteration or in addition—begins to indicate his own conception of Brutus. Here the changes and additions are, in sum, important. The course of reasoning by which Brutus arrives at the conclusion that Caesar must be "prevented" is Shakspere's. Therein several items are noticeable. Here is nothing of the democratic indignation of Cassius against Caesar's pretentions; it is abstract rather than immediate, and intellectual rather than practical. His cogitations are those of a remote student rather than of one plunged into the midst of affairs. Yet so inconclusive is the analogy by which Brutus convinces himself —what else should a man do but turn his back to a ladder and look upward when once he has attained the topmost round?— that one thinks Shakspere can only be making fun of his mental processes. Apparently, it is the cumulative effect of the many letters purporting to come from Roman citizens and saying what

Rome expects from a man of the reputation of Brutus, which finally makes up his mind. The speech of Brutus before the entrance of the conspirators into the garden is Shakspere's. In it he expresses his natural distaste for underhand deeds.

The conspirator scene, dominated by Brutus, is characterized by his three refusals to the three suggestions of Cassius—that they bind themselves by an oath, that they ask Cicero to join them, that they kill Marc Antony also. Only the first of these is an invention. The answer of Brutus to this suggestion of Cassius shows a lamentable idealism which may have important consequences—because he needed no oath himself he assumes that no one else would. The other refusals are more significant in that they are direct changes from Plutarch. There the conspirators at last and reluctantly came to the unanimous agreement to leave out Cicero lest his well-known deliberation and caution should delay them, since their best chance is to strike at once; besides this, they agreed that his age and the lack of courage naturally attendant upon it, if nothing else, might interfere. In the play, the objection of Brutus, phrased with unaccustomed crispness, is based solely upon the ground that he will never follow anything begun by other men. It is a remark which characterizes the vain-glory of Brutus quite as much as it does that of the orator. For Cassius is, in the public eye, the only near-rival of Brutus in the conspiracy as it now stands, and Brutus has reason to rely on his ability to talk down Cassius. The change in the third refusal is even more indicative. In Plutarch, Brutus had held out against the other conspirators on the grounds of justice and also of hopes of a change in the man. He said that Antony being of generous nature, a lover of honorable distinctions and of fame, would, with Caesar gone, join his countrymen in seizing hold of freedom and be led on by them through emulation to do what was good. Here, his first reason, his objection to shedding more blood than was necessary, but follows Plutarch's frequent statement to that effect. The second reason, however, gives us a professional moralist who knows little of men—because Antony is given to sports, to wildness, and much company, he is not to be feared. Plutarch says that in sparing Antony it must be admitted Brutus incurred the imputation of strengthening against the conspirators a dangerous and irresistible enemy. In this scene, Shakspere adds to this blunder the impression of a man whose conceit and whose worldly ignorance may betray him, and who, at any rate, is not willing to listen to anybody else's opinions.

The exquisite colloquy between Brutus and his wife, is, expressed or implicit, all in Plutarch. There, too, is the characterization of Portia in entirety. Nevertheless, Shakspere in handling this dialog and emphasizing the tender side of Brutus has emphasized also something else. The man resorts to specious evasion when he is disinclined to a direct answer. He does not tell Portia that he will not inform her what is troubling him; he merely puts her off, hoping that she will become discouraged. This is not in the original incident, nor is this trait of Brutus to be found in Plutarch.

In the third act, the only new item before the death of Caesar cannot be interpreted otherwise than as an additional stroke of self-righteousness. "I kiss thy hand, but not in flattery, Caesar." One may imagine the confusion of Brutus had Caesar said, interrupting him as he had Metellus, "In what then, Brutus?" The less righteous Cassius offers no excuse or protest—he presses close and kneels before Caesar in accordance with the plans of the conspirators, that is all. There is no further change from Plutarch, although some manipulation of his material for other purposes, until the entrance of Antony's servant. The colloquy of Brutus with him and later with Antony is Shakspere's. The only material it utilizes from the biographer is as follows: "After this a discussion arising about the will of Caesar and his interment, and Antonius demanding that the will should be read and that the body should be carried forth not secretly and without due honors, so that this, too, might not irritate the people, Cassius violently opposed it, but Brutus gave way, wherein he was considered to have made a second mistake." The scene harps constantly on the foolish magnanimity of Brutus, thrown into bold relief by the discernment and practicality of Cassius. Brutus at once upon the politic supplication by the servant is confident of Antony's friendship; he offers Antony a Barmecide feast of kind love, good thoughts, and reverence—against the quick assurance by Cassius of an equal voice in the disposing of new

offices; he gives immediate assent to Antony's request, and upon
the expostulation of Cassius silences him with the magnificently
Brutian reply, "I will myself into the pulpit first." Shakspere
has even taken from Plutarch Antony's own craftily-proposed
reason for honoring Caesar's body in the customary public
funeral, and transferred it to Brutus—an excellent indication of
how he regarded the over-simplicity of the mind of Brutus.
But as if to leave no doubt of the matter, he makes Brutus
follow up the imprudent permission by a remark which superbly
illustrates his childish reasoning or lack of reasoning, "You shall
not in your funeral speech blame us but speak all good you can
devise of Caesar." As if Antony could do one without accomplishing the other! Complacency and foolishness could scarcely
go further than in this scene and permit a hero to retain his hold
upon the sympathy of the audience. But the lofty and humane
utterance of Brutus in other parts of the scene so extends its
influence over his later behavior that the effect is adroitly counter-
acted. In the next scene occurs the oration of Brutus on which
he so confidently relied to smother, and to smother in advance,
the emotions which Cassius told him Antony would arouse; and
this is to be accomplished by a statement of "the reason of our
Caesar's death." The juxtaposition here of reasons against
emotions, beside affording dramatic anticipation of the nature
of the two orations, is in itself a fine stroke in Shakspere's characterization of Brutus. He, a public orator, seeking to nullify
emotions with reasons! The oration proves, however, better
than it threatens. In Plutarch, he had made two speeches on
successive days, to which the people had listened in silence and
in an attitude of great respect. For this second, Appian provided words. The style was syllogistic and the text was,
"There is no true Roman who would not choose to die rather
than be a bondman; if Caesar, then, threatened not our liberty,
we are forsworn; but if he did, we have rightly killed him."
From the hints in Appian and in Plutarch's earlier description of
his brief compendious style, comes, then, the excessive formality
of its manner (a manner peculiarly fascinating to any euphuist).
But style and text granted, the bulk of the speech is Shakspere's.
Nor is its formality by any means cold, as has been so often said,

except by comparison with that which is to come. On the contrary, it is both direct and passionate and ends in a most appealing climax. It is an epitome of what is best in Brutus. Yet with masterly hand, Shakspere contrives to make it all this and at the same time an illustration of the temperamental weakness of Brutus and his unfitness to lead men. For Brutus addresses his speech only to people who have the same idea of honor as himself and as confidently rely upon it as he does upon his own. The pathetic magnanimity of Brutus and his utter foolishness in having afforded Antony so dangerous an opportunity, receives a reinforcement in his quiet departure from the scene. He does not even stay to make sure that Antony will keep his promise!

The next appearance of Brutus is in the second scene of the fourth act where he meets Pindarus, sent on in advance of Cassius and his army. This scene is an invention, and its dramatic purpose is preparation for the quarrel scene. But its contribution to the dramatist's conception of Brutus is significant, since there is no warrant for it in Plutarch. It does not appear there or in the play that Brutus has the slightest ground for his assertion that the friendship of Cassius is cooling. The annoyance of Cassius at the, to him, inexplicable position taken by Brutus would be sufficient to account for his receiving the messenger with merely formal courtesy. Indeed, in view of the provocation given by Brutus, he has showed surprising self-control. Thus the accusation of Brutus, rounded off with his customary sonorous moral generalization, is quite outrageous; and equally flagrant from the point of view of military discipline. It was his business as fellow-general if not as friend, to conceal whatever dissensions had arisen. Yet the loyalty of Cassius is discredited by Brutus to his own under-officer as indiscreetly as the behaviour of Cassius has been censured to the latter's servant. From the mouth of the man who has just uttered these lofty moral analogs how equivocal and self-righteous sounds his answer to the direct and immediate charge of Cassius! "Judge me, you gods! wrong I mine enemies? And if not so, how should I wrong a brother?" And then, characteristically careful of his own dignity, he reminds the impulsive Cassius of what he himself has, at his convenience, forgotten the moment before, that their wrangles should be kept strictly private.

For the quarrel scene, Shakspere draws not only upon Plutarch's report of the quarrel but from hints of the two characters scattered throughout the lives of Brutus, Caesar, and Antony. Of the quarrel the account is as follows: "Now, as is wont to happen among many friends and commanders, causes of difference had arisen between Brutus and Cassius, and suspicions; and before they did anything else, immediately on their arrival at Sardis, they entered into a room by themselves and closed the door, and no one being present, they began with blaming one another and then fell to proofs and charges; from this they came to tears and passionate expressions without restraint, so that their friends, wondering at the roughness and violence of their anger, feared lest something should happen; but it was forbidden to approach them." In its main outline the scene but dialogs this account. Not until the following day did the Lucius Pella incident take place. Brutus had publicly condemned and declared him infamous, sustaining the charge brought against him by the people of Sardis with taking money unlawfully. "This affair caused Cassius no small pain; for a few days before when two of his friends were convicted of the same offense, he had privately admonished them but publicly acquitted them and continued to employ them. Accordingly he blamed Brutus as being too strict an observer of law and justice at a time which required politic conduct and conciliatory measures. But Brutus told him to remember the Ides of March on which they killed Caesar, who was not himself oppressing and plundering everybody, but supported those who did it, so that if there was any specious pretext for overlooking justice, it would have been better to bear with Caesar's friends than to allow their own friends to do wrong." Such, concludes Plutarch, were the principles of Brutus —naively forgetting that he had recorded that Brutus was eager to make use of the money which Cassius had raised by the only means in his power. The question now is, did Shakspere naively forget it also? Or does he depict here, as he seems to have depicted all along, a self-righteous self-deceived man, platitudinizing his way through an equivocal position?

Shakspere had read in the 'Life of Brutus' that when they were in Smyrna Brutus had demanded a share of the money which

Cassius had collected, but the friends of Cassius did not wish him to give up the money. "What you save by economy and get with odium," said they, "it is not fair that he should take and apply to gaining popularity and gratifying the soldiers." Yet Cassius had not listened to them and had given him a third part. Shakspere had read also that Brutus demanded money of the Lycians, even though it was a great deal less than Cassius had demanded of the Rhodians. These two statements could hardly have failed to impress an earnest inquirer into the character of Brutus, on his guard against the apparent partiality of Plutarch just expressed in the comment which closes the Lucius Pella incident. In the play, the sole cause of the dispute is the matter of the money, aggravated by the condemnation of Pella. As it stands then, Brutus quarrels with Cassius simply because he was not furnished with money for his legions. He says he is too honorable himself to raise money by mulcting peasants and suggests that this is the source of the money in the possession of Cassius which he desires to use. Surely, this is a stroke engraved by Shakspere in deep irony for the self-righteousness of Brutus. Furthermore, all of the generosity and all of the affection manifested in this scene are displayed by Cassius. Brutus makes an outrageous accusation against the honesty of his fellow-general and friend; puts into his mouth words never uttered; is, even if he has a better command of himself, the more resentful and the more violent of the two; and refuses the first attempt of Cassius at reconcilation—yet finally, when he comes down from his perch, does so with a remark which indicates ungenerosity and self-deception to the highest degree, "Do what you will, dishonour shall be humour. O Cassius, you are yoked with a lamb!"

As the imprudence of Brutus in the Antony scene had been more glaring because placed against the practicality of Cassius, and his unfairness here more blamable when compared with his friend's behavior, just so Shakspere contrives to extol Cassius in the episode which follows the quarrel. In Plutarch this interruption had indirectly brought about a reconciliation; in the play it serves little dramatic purpose. Had it come midway in the quarrel instead of at the end, it would have heightened the effect of the scene. Shakspere, doubtless employing it merely for its picturesqueness, still makes it bear its contribution to the characterization of the men. The two brief speeches of Brutus are in the same key of petulance, while the two of Cassius—of laughter and of disdainful excuse for the poet—throw the little episode entirely in his favor. The death of Portia is transferred from the very end of the Life of Brutus, nor does Plutarch mention its effect upon her husband. The exquisiteness of the scene is for both characters notable. Yet even here the generous devotion of Cassius is manifest; and though Brutus behaves with great and simple dignity, his later conduct with Messala cannot be acquitted, Stoic though he was, of that theatricality and excessive care for his reputation which has characterized him throughout.

The tactical blunder of Brutus in forcing Cassius against his judgment to give battle at Philippi is in many ways increased by the manipulation of the Plutarch material. Octavius in the next act says that Antony scouted the idea of the enemy leaving the better position in the hill country to come down to battle on the plain. Plutarch does not mention this particular aspect of the matter. The brief altercation between the two generals of the Caesar faction seems inserted merely for the purpose of showing how much firmer Octavius could be when opposing his will to Antony's, than was Cassius with the opinionated Brutus. Again, in the last act, Cassius calls Messala solemnly to witness that like Pompey he is compelled to stake their whole venture upon one throw. This speech is in Plutarch, it is true; yet, emphasized by the recollection that Cassius had claimed to be a more experienced soldier than Brutus, it gains here a new stress. Too soon, indeed, was the truth of his assertion demonstrated. In the light of that demonstration, how emptily reverberates the lofty generalization on life with which Brutus, as usual, browbeats into submission any opposition to his will!

Plutarch records that when Cassius asked Brutus what he intended to do with respect to flight or death if they should be defeated, Brutus answered that when he was young and inexperienced and neglectful of many matters of philosophy, he blamed Cato for killing himself, thinking it unbefitting a man to withdraw himself from his daemon and to skulk away; but now he was of different mind, and if the deity should not determine in their favour he would withdraw content with fortune. Shakspere has handled this speech with a marked alteration, and it cannot be by chance that he makes Brutus evade in high-sounding language until the insistent Cassius puts the question in the baldest terms. This, taken in connection with the previous evasions of Brutus in their first colloquy and with his sonorous putting-off of his wife in the garden, seems to show Shakspere's idea of a salient trait. Noticeable is it, too, that only the thought of his reputation in Rome wrings from him his secret decision; and that here, as often, Brutus speaks of himself in words that one could wish came from another.

In Plutarch's account of the battle, the greater part of the army rushed against the enemy without waiting for the word. This was no fault of their commander, but the speech of Titinius, "Oh, Cassius, Brutus gave the word too early," conveys the impression that Shakspere wanted Brutus to make another military blunder. In the midst of the battle Titinius could not have known the truth but the speech uncorrected is a decided slip on Shakspere's part unless he intended it to tell against the generalship of Brutus. Plutarch says he blamed the soldiers mildly for not having waited for the word and promised them the two cities Thessalonica and Lacedaemon for plunder. This last, comments the biographer, is the only thing Brutus is charged with that admits of no defense; and excuses him by saying that in so hazardous a state of affairs he was compelled to employ those who were with him and to do and say many things according to their pleasure. Now, this defense is so similar to that which Plutarch assigns to Cassius about the condemnation of Lucius Pella that it must have proved another challenge for any careful reader like Shakspere to weigh Plutarch's estimate of Brutus upon his own scales. His suspicions aroused, it needed only Plutarch's Comparison of the Lives of Dion and Brutus to confirm and enlarge them. In the 'Life of Brutus,' Plutarch, poised between his bias for Brutus and his custom of telling the evil as well as the good of his subject, blows hot and cold in a somewhat bewildering way. But on the whole he so emphasizes his virtues and passes without comment those faults which he mentions, that Shakspere, possibly ignorant of Cicero's accusations against Brutus, may have derived an impression of the very virtues that might have for him the greatest personal appeal. But when the dramatist came to read the Comparison, he must have smelt a rat. For there Plutarch's partiality for Brutus is hard beset by his patriotism for Dion; and not only does he allow himself to mention some faults of Brutus unmentioned before, but condemns him for them. Plutarch repents instantly and repaints the picture in more flattering terms, it is true, but the damage is done for anyone not hopelessly of his way of thinking.

Only once in the entire course of the play—for his omission of Plutarch's strictures upon the man's generalship is probably dictated by consideration of time and place—has Shakspere unmistakably changed the Plutarch material to favor the character of Brutus. His last words to the little group just before his suicide, Shakspere has fortunately lightened of some of their complacent self-righteousness and made of them a wholly admirable and sympathetic speech. But his final words to any human ear are extraordinarily uningratiating. In Plutarch, as in the play, Strato holds his sword at his earnest request. Strato, says Plutarch, was his instructor in rhetoric and later showed himself of noble and courageous temper. Shakspere speaks of him only in the terms one would use of a servant, it is true; but even so, Brutus addresses him in amazingly tactless and patronizing words. "Thou art a fellow of good respect, thy life hath had some smatch of honor." In the 'Life of Antony' it is recorded that Antony, standing over the body, upbraided it gently for the death of his brother; that he caused it to be wrapped in the most costly of his purple vests and defrayed the expenses of a funeral. And in Chapter XXIX of 'Brutus,' Plutarch writes: "But as to Brutus, many persons had heard Antony say he thought Brutus was the only person who conspired against Caesar because of being moved by the splendor and apparent noble nature of the deed, and that the rest combined against the man because they hated and envied him." Thus Shakspere found Antony's magnanimity amply recorded, and no unique significance can be ascribed to the beautiful eulogy. Almost all the other heroes of his plays receive praise from their enemies (whether it befits their character, as in Antony's case, or not). Sometimes, indeed Shakspere's mechanical and unpsychological employment of what might almost be called his favorite trick, is exasperating. Certainly here, for two reasons then, we may not gather from it that he had any great approval of the character of Brutus.

Far different is it with Cassius. He seems much to have admired this vigorous, impulsive, and generous man. It cannot be said that he has developed the portrait as found in Plutarch, only that as a characterization and a dramatic personage he has made greater use of him. In the opening scenes, as often happens in Shakspere, Cassius promises to become even more important than he is. His passionate and splendid speeches on his first appearance are invented, together with his almost equally vigorous speeches to Casca on the night of the storm. All of the doings and sayings of Cassius in Plutarch illustrate the practicality of the man, and upon this key Shakspere when he manipulates the Plutarch material constantly plays. The necessity of dramatic effect would not in itself have compelled Shakspere to give, or at least suggest, the entire responsibility of Cassius for the instigating letters which in Plutarch are written to Brutus by many Roman patriots; nor to focus upon him the general desire of the conspirators to kill Antony. Though they are also employed for purposes of the sharp concrete contrast which is the secret of the play's success, they are strokes in the characterization of the man. That his devotion to Brutus should have been disparaged because he was willing to convert his friend to his cause by utilizing a leading trait of that friend's character, is as surprising as that his patriotism should have been belittled on account of his personal antagonism and envy for Caesar. Even the enemies of Brutus attributed to Brutus whatever of good the act brought with it and the worst that happened they attributed to Cassius, writes Plutarch; but he does not do so himself. On the other hand a passage wherein he compares the two is noteworthy. "But Cassius, who was a violent-tempered man and rather on his individual account a hater of Caesar than on the public account a hater of the tyrant, inflamed Brutus and urged him on. Brutus indeed, is said to have been discontented with the dominion, but Cassius to have hated the dominator; and Cassius had various

grievances against Caesar. [He then narrates one of the grievances and continues] Now they say that this was with Cassius
the main cause of his conspiring; but they say so untruly. For
there was from the beginning in the nature of Cassius a certain
hostility and dislike to all the race of tyrants, as he showed when
he was still a boy and went to the same school with Faustus, the
son of Sulla." Narrating the incident, he concludes, "Such was
the character of Cassius." And later he writes: "When Cassius
was trying to move his friends against Caesar, they all assented,
provided Brutus would take the lead; for they said that the
undertaking required nor hands nor yet daring, but the character
of a man such as Brutus was... for it would be said that Brutus
would not have rejected all share in the thing if it had a good
cause." Assuredly, none of the acts of Cassius in the play give
ground for the lower interpretation his character has often received. Upon inspection this seems to rest mainly in two items.
The first is found in the three unfortunate lines in his soliloquy
after he has broken to Brutus the news of the conspiracy and
Casca has narrated the attempt to crown Caesar—"Therefore,
it is meet that noble minds keep ever with their likes; for who so
firm that cannot be seduced." Even when read sardonically,
these lines do not seem to suit Cassius. It is perhaps the only
place in the play where Shakspere yields to his constant temptation to insert in the mouth of a character a social generalization
which the situation suggests to him but would not to the person
speaking; yet it is of all places the most damaging. The second
item is more consciously intentional on Shakspere's part. Plutarch narrates that Caesar, in spite of his affectionate regard for
Brutus as his son, was not altogether without suspicions of him
and matter of complaint against him; and had said of Antonius
and Dolabella that it was not sleek and long-haired men that
gave him trouble but those pale and lean fellows, meaning Brutus
and Cassius. As Caesar in the drama finds them both together
on his return from the games, Shakspere might, without any
change, have made Caesar apply his remark to both of them.
That he did not do so, was probably for no weightier reason than
that it would not suit the figure of the actor who played Brutus;
but the remark, being made of Cassius alone, has assisted in the

assignment to him of a lower motive in instigating the conspiracy as a discontented nature seething with bitter thoughts. So far from condemning Cassius, Shakspere has—whether crowded for space or not—suppressed some unfavorable items. Notable among these is the statement that in the first battle he showed little vigor and judgment and wasted time. The similar adverse comment upon Brutus, Shakspere has suppressed also but he has suggested one which Plutarch did not furnish him.

Thus the actual changes Shakspere made in the Brutus material and their contrast with those made in the Cassius material, all look one way. He apparently had no intention of further idealizing the character of Brutus, but, rather, discerned the partiality of Plutarch and made a juster estimate. It is an estimate which curiously approximates the researches of Drumann and the strictures of Long centuries later. "Of enlarged political views he had none; by the persuasion of others, not his own resolve, he became an assassin in the name of freedom, which meant the triumph of his party, and in the name of virtue, which meant nothing; he dreamed of success and forgot the means; his mind was a barren field on which no culture nor philosophy of others could raise an abundant crop, and he had ever ready in his mouth something that others had said; he thought that justice perished with him, but conscience was his tormentor, for truth was stronger than the illusions of self-imputed virtue; he was one of those who deceive themselves into a belief in their own virtues because they are free from other people's vices."

IV

Shakspere dramatizes the story with little more change than that involved in the change of technic—a change more considerable then, of course, than it has ever been since. The only mark of his own which he has left there, an interpretation of the character of Brutus differing from Plutarch's, is impressed so uncertainly and so neutralized by counteracting items that it has habitually been misread. Beyond the giving of a twist of his own to the leading character and the imparting of individual touches to some of the minor functionaries of the story—necessary in drama though not in narrative—the material has passed through his mind and received no imprint of its passage. The story, so essentially dramatic, creates no different impression of liveliness or artistic achievement, nor of human complexity, of the plot spun by men's passions and how "we are betrayed by what is false within." The old biographer is not bettered by the dramatist who but followed his blazed trail. It was a trail perhaps more aptly contrived for the theater than any other narrative ever written, for Plutarch was one of the greatest dramatists that never wrote drama—history being to him only a field for the exposition of character contrasts and the mixed good and evil of men. Whoever prefers Shakspere to Plutarch prefers poetic drama to prose biography, that is all. Granting the facts and the people of Plutarch—the arrangement of the story, its condensation and selection of incident are but right journeyman's work, however distinguished for its time, a time when theatrical technic was all in the making. Only upon the changes and additions of Shakspere may rest any claim for his dramatic genius.

It is necessary, then, to find out what these are. Shakspere read not only Plutarch in entirety, but all the sources of information on Caesar and his times which he could lay hands upon. He read Appian, Dio, and other Latin authors; his obligations to them and to more modern writers are collected by Professor Sykes in his notes upon the play.[1] Shakspere's departure from his authorities will, with the exception of those before noted, be enumerated as briefly as possible in a detailed examination of the story.

The conventionally Elizabethan tradesmen and the spirited speeches of the protesting tribunes at the opening of the play are Shakspere's. Plutarch provided him with the incidents of the tribunes' stripping the images and of their subsequent punishment by Caesar. Shakspere achieved more prominence for Calpurnia by making her one of the women to be touched by Antony in his sacred course. Casca's narration of the offering of the crown is a mosaic of Plutarch; his humor, so well sustained here and later, is an invention. Shakspere, after the fashion of

---

[1] Julius Cæsar. Edited by F. H. Sykes. Scribner's Series of English Classics. New York, 1909.

the Elizabethan stage, increased the tragic atmosphere by one of his Oldest Inhabitant storms, so constantly occurring in his serious work. Plutarch spoke instead of the brightness of the moon that night; but he mentioned, though in various places, all the omens and portents. The talk of Cassius and Casca is an invention, though what they say of Brutus is found in Plutarch. The calm speech of Cicero is taken from his Divination.

Lucius is an invention, together with his master's relations with him. The query of Brutus as to the date is Shakspere's fine device to show the direction of his thought, to remind the audience of the soothsayer and thus increase its expectation of the tragic event he has bidden Caesar beware of. Shakspere brought the conspirators in a body to the garden of Brutus. It is unfortunate that he did not hit upon some equally casual matter with which Casca and Cinna might have filled up the interval while Cassius and Brutus whispered together. Since both are citizens of Rome, the discussion about where the sun rises is not particularly happy; nor does Shakspere here allow Casca to display his characteristic humor, so pithily shown later in his acquiescence in the decision of Brutus to leave out Cicero. Shakspere invented the plan to circumvent Caesar by the flattery of Decius in case he should, alarmed by the prodigies, decide to stay at home. In Plutarch, Brutus went to the house of Ligarius; but otherwise the incident is practically the same. The 'Life of Caesar' says that upon the adverse report of the augurers he determined to send Antony to dismiss the senators. Thus Shakspere, in making Caesar decide to go in spite of· it, emphasized his courage; his attitude toward the portents and Calpurnia's fear are in the account. Shakspere scored, though not without Plutarch's warrant, an ironic stroke in the portrait of Caesar by making him susceptible to flattery. It was for the same purpose of humanizing the superman that he, apparently, invented the deafness in one ear. In Plutarch as here, it was Decius who overcame Caesar's resolve to humor his wife; but there he did it by the satire and veiled threat, which Shakspere utilized also, rather than by flattery. For this the opportunity is invented in the dream of Calpurnia, whose dream in Plutarch is different. Shakspere's dream serves not only this purpose

but the far more effective one to an Elizabethan audience of
visibly coming true. Despite dexterous original touches and
phrases in the early part of this scene, it is nevertheless very near
Plutarch; and his are its two most telling lines, the one rephrased
and the other unchanged—"Cowards die many times before their
deaths" and "Break up the Senate till another time when
Caesar's wife shall meet with better dreams." The coming
together at Caesar's house of all the conspirators (save Cassius)
is not in Plutarch. It heightens the expectation, provides opportunity for another enrolment, adds tragic irony to Caesar's
death by the hands of those he had just treated as friends and
regaled with wine, and—not less importantly—furnishes Brutus
with a fine sympathetic closing speech. The Artemidorus incident with the letter presented as a petition is in Plutarch, but not
the wording of the letter. In conveying the information Shakspere again enumerates the conspirators.

The Portia incident is narrated in the Life of Brutus. He, in
the Senate House, before the assassination, had news that his
wife was dying; and his stoicism here probably gave Shakspere
the hint for his behavior in the play when he gets the tidings of
her death. In reality, however, she had only swooned. "For
Portia, being very careful and pensive for that which was to
come, and being too weak to away with so great and inward grief
of mind, she could hardly keep within, but was frighted with
every little noise and cry she heard... asking every man that
came from the Market-place what Brutus did, and still sent
messenger after messenger to know what news." The scene is
exquisitely graded by the introduction of Lucius and the humor
that he occasions. It is also most effectively placed. By it
Shakspere both heightens and delays the action; and his further
introduction, of the soothsayer, serves the same purpose and knits
that person to the story in masterly fashion. By this reminder
of his first appearance, we are made ready for his third.

This, too, is placed precisely. For Artemidorus with the same
purpose of warning Caesar against his doom interrupts what the
man is about to say and is himself interrupted by the prepared
Decius; and Caesar passes on unaware of the real intentions of
all three. The sublimity, or grandiloquence, of Caesar's answer

to Artemidorus is a fine invention. In Plutarch, Caesar is prevented from reading the letter by the number of people who wish
to speak to him. Shakspere makes it seem as if the conspirators
had fortified themselves against just this unlucky mischance.
Plutarch's incident exhibits more irony, in that Caesar carried
the letter of Artemidorus into the Senate House with him and
several times sought to read it, retaining it alone among all that
had been presented to him; but this would not have lent itself
to a clear stage presentation without the loss of valuable time.
Shakspere so manipulated the incident that it becomes one of the
finest devices in his entire theater. It causes the interruption of
the soothsayer, who has just told Portia that if his feeble strength
can contrive the opportunity in the crowd, he will beseech Caesar
to befriend himself; it indicates how carefully the conspirators
have buttressed their plot; and it procures a moment of supreme
irony. Thus, it is a splendid instance of how Shakspere could
on the occasions when he troubled to do so, take material already
dramatic and heighten it to its limit.

The Popilius Lena episode is in Plutarch. There Brutus as
well as all the rest feared the plot was discovered, and Cassius
and some others had already seized their daggers when Brutus
called the attention of Cassius to the cheering expression of the
senator's countenance. There is, however, no hint in Plutarch
that they drew their daggers for the purpose of killing themselves;
and Shakspere makes noble use of this episode as foreshadowing
of the final scene in which the practical Cassius again anticipates
disaster wrongly and is beforehand with death. As in Plutarch,
Trebonius draws Antony away and the conspirators utilize the
pretext of Metellus Cimber to close round Caesar; but Plutarch
only says that Caesar repulsed them individually and finally rose
in displeasure. The wording of the scene, and the vaunting speech
of Caesar are Shakspere's. Ibsen, with his love of forecasting
symbols, could not perhaps have resisted cluttering the great
moment of this scene by embodying Plutarch's statement that
so many daggers were let fall upon one man that the conspirators wounded each other, and among them Brutus caught a blow
upon the hand. But Shakspere in his embarrassment of riches
fortunately let many nuggets drop. As Professor Sykes points

out, the expression "*Et tu Brute*" had already become a conventional phrase and occurs in 'Richard Duke of York,' 1595, and doubtless had been familiarized by Edes's Latin play on Caesar. Shakspere made Brutus solemnly exhort his friends to bathe their hands in Caesar's blood (an exhortation doubtless literally carried out on the Elizabethan stage) in order that Calpurnia's dream might come true; but the hint for the impressive democratic demonstration is in Appian as well as in Plutarch. Probably from it, Shakspere built backward to the dream itself; if so, it is a rare piece of ratiocination. The invention of Antony's servant accomplishes the customary condensation of time in a dramatization, for in Plutarch several events in several localities took place. Shakspere utilizes the scene not only to quicken his story but to enforce the characterization of Brutus and Cassius, and to make the preliminary sound upon the note with which Antony opens his public speech. The glorious remainder of this scene after Antony's entrance until he asks the privilege of producing Caesar's body in the market-place and speaking in the order of the funeral, is Shakspere's. Therein his craft and wariness is tellingly prefigured. Sparring for the safe word, he gains time and a possible lead by allowing himself to be overcome with the sight of Caesar's body; then knowing well that he can rely on the promise of safety, he offers them his own body. In his reply to the humane and piteous speech of Brutus and the quick practical offer of Cassius, we have the last impressive roll-call of the conspirators and another glimpse of the alertness of his mind in the adroit anticipation of what suspicions they may have of his honesty. Again he awaits a lead by allowing his apparently genuine grief for Caesar to overcome him. Antony's soliloquy after the departure of the conspirators is Shakspere's. That portion which predicts the civil strife, it is unfortunate that the dramatists did not reserve until the end of scene second. Placed there and with scene third omitted, it would have made an adequate bridge to the events of the fourth act. In Plutarch, Octavius does not come to Rome until later; and the condensation for dramatic purposes is of course inevitable. But the introduction of Octavius here, by means of his servant, has the effect of further focussing the suspense of the next scene by making its consequences heavier if

Antony succeeds in his announced plan of inflaming in his oration the people of Rome against the conspirators.

The second scene of the third act lives, moves, and has its being solely in the contrast of the two orations. The first completes the story of the murder, the second decisively begins the story of the revenge. Shakspere could not, of course, make use of the two extra speeches of the anti-Caesar party mentioned in Plutarch, the second speech of Brutus and one of Cinna in which he preferred charges against Caesar. When Cinna began to speak, the people broke out so passionately against the murderers that they returned for safety to the shelter of the Capitol. On the following day the situation became less perilous for them, as the Senate returned thanks to them for their deed. But they also conferred honors upon Antony for saving the State from civil war by his reconciliation with them. Thus, Brutus was no longer in a position to prevent Antony from saying what he pleased in his oration. Shakspere, wisely omitting all this, neglected to provide some reason for Antony's being allowed to break his promise unmolested; and it is the only loose end in the play. Even a confirmed idealist like Brutus would not have gone quietly home, letting Antony speak as he pleased—to say nothing of the practical Cassius who foresaw too well the intentions of the man. The demands of the scene, if nothing else, would have forced Shakspere to depart from Plutarch in making the speech of Brutus find ringing response from his auditors. For unless Brutus is successful, the whole point is blunted of Antony's cautious tactics —without which the anticipation aroused in the previous scene would be fustrated.

It has been the custom to say that Shakspere built the prodigious speech of Antony out of a few meagre hints. So inevitably does it appear the utterance of the man himself, however, that one is not surprised to find the entire material scattered throughout the several authorities which Shakspere consulted. The 'Life of Brutus' narrates that Antony, seeing the masses were stirred by his speech, changed their feeling into compassion and, taking the blood-stained vest of Caesar, he unfolded it and showed the rents and the number of the wounds. The 'Life of Antony' says that when he saw the people were very glad and desirous also to hear Caesar spoken of and his praises uttered, he mingled his oration with lamentable words, and by amplifying matters greatly moved their hearts and actions unto pity and compassion; to conclude his oration, he unfolded before the whole assembly the bloody garments of the dead, thrust in many places with their swords, and called the malefactors cruel and accursed murderers. Appian says that Antony noted the effect of Caesar's dead body on the people before he spoke. Dio supplies everything that is left. In his account, Caesar's praises, his amiability, his sincerity to his friends, his campaigns and triumphs, and the money and tribute these brought to Rome, his paternal care of the people, his death at the hands of those whom he had benefited and loved, his rent robe—all of these are itemized. Shakspere has but shifted Plutarch's announcement of the testament to the end of the speech. It is an important change, it is true, but one dictated by any consideration of climactic effect upon the auditors. The sole item, then, not supplied by his authorities is the suppliant beginning of the speech and this in the play was necessitated by the conditions of his speaking at all; but even so his authorities supplied him with the cautious change of mood on Antony's part as he went on. Even Antony's pun on "brutish" comes from Plutarch's Caesar, where Caesar himself had made it. Yet this speech—admittedly supreme in its phrasing, its progress, and its oratorical temper—is repeatedly said to have been Shakspere's invention out of the scantiest hints. It must be admitted that if Antony's speech had come down to us, it would, independently of its wording, be pronounced one of the world's masterpieces of oratory for the sagacious selection of its items; and it is interesting to note that it is for this and its barometric sensitiveness to its audience that critics have chiefly praised it. The result of the speech is narrated in Plutarch.

The Cinna-the-poet episode occurs both in the 'Life of Caesar' and that of Brutus. It is doubly unfortunate that Shakspere yielded to the temptation to include it. Though its termination is violent, one needs no further impression that the crowd means mischief to Brutus and Cassius; and the thing that would keep it from being an anti-climax, the actual tearing to pieces of Cinna,

could not have been convincingly presented even upon the
childishly violent Elizabethan stage. As it is, nothing can differentiate it from the last scene of hubbub. Except for its conventional Elizabethan humor, then, it could have afforded small
satisfaction to the audience for which it was written. But chiefly
it performs a decided disservice to the plot. It makes the gap of
time and difference of material all the more frustrative of the
continuity of interest. Since the mob has done this to Cinna-
the-poet only for his unlucky name, what will they do to Brutus
and Cassius when caught? Instead we see no more of the mob.
But Shakspere a true Elizabethan, like Plutarch a true Greek of
his time, could never resist a dream. Plutarch's dream is the
more dramatic and imaginative—that Caesar had invited the
poet to supper and being refused had laid hold of his hand and led
him unwillingly to a vast and gloomy place. Shakspere's dream
is more briefly spoken and more obvious, but its effect is similarly
in accord with the tradition of dreams.

Act four consists of two scenes, for the second and third would
on the Elizabethan stage be played as one. The first concerns
the Caesar party, the second the conspirators; and the principle
of contrast governs the selection of material for the first scene,
though the effect is somewhat obscured by the profusion of material in the second. The detailed narrative in the Lives of Brutus
and of Antony is of necessity mightily condensed, following the
plan already selected from the Life of Caesar. This, as has been
noted, passes at once from the results of Antony's speech to the
omen-and-phantom harassed end of Brutus and Cassius. In
order to proceed to this catastrophe it was necessary to show us
the two parties at war; and, besides this, there was an entire
act to fill up. This the dramatist did by giving us a glimpse of
both sides in accordance with the principle of contrast in its
simplest terms, as in Henry V on the night before the battle
between the French and the English. Fortunately here he was
reduced, however, to no such childish material. For the first
scene Plutarch gave him the picture of the Caesar party united
and merciless. When Antony, Octavius, and Lepidus agreed to
bury their differences, they cemented their union by mutual
sacrifices. Plutarch underscores the moment by an unusual

personal comment. "I think nothing could be more savage and cruel than this exchange." Shakspere gave Antonia a son that he might be sacrificed, the brother of Lepidus is mentioned in Plutarch. It is not recorded in Plutarch that Antony and Octavius cut down Caesar's bequest in order to raise money—indeed, their first difference had come about because Octavius, in order to further his own cause, demanded from Antony the money to pay the citizens their inheritance. Plutarch does say, however, that Antony was entrusted by Calpurnia with all the gold Caesar had by him in the house and with his memoranda and that Antony inserted in the latter what entries he pleased. The hint of Antony's making free with Caesar's intentions Shakspere turned into terms of money apparently for the sake of a parallelism with the conference of the conspirators in the next scene. The cool talk about their fellow-triumvir, between Antony and Octavius after his exit, might be more pointed, but this invention of Shakspere's appears intended to further the impression that they will let no personal ties stand in their way, and thus to increase the contrast in the coming scene where the condemnation of the policy of Brutus by Cassius receives impetus on account of his friendship for Lucius Pella. In Plutarch, Lepidus, left in Rome when Antony and Octavius set out for war, disappears as here from the immediate story; his only service to the play is, thus, dearly purchased.

The marvellous quarrel scene, in itself transcendent, does not promote the plot. Shakspere's chosen scheme demanded that he mark time for almost the entire fourth act. The interval could not have been filled in better, but the drama is not advanced in the least. We have already had several differences between Brutus and Cassius, and foresee too well in this case, as in the more organic difference that follows, what will be the outcome. As has been noted elsewhere, Shakspere has boiled the two disputes of Plutarch into one and made the sole cause of the dispute the matter of the money, in order to sharpen the contrast which the two scenes are intended to present.

The colloquies between Brutus and his attendants and Brutus and his page are inventions. The mildness and humanity of Brutus are constantly reiterated by Plutarch, and Shakspere

utilizes these traits to follow his custom of softening the harsh outlines of his heroes by the display of a milder side. The delightful
humorous touch of the misplaced book has the same effect; and
Plutarch often noted that Brutus in his campaigns read late into
the night. In dismissing the attractive Lucius from the account,
it may not be amiss to note that he is the only child in Shakspere
whose mental agility does not forfeit naturalness and whose
sophistication does not repel. The ghost episode, except for the
change of daemon, follows Plutarch, even to its disappearance
upon the bold reply of Brutus—an idea which Shakspere made use
of again in Macbeth.

To obtain the contrast for which only it seems intended, the
firm insistence of Octavius that he will take the right hand of the
field whether Antony consents or not, is placed so badly as to
appear pointless. Plutarch says that Brutus asked Cassius to let
him command the right wing, which was supposed to be more
appropriate for Cassius on account of his experience and age, but
Cassius granted even this. Shakspere's intention in transferring
this incident to Octavius and Antony is plain; but it also affords
an illustration of how he sometimes forgot in dramatizing that
his audience had not his authorities before them, and only half
executed his idea. The defiant parley between the two armies,
their sober exit, and their piece-meal re-entrance for battle are
conventionally Elizabethan. After the apparition of the ghost,
Cassius had encouraged Brutus by telling him that the doctrines
of Epicurus did not permit a belief in daemons, but the several
bad omens which preceded the battle, Plutarch says, gradually
withdrew even Cassius himself from the Epicurean disbelief in
portents. He mentions also that the day of the battle was the
birthday of Cassius. The beautiful exchange of farewells and
the fine closing speech of Brutus are Shakspere's.

In Plutarch's account of the battle, Octavius was not present
by reason of sickness and some even said that Antony was not
there but only came up afterwards to join in the pursuit. All this,
of course, would have been impossible equally to dramatic interest and to the Elizabethan mode of conducting stage-warfare.
Plutarch notes also that when the soldiers of Brutus were victorious, they rushed straight to plunder without coming up to help

Cassius—an ironic trick which fate played upon the idealist that Shakspere has foregone. The episodes of Titinius and Pindarus are identical with the Plutarch narrative, but the beautiful action of the former in removing his garland and crowning the dead general is Shakspere's. The speech of Brutus over Cassius, Shakspere has merely re-worded. That night, says Plutarch, the phantom again appeared to Brutus but spoke not. In Plutarch is the hint for the battle-cry of Young Cato, which suggested to the dramatist the battle-cry of Brutus also. The incident of Lucilius passing himself off as Brutus (a device Shakspere had already employed in his History plays) is narrated in Plutarch, together with Antony's generous response. There, too, is the incident of Statilius given at length. In Plutarch's account, Brutus, near a large rock in a hollow spot, spoke in the course of the night to his slave Kleitus; the fellow kept silent and shed tears, and Brutus turned to his shield-bearer Dardanus and privately said something to him; at last, employing the Greek language, he addressed Volumnius and reminding him of their philosophical studies and discipline, urged him to put his hand to his sword and aid him in the thrust; Volumnius refusing and the rest being in the same disposition, and someone saying they must not stay there, Brutus sprang up and said, "Certainly we must fly, yet not with the feet but with the hands"; offering his right hand to each with a cheerful countenance, he said that he felt great pleasure that no one of his friends had deceived him...Plutarch relates that Octavius received Strato out of appreciation for his loyalty to Brutus, just as Antony had received Lucilius.

It will be seen that Shakspere, in the material which he gathered from so many sources, has made here no large and alchemic alterations such as supremely illustrate his dramatic genius in the manipulation of the material of Othello. But the minor changes he has made are all dictated by a desire for immediate theatrical effectiveness, or, better still, by a continuous dramatic design. There are almost none of the hit or miss changes and none at all of the raw chunks of narrative taken over without any change whatever, which much of his other dramatization displays. Nor does the play exhibit, in large, the triumphant technic of Othello, though it has not on the other hand the great

infirmity of that play—perhaps the gravest of which great drama
is capable—the sacrifice of characterization to plot. It is on the
minor manipulations of 'Julius Caesar' that any claim for Shakspere's dramatic genius must rest. The general disposition of
the canvas, though notable, is far less important. His massing
of the characterization and of the wealth of theatric episode
furnished by his authorities, shows fine mastery of the fundamental principle of contrast. This principle, after his mechanical
employment of it in his early plays and his confusion of it with a
rigid symmetricality, he had begun to wield more artistically in
'Henry IV'; and it may be said that he reached his highest utiliza-
tion of it in 'Julius Caesar' and never again exhibited an equal
mastery. Also, he never before or after constructed a play which
from scene to scene is so compact and close-knit. But for both
of these excellences, it may be maintained with some show of
indisputability that Plutarch is largely responsible. Contrast
is everywhere underscored in Plutarch, and only in the two conferences of the rival generals has Shakspere increased it in any
manner which may be termed distinguished; as for compactness,
what should be the business of dramatization if not to dovetail
the episodes selected from the narrative? Upon the minor devices
of the play, then, must rest any claim for whatever of veritable
dramatic genius Shakspere has here exhibited.

And these are of a nature to sustain that claim. In his manipulation of the agitation of Portia to heighten and prolong the
suspense before Caesar's death, together with the introduction
of Lucius and the soothsayer in the scene; of the Artemidorus
incident to fill three high dramatic functions; and in his invention
of Calpurnia's dream with its flattering interpretation by Decius
and its real fulfillment in such way as to include the democratic
demonstration by the Brutus faction in Plutarch; of the series of
enumerations of the conspirators, so naturally contrived and with
such cumulative dramatic impressiveness; of the incident of
Portia's death in its effect upon Brutus and Cassius; of the apparition of Caesar's ghost in order that his avenging spirit may dominate the play and crystallize the statements to that effect in
the beginning, middle, and end of the play; of the crowning of the
dead Cassius with the garland of Titinius—all these may justly

be called manifestations of genius. With them, though less independently, may be put the superb handling of Antony's craft in the Capitol. This, it is true, is only carrying out the Antony of the oration; but with what sure and accomplished artistry it is presented.

Against this array of splendid successes may be placed the few minor slips in technic which have been noted. The only one of first importance is the failure—so easily remedied in the material Shakspere himself has supplied—to establish an adequate transition at the end of the third act to the new interest of the rest. What other play of Shakspere's can show fewer technical errors? And, finally, Shakspere has here achieved the greatest technical triumph of drama, although one that it shares with other forms of narrative—the dramatization of his audience. He has kept its sympathy in fluid state, flowing toward and ebbing from each of the four principal characters at his will. Brutus, Cassius, Antony, Caesar—we are made to approve and to condemn turn by turn. Never does he allow our attitude to become static. This, too, he has accomplished not as in the best of his other plays, occasionally or merely by side-scenes interpolated for that purpose, but from beginning to end and in the very fabric of the story. To a great extent this flux of sympathy is produced by Plutarch who insistently paints men as praiseworthy and blamable, but the dramatist has pointed and increased his material seemingly with this aim chiefly in view in his characterization.

V

There are, however, other ways in which the workmanship of this play entitles it to head the list.

It is his only lucid tragedy in diction. Verbal obscurity in any writing is inexcusable, and is more inexcusable in a dramatist than in any other writer. What he says must be comprehended immediately and by the ear only. Consequently the lucidity of 'Julius Caesar' should not be mentioned as a distinguished mark in its favor, were he not elsewhere frequently obscure. A verbal virtue somewhat more positive is the unique absence in this play of that foppery and windiness of phrase which were equally

Shakspere's habit. There is little here of "My determined voyage is mere extravagancy" (when Sebastian means only that he is going to roam about a bit) or of "Pity like a naked new-born babe striding the blast or heaven's cherubim horsed upon the sightless couriers of the air shall blow the horrid deed in every eye that tears shall drown the wind." One is merely a mincing way of saying a necessary commonplace; the other is a booming collection of words which, though saying little that is analyzable, has yet the emotional effect desired and makes excellent mouthing, after the fashion of all the Elizabethan dramatists. But in this play Shakspere fortunately contents himself with saying a thing in a commonplace way when it is a commonplace thing that needs to be said, and with hitting a precise meaning, not less declamatory than the other, when he has a more emotional thing to say. In lucidity and in restraint of language, then, this play is in view of the rest of his work pre-eminent. Again, though it has none of the sheerly dazzling patches of poetry found elsewhere, it is distinguished throughout, as is no other play of his, by a uniform poetic excellence. Its diction alone, therefore, would entitle it to foremost rank. It is equally distinguished by lucidity of statement. Everything is explained. That chief of Elizabethan falsities by which the dramatists obtained the highest degree of emotion with the least degree of explanation, the Determined Villain, does not appear in this play. Here each person has his own human reasons for his behavior and justifies it accordingly. There is no unaccountable emotion in 'Julius Caesar.' At the most, only the departure of Brutus from the market-place is left dangling. When the Elizabethan drama did not blink rationalization altogether, its explanation was frequently preposterous even in its most notable plays, as Shakspere is in 'King Lear' for example. The story of 'Julius Caesar' does not get itself along by the employment of unreal, crude, or absurd expedients. Here are no implausible overhearings, letters, or any of the other shifts of a primitive stage by which Shakspere habitually avoided plot-work; nor is the plot carried forward by those kindred tools of an indolent dramatist, confidants, soliloquies announcing the past actions and the future intentions of the character, and asides—the last two of which so greatly detract from the technic of Othello. When we take into consideration the nature of his stage and the demand of his audience, it is surprising that Shakspere should have made his stories as credible as they are; but 'Julius Caesar' exhibits an approximation to modern standards found in no other of his plays. The coherence and completeness of statement here, like the lucidity of its language, is unique. We know all we need to know about this story to understand and appreciate it; there are no gaps or weak places anywhere in our information. Of what other Shaksperian play can this be said?

'Julius Caesar' caters more discreetly to declamation than any other of his plays. The Elizabethan stage was of necessity a declamatory one. But it refused even in the beginning to abandon itself to the classical influence which made of the pieces of Racine and Corneille but a series of declamations. It early became the English dramatic ideal not to allow, in this manner, literature on the stage to interfere with life; and the nearer a dramatist came to that ideal the more successfully he purveyed to the public. Sounding speeches were highly desirable but only when they did not interfere with the movement demanded by the scene. Shakspere never failed to utilize a legitimate opportunity for declamation but he frequently failed to perceive when the scene did not provide one. 'Julius Caesar' forces nobody to stand around seeking to sustain his emotion by facial expression or gesture while some one declaims. And often in Shakspere this some one is a subordinate personage who arrests the action of his betters and forces them to defer their emotions to a more convenient season. In the detailed expression of emotion, then—just at that point where the Elizabethan drama of necessity scored highest—Shakspere is in 'Julius Caesar' more dramatic than he is in any other play, certainly than in any other tragedy.

As dramatist, his greatest weakness was dramatic irrelevance. He insisted on pursuing any idea that turned up until he said his say about it, regardless of the moment. He intruded ideas or moods impossible to the character under the circumstances or even impossible to the character at all. One has often occasion with Shakspere to recall Mr. Owen Seaman's delightful parody of Maeterlinck: "The true force of the drama lies not in making your characters say the things that are indispensable to the situation but in making them think the thoughts that do not occur to them." Modern stage-versions of Shakspere slash long speeches, not only for the reason that their length kills the situation, but because they so frequently allow the emotion to leak away in irrelevant and often vaguely expressed thought. Nowhere in this play, with the exception of three lines in the soliloquy of Cassius, does Shakspere speak on his own account; and it is a temptation he never elsewhere so consistently resisted.

There is in 'Julius Caesar' no dead wood. There is none of the redundancy, prolixity, or superfluity of the other plays. This to the end of Shakspere's life was always a matter of fortune. Nothing is more surprising in the many surprising paradoxes of his achievement than that a man who had had a long theatrical career as actor and manager and who had written many supremely successful plays, could have thought he was duplicating the special success of Beaumont and Fletcher by his work in the last act of 'Cymbeline.' He tried for a series of surprising situations in the *dénouement;* and each one compels the actors not for the moment concerned to be studiously oblivious to what is going on, and each one necessitates an explanation at length of what the audience knows already. There is nothing of either of these faults here. The play has even the merit, unique among his tragedies, of being done when 'tis done, or, at least, of being done quickly. It is his only tragedy of which you can say there is nothing too much of anything. It is his only tragedy, almost his only play, of which the original version and the present acting-version can be the same. This is in spite of the considerable fact that the entire last act—showing a battle in the conventional and, for the most part, the only way possible to the platform of the Elizabethans—has become the most futile and even the most ridiculous of all the archaisms caused by the furniture and conduct of the modern stage.

Shakspere never gets in any other play the largeness of human sympathy here. You are made to admire idealism, yet it is the cause of the failure of Brutus; had he not been blinded by it, he would not have rejected the practical suggestions of Cassius, yet the practicality of Cassius caused his unnecessary death and turned what might have been victory, won by the idealist Brutus, into defeat; Caesar is both sublime and petty; Cassius and Antony consciously utilize their most genuine emotion to gain their own ends, just as Brutus is constantly dodging the issue by the employment of large moral statements in which he nevertheless believes.

Yet, as we review Shakspere's manifold obligations to Plutarch and to others in this his least original play, all these superlatives of which 'Julius Caesar' is worthy can but point a question in our minds. Where else has he so completely grasped a set of people and made their actions so intelligible? That Shakspere, like some other great men in theatrical history, always found it easier to exercise his dramatic genius on work done by other men, is granted; it is granted also that Plutarch gave him people and action more realized than did any other of his authorities. Could he, unaided, have accomplished a play so entirely mastered as this? One perhaps may venture to say, as was said of the Almighty with the strawberry, doubtless yet doubtless he never did. Matthew Arnold would not forgive the profanation of the line from his rapt sonnet—but "we ask and ask, thou smilest and art still."

XI

PAROLLES

By GEORGE PHILIP KRAPP
Professor of English

PAROLLES

Parolles enjoys the bad eminence of being one of the least likeable of all Shakspere's characters. Other persons in the plays stir deeper feelings of aversion or of uncertain admiration, but Parolles is one of those obnoxious creatures who make themselves too conspicuous to be disregarded and yet must be scorned and despised. The critics are at one in finding 'All's Well' one of the least agreeable of Shakspere's plays, and Parolles one of the least agreeable of the persons in the play. And yet it is not probable that Shakspere set himself the task of writing an unpleasant play in 'All's Well,' or that he conceived Parolles as merely a horrid example of all that is mean and contemptible. If that were so, it is doubtful if Shakspere would have thought the character worth putting into a play. Parolles is bad enough, but he is not altogether without excuse to offer for his existence. For one thing, we note that he seems to be held in higher esteem by some of the characters in the play than he has been by later readers of it. Perhaps it is no high commendation to be patronized by Bertram, but to be endured by Helena is something. He would be a rash advocate who should attempt a eulogy of Parolles, but there may be a word of explanation to be said in placing him more precisely in the social group where we find him than his critics have sometimes done.

One consideration has been almost universally drawn into the critical discussion of Parolles which seems quite irrelevant. This is the endeavor to connect him with the genesis of the character of Falstaff. It has often been assumed that Parolles is a kind of preliminary and unsuccessful Falstaff, "the first slight sketch for Falstaff," as Brandes describes him,[1] and that having Falstaff, we may neglect Parolles. Now this assumption rests in the first place upon several doubtful chronological hypotheses. It is by no means certain that 'All's Well' is the same play, in a revised

[1] Brandes, *William Shakspere, A Critical Study,* II, 67.

form, as the lost 'Love's Labour's Won,' and consequently by no means certain that the first composition of 'All's Well' antedates the composition of 'Henry IV.' But granting that 'All's Well' and 'Love's Labour's' are the titles of one and the same play, there is nothing to prove that Parolles was in the earlier version of the play, or if there, that it was the same character as we find it in the extant version. Parolles does not appear in the source from which the main fable of 'All's Well' was derived, and how or when he came into the play is entirely a matter of guess-work. So far as the chronological evidence goes, one might as reasonably argue that Falstaff was a preliminary study for Parolles.

And this assumption, in a way, has also been made. For it has been asserted that Parolles is merely the dregs of the character of Falstaff, fashioned out of the left-over materials of Shakspere's imagination and thus betraying weakness and lassitude of invention. He has been characterized by Professor Brander Matthews, for example, as "only a variant of the braggart," "a diminished replica of Falstaff, done without gusto or unction."[1] But is not the resemblance between Parolles and Falstaff mainly one of externals? The flavor of the personality of Parolles is different from that of Falstaff, less full-bodied perhaps and certainly more pungently satirical. And one may reasonably refuse to believe that Shakspere repeated characters as mechanically as this identification of Parolles and Falstaff implies. By the same argument, Falstaff himself would be a replica, even though an enlarged one, of Don Adriano, for Falstaff and Don Adriano have the same characteristics in common as Falstaff and Parolles. But assuredly neither Parolles nor Falstaff is cast in the same mould as this more conventionally typical boasting soldier.

With all allowance for the significance of chronological groupings and for conventional dramatic types of character, it seems that, such as they are, Parolles is capable of standing on his own legs. The traits he has in common with Falstaff, and also with Don Adriano, are very general. All three are soldiers, are cowards, are braggarts, and each is the victim of a practical joke. But there are various ways of being a soldier, a coward and a braggart, just as there are various ways of being the victim of a

---

[1] Brander Matthews, *Shakspere as a Playwright*, p. 225.

practical joke. The differences between Parolles and Falstaff, at least, are as great as one usually finds them between two persons of a generally similar class in real life. Don Adriano seems the most literary and least real of the three. Parolles may not be a minutely faithful photograph of contemporary reality, he may owe something to the traditional comedy character of the boastful soldier, but at the same time there can be little doubt that he suggested to Elizabethan audiences more intimate associations than with a general literary tradition or with other characters of the Shaksperian drama.

Externally, there is one important difference between Parolles and Falstaff to be noted. By birth at least, Falstaff is a gentleman, but there is nothing in the play to indicate that Parolles is anything but a climber. He is a follower of Bertram, not a companion or associate. The gentlemen in the play do not joke and play with him as do Hal and his friends with Falstaff. He is merely the victim of their pranks, not a participant in them. He seems to be endured among gentlemen for certain qualities that made him entertaining, but he has no prescriptive right to the enjoyment of such society. As soon as he ceases to be amusing, he is cast aside and easily disgraced out of existence. One might question whether this treatment of Parolles is to be regarded as indicative of that aristocratic attitude towards his characters which in other instances has been noted in Shakspere's plays. The treatment which Parolles receives is certainly hard and unsympathetic, but under the circumstances could it well have been otherwise? It is not merely that the fate of Parolles is true enough to life, since it has been the portion of many a hanger-on to the fringes of gentility. Shakspere might easily have given the character a somewhat more pleasing aspect if the conventions of his subject had permitted. But in 'All's Well' Shakspere was not writing a picaresque romance in glorification of roguish wit and ingenuity. What he was writing was a formally constructed play in which royalty and high nobility occupy the chief places and in which the unsympathetic portrayal of an ignoble, pretentious character was an almost necessary consequence. One must hesitate, therefore, to look upon the treatment which Parolles received too much in the light of a personal condemnation or expression of opinion. If it were, Shakspere might be open to the accusation of fouling his own nest, for Parolles is just the sort of person he might be supposed to understand and to sympathize with. Shakspere was probably neither a soldier, a coward, nor a braggart, but was he not, at the time this play was written, rising in the world by his wit, just as Parolles was endeavoring to do? And in the world in which Shakspere lived, is it likely that a rogue, if witty, would be disposed of as harshly as Parolles is in the play? It should not be forgotten that Parolles, also, is a poet (IV, III, 355), and if we may be allowed to guess a little as to what would have been consistent with his character, of the same school as Shakspere. In the sonnet which he "writ to Diana in behalf of the Count Rousillon," it would have been quite in keeping if he had practiced the same fashionable devices of style as Shakspere had employed in his own sugared sonnets. For there is no question that Parolles was just such another lover of aureate diction and the ornamental poetic style as Shakspere.

An equally important difference between Parolles and Falstaff lies in the fact that the latter enjoys a joke upon himself as much as any one else. He sheds a practical joke as easily as a duck sheds water. But Parolles succumbs under similar treatment. He is made of quite different stuff, and nothing short of an entire re-creation could make a Falstaff out of him. It is impossible to think of Parolles mellowing into Falstaff, because he is entirely lacking in humor, that invaluable preservative of old age and corrective of the false judgments of youth. When he falls into decay, to put it mildly, he smells "somewhat strong" of Fortune's displeasure. The quality which makes him temporarily entertaining is not humor, but a kind of intellectual briskness and smartness which does well enough for the diversion of an idle moment, but which makes little appeal to sympathy and a poor foundation for a solid structure of character. You cannot laugh with Parolles—at times you can scarcely laugh at him. Both Parolles and Falstaff know they are cowards, but the knowledge does not worry Falstaff. Parolles, however, tries to reason away his cowardice. This defect in his nature is a queer puzzle, even to himself, and he endeavors to make himself extraordinarily brave and effective by thinking himself into an honorable situation. His fatal error arises when he tries to realize this intellectual ambition in action, and he thus deceives himself in a way of which Falstaff would never be capable.

Helena is fully aware of the weaknesses of Parolles, and yet she declares that these "fix'd evils" in him are so apt to the man that they take precedence over "virtue's steely bones." In plain English, Parolles is a light weight, even worse, but he knows how to dress himself up in a way which makes you overlook the fundamental defects of his character. He is like a French novel, vicious but tolerated for its style. And he suggests again the old courtly theme of debate as to the relative merits of nature and nurture. Not born to virtue, it is by nurture that Parolles is endeavoring to lift himself by his boot-straps, but the play takes the courtly point of view that nurture alone is but a feeble support.

The particular virtue which Parolles cultivates is one of manner. In the text of the play it appears as vivacity and novelty of phrase, sometimes shallow, sometimes genuinely witty. Parolles is a soldier only because gentlemen usually were soldiers, but in truth his tongue is mightier than his sword. He is a soldier-wit, like George Pettie, Barnabie Riche, Gascoigne and dozens of others in Elizabethan days. He first appears upon the scene in a wit combat with Helena, the subject matter of which is supposedly "smart," but to most readers now is merely revolting. It should be judged, however, not for its matter, but its manner. Parolles is here "a great way fool," but an acute fool. Pompous words are not his stock in trade, as with the traditional boasting soldier. He speaks a courtly idiom, which by Shakspere's day had ceased to be learned and pedantic. A "snipt taffeta fellow" in speech as well as dress, he knows how to use the language of the smart set of his day. Perhaps what he says is not more witty than most smart talk, which depends largely for its effect upon its freshness and its superiority to contemporary morals. The reader a few generations from now will perhaps equate it with discussions of divorce and similar topics as they appear in present-day high society novels. The level of taste seems to be about the same.

The relations of Bertram to Parolles are those of student and mentor. Bertram is young and ignorant of the ways of the world, and he believes in Parolles' assumption of wide human experience and of knowledge of the proprieties of worldly conduct. It is not a hopeful situation for Bertram, but after all, what Parolles is to teach his pupil is not virtuous action, but the exterior ornament and dress of action. When Bertram says good-by to his comrades in arms abruptly, Parolles directs him how to take a more "dilated farewell." The plain and honest phrase of the old Lafeu he translates into an elegant style befitting the gallant courtier. Lafeu is the cloth-breeches of Greene's allegory, and Parolles the velvet-breeches. "Will this *capriccio* hold in thee?" he asks Bertram in a fine Italianated phrase. Bertram, being a young spark, and not too penetrating, accepts Parolles at his surface valuation. But Lafeu immediately starts a quarrel by questioning Parolles' gentility. The soul of this man is his clothes, he tells Bertram, with a great show of interest in Parolles' tailor. A fine manner, in Lafeu's opinion, does not make Parolles a fit companion of counts. "You are more saucy with lords and honourable personages," he tells him, "than the commission of your birth and virtue gives you heraldry."[1] But Parolles insists that his virtue does not lie in his birth, that he is fit companion for Bertram or any count—for all that is man. A higher claim than this no up-start courtier could make.

The reader has long been prepared for the final undoing of Parolles in the fourth act. Only Bertram has been blind to the innate viciousness of his follower, but Helena, Lafeu and Bertram's comrades in arms have seen through him. What little sympathy one may have had for him flies to the winds when we learn in the third act that he has been reporting "but coarsely" of Helena in Florence (III, v. 59). As an act of mercy, Bertram's friends finally decide that his eyes also must be opened. They tell him that Parolles is the "owner of no good quality worthy your lordship's entertainment," but only an ocular demonstration will suffice to redeem Bertram. The practical joke is accordingly planned and carried out with such perfect success that the bright bubble of Parolles' courtly pretensions is forever exploded. But he remains the same Parolles as before. He had set for himself the task of achieving a place among gentlemen by his wit. He had

[1] Act II, Scene iii, 1. 277.

failed, "crushed with a plot." He therefore puts aside his sword, cools his blushes, and sets out in search of a new world where he can thrive by foolery. "There's place and means for every man alive." He has not been wounded in any vital spot, only convicted, as he thinks, of an error in judgment. One is not surprised to find, however, that he thrives but meanly in his new world. He runs the regular progress of the witling from presumption to decay. He is sure that his merits have never received their deserts, that he has been "cruelly scratch'd" by fortune, but in the end he is glad to accept a meal at the hands of his old enemy Lafeu.

If we may judge from contemporary reports and other evidence, the character of Parolles found many counterparts among the young wits of the day. In the last quarter of the sixteenth century, a new type of character appeared in English life. The way to eminence for those who were not born to distinction had hitherto been along the road of serious scholarship, especially theological scholarship, supported of course by solid morality. The Reformation, however, had destroyed the old ecclesiastical system, and the state had helped itself so generously to the treasury of the church that little was left with which to reward aspiring scholars. The Renascence had also emphasized many non-theological activities; and now brilliance, dash, a fine manner, came to be so highly esteemed that they often took the place of the more substantial virtues. Young university graduates thronged to the city with the intent of coining their brains into gold. They had an extravagant belief in the sufficiency of genius, and genius they considered to be only distantly related to morality. Nor did they clearly distinguish genius from ingenuity. Conventional morality, indeed, often remained, and was converted into an ornament of style. The heroes of Lyly's novels, model fine gentlemen, always have a neat moral at the tip of their tongues. It is astonishingly easy for them, however, to recover from a violation of honorable principle. And ingenuity as a substitute for genius is illustrated on every page of the writings of the fine stylists of the school of Pettie and Lyly. It was a natural enough survival from humanist theory, which had made a good Ciceronian style of sufficient virtue to save in this world and the next. At bottom what the

Elizabethan painters of contemporary high life cultivated was a certain liveliness of fancy and phrase, an expression that had point and finish. The prime requisite of the fashionable hero was to be clever, to be animated, and interesting, and above all, not too precise. One of the most commonly expressed opinions among the Elizabethan wits was that the genius is free, that he must taste of both the good and evil fruit of the tree of knowledge and must follow wherever his star might lead him. Greene's 'Vision' contains an instructive comparison of Chaucer with Gower, the latter standing for the learned and well-regulated moralist, the former for the expansive genius who sometimes forgets the demands of common decency. A perfunctory approval is given to Gower, but the defence of the free wit of Chaucer, as Chaucer was conceived by the Elizabethans, comes more directly from Greene's heart. And similar ideals of conduct we find illustrated elsewhere, not only in Elizabethan fiction, but also in real life. A philosophy of behavior which took so little account of the judgment of society was bound often to result in sordid failure, for genius, even when real, has always been of uncertain value and never sure of its reward. The biographies of Marlowe, Nashe, Greene and many others, all point the lesson of the final disaster of wit that is hoist with its own petard. Shakspere has justified the fate of Parolles by emphasis upon his lack of honorable principle and substantial character. Poetic justice demanded this of him. But would he have justified the fate of Marlowe, Nashe and Greene in the same way?

The conflict of ideals as it was exemplified in the Elizabethan literary world is well illustrated in the correspondence between Nashe and Harvey. The latter continually insists upon moderation, learning and serious elevation of tone as essential to good style. The solid morality of Cheke and Ascham and the chivalric honor of Sidney he looks upon as the ideals of conduct to be cultivated. Nashe, on the contrary, finds the old morality stupid. He pins his faith to natural quickness of perception and ability to strike off the novel and interesting phrase. Too much study, he concludes, throttles genius, which must follow its bent at any cost and above all must never be "soft and mediocre." Harvey returns with the objection that the "new-new writers" depend merely upon "a knacke of dexterity," that they ignore art and discipline. He complains that people no longer respect the painful student. And he declares that if you seek out the arch-mystery of "the busiest Modernistes," of whom Nashe is his dread example, you shall find it "nether more nor lesse then a certayne pragmaticall secret, called Villany." Scholars, he continues ironically, are fools for laboring over their compositions—"the book-worme was never but a pickgoose." It is the villanist who knocks the nail on the head and goes farther in a day "then the quickest artist in a weeke"—almost a repetition of Helena's comment on Parolles. The defence of himself which Harvey puts into the mouth of the villainist is that he takes life as he finds it. "Life is a gaming, a iugling, a scoulding, a lawing, a skirmishing, a warre, a Comedie, a Tragedy, the sturring witt, a quintenessence of quicksiluer; and there is noe deade fleshe in affection or courage." Stability and solid virtues, continues this ironical defence, are of little avail; what counts is ingenuity, wit and vivacity. "Try, when you meane to be disgraced; and neuer giue me credit if Sanguine witt putt not Melancholy Arte to bedd."[1] With such sentiments as these, Parolles is in complete accord. "Simply the thing I am," he says, "shall make me live" (IV, iii, 369). The world is his orange; and if he can not make a hole in one place, he can in another; for are there not place and means for every man alive?

To the Elizabethan audience witnessing a performance of 'All's Well,' it seems probable that the comparison which the character of Parolles suggested was not with any Miles Gloriosus or with Falstaff, but with those villainist and modernist time-servers who walked the streets of London in gaudy splendor. If so, Parolles may not be regarded as merely an echo of the braggart soldier of Renascence comedy or a weak reproduction of Falstaff. He seems rather a transcript from Elizabethan life. He has his virtues, for after all his distinction of style in itself is not without merit. He really has the gift of phrase, as so many Elizabethan wits had. And his style seems meretricious only when it is measured by a different standard from its own, by the standard of the downright simplicity of the blunt English style.

[1] Gregory Smith, *Elizabethan Critical Essays*, II, 254-5.

By the same test, however, the most highly prized Elizabethan literature would suffer. There was a reason for enduring Parolles, even for finding him interesting. The question, however, how far his accomplishments justify his existence goes back to deep questions of art and morality. So far as 'All's Well' is concerned, the moral of the character of Parolles, if there is one, seems to be that style is not enough to procure the salvation of a man.

XII

A NOTE ON THE HISTORY PLAY

By CHARLES SEARS BALDWIN

Professor of Rhetoric and English Composition

A NOTE ON THE HISTORY PLAY

The idea that the history play is perennial has lately been confirmed anew by the rapid spread of historical pageantry and by the popularity of motion pictures strangely recalling in matter and form the Elizabethan "histories." To say that neither of these is properly drama is to beg the interesting question whether history remains vital for the stage, a question too large to be answered in terms of form. To criticism preoccupied with the evolution of forms the "histories" may easily seem to have yielded full fruit and faded before Shakspere's death. Shakspere himself, but for whatever share he had in 'Henry VIII,' wrote no "histories" after 1600. It is easy to infer that he outgrew the form; it is truer to say that history kindled his tragedy. More remarkable in the "histories" than any definiteness of form is their habit of verse and their preoccupation with tragedy. Emphasized by Marlowe, this tragic interpretation of history was carried forward by Shakspere. Even 'Lear' and 'Macbeth' were for an Elizabethan but the more tragic because they kept a dramatic interest very definitely historical. 'Richard II' and 'Lear,' then, instead of being segregated as two distinct forms of which the earlier was dispossessed by the later, may both be called history plays in that both conceive drama historically. The falls of princes, still connoted in Elizabethan English by the word tragedy, supplied most of the themes, early and late, of Elizabethan poetic drama. In a large sense we may speak of Elizabethan tragedy as representing history in poetry, and of the historical conception of drama as idealizing human passions in great figures of the past.

The conception is old. Is it primitive or primary? Early drama, however various its forms, generally represents and always idealizes the past. Its personæ are grandiose figures which through being traditional readily become types, as Orestes of the avenging son. But some evolutionists would have us see

further a general and normal development of drama away from
this toward a representation more and more realistic, not only
in staging and scenery, but in characterization. The form
thus evolved interprets to us directly the men and women that
we know now, and interprets them as individuals. In this view
the history play is outworn. But is realistic presentation of
highly individualized contemporaries a culmination of dramatic
development, or only a phase of dramatic interest? That we
too, after smiling at old critical disputes, should try in our turn
to bound the field of drama would be ironical. What we have
to ask rather is whether history on the stage has continued and
still continues to move audiences. And that history plays have
not lost their hold, that they are now more than revivals relying
on spectacle and archaeology, should not be doubted even by
evolutionists.

To say nothing further of the rapid development of pageantry,
'Cyrano de Bergerac,' which in romantic conception and interest
is very like an Elizabethan play, is one of the great stage successes
of yesterday. The most sustained achievement of Synge is his
'Deirdre.' Stephen Phillips sought a past still more remote;
and the youngest of Italian dramatists, Sem Benelli, is busy with
the Lombards, while his Renaissance pageantry, history now for
us and conceived historically, has been bringing once more to the
stage the stir and intrigue, the vivid passion and plot, that support the figures of Juliet and Othello. That playwrights and
audiences should still seek this old interest is beyond the com-
prehension of the intellectuals. Is there only coincidence in the
fact that the most outspoken detraction of Shakspere in our
time has come from a dramatist who uses history on the stage for
satire? Certainly the vitality of the history play must be
doubted by those who see history only in this light. Not so is it
seen by the crowd. Ready as an audience is for stage parody,
it is far readier for hero-worship. That modern drama has succeeded with documentary realism does not make the theater
any less the home of romantic idealism. That audiences will
feed on the facts of to-day does not mean that they have lost
their appetite for the ideals of the past. Their appetite has always been for both, from the days when real English yokels

were foisted into sacred story—nay, from the days when the Greeks who laughed with Aristophanes at their demagogs and their great philosopher felt none the less the answer of their race to the call of its heroic tragedy. Joan of Arc has passed into motion pictures; but she will not leave the greater stage, or all signs fail.

Shakspere reminds us after three hundred years that the appeal of the stage is largely communal. No one better than he has understood drama as answering national emotions. Far from clouding his plays for us, his communal appeal enhances them. It is this that shines through the accidents of time. The manner here and there is antiquated. The local and temporary is lost for the stage; it can be recovered, as in Aristophanes, only by study. This too was dramatic for its time, as for us our passing concerns, which will fade as quickly. Even the larger occasion may be partly lost. We cannot quite thrill with the old insular pride. But what is traditional still speaks, and what is national is felt in terms of our own nationality, as Swiss 'Wilhelm Tell' speaks through German Schiller to the nationality of many races. In no aspect is Shakspere more convincingly dramatic than in the carrying power of his representations of history. If we include the whole historical conception of drama as representing personages in the perspective of the past, then we must be the more deeply convinced that the communal sympathy with tragic failure and the communal sense of poetic justice will continue to feel in history the moral weight of drama.

For no dramatic interest can be more confidently called permanent than the historical. It is no contradiction of this to say that drama is at all times intensely present. The two statements are complementary aspects of a single truth. Drama is, indeed, peculiarly bound to the forms and language of its own day; but what it thus utters is not only the affairs of its day, but all that lived to make this day good for us, or warn us against perversion, or give us hope for the morrow. Projecting the past in the light of the present, drama can translate tradition into vision. It can enlighten communal consciousness and give to communal aspiration the same rekindling that we feel on great occasions in oratory. Here is the motive of the oratory in the old "histories." That such passages as "This royal throne of kings, this sceptred isle,"[1] "Once more unto the breach, dear friends," the Crispin Crispian speech, and "We are but warriors for the working day,"[2] have become hackneyed in schoolboy declamation proclaims them hymns for generous youth. They echo the robustious oratory of their dramatic type no more clearly than they answer the popular interpretation of history. The emotional significances of history are conveyed through persons; and the greater historical figures are part of our faith. This is not the day to rule patriotism from the stage.

It is not accidental that history plays, whether tragedies or not, have usually been written in verse. This is their language, as for Shakspere and Racine, so for Schiller and Hugo, and to-day for Rostand, Phillips, Synge, Benelli. An agreement so long and so wide should suggest more than the Greek or the Elizabethan convention of tragedy. Obviously verse is appropriate to historical dignity. It is part of what we expect. In spite of sad experience with dull ceremony and pretentious metrical oratory, we come to history plays more than ready for a diction that in itself removes them one degree from conversation. We welcome the verse as we welcome the pageantry and pomp. Together, perhaps, they will unspell the vulgar jostle and cry.

Beyond this we become aware, even from reading, much more from hearing, that the verse subtly and constantly enhances the emotion by enriching the connotation. It is not merely rhythm added to force, though how much rhythm, even in prose, is worth dramatically every good actor knows. It is not even poetry added to drama. It is an element permeating and integral. Good dramatic verse, to say nothing of the best, is not a lyrical addition, not a decoration, but as truly a dramatic means as the other means of characterization. The tradition of the Comédie Française lays distinct stress on the rendition of dramatic rhythms. Dramatists primarily lyrical, Tennyson for instance, may indeed fall short with this as with other dramatic means; but that the best parts of *Becket* are enhanced by the verse

[1] *Richard II*, II. i. 40. Something of this typical oratory was heard no longer ago than 1911 in Benelli's *Rosmunda:* "Verona! Verona, ti veggo e sento!" Act II, page 65 of the Treves edition.
[2] *Henry V*, III. i, 36. IV. iii, 40. IV. iii. 108.

dramatically will be granted by any one who heard the lines from
Ellen Terry. And the test, of course, is the verse of greater
dramatists. Shakspere's verse control has been sufficiently
praised for range and freedom. His secure freedom should be
interpreted, not merely as variety, but as dramatic adaptation.
Within the bounds of a single meter he enhanced rhythmically
the quarrel of Brutus and Cassius,[1] Lear's summons to Regan,[2]
the sudden agony of Othello's doubt,[3] and Macbeth[4] sinking
under his sin. To know how far verse can be dramatic one need
only hear Shakspere from a great actor. This, in so much that was
beautiful and strong, is the most vivid memory of Booth. The
desire of the men and women of the stage to play Shakspere is
something more than ambition for traditional star parts or for
sword and cloak; it is the artist's instinct for lines that liberate
all his dramatic powers.

Such dramatic handling of verse Shakspere gained slowly.
His earlier work in "histories," whatever its extent, did not
liberate their verse from oratorical monotony. Nor is the verse
of 'Richard II,' any more than the other means of characterization, superior to Marlowe's in 'Edward II,' though 'The Merchant
of Venice' about the same time shows both rhythmical differentiation of character and rhythmical variety for mood. In
'Henry V' his metrical advance is mainly in better harmonizing
of the old oratory. Only now and then, as in Henry's reply to the
ambassadors of the Dauphin,[5] we feel a movement freer and more
significant. Lest we be reading into these passages our memories
of his greater history plays, we may turn to the first part of
'Henry IV.' Here certainly are greater range and flexibility
and, in the characteristic rhythms of Hotspur throughout the
play, control of a new dramatic resuorce.

To what lengths Shakspere used this resource is seen in
'Othello,' perhaps the extreme instance of verse used dramatically. That metrical audacity, which has left pedagogs count-
ing syllables in vain and sharpened the critical scrutiny of the
text, is the delight of actors. They feel in these shifting rhythms
an emotional expression as direct and physical as gesture.

[1]'Julius Caesar', IV. iii. 35.   [2]'Lear', II. iv. 89.   [3]'Othello', III. iii. 90, quoted below.
[4]'Macbeth', V. v. 9-29.   [5]'Henry V', I, ii. 260.

Read so, the brawl manipulated to Cassio's disgrace—and the instance is not exceptional—has rhythmical effects almost separably dramatic. Iago's rapid instructions to Roderigo, his fomenting of the fight, the dignity of Othello's anger, are hardly more remarkable in action and in structural placing than in tempo and phrasing.

Iago. (*Aside to Roderigo*) Away, I say; go out, and cry a mutiny.
Exit Roderigo.

Nay, good lieutenant,—God's will, gentlemen;—
Help, ho!—Lieutenant,—sir,—Montano,—sir;—
Help, masters!—Here's a goodly watch indeed!
Bell Rings.

Who's that which rings the bell?—Diablo, ho!
The town will rise. God's will, lieutenant, hold!
You will be sham'd for ever.
Re-enter Othello and Attendants.

Oth.   What is the matter here?

Mon. 'Zounds, I bleed still; I am hurt to the death.
He dies!

Oth. Hold, for your lives!

Iago. Hold ho! Lietenant,—sir,—Montano,—gentlemen,—
Have you forgot all sense of place and duty?
Hold! the general speaks to you; hold, for shame!

Oth. Why, how now, ho! from whence ariseth this?
Are we turn'd Turks, and to ourselves do that
Which Heaven hath forbid the Ottomites?
For Christian shame put by this barbarous brawl.
He that stirs next to carve for his own rage
Holds his soul light; he dies upon his motion.
Silence that dreadful bell; it frights the isle
From her propriety. What is the matter, masters?
Honest Iago, that looks dead with grieving,
Speak, who began this? On thy love, I charge thee.[1]

The dramatic gain in this flexible adaptation can be felt fully by looking back to the narrower metrical range of even the most dramatic lines in Marlowe's *Edward II*. The passage is otherwise fairly similar.

[1]'Othello,' II. iii. 157-178.

Gav. Base, leaden earls, that glory in your birth,
   Go sit at home and eat your tenants' beef;
   And come not here to scoff at Gaveston,
   Whose mounting thoughts did never creep so low
   As to bestow a look on such as you.

Lan. Yet I disdain not to do this for you.
      Draws his sword and offers to stab Gaveston.

K. Edw. Treason! treason! where's the traitor?

Pem. Here! here!

K. Edw. Convey hence Gaveston; they'll murder him.

Gav. The life of thee shall salve this foul disgrace.

Y. Mor. Villain! thy life, unless I miss mine aim.
      Wounds Gaveston.

Q. Isab. Ah! furious Mortimer, what hast thou done?

Y. Mor. No more than I would answer, were he slain.
      Exit Gaveston with Attendants.

K. Edw. Yes, more than thou canst answer, though he live;
   Dear shall you both abide this riotous deed.
   Out of my presence! come not near the court.

Y. Mor. I'll not be barred the court for Gaveston.

Lan. We'll hale him by the ears unto the block.

K. Edw. Look to your own heads; his is sure enough.

War. Look to your own crown, if you back him thus.

Kent. Warwick, these words do ill beseem thy years.

K. Edw. Nay, all of them conspire to cross me thus;
   But if I live, I'll tread upon their heads
   That think with high looks thus to tread me down.
   Come, Edmund, let's away and levy men,
   'Tis war that must abate these barons' pride.[1]

Thus the metrical latitude of 'Othello' should not be thought of as impatience, nor as the challenge of a free spirit. Lines such as—

   Excellent wretch! Perdition catch my soul,
   But I do love thee! and when I love thee not,
   Chaos is come again.[2]

and

   On horror's head horrors accumulate.[3]

defy only a mechanical prosody; they do not, as verse less surely controlled has sometimes done for the same reason, and as Mar-

[1]'Edward II', II. ii. 74. [2]III. iii. 90. [3]III. iii. 370.

lowe's shrill "Treason! treason! where's the traitor?" violate the sustaining metrical movement. But their motive is purely dramatic. Rarely throwing out the stride that sustains the movement of the whole, they shift, stretch, or check it in order to suggest the emotion of the moment directly by its rhythm.

Shakspere's accommodation of dramatic rhythms to metrical pattern is represented, more typically than in the extreme case of 'Othello,' by 'Lear' and 'Macbeth.' The meter of 'Lear,' though distinctly more reserved, is played no less dramatically. The verses spoken by the king, finely differentiated throughout for character, carry to its full dramatic height his outbursts of passion, as in his summons [1] to Regan. The rhythms rise and fall with the mood, breaking and stammering, subsiding to the normal beat, quivering again. So few instances can exhibit only the effects most obviously dramatic. To the attentive ear the finer and more pervasive adaptations are no less significant.

Nor is even this the final cause of verse in history plays. They have demanded verse to enhance their characterization because that characterization is essentially poetic. History is incarnated to be idealized. The great figures of the past, remote from the urgencies of our confusing present, confirm our faith that man may dominate and direct his world for good, or, when they too fail, reveal with larger truth the tragic flaws of humanity and the hope of its regeneration. History plays are poetic in diction ultimately because they are poetic in conception, as Greek drama was at once history and poetry. Their heroes are personal forces of good or evil. The fundamentally dramatic assertion of personality becomes a poem of aspiration or warning. The great men and women in whom this vision of humanity is realized are recreated in our image, indeed, but in such wise as to answer our faith.

'Tis opportune to look back upon old times, and contemplate our Forefathers. Great examples grow thin, and to be fetched from the passed world. Simplicity flies away, and iniquity comes at long strides upon us. We have enough to do to make up our selves from present and passed times, and the whole stage of things scarce serveth for our instruction.[2]

[1] II. iv. 89—122.
[2] Sir Thomas Browne, *Hydriotaphia*, The Epistle Dedicatory.

XIII

THE CHARACTER OF HENRY V AS PRINCE AND KING

By JOHN WILLIAM CUNLIFFE

Professor of English and Associate Director of the School of Journalism

THE CHARACTER OF HENRY V
AS PRINCE AND KING

There is always something new to be said about Shakspere, because the amazing vitality of his work has given it the power of presenting itself to different minds and different ages in ever-varying shapes. The fundamental human emotions remain the same, and secure for his great dramas their universality of appeal, but manners and morals change, and with them the taste of the public and the views of the critics. There is probably no play of Shakspere's which a modern audience approaches with the same mood as the people to whom it was originally presented, for we have not the same customs or the same ideas. Yet the dramatic form and the extraordinary objectivity of Shakspere's genius in that form have saved his work from the wastage of time more than that of any other English poet—perhaps more than that of any other poet. Writers who delivered their message to their age more directly have suffered more in this respect, either from the absorption or from the rejection of their particular point of view, or again from the alienation of the public mind from the particular form of art in which they expressed themselves. Some of Shakspere's plays have lost their hold on the general public for these or like reasons—'Love's Labour's Lost' is a conspicuous example—but others have gained in significance because later generations have seen in them meanings which were hidden from his own time, and were perhaps not altogether clear to Shakspere himself. The Shylock of the modern stage, for example, as Professor Stoll has forcefully reminded us, is not the Shylock of the Elizabethans—perhaps not Shylock as Shakspere conceived him. I say "perhaps" as to this latter point, because dogmatism on this issue seems to me peculiarly dangerous. Do we know that Shakspere conceived his characters with the hard clear outlines, say of Ibsen, and not rather as we see the people about us, infinitely complex, and variable with the ever-flowing and ever-

changing current of life? If we judge his methods from the results
of his imaginative toil—and it is all we have to judge from—it
seems as if his aim were first to make his characters live and then
to make them dramatically effective for the particular story—
perhaps even for the particular incident—he had to deal with in a
given play or a given scene. If this is so—and while it is a mere
deduction as to which there will be differences of personal opinion,
I do not see how it is possible to establish the contrary—the
modern spectator or reader is left free to enjoy the play in his
own way—to sympathize with Shylock in his tragic fall or with
Antony and Cleopatra in their magnificent self-destruction, if
he is so inclined. What if the Jacobean audience saw in the latter
play only an obvious moral—which may be doubted—we are
not debarred from enjoying the deeper and wider significance we
find there. Shall Falstaff be to us merely a drunken, lying cowardly
swashbuckler with a huge paunch and a witty tongue because this
was all the Elizabethan groundlings saw in him? Nay verily,
we of the twentieth century prefer the humorous philosopher
Professor Bradley conjures from the Shaksperean page, and are
ready to believe that Shakspere's genius put him there before the
keen critical insight of the Oxford professor released him from
some of his earthlier trappings. Historical criticism has its rights
and its uses, but do not let us allow the fear of interpretative
anachronism to restrict our enjoyment of supreme art. Let us
know by all means how Shakspere's characters appeared to
Shakspere's age—let us try to make out, as far as we can, how
Shakspere himself conceived them; but after all the one great
question for us is the impression they make on our minds as we
see them across the footlights or imagine them rising from the
printed page. It may be in part our imagination as well as
Shakspere's—the ablest dramatist is dependent on the "imaginary forces" on which he works and is only a partner in the "great
accompt." We must indeed guard ourselves against allowing our
imagination to run counter to Shakspere's conception and thus
create inconsistencies which are not to be found in the text. We
cannot study the text too closely, and we must not reject any aid
that may be offered us in sources or stage-traditions, in contemporary customs or prevailing beliefs and opinions which

Shakspere may have shared or by which he may have been influenced. But within these limits and with these helps we are free to form our own conception of the characters to which Shakspere gave the breath of life.

In illustration of these principles, which are, if they are sound, of general application to Shakspere's dramatic work, I wish to discuss in some detail the character of Prince Harry, afterwards Henry V, as presented in the two parts of 'Henry IV,' and the play which rounds out their story. At the very beginning I bow to historical criticism by acknowledging that the right way to proceed is to ask first what conception of the character prevailed in Shakspere's time and on the Elizabethan stage before Shakspere undertook to present it. As to the first point we have very clear leading. With that most difficult of all problems, the ascertainment of the actual truth, we are not here concerned. It is enough for us to know what form Henry's character had taken in the popular mind and in the historical authorities to which Shakspere had access. Some modern historians have been inclined to question the stories of Prince Henry's dissolute youth, arguing that he was too busily engaged in military campaigns and affairs of state to have had time for riotous excess; but in Shakspere's day the tradition of Henry's youthful wildness was firmly established and generally accepted. The legend, if such it must be called, rests upon slight contemporary evidence, but it is nevertheless of a highly respectable antiquity. Tito Livio da Forli compiled about 1436 or 1437 a 'Vita Henrici Quinti' which may be said to be almost official, since it was done at the command of Duke Humphrey of Gloucester, whom the writer served as "poet and orator."

Veneria et martialia mediocriter secutus et alia quae militaribus licentia praebere solet quoad rex illius pater vixit

is the official historian's phrase.

During his father's lifetime he followed, in moderation, the pursuits of Venus and Mars and others which licence commonly offers to soldiers.

An English translation of the 'Vita,' written in 1513 by an anonymous author, and first printed in 1911 as edited by C. L. Kingsford, adds further particulars, for which he claims the authority of James Duke of Ormonde (1392-1452), who was knighted by Henry V on the way to Agincourt and was later appointed by him Lieutenant of Ireland.

He delighted in song and musical instruments, he exercised meanly [in moderation] the feats of Venus and of Mars, and other pastimes of youth, for so long as the King his father lived; by whose life (as I have learned of the credence before rehearsed, and also as the common fame is) accompanied with some of his young lords and gentlemen [he] would wait in disguised array for his own receivers, and distress them of their money. And some time at such enterprises both he and his company were surely beaten; and when his receivers made to him their complaints, how they were distressed and robbed in their coming unto him, he would give them discharges of so much money as they had lost, and besides that, they should not depart from him without great rewards for their trouble and vexations. And he that best and most manly had resisted him and his company in their enterprise, and of whom he had received the greatest and most strokes, should be sure to receive of him the greatest and most bounteous rewards.

The counterpart of this tradition is, of course, that of Henry's sudden conversion, for which the earliest authority is Thomas Walsingham, writing within six years of Henry's accession:

Repente mutatus est in virum alterum.

The phrase is repeated or varied by one chronicler after another. The 'First Life of Henry V,' as its editor, Kingsford, calls it, elaborates the theme with details of the dismissal of "all those young lords and gentlemen that were the followers of his young acts," and Robert Fabyan, writing independently about the same time (he died in 1513 and his Chronicles were published in 1516) says:

This man, before the death of his father, applied him unto all vice and insolency, and drew unto him all rioters and wild disposed persons; but after he was admitted to the rule of the land, anon and suddenly he became a new man, and turned all that rage into soberness and wise sadness, and the vice into constant virtue. And for he would continue the virtue, and not to be reduced thereunto by the familiarity of his old nice company, he therefore, after rewards to them given, charged them upon pain of their lives, that none of them were so hardy to come within ten mile of such place as he were lodged, after a day by him assigned.

Through Fabyan the tradition passed to Hall, and through Hall to Holinshed, who had also access to the 'First Life,' as he himself tells us, in a copy belonging to John Stow. It was, no doubt, in Holinshed's second edition of 1587 that Shakspere found his historical authority, for from this edition he took directly many phrases as well as speeches and incidents in 'Henry V,' but he must long have been familiar with the popular tradition which Holinshed's lines embody:

This king even at first appointing with himself to show that in his person princely honors should change public manners, he determined to put on him the shape of a new man. For whereas aforetime he had made himself a companion unto misruly mates of dissolute order and life, he now banished them all from his presence (but not unrewarded, or else unpreferred); inhibiting them upon a great pain, not once to approach, lodge, or sojourn within ten miles of his court or presence   .   .   .

It will be noticed that in the above passage the charges of dissoluteness are restricted to Henry's companions, the Prince himself being kept free, and in an earlier passage in Holinshed's second edition, apparently inserted by Abraham Fleming, we have a further apology making a similar restriction:

Thus were the father and the son reconciled, betwixt whom the said pickthanks had sown division, insomuch that the son, upon a vehement conceit of unkindness sprung in the father, was in the way to be worn out of favor. Which was the more likely to come to pass, by their informations that privily charged him with riot and other uncivil demeanor unseemly for a prince. Indeed he was youthfully given, grown to audacity, and had chosen him companions agreeable to his age; with whom he spent the time in such recreations, exercises, and delights as he fancied. But yet (it should seem by the report of some writers) that his behavior was not offensive or at least tending to the damage of anybody; since he had a care to avoid doing of wrong, and to tether his affections within the tract of virtue; whereby he opened unto himself a ready passage of good liking among the prudent sort, and was beloved of such as could discern his disposition, which was in no degree so excessive, as that he deserved in such vehement manner to be suspected.

It is evident from Shakspere's use of the word "pickthanks" ('1 Henry IV,' III, ii. 25) that he had this passage in mind when he wrote Prince Henry's apology to his father, and indeed Shakspere's whole conception of Henry's character is based on Holinshed. Youthful indiscretion, foolhardy enterprises, random adventures, low companionships, both admit, but no vices. Shakspere's "mirror of all Christian kings" ('Henry V,' II. Ch.

is Holinshed's majesty "that both lived and died a pattern in princehood, a lodestar in honor, and mirror of magnificence; the more highly exalted in his life, the more deeply lamented at his death, and famous to the world always."

This is the more remarkable because Shakspere, when he wrote 'Richard II,' had already made up his mind as to the dramatic effectiveness of this adventurous side of the young Henry's character. In this earlier play he goes out of his way to bring in the following lines, apparently intended to serve as a link between 'Richard II' and '1 Henry IV,' which Shakspere, no doubt, already had in mind:

> *Boling.* Can no man tell me of my unthrifty son?
> 'Tis full three months since I did see him last;
> If any plague hang over us, 'tis he.
> I would to God, my lords, he might be found;
> Inquire at London, 'mongst the taverns there,
> For there, they say, he daily doth frequent,
> With unrestrained loose companions,
> Even such, they say, as stand in narrow lanes,
> And beat our watch, and rob our passengers;
> Which he, young wanton and effeminate boy,
> Takes on the point of honour to support
> So dissolute a crew.
> *Percy.* My lord, some two days since I saw the prince,
> And told him of those triumphs held at Oxford.
> *Boling.* And what said the gallant?
> *Percy.* His answer was, he would unto the stews,
> And from the common'st creature pluck a glove,
> And wear it as a favour; and with that
> He would unhorse the lustiest challenger.
> *Boling.* As dissolute as desperate; yet through both
> I see some sparks of better hope, which elder years
> May happily bring forth . . .
>
> ('Richard II,' V. iii. 1-22)

This is Shakspere's nearest approach to direct reflection upon Prince Henry's moral character, and it is limited to an impression, perhaps exaggerated, in the mind of an anxious father, and the report of a reckless speech suggesting the young prince's contempt for courtly ceremonial, and so far likely to win sympathy from the audience, notwithstanding the extravagance of its expression. This is in striking contrast with the picture presented in a play

already in possession of the stage, the 'Famous Victories of
Henry the Fifth,' which Shakspere evidently knew, as he was
slightly indebted to it. This old play, which is a rough and art-
less piece of work covering in twenty short scenes the same ground
as Shakspere's three plays, begins with the traditional robbery
of the receivers, who, after giving Henry a sound thrashing in his
disguise as a footpad, are later bullied by him into silence in his
character as a true prince. He goes off with his companions to
spend the proceeds of the robbery in "the old tavern in Eastcheap," remarking:

> There is good wine: besides, there is a pretty wench
> That can talk well, for I delight as much in their tongues
> As any part about them.

In the next scene the jovial crew fight in the wineshop with the
pots and afterwards in the street with their swords. "For the
space of half an hour there was such a bloody fray as passeth, and
none could part them until such time as the Mayor and Sheriff
were sent for, and then at the last with much ado they took them,
and so the young prince was carried to the Counter." Released
by command of his father, who nevertheless praises the Mayor
and Sheriff for their faithfulness, young Henry interferes to
prevent the condemnation of a convicted thief, one of his companions, and is sent to the Fleet for giving the Judge a box on the
ear in open court. Then comes the reconciliation with the King,
whose death follows immediately, and Henry dismisses his old
companions, receives the Dauphin's tun of tennis balls, and departing for France makes the Judge Protector of the Realm during his absence. Agincourt and the wooing of Princess Katharine
follow hard after and bring the play to a close.

Shakspere, following the lead of Holinshed, deals with the
matter very differently. Vice is condoned by humor in the
inimitable creation of Falstaff, and the Prince's exchanges of
banter with him in the first scene in which they appear are a
mixture of wit and sound morality. Henry at first declines the
invitation to highwaymanship. "Who, I rob? I a thief? not I, by
my faith," and he is only persuaded "for once" in his days to be a
madcap by the proposal that "for recreation's sake" he and Poins

shall rob the other four of their ill-gotten gains. After the adventure has served its purpose in developing Falstaff's humor to its fullest extent, Henry says, "The money shall be paid back again with advantage"; but Shakspere does not allow even the introductory scene to close without making clear to his audience the light in which Henry's youthful escapade was to be regarded. The following passage is in soliloquy and brings out the underlying seriousness of Henry's character, which has been more than once suggested in the preceding dialog:

> I know you all, and will awhile uphold
> The unyok'd humour of your idleness:
> Yet herein will I imitate the sun,
> Who doth permit the base contagious clouds
> To smother up his beauty from the world,
> That, when he please again to be himself,
> Being wanted, he may be more wonder'd at,
> By breaking through the foul and ugly mists
> Of vapours that did seem to strangle him.
> If all the year were playing holidays,
> To sport would be as tedious as to work;
> But when they seldom come, they wish'd for come,
> And nothing pleaseth but rare accidents.
> So, when this loose behaviour I throw off
> And pay the debt I never promised,
> By how much better than my word I am,
> By so much shall I falsify men's hopes;
> And like bright metal on a sullen ground,
> My reformation, glittering o'er my fault,
> Shall show more goodly and attract more eyes
> Than that which hath no foil to set it off.
> I'll so offend, to make offence a skill;
> Redeeming time when men think least I will.
>
> ('I Henry IV,' I. ii.218-240)

Shakspere's apparent vindication of Henry's character in this passage is very far from satisfying modern critics. Professor Bradley, discussing Henry's "rejection of Falstaff" says of it:

. . . In his first soliloquy—and first soliloquies are usually significant— he declares that he associates with them in order that, when at some future time he shows his true character, he may be the more wondered at for his previous aberrations. You may think he deceives himself here; you may believe that he frequented Sir John's company out of delight in it and not

merely with this cold-blooded design; but at any rate he *thought* the design was
his one motive.   And, that being so, two results follow.   He ought in honour
long ago to have given Sir John clearly to understand that they must say
good-bye on the day of his accession.   And, having neglected to do this, he
ought not to have lectured him as his misleader.   It was not only ungenerous,
it was dishonest.   It looks disagreeably like an attempt to buy the praise of
the respectable at the cost of honour and truth.   And it succeeded.   Henry
always succeeded.

And again:

.   .   .   This same strain of policy is what Shakspere marks in the first
soliloquy in 'Henry IV,' where the prince describes his riotous life as a mere
scheme to win him glory later.   It implies that readiness to use other people
as means to his own ends which is a conspicuous feature in his father;
and it reminds us of his father's plan of keeping himself out of the people's
sight while Richard was making himself cheap by his incessant public appearances.   And if I am not mistaken there is a further likeness.   Henry is kindly
and pleasant to every one as Prince, to every one deserving as King; and he
is so not merely out of policy: but there is no sign in him of a strong affection
for any one, such an affection as we recognize at a glance in Hamlet and
Horatio, Brutus and Cassius, and many more.   We do not find this in 'Henry
V,' not even in the noble address to Lord Scroop, and in 'Henry IV' we find,
I think, a liking for Falstaff and Poins, but no more: there is no more than
a liking, for instance, in his soliloquy over the supposed corpse of his fat
friend, and he never speaks of Falstaff to Poins with any affection.   The truth
is, that the members of the family of Henry IV have love for one another,
but they cannot spare love for any one outside their family, which stands
firmly united, defending its royal position against attack and instinctively
isolating itself from outside influence.   (pp. 257-8)

So, too, Masefield:

.   .   .   Prince Henry is not a hero, he is not a thinker, he is not even a
friend; he is a common man whose incapacity for feeling enables him to change
his habits whenever interest bids him.   Throughout the first acts he is careless
and callous though he is breaking his father's heart and endangering his
father's throne.   He chooses to live in society as common as himself.   He
talks continually of guts as though a belly were a kind of wit.   Even in the
society of his choice his attitude is remote and cold-blooded.   There is no good-
fellowship in him, no sincerity, no whole-heartedness.   He makes a mock of
the drawer who gives him his whole little pennyworth of sugar.   His jokes
upon Falstaff are so little good-natured that he stands upon his princehood
whenever the old man would retort upon him.   He impresses one as quite
common, quite selfish, quite without feeling. When he learns that his behaviour
may have lost him his prospective crown he passes a sponge over his past, and

fights like a wild cat for the right of not having to work for a living. (pp. 112-113)

There is a touch of exaggeration here, in protest against the received Nineteenth Century view—a protest which had been already voiced by Mr. W. B. Yeats in 'Ideas of Good and Evil':

> . . . To poise character against character was an element in Shakspere's art, and scarcely a play is lacking in characters that are the complement of one another, and so, having made the vessel of porcelain Richard II, he had to make the vessel of clay Henry V. He makes him the reverse of all that Richard was. He has the gross vices, the coarse nerves, of one who is to rule among violent people, and he is so little 'too friendly' to his friends that he bundles them out of doors when their time is over. He is as remorseless and undistinguished as some natural force, and the finest thing in his play is the way his old companions fall out of it broken-hearted or on their way to the gallows; and instead of that lyricism which rose out of Richard's mind like the jet of a fountain to fall again where it had risen, instead of that phantasy too enfolded in its own sincerity to make any thought the hour had need of, Shakspere has given him a resounding rhetoric that moves men, as a leading article does to-day . . . (pp. 126-127)

These criticisms of Henry's character were all written during the first decade of the present century, and so far as Professor Bradley and Mr. Yeats are concerned were worked out independently, as the dates of composition show; Mr. Masefield acknowledges general indebtedness to the other two, but he is too original a thinker not to have his own opinion. The three views have obviously much in common, and it will be convenient at this point to suggest some of the reasons that underlie the change from the generous appreciation of Henry's character as Shakspere depicts it, to this attitude of cold or hostile criticism. In the first place, we are no longer sensible of "the divinity that doth hedge a king," and we apply to Henry the same standards as to other men. When his father deplores the "indirect crook'd ways" by which he gained the crown and Henry replies:

> You won it, wore it, kept it, gave it me;
> Then plain and right must my possession be,

it is a position we can understand; but when in answer to Henry's adjuration, the Archbishop of Canterbury enters into an elaborate argument as to Henry's claim to the throne of France, the plea does not move us—does not even interest us. We cannot forget that the reigning French king's right rests upon the same foundation as Henry's own right to the crown of England, the right of possession and continuance, and the acquiescence of his subjects. We are conscious too, that neither the Archbishop's nor Henry's view is disinterested. In the case of the Archbishop, Shakspere has devoted the opening scene to making this abundantly clear. In the case of Henry, his father's dying advice was "to busy giddy minds with foreign quarrels," and Lancaster's closing speech in '2 Henry IV' is equally significant:

> *Lan.* I will lay odds that, ere this year expire,
> We bear our civil swords and native fire
> As far as France: I heard a bird so sing,
> Whose music, to my thinking, pleas'd the king.
>
> ('2 Henry IV,' V. v. 111-114)

To us, Henry's attack upon France is merely a war of conquest—no more and no less—and his valor, whether as prince or king, stirs us simply as a warlike quality without regard to the cause in which it is displayed. We can not regard the rebellion of the Percies as a heinous offence, and the terrible threats Henry utters against the citizens of Harfleur only provoke our sympathy for them; so far as he himself is concerned, we can only hope that he did not mean what he said, but was using guileful rhetoric to cow the burghers into prompt submission.

Similarly, Prince Henry's wildness must be justified or excused to us like the wildness of any other young man; if he were merely self-indulgent, we should be inclined to make the customary allowances for youth, and even to make some special excuse for the peculiar temptations of his position. Above all, we should readily forgive his liking for the society of Falstaff, whose character has evidently been created by Shakspere to account for and take the edge off Henry's dissipations. But when the Prince pleads, in soliloquy, that his "loose behaviour" is not idle at all, but a deliberate scheme for political ends, this avowal of a cold disposition alienates our sympathy more than any idle flashes of youth, because we no longer hold in esteem the aim to which, according to Henry's excuses to himself, his course of duplicity was steered. It is not that nothing would justify such a course, according to our standards of conduct, but that the particular reason given seems insufficient—not a really high aim, but mere selfish ambition.

Again in the fine soliloquy before Agincourt, ending:

> And but for ceremony, such a wretch,
> Winding up days with toil and nights with sleep,
> Had the fore-hand and vantage of a king.
> The slave, a member of the country's peace,
> Enjoys it; but in gross brain little wots
> That watch the king keeps to maintain the peace,
> Whose hours the peasant best advantages.
>
> ('Henry V,' IV. i. 295-301)

we are keenly conscious of the fact that Henry thoroughly enjoys being king and is doing everything in his power to seat himself firmly on the throne; he does not really wish to change places with the peasant, any more than the great landowner or manufacturer wishes to change places with the people who work for him, however much envy he may sometimes express of their freedom from responsibility.

Another element in Henry's character which the modern reader takes very differently from the generation for which the play was written is his religiosity—I can find no more accurate word for the mixture of official piety with what Professor Bradley describes as superstition. Certainly, such passages as

> O God of battles! steel my soldiers' hearts;
>
> ('Henry V,' IV. i. 306)

and

> . . . O God, thy arm was here;
> And not to us, but to thy arm alone,
> Ascribe we all!
>
> ('Henry V,' IV. viii. 111-113)

strike us with a sense of incongruity when we remember Henry's command just before:

> Then every soldier kill his prisoners

and his threat:

> Besides, we'll cut the throats of those we have
> And not a man of them that we shall take
> Shall taste our mercy.

One calls to mind the satirical despatch perpetrated by an English humorist in the name of the first German Emperor:

> Dear Augusta
> Another buster!
> Ten thousand Frenchmen sent below,
> Praise God from whom all blessings flow.

More recent examples of Tsar or Kaiser may also occur to us. No doubt Henry's religious fervor is thoroughly in character, and was a historical fact, but it no longer appeals to us as it did to the men of Shakspere's own day.

Another and perhaps more debatable point is his humor, as to which Mr. Masefield is especially severe in the passage above quoted. He says further:

> Henry V is the one commonplace man in the eight plays. He alone enjoys success and worldly happiness. He enters Shakspere's vision to reap what his broken-hearted father sowed. He passes out of Shakspere's vision to beget the son who dies broken-hearted after bringing all to waste again.

> "Hear him but reason in divinity,"

cries the admiring archbishop. Yet this searcher of the spirit woos his bride like a butcher, and jokes among his men like a groom. He has the knack of life that fits human beings for whatever is animal in human affairs. (pp. 121-122)

It must be confessed that to a modern taste Henry's sallies of wit, whether as prince or king, are not of the most refined sort. He has a love for that most detestable kind of joke called practical; and his wooing of Katharine, though full of humor and a certain bluff overbearing hilarity, has nothing princely about it. For an ideal hero, even for an ideal sovereign, thinking people of our age would demand something different.

When all these deductions and exceptions are allowed, what is there left for us of "the mirror of all Christian kings?" Obviously nothing that has been said detracts from Shakspere's portrayal of the character, which still stands four-square to all the winds of heaven. On the contrary, while the esteem in which such a character is held has changed, the character as Shakspere has portrayed it becomes on closer consideration more human, more vivid, more interesting. When we regard Henry no longer as an ideal hero but as a man subject to the limitations of his time and with some personal shortcomings of his own to boot, he becomes all the more real to us, and the more worthy of our attention. For the predominant feature in his individuality Professor Bradley has, I think, hit upon the right word when he describes Henry as "the most *efficient* character drawn by Shakspere." The word carries with it familiar connotations and limitations which are by no means out of place in this connection. Henry is efficient after the manner of a modern captain of industry, although his efficiency is directed not to the management of a great railroad or trade combination or financial enterprise, but to the ruling of a kingdom. This is his overpowering concern from the very beginning, and accounts for the explanation he offers, to himself and to the audience, of his association with Falstaff and his crew. The explanation may be, as Professor Bradley suggests, a piece of self-deception, though I do not think it so; but clearly Shakspere meant us to realize from the very first that the one idea Henry had in mind was that he was to be king of England. The policy of reserve and distance which his father commends does not appeal either to his reason or to his natural disposition, and has not been, as the old king seems to think, justified by its results. Prince Henry has none of the sentimentalism of Richard II, to whom his father compares him, and the resemblance in their courses is merely superficial. With his boon companions Henry never forgets that he is a prince, and he does not let his companions forget it for long. He is always master of himself and of them. Even in his most expansive moments there is a touch of condescension rarely absent in social intercourse between people of high rank or position and those whom they account their inferiors. We might like him better if he were more genuinely open-hearted, but Shakspere has not so represented him.

Henry's consciousness of kingship carries him unfaltering through the difficult interviews with his father. As he expects submission from others, he pays it to the wearer of the Crown except in so far as submission would interfere with his own plans for the future. His own ideas as to the methods of sovereignty are so different from his father's that there can be no true com-

munion between them.   It is only in face of a common danger
or in moments of tense natural emotion that they are really at one.
Henry saves his father's life at Shrewsbury, but he does not fail
to draw his father's attention to the fact, as a proof of the sincerity of his affection; and the moment he thinks the breath is out
of his father's body he seizes upon the crown as his by right divine:

> This from thee
> Will I to mine leave, as 'tis left to me.

His father's scruples as to the "indirect crook'd ways" by which
the crown was gained trouble him not a whit:

> My gracious liege,
> You won it, wore it, kept it, gave it me;
> Then plain and right must my possession be:
> Which I with more than with a common pain
> 'Gainst all the world will rightfully maintain.

For a monarch imbued with these ideas, and in the mood induced by his father's death and his own accession, the dismissal
of his quondam followers is inevitable.   It was a political necessity
and a fore-ordained part of Henry's plan.   He carries it out with
the forthrightness and thoroughness of a plain, direct nature
strongly stirred; the harshness he shows, so little to the taste of
modern critics, is entirely in accord with his character and with
the situation.   The expectations Falstaff expresses with infantine
eagerness when he hears of Henry's accession show that any
other course would have been impossible, and Henry was not the
man to do things by halves.   Again, one might wish for more
subtlety, more delicacy, a flash of finer feeling, an expression of
regret, a realization of the effect of his decision upon its victims—
but these are not elements of Henry's character as Shakspere has
represented it, and would not have been consistent with the
historical facts he had to present to his audience.

In 'Henry V' the character is further developed upon the lines
Shakspere has already laid down in the preceding plays.   His
energy and ambition find a natural outlet in the war with France,
and he is doubtless fully aware of the political expediency of the
course recommended by his father, "to busy giddy minds with
foreign quarrels."   He seeks the official sanction of the Arch-

bishop, no doubt again as a political expedient rather than to solve any doubt in his own mind—his mind was not given to doubt; he knows beforehand the answer the Archbishop will make and the special reasons he has for making it. To admit this is not to accuse Henry of hypocrisy. He is not troubled, any more than a modern capitalist on the eve of a great undertaking, with moral misgivings; he accepts the law as it is expounded by the traditional authorities, all the more readily, no doubt, because it falls in with his own inclinations and interests. In the conduct of the campaign he shows the same practical temper. He uses horrible threats to induce the citizens of Harfleur to yield promptly, but enjoins mercy to all when they do yield. He knows that "when lenity and cruelty play for a kingdom, the gentler gamester is the soonest winner," and therefore gives express charge that "in all our marches through the country, there be nothing compelled from the villages, nothing taken but paid for, none of the French upbraided or abused in disdainful language." But when at Agincourt the defeated enemy threatens to gather head again, he bids "every soldier kill his prisoners." He sees directly to the aim he wishes to attain and takes without hesitation the means necessary to accomplish it.

Henry's religion is of a piece with his morals. It is the conventional religion of his time. Why should one expect it to be otherwise? It would be idle to expect from him the philosophical subtleties of Hamlet or the profound reflections of Prospero or the poetic vision of Macbeth. His conversation with the soldiers as he wanders through the camp in disguise on the eve of Agincourt and his subsequent meditations in private run on the familiar theme of the responsibilities of kingship, and hardly rise above the commonplace. The horrors of war indeed obtain a passing reference in the adjuration to the Archbishop before the campaign, already planned, is entered upon. They are effectively used by Henry as a means of bringing the citizens of Harfleur to prompt submission. But when one of the soldiers before Agincourt proposes to call the king to a reckoning for "their wives left poor behind them . . . their children rawly left," Henry answers with an argument conceived in the spirit of medieval theology, "Every subject's duty is the King's, but every subject's soul is his own." It is the soldier's account of heaven that occupies Henry's mind, not the bereavement and suffering of their families; and the moment he is left alone he throws off the burden of spiritual responsibility for himself as decisively as he has rejected it in argument.

> Upon the king! let us our lives, our souls,
> Our debts, our careful wives,
> Our children and our sins lay on the king!
> We must bear all. O hard condition,
> Twin-born with greatness, subject to the breath
> Of every fool, whose sense no more can feel
> But his own wringing! What infinite heart's ease
> Must kings neglect, that private men enjoy!
> And what have kings, that privates have not too,
> Save ceremony, save general ceremony!

Although Shakspere has not endowed Henry with any deep spiritual insight, he has given him a common sense appreciation of the value of common virtues and common things; he is not deceived by mere appearances. He is not blind to the penalties of high office, and his consciousness of kingship does not mislead him into an exaggerated estimate of his own personality. "All his senses have but human conditions: his ceremonies laid by, in his nakedness he appears but a man; and though his affections are higher mounted than ours, yet, when they stoop, they stoop with the like wing." It is this essential humility which redeems Henry's conventional piety as expressed in his prayer before battle and his ascription of the victory to the special interposition of Providence.

> Come, go we in procession through the village
> And be it death proclaimed through our host
> To boast of this or take that praise from God
> Which is his only.

Fluellen's matter-of-fact reference in this passage to the help of the Deity, "Yes, my conscience, he did us great good," suggests that Shakspere was not himself oblivious of the human elements of the great struggle. There is nothing to justify us in assuming that in ascribing this attitude to Henry, Shakspere did more than follow historical tradition and invest his hero with qualities which he knew would be acceptable to his audience. Shakspere has indeed clothed Henry's commonplace thoughts with beauty, just as he has expressed Henry's patriotism in imperishable lines which still stir the blood. In both cases he was the dramatic artist appealing to current religious and political sentiment, and the charm and vigor of the expression keep their emotional hold on people whose minds are no longer affected by the intellectual assumptions which the passages imply.

Henry's humor, as has been already suggested, is somewhat too robust "for this refined age." But the wooing scene is undoubtedly effective. With Katharine as an equal in rank—and, moreover, one who does not entirely understand what he is saying—Henry is more himself than in any previous scene, and we get a glimpse of him as a man which rounds out our appreciation of him as prince and king. Masefield's strictures on Henry in this situation seem to me much exaggerated. He is masterful, downright, bluff, good-natured; he is not delicate or refined, but he is not indelicate, according to the less squeamish standard of Shakspere's time. The dramatic irony of the passage about the "boy, half French, half English, that shall go to Constantinople and take the Turk by the beard," takes the edge off its directness; and Katharine's reply leaves it doubtful whether this long speech was supposed or intended to be understood by her. Henry was enjoying an unaccustomed freedom of letting himself talk. Shakspere had promised his audience at the end of 'Henry IV,' Part II, to make them merry with fair Katharine of France, and he fulfilled his promise in a fashion still highly effective with the unsophisticated, and of added interest because of the light it throws on Henry's character.

Finally, as a matter of literary curiosity rather than as a necessary factor in the appreciation of the play, one may ask the question, "How far did Shakspere approve of Henry's character, regarded not as an artistic achievement but as a living soul he had himself created?" Shakspere was not in the habit of labelling his characters or their qualities for the moral edification of his audience, and the question may be unanswerable in any definite, precise way. There is nothing to show that Shakspere drew Henry lovingly, as we are inclined to fancy he did his great tragic characters, Hamlet and Othello and Macbeth, because he seems to us to have put into them something of himself. It appears rather that he accepted Henry as a national hero, and presented him as such to the public of his day. Henry's character has solid qualities which Shakspere must have admired, and he has made him the instrument of a ringing rhetoric which resounds through the long avenues of time. Three centuries after the play was first produced, one of the greatest of American actors almost ruined himself financially in the attempt to give it a fitting revival; and in this year of Grace, 1915, the English soldiers in the trenches of Flanders have recited its stirring lines to encourage each other to the assault. When we remember that 'Henry V' addressed itself in a peculiar fashion to the spirit of the Elizabethan age, when we recall the enormous changes in political, social and religious opinion that have taken place since, the amazing thing is that the play still appeals to a modern audience and that the breath of life with which Shakspere inspired Henry's heroic figure has preserved him, not indeed as an ideal, but as a human personality with striking resemblances to people whom, under very different conditions, we see about us at the present day. It is his common humanity that endears him to us, his high courage, his modesty, his plain-speaking, his good-humor, and his practical common-sense.

XIV

SCHOOL PRODUCTION OF SHAKSPERE'S PLAYS

By ALLAN ABBOTT

*Assistant Professor of English
in Teachers College*

SCHOOL PRODUCTION OF SHAKSPERE'S PLAYS

What Shakspere himself thought of boy actors is apparently clear from the "little eyases" passage in Hamlet; even Hamlet and Rosencrantz can for once find common ground, in scorn of their elocutionary excesses and their impertinence in offering to compete with regular actors. Shakspere, to be sure, had something at stake; the boys carried it away, Hercules and his load too; in days when all the popular playwrights were composing for the children of Paul's, the management of the Globe might well have looked at these forward lads much as a Broadway producer regards the moving pictures. The indignation of Hamlet and Rosencrantz is reserved for boys on the professional stage; it does not touch what must have been a commonplace to Shakspere, the performance of academic plays within school and college walls. The endebtedness of Shakspere and his colleagues to these school performances must have been evident to him, as to us. While he may have lacked the knowledge now at hand of the well marked steps from the school play in Latin, as an aid to language study, through the schoolmaster's translation, adaptation, or imitation of the Udall or Mulcaster type, to the establishment of the traditions of Plautus and Terence and Seneca on the public stage, he cannot have escaped knowing that Kyd and Lodge had been Merchant-Taylor boys under Mulcaster; that Lodge and Peele had both acted at Oxford and had begun their career as dramatists by writing for school and college production; indeed, that the Senecan rhetoric of his own early tragedies, and the euphuism of his early comedies, had a direct ancestry in the academic play. Not only among dramatists but at court, and among thinking people generally, such plays were looked upon with serious consideration.

The values assigned to school plays in Elizabethan times may afford some suggestion of value in considering similar productions in modern schools. From the original aim to afford practice in spoken Latin came a similar elocutionary purpose with regard to English. This purely academic aim expanded until, as summed up by Bacon, it included the development of the memory, voice, good pronunciation, decent carriage of the body, gesture and assurance. Educational reformers like Comenius saw larger possibilities—what in the educational language of to-day would be called social values. "There must be movement, spontaneity, sociability, friendly emulation, distinct rules, good example, and relaxation of mind." In the minds of the boys and their masters, meanwhile, the frequent opportunity to act before the court aroused a natural ambition not to bore the court, and so led to active study and experiment in dramatic art. One cannot doubt that the serious attention to acted classical drama in the schools of Shakspere's time and earlier brought a rich return to the boys individually, and reacted favorably on the developing drama of the age.

In our own day, the eminent place then held by Plautus and Seneca as models for dramatists to follow has been lost; one can but wonder if a similarly stimulating force in modern education might not be found in the acting of Shakspere, with a frequency and seriousness of purpose far from common in our schools. All the ends, both of pleasure and profit, whether elocutionary or social, as enumerated by Bacon and Comenius, are as much to be desired as ever; and they can be attained through Shakspere far more effectively than they were through the classical plays, just in proportion as Shakspere more adequately embodies the life and ideals of our own race. Furthermore, a growing realization that drama lives not in books but only in action, and that in most communities even the half-dozen stage favorites of Shakspere are seldom seen, and the other plays never, gives our schools the social motive to maintain their claim to community leadership by keeping these plays, our greatest literary inheritance, alive in the hearts of men.

Unhappily, however, many school boys exhibit a marked reluctance to produce Shakspere at all; and unless this reluctance can be overcome, either by bringing them nearer to Shakspere or Shakspere nearer to them, it may spread—if it has not already done so—to an equal disinclination to attend the plays or to read them.

The schoolboy's unwillingness to act Shakspere is traceable to current traditions of school dramatics, of professional acting of Shakspere, and of class-room teaching. Dramatics, in too many schools, are conducted with no worthy or particularly interesting end in view; the range is apt to be from vaudeville or vapid farces of what passes for college life, to the reproduction of recent comedies of the public stage. In the latter case, long periods of rehearsal under anxious coaching, helped by visits to the professional production, may result in a rendering nearly as effective as that of a third-rate road company, but lacking for the actors value commensurate with the time spent, because the work has been wholly imitative, never creative. The second tradition, that of Shakspere on the stage, makes any such imitation in the case of his plays wholly out of the question. We think of Shakspere's characters as performed by leading actors at the height of their career; they connote Southern and Marlowe, Forbes-Robertson, Irving and Terry, Arnold Daly and Ada Rehan, and a host of others. And on the staging side, they suggest increasingly elaborate productions after the manner of Irving and Tree, brilliant in conception, rich and complicated in their use of all the resources of the electrically lighted picture-frame stage. Anything a school could attempt in imitation either of the acting or the staging must fall hopelessly short. Finally, the tradition of teaching is, not infrequently, that of poring over the text of a single play, week after week, expounding its vocabulary, analyzing its structure, weighing what pseudo-philosophical critics have found in it, handling it, in short, as a treatise rather than as a play. When a teacher suggests acting Shakspere, the boy is apt to fear it will prove more instructive than amusing. So, finding himself between the devil of competition with the "scenic production" of the professional stage, and the deep sea, in which he too long has floundered, of class-room analysis, and lacking any experience of creative dramatic work which might embolden him to take Shakspere into his own hands and interpret him in terms of his own boyish experience, he turns back, naturally enough, to farce or minstrel show.

That this is not the situation in all schools, that on the contrary some have played Shakspere for years, not only with pleasure to the audience, but with stimulating reactions on the actors, may encourage an attempt to outline some of the principles of selecting, arranging and staging Shaksperian plays so as to bring out their great and particular values for high school boys. And these principles all reduce themselves to one—namely, to cut loose from all tradition, academic and theatrical, and to interpret the plays with independence and boldness in terms of schoolboy life and thought. Academic life is notoriously conservative and respectful, not to say worshipful, of the great men of old; it tends to solemnify even the humor of an earlier age. It would do us no harm to take a hint from the title page of Kirkman's Drolls (among which appeared the "merry conceited humours of Bottom the weaver")—"shewn for the merriment and delight of wise men and the ignorant.....by Several Stroleing Players, Fools and Fidlers and Mountebanck's Zanies with loud Laughter and great Applause." This promises drama, at least; for what is drama, if not the moving of an audience to emotional response? The "Mountebanck's Zanies" knew enough to select such plays and parts of plays as they could make effective emotionally; and they had their reward, not only from the ignorant, but from wise men.

The essential thing, then, in selecting and arranging a Shaksperian play for school performance, is to find one that has dominant emotional qualities with which the boy is in hearty accord; that is funny with his fun, tragic with his grief, stirring with his ambitions; and to simplify the expression of these emotions by omitting scenes of too great maturity or complexity, by cutting down the rhetorical speeches and witty flourishes, even the passages of sustained thought or poetry, that would have for him an intellectual rather than an emotional appeal. It will help the conscience, in this ruthless cutting, to recall how little respect the Elizabethans had for the integrity of their own texts, and how far we now are from the taste of that time, which demanded plays crowded with every incident, character, and effect that could be drawn in.

Taken frankly at their simpler and more obvious emotional values—those values that would have reached the part of the audience in the Yard—Shakspere's plays cover a considerable range of a boy's mental life. A glance through those that are at all possible for this purpose will reveal the dominant emotion, and the aspects that should be "played up" in schoolboy production.

Of the comedies, those most frequently played professionally— 'As You Like It,' the 'Merchant,' 'Much Ado'—are essentially romantic-heroine plays, plays for a company with some brilliant actress at the head; and so less suited to school boy production than others. 'Midsummer Night's Dream,' given in schools often enough, is best adapted to elementary schools and girls' schools, the mature high school lad being somewhat impatient of fairies. The 'Tempest' is very alluring to a coeducational school that has strong courses in music and art; stressing scenery and costume, dance and song, a very pretty spectacular play could be produced; but the emotional tone is distinctly mature— Shakspere himself came to it late. But 'Love's Labor's Lost,' the 'Comedy of Errors,' the 'Shrew,' 'Merry Wives,' and 'Twelfth Night,' are very boyish in their appeal, and if adequately cut, not too difficult to act.

'Love's Labor's Lost' is built around a boyish idea, the vow to keep away from girls. Any boy could understand that—it is normal adolescent psychology. The plot unfolds simply enough; the characterization—what there is of it—presents no difficulties. Biron himself acts just like a clever schoolboy; and Armado and Holofernes are caricatures of the type boys draw in their text books. The verbal humor and parody on which the play depends, Holofernes' scraps of school Latin, the Malapropisms of Costard and Dull, the quibbles and smart retorts of the principals, are quite in the approved manner of schoolboy wit. Such wit at great length grows tiresome; whole scenes, and many scattered passages, can be cut away—the last scene, for instance, is twice as long as Shakspere ever allowed himself to make a comedy scene again—but a well chosen hâlf of Love's Labor's Lost should be very good fun with a bright school cast.

The 'Comedy of Errors' is boyish in another way, and is so short it hardly needs cutting at all. Its frankly farcical appeal, its double confusion of identity, its frequent quarrels and thrashings, are all very near the rough physical humor of the boy. Of course the Dromios make the play, and to throw them into even sharper relief it is possible to reduce the longer speeches, the complication of the wives, and the including story of the parents.

The Shrew seems to demand an actress with both wit and charm, an Ada Rehan. But does it, in its essentials? Katharine is after all the prototype of the too clever and tyrannical girl whom the boys fear while they admire, and would like to humble. In the hands of a great actress, she is far more; but even at this, she is sufficient to make the play. The Induction may be omitted, and the Bianca story suggested with just enough detail to account for the main situation, rather than developed in full.

The 'Merry Wives of Windsor' resolves itself, for boys, into the three tricks against Falstaff, taken just as pranks. The jealous humours of Ford, the bombast of Pistol, the Welsh fritters that Evans makes of his English, are not as amusing now as when they were written; they, and the sub-plot of the wooing of Ann Page, can be greatly reduced; so can much of the dialog in the Falstaff scenes. The play as it stands runs to twenty-eight hundred lines, far too long for school performance.

'Twelfth Night' has a much greater variety of comedy elements than any of the earlier plays, yet it remains for the most part within the court of boydom. Fortunately, the diverse elements are distributed among contrasting characters; Viola, to be sure, ranges from grave to gay, and touches all the plots in turn, but Viola makes no such demand on a boy actor as would Rosalind or Beatrice or Portia, especially if the romantic element be reduced. A school performance would at least be free from the common fault of professionals in this play, that of taking the romantic elements too seriously; making the shipwreck a real tragedy, and the sentimental duke (whose mawkishness gets from boys the same response it did from his courtiers) a true lover playing for sympathy. The Toby-Malvolio elements can be played by boys practically in full, with great gusto. The clown's part demands cleverness and good fellowship of a kind common among schoolboys, together with a singing voice not so common, yet not beyond hoping for. Cutting should result in suppressing, in large measure, the Duke, Sebastian, and Antonio, and as in the other plays, omitting the verbal quips dear to the Elizabethan mind.

Of the history plays, the best suited to school production are those centering about Henry V. The play of King Henry V itself has the advantage of consisting almost wholly of splendid declamation of simple, if somewhat Jingoistic, patriotism, and the disadvantage of assigning all these speeches to the same actor. Some of Henry's speeches would surely have to be sacrificed, in view of the limitations of schoolboy memory and declamatory power. But the need for supporting pantomime by large numbers of armed followers affords a great number of the pupils opportunity to shine in armour and to thrill with patriotic ardor at little expense of the intellect. The camp scenes, like the low comedy scenes in the earlier plays, contain enough boisterous horse-play and obvious burlesque of character-types to please. Pistol needs to be partly suppressed, as his humours are mainly Elizabethan; but in the main, the adaptation of the play would consist of reducing the burden on the boy acting Henry, omitting the nondramatic conferences and parleys, such as the greater part of Act I, and working up the rest into a military pageant. In one school performance, scenes from Henry IV, Parts I and II, were combined with parts of Henry V, exhibiting the change in the scapegrace hero in a single play, instead of the Shaksperian trilogy. One has to choose, in this case, between overcrowding the plot and too great sketchiness; on the whole, it seems better to make a separate play of the roystering prince scenes from the earlier plays.

The declamatory nature of Henry's battle speeches suggests several of the tragedies as equally possible. 'Coriolanus' has been very effectively given in a boys' school; the patriotic atmosphere, the bickerings and jealousies, the violent unreasonableness of the mob, the self-will and the injured pride of Coriolanus, are all sufficiently objective to appeal strongly. The needed reduction of over-elaborate Elizabethan rhetoric was accomplished by cutting down speech after speech to the opening few lines. 'Julius Caesar,' for obvious reasons, is the one tragedy most often attempted; it invites unfair comparison with great actors, especially in the parts of Brutus and Antony, but even these parts, taken for their simpler and more fundamental values, can be acted by boys with effective power, and the fine declamatory passages, the patriotism, the analysis of civic ideals and political methods, and the spectacular features of mob and army, will reach the hearts of boys and may be vigorously portrayed by them.

The play that, were it not for the halo of scholarly debate and of unapproachable ideals of stage representation surrounding it, would be most tempting to an ambitious school is, if one may dare to say it, Hamlet. Could we but strip our minds of all memories of Forbes-Robertson and Irving and Booth, of all the philosophy of Goethe and Coleridge and Schlegel, of all that the romantic turn of modern thought has read into the play, might we not see it much more simply, and perhaps more nearly as Shakspere meant? Whatever the gain in philosophic power, there is surely a loss in dramatic truth, when Hamlet must be presented by a man of ripe maturity, whose hesitation before his life problem may well make the judicious grieve. For after all, Hamlet, whether eighteen or thirty or somewhere between, is a student suddenly called to a man's responsibilities; as a school boy once said to the writer, "Hamlet is a young man's story; we fellows are just finding out there is trouble in the world for us to face, and that's what Hamlet had, too." The more mature, thoughtful type of school or college lad is apt, like Hamlet, to try to erect his particular experiences into universals; to philosophize, pessimistically, on this world and the next; to dally with the thought of suicide; to be blocked in necessary acts by mistrust of others, of himself, of the supernatural; yet to remain so far from confirmed in this mood that he can still excel in manly contests of strength or of wits, can take pleasure in the art of the theater and the news from town, and when the immediate need comes, can act with manly vigor. Yes, I should like to see a thoughtful school or college boy in Hamlet.

If discarding the accretions of modern thought brings Shakspere nearer to the boy, and perhaps nearer also to his own times, all the more may discarding modern stage methods do so. The objection to any attempt to reproduce Beerbohm-Tree stage pictures is not alone the utter impossibility of success; it is that even when successful, these pictures kill the play. Not even the best actors can talk them down. School productions are happily free from this temptation; they may approach in this respect also the admirable amateur standard of Kirkman's Drolls, which were played in Bartholomew Fair in London and divers country fairs, and apparently almost anywhere else, indoors or out.

The outdoor production has heretofore been most successful in schools. Conditions are more free and natural; there is less temptation to imitate the artificialities of the theater, more need for unrestricted and bold impersonation, for letting oneself go. Moreover, there has been stimulating example, in the outdoor productions of players like Mr. Greet and the Coburns, with whom the play, not the staging, is the thing. Outdoor production is to be recommended wherever a school is so fortunate as to have the few essential conditions. These are: a reasonable hope of settled weather at the time the play is to be given; absolute quiet in the surroundings—there can be no acting against the clatter of trolley cars; a slightly hollowed lawn sloping gently down to a background of trees or knoll or rock; and adequate light. With clumps of shrubbery—preferably natural, but if it must be, placed on purpose—for wings and tiring-house and a few moveable benches and tables, the play may be given all the better for lack of stage, curtain, or set scenery.

Within doors, the very difficulties of the school auditorium or gymnasium floor, that are the bane of most school dramatics, may be the making of the Shaksperian play. The recent theatric art that has developed since Gordon Craig began his experiments affords two types of staging that are at once more practicable under school conditions, and more close to Elizabethan practice, than modern staging with flat scenery; these are the curtain and the screen settings. In principle, they are alike in that they consist of simple, harmonious backgrounds, neutral in tone, that do not definitely locate the scene; the platform so decorated corresponds exactly to the Shaksperian unpropertied forestage. Against this neutral background, which may be illuminated so as to suggest the emotional tone of the scene, the actors stand out in strongly colored and characterizing costume; they do not have to compete with the setting, but are thrown into relief by it. Where definite indication of place is desired—and this will be in comparatively few scenes—the scene is symbolized by one or two simple, effective properties; a shrub here, a garden bench there. The imagination readily expands these so that the whole stage becomes their proper location. It is sometimes possible on a school platform to approximate the Elizabethan stage even more closely, by arranging an inner stage more fully propertied; but there is danger here of diverting attention from the actors to the decoration. Simple curtains or screens are better.

The various kinds of simplification suggested throughout this essay—simplifications of staging, of plot, of dialog, of character interpretation—should at least have the effect of removing from the schoolboy's mind apprehensions arising from the more severe standards of the classroom and the theater. Will they also remove the qualities that make Shakspere what he is—that make him worthy of study or representation at all? Not if the simplifications are made in a spirit of sincerity and truth; of truth to human nature, especially boy nature, as we have insight to understand it, of sincerity in demanding of the boy actor adequate expression of the emotions, and those only, that befit his time of life. His lighter emotions—the boisterous fun of rough and tumble farce, the delight in caricaturing familiar types, that tang of witty retort, pun, or verbal distortion, those staples of school-boy humor—Shakspere affords in astonishing abundance. We like to say, when on our academic dignity, that he wrote such scenes to please the rabble in the pit; but the zest, the gusto, with which they are written, the vitality with which the Dromios, Falstaff and Toby, Fluellen and Bottom, survive the centuries, compel us to admit in more intelligent moments that he wrote them to please himself. And on the more serious side of boyish life and thought—more serious, often, in its tragic facts, in its passionate ideal, than we oldsters remember—there remains after all reasonable subtractions much that the boy can get from Henry's simple manliness, from the conflict of political ideals in the Roman plays, from Hamlet confronting the eternal problem of manhood's responsibilities, to establish his feet on a road that climbs high and far.

XV

AMERICAN EDITORS OF SHAKSPERE

By Harrison Ross Steeves

Assistant Professor of English

AMERICAN EDITORS OF SHAKSPERE

Scholarship has always seemed to the mind of the outsider to be made up in no small measure of dry-as-dust pursuits; and as a natural corollary to this suspicion, one is likely to find a very strong conviction that the study of scholarship itself is something in which there can by no possibility be a saving interest. One might imagine Dr. Johnson, if he lived to-day, transferring his distaste for the "mere antiquarian" to the mere bibliographer. There is some reason, too, in the general prejudice, as one can easily find out if he will glance over the bibliography of a subject foreign to his own interests. Shaksperian scholarship, however, is as little touched by the inevitable dullness as any subject could possibly be. It has assets of interest in its bulk, its vitality, its personalities, which are to be equalled only in the history of classical scholarship; and this makes its history, or any light upon its history, something more than a matter of merely pedantic concern. The editing of Shakspere has almost always turned out to be a very human occupation. Why, it may be hard to say, unless because of some occult transfusion of the playwright's humanity. Shaksperian scholarship is in itself of highly dramatic interest, colored with controversies, grim or comical, punctuated with wrecked reputations. It is also, for the literary student, a more or less adequate measure of the intellectual temper of whole peoples and periods.

The history of American Shaksperian scholarship, in particular, is of interest to Americans for other than merely patriotic reasons. It is a valuable record of the growth of our literary needs and critical views, and an index of the development of scholarly purpose generally. Looking, then, at the history of editions of Shakspere in America as a review of the general flux of comment and controversy, rather than as a tally of the changes in textual scholarship, we may hope to find in what America has done with and for Shakspere some light upon personalities, and upon the development of American literary taste; and we may be able to measure in a general way the extent of the independent scholarly contribution of American editors.[1]

American Shakspere scholarship has, in the main, followed the trend of British and German scholarship from romantic criticism and commentary, and minute exposition, to restrained and conservative textual editing. There were of course no developed scholarly traditions in America during the period when Shaksperian study was emerging from opinions and fancies into a matter of intelligent interest. With the intellectual expansion of America in the first half of the nineteenth century, however, it was inevitable that the industry of Malone and his successors should be reflected in the work of American scholars. Even so, to-day the strictly American editions of Shakspere could be numbered almost upon one's fingers; yet it is no mere pretension to say that at least two of these editions, Grant White's and Furness's, have had a conspicuous critical importance.

The first complete edition of Shakspere printed in America comes relatively late in our history as a publishing nation, yet it possesses the distinction, according to Mr. Jaggard, of being "the first printed outside of the British Isles." The primacy of this edition is more conspicuous because of the fact that the frontispiece to the first volume, an embellished engraving of the Chandos portrait, was the first portrait of Shakspere published in America. The issue is now exceedingly rare; only twelve copies are known to exist, of which four are imperfect. A perfect set was offered by a New York bookseller in 1904 at two hundred and fifty dollars, probably a higher price than could be got for any other edition subsequent to the four folios.

The text of this edition is evidently an eclectic one, as it is stated in the preface to be "taken from the latest and most ap-

---

[1] A history of American editions of Shakspere, not wholly complete, even for the period it covers, but a fairly adequate view of the subject, was published by Dr. Karl Knortz in 1882. Miss Jane Scherzer's admirable bibliographical analysis of American editions down to Richard Grant White's was printed in the *Publications of the Modern Language Association of America* in 1907. The writer did not see Miss Scherzer's study until his own investigations were practically completed; the limitation of the period which Miss Scherzer has covered, however, and the fact that the emphasis in her article was placed upon questions of text, seem to justify the publication of the present paper, which differs from hers, in addition, upon some questions of opinion.

proved London editions." The "apparatus" of the edition, however, is so slight, and so badly proportioned to the questions of
importance connected with the separate plays, that it is practically useless. There are no explanatory notes, for, as the editor
naively remarks, "An American reader is seldom disposed to
wander through the wilderness of verbal criticism." All the
comment upon the plays is confined in the main to a paragraph
or two of quotation, generally from Johnson, at the end of each
play. There is a glossary; but its adequacy may be judged from
the fact that the editor's difficulties with words of doubtful significance were surmounted by omitting them entirely. *Scamels*,
kibes, *armegaunt* and *ribaud'red*, to take a few as to which an
investigator might naturally feel some curiosity, simply do not
appear.

A very curious fact with regard to the American editor's preface is that at least two-thirds of its bulk is devoted to an
elaborate defense of Shakspere against the charge of immorality.
The defense is supported principally by the contention, frequently
reiterated, that the writers of the Restoration and the Eighteenth
century were a great deal worse. This question of morality,
together with that of the underlying sincerity of Shakspere's
aims is to the editor a very grave one. "The fools of Shakspere,"
he says, "are always despised, and his villains always hated. If
any one of the vicious characters in this writer can be termed
seductive, it must be Falstaff; yet he is on every occasion overwhelmed with such ridicule and contempt that no reader can envy
his situation, and Shakspere, in the sequel, dismisses him to an
excess of neglect and ignominy that may hurt the sensibility even
of the severest moralist." The conclusion of the discussion is that
we have in Shakspere so glittering an array of moral sentiments
that we can be quite sure of his soundness; though we must
admit that he is the victim of the very frivolous manner of his
age.

There is, on the whole, little reason for pride in the scholarship
of this first American edition. Those who had it in hand were
simply not equipped to discern or to satisfy the needs of the average reader of an old dramatist; so it is in a way distinctly more
encouraging to find the next publishers of Shakspere drawing

freely and admittedly from the best of contemporary British scholars.

The Philadelphia publication was followed by an eight volume Shakspere published in Boston, in 1802-4. This edition, however, is reputed to be a reprint of that of Edinburgh, 1792. The third American edition, issued in Philadelphia in 1809, was nominally from Isaac Reed's edition, but it is said by the compiler of the catalog of the Barton Collection that Joseph Dennie exercised some editorial discretion upon the work. Two other editions were issued, one in Boston in 1813, and one in New York, in 1821, both based on Reed, and both reprinted once; but these, like their predecessors, laid absolutely no claim to constructive scholarship. The editors seem in no case to have done anything more than use their ingenuity upon the material accumulated by British editors, particularly Malone, Steevens, and Reed.

An edition appeared at Boston in 1836, however, which was in some respects original. Although no editor's name appears in any part of the edition, it is known that O. W. B. Peabody saw the publication through the press. He based his text upon the First Folio, re-editing Singer's notes, and using his introductions to the separate plays. He also abbreviated Charles Symmons' life of Shakspere, which had appeared originally in Singer's Chiswick Edition of 1826, and supplemented this shortened biography with a reprint of Collier's 'New Facts regarding the Life of Shakspere.' This was, in fact, the first form in which the 'New Facts' appeared in the United States. Peabody's edition is plainly not of high importance, as it involved nothing more than the working over of material then very much esteemed; for Singer's edition was at that time in great demand, and was reprinted frequently in America.

In the decade between the publication of Peabody's edition and the completion of Verplanck's, in 1847, three other American imprints appeared, differing in no essential respect from previous eclectic editions. The distinction between a pirated edition and one which makes legitimate use of the accruing fund of scholarship is of course not always wholly clear; but for our purposes we may assume that original editorial work should involve more than the exercise of mere discretion upon questions of historical fact, criticism, and conjecture. For this reason it may be said that down to the time of Peabody possibly, Verplanck certainly, no such thing as original Shaksperian scholarship existed in America.

Verplanck had only slight access to the remoter sources of information, and embarked upon his edition with no intention of contributing further to the sum of knowledge and conjecture than the majority of his predecessors in America had done. His own sincerity and literary interest, however, enabled him to produce finally an edition which, although not masterly in a purely scholarly sense, still is consistent and intelligent in its handling of fundamental problems. Verplanck's edition was brought out in three volumes by Harper and Brothers, New York, from 1844 to 1847.

Bred in New York, with the independence and the traditions of the society of the place—including, then, education at Columbia—Verplanck had a multiplicity of interests and occupations which, however much they may have contributed to his experience of men and affairs, were scarcely likely to set him up as a critical editor. His principal distinction came from his professorship in the Evidences of Christianity at the General Theological Seminary in New York, and his later service as a member of the State legislature. He was also a rather fertile writer upon topics of public interest, legal, educational, historical, political, literary and religious.

The principal items in Verplanck's equipment for the editing of Shakspere were his courage and his common sense. He himself was sceptical of the need of a new edition of Shakspere, and especially of an American edition. This edition was, in fact, projected as in no sense an editorial departure, but as an "elegant" publication in the early Victorian manner. Verplanck accepted the Harpers' proposal that he should bring the work out, with the ingenuous admission that recent editorial work, especially that of Collier, would make it "not at all difficult" to produce an acceptable issue. Collier's text, indeed, was actually made the basis of Verplanck's; but, as the work progressed and Verplanck found himself differing from Collier, he started upon independent investigation, the fruits of which

are embodied in his introductions to the separate plays. His
textual policy was simple and sane—to defer to the First Folio,
but not to idolize it, to accept reasonable emendations, and to
retain all the readings in which there was any possible meaning.
In his use of notes, Verplanck followed the custom of most of his
predecessors in appropriating comment from Malone, Knight,
Collier and others, following the unwise practice of not men-
tioning the editors he quoted, but signing his original notes.
His annotations are in the main sensible and not superfluous;
and his introductions show undoubted capacity to weigh the
evidence at hand, especially with reference to the various periods
of Shakspere's production.

It is not, after all, surprising that the theologian and legislator
possessed qualities as an editor at once fairly philosophic and
judicial. In spite of the fact that Verplanck was unfortunately
free from most of the strictly professional qualifications of the
editor of Shakspere, he nevertheless gave to his readers thoughtful and at times penetrating comment. Whipple, indeed, has
said that Verplanck's introductions were "the first connected
attempt to trace out Shakspere's intellectual history and character." It was impossible, however, that a piece of work undertaken so lightly should rank very high. With all Verplanck's
seriousness and industry, the fact remains that his edition is
lacking in originality and in scholarship, and is therefore not to
be placed in the same class as the editions of two of his immediate
successors, Hudson and Grant White.

Henry Norman Hudson, who, while he was laboring as a
farm-hand, earned and borrowed the money to attend. Middle-
bury College, was afterwards successively teacher, preacher,
and itinerant lecturer. With an intense attachment to the works
of Shakspere and a literary taste of some purity he produced a
series of lectures upon Shakspere which he delivered in the South
and Middle West in 1843, while these sections were still young
in culture. Hudson succeeded in gaining an audience in Boston,
and after his acceptance there, it was not a difficult thing for him
to carry his success to the other important Eastern cities. His
lectures were published in 1848; and with the added reputation
that this publication gave him, he undertook to edit a new

Shakspere for Monroe and Company of Boston. This edition, generally regarded as the first in America of anything like scholarly seriousness and magnitude, was brought out in eleven volumes from 1851 to 1856.

The particular qualities which made Hudson a competent editor of Shakspere were those which made good English critics in the generation preceding his own. He was an admiring follower of Coleridge, whom he frankly looked upon as the greatest of the critical order. What Hudson had already given a nation aspiring for things intellectual, he gave again in his edition of Shakspere's works; but his introductions, embodying much of the substance of his lectures, must be admitted to be considerably superior to his notes. Looked at, however, from the standpoint of Hudson's purpose— to produce not a scholar's edition, but a popular one—even the notes may seem to have a real value, although their bulk is rather embarrassing to the reader, their obviousness is frequently rather irritating, and they are in some instances careless and even absurd.

Hudson's edition was modeled generally upon Singer's Chiswick edition of 1826, both in form and plan. The editor began, indeed, simply to re-edit this text for American readers, but, like Verplanck, altered his purpose when the fatal impulse seized him to make his own text. He announced his editorial policy as conservative, his text being based when possible upon the 1623 Folio—but not too conservative, since, to his mind, both Collier and Knight had erred upon that side. What is most alluring in Hudson's prospectus is his resolution to make his notes both simple and compact. Alas for the good intention; they are only less to be criticised upon these lines than those of his predecessors. Enlightened as he was upon the need of a new principle of annotation, his own notes, especially the etymological ones, are very frequently intrusive, and sometimes controversial and even provocative. Speaking generally, they tempt one to the belief that his sense of his own erudition was more present with him than that of his readers' needs; for many of the notes shed more light upon the habits and institutions of the Elizabethan age than upon the text itself. In addition, he adopted the very unsound practice of signing only his own annotations, and this practice, of course, concealed the sources of much of the editorial comment.

It is fair to Hudson, as well as a tangible justification for these criticisms, to cite an annotated passage taken almost at random from his edition.   In the concluding lines of Act IV of the 'Two Gentlemen of Verona,' Julia, looking upon Silvia's picture, is soliloquizing:

> Her hair is auburn; mine is perfect yellow:
> If that be all the difference in his love,
> I'll get me such a colour'd periwig.
> Her eyes are grey as glass; and so are mine:
> Ay, but her forehead's low, and mine's as high.
> What should it be that he respects in her,
> But I can make respective in myself,
> If this fond love were not a blinded god?
> . . . .
> . . . . O thou senseless form!
> Thou shalt be worshipp'd, kiss'd, lov'd, and ador'd;
> And, were there sense in his idolatry,   .
> My substance should be statue in thy stead.

By way of comment on the word "periwig," Hudson takes pains to tell us that "false hair was much worn by ladies in Shakespeare's time," and quotes two fairly long passages to prove it. "Grey eyes," he explains, "were what to-day we call blue; glass was at that time of a light blue tint." Clearly, neither of these notes throws any real light upon the substance or the purpose of Julia's speech. "A high forehead," he continues, "was then accounted a feature eminently beautiful. Our author, in the 'Tempest,' shows that low foreheads were in disesteem: 'Apes with foreheads villainous low.' " This fact, however, could scarcely be put more plainly than in Julia's words. The lines,

> What should it be that he respects in her,
> But I can make respective in myself,

he paraphrases: "What he respects in her has equal relation to myself"; certainly a very bad interpretation, though that is beside the present point.[1]   In explaining 'statue,' which would

---

[1] In the Harvard Edition, 1880, Hudson gave a more acceptable definition of *respective: respectable*. Even this, however, is evidently not the meaning that the context would indicate, i.e., to be respected.

appear simply from the context to mean '*picture*,' he once again descends to the tedious business of quoting two passages from Stowe and Massinger to prove the correctness of a fairly obvious gloss. It cannot be denied that it is largely because of such over-scrupulous annotation that an editor of to-day can confine almost all the necessary information upon these points to an indexed glossary; but such annotation also shows the flash of truth in Lowell's remark, that "he who loves the comic side of human nature will find the serious notes of a variorum edition of Shakspere as funny reading as the funny ones are serious."

Hudson's credulousness as to the need of minute emendation is in a way a reflection of his veneration for the word. Happily, however, the next generation of scholars were to succeed in removing from the ordinary text the machinery of conjecture which so often impeded reading and therefore affected the reader's interest. Akin to Hudson's reverential feeling for all that demands explanation, is a tendency to pious idolatry of Shakspere, especially in the 'Life,' which appeared in his concluding volume. This idolatry is seen in a rather rash disposition to interpret historic facts in terms of character, and in the assumption of uniform excellence of purpose and workmanship throughout all the plays. Here again, of course, one can hear the echoes of Coleridge. In these faults, however, Hudson was scarcely behind his time in critical view and habit.

It must not be supposed from these strictures that Hudson's edition went unwelcomed or unpraised. On the contrary, his contemporaries, and not only those in America, were much impressed with its merits. If he was at times paternal in his attitude toward his reader, or too expansively eloquent in his praise of his subject, we should in justice to him consider his readers—not so cultivated but that even Dickens could point out their deficiencies. That Hudson's editorial work is unnecessarily "aesthetic," and at times didactic, is no sign of his failure to adapt himself to his readers, but quite the reverse. The man who had lectured with distinction to hundreds of typical American audiences of that day could scarcely be accused of ignorance of their mental make-up. Criticism of Hudson is in fact an arraignment of our intellectual status in the mid-century:

Hudson's capacity as an editor was, and is, in some respects high. He was not wanting in erudition, nor in acumen: witness his distrust of the readings of Collier's 1632 Folio; and his faults are, when we sum them all up, largely those of supererogation.

In his descending years Hudson appeared again as editor of Shakspere, first in 1870-74, in an edition adapted to school purposes, and afterwards in the Harvard Edition, issued in 1880 as a careful revision and rearrangement of his first issue. It does not need an intensive examination of this last edition, however, to show that the aging scholar belonged to a past generation of Shakesperian students.

Another edition which must be recorded as an American edition is George Long Duyckinck's issue of Collier's 'Works of Shakespeare,' which appeared in London in 1853. Duyckinck's edition, in eight volumes, was published in New York in the same year. The text of Collier's edition of 1853, it may be remembered, was that of the so-called corrected Folio of 1632, the authority of which has, of course, wholly disappeared in the light of expert scrutiny. Since Collier's second edition contained no notes whatever, Duyckinck took all his preliminary material from Collier's first edition, of 1844, and referred to this edition also for purposes of textual comparison. The notes to Duyckinck's edition were garnered from the works of practically all the contemporary scholars, including Collier, Knight, Dyce, Halliwell, Verplanck, and Hudson, and there are a few instances in which he supplied notes himself. It will be readily seen from this description that Duyckinck's editorial labors contributed little to our stock of information or conjecture; and the fact that his work is attached to a notoriously corrupt text almost entirely vitiates any value it might otherwise possess. Another publication of Collier's "corrected text," with eclectic notes, was that of J. L. Jewett, published in New York in 1855.

The American edition which has generally been accepted as possessing a merit and importance comparable with that of the best British editions, is Richard Grant White's, published in twelve volumes, from 1857 to 1866. Its reputation is not altogether misjudged, although, as Miss Sherzer has pointed out, the basis of its merit is insight and general carefulness in workmanship, rather than originality or distinctly new critical purpose. White was diversely and largely endowed as an editor. He came of the oldest New England stock, was the heritor of cultivated traditions, possessed fine aesthetic perceptions in many fields of art—in the plastic arts and music in addition to literature—and had felt enough of the pinch of necessity during his early years to save him from dilettantism. His edition was the product of many years of industrious study of Shaksperian scholarship, and for this reason had little of the superficiality and pretentiousness of Hudson's.

The preface of White's edition is an intelligent announcement of the canons of editing which he recognized, few of which, and those the less significant, were wholly new. Even though White is in no important sense a pioneer, the fact remains that both in purpose and practice, he shows a knowledge and command of the business of editing which made his edition decidedly superior to any that had hitherto appeared in America. "At best," he wrote, "an editor, like a physician or a lawyer, is a necessary evil," and working upon this conviction, he made his particular task the avoidance of the unnecessary. On the other hand, he expressed a firm faith in the dignity and prerogatives of the editor, as laid down by Porson; and upon this faith he built a sound and generally intelligent system of critical practice. Recognizing Shakspere scholarship as a special problem, he accepted the 1623 folio as in general the most authentic text, but made full allowance for the authority of the quartos. In many matters of editorial detail he endeavored to introduce, and did introduce, consistent handling of the text. He insisted, for example, upon the retention of orthographic and grammatical forms, even where they were unusual, or, from the modern standpoint, wrong; and this because he saw these forms as concrete records of usage and linguistic flux. It was he who first followed with consistency the original printing of the full and contracted forms of the past participle in *ed*, and who pointed out the special nature of the elision in such words as *sland'red*, not merely because the meter was in many cases affected by carelessness upon this point, but because such forms indicated, if not a customary, at any rate a preferred pronunciation. He was the first to insist upon the preservation of *it* in the possessive case. Care upon these points shows a distinctly high sense of what is or is not important. In addition he was sponsor for some improvements in editorial practice. All the notes which he quoted, for example, were identified by their authors' names, although the tracing of authorship was in some cases very laborious. He endeavored to give a history of important emendations and glosses, and to give authentic credit for restored readings. Considering the lack of system of previous editors, with regard to such matters—or the lack of honesty, as Halliwell called it—White's departure in these respects is an important assertion of scholarly conscience.

White's particularity, however, had definite and sensible bounds. "It has been a point in the preparation of this work," he says, "to give results rather than processes." The edition contains a minimum of annotation for the general reader, but a nearly complete record of textual variants, for it had the large design of meeting also the wants of scholarly readers. Aesthetic comments find no place whatever. This is "a department of Shaksperian literature," he observes, "with which my acquaintance is merely casual, and very limited. In the purely editorial part of his work, it is, in my judgment, an editor's business simply to enable the reader to possess and understand his author."

In a word, White's policy is the combination of common sense with the increasingly strict requirements of modern scholarship. It is not epoch-making in the sense that its scholarship is impeccable; but if any single edition clearly marks the transition from the early Victorian to the modern sense of editorial responsibility, White's is that one.

The specific merits and faults of this edition have been covered very adequately in Lowell's distinguished review;[1] so it is scarcely necessary here to deal with them extensively. Briefly, Lowell has very warm commendation for White's judgment, critical discrimination, and restraint. The edition is to his mind, "distinctly better than its predecessors," and this pronouncement must be kept in view in the face of the fact that Lowell produces a rather startling array of questionable emendations, and attacks

---

[1] *Atlantic Monthly*, III, 111-21, 241-60. Miss Sherzer has given a résumé of the important points in Lowell's criticism.

the editor forcefully with regard to his etymological notes and
his disordered views of Shakspere's pronunciation.   Lowell's
specific objections to White's readings are generally well taken,
although the particular instance upon which he rests the burden
of his case—the retention of *chroniclers* instead of *coroners* in 'As
You Like It,' IV, i, 105—is still open to scholarly opinion. With all
the faults before us which Lowell enumerates, however, the fact
remains that he regarded the edition as distinctive and thoroughly
worthy.   It seems, therefore, quite wrong to deny it a special
eminence simply because the editor exhibited lapses in what was
frankly and in the strictest sense editorial work; for as against
these lapses, we have for the first time a generally consistent and
practical adherence to the lines of editorial policy which he
adopted—and these constitute, in the main, a definition of the
purposes and methods of modern scholarship.

It has already been pointed out that White's Shakspere was
"designed to meet the wants of all readers"; and the fact that the
editor has so successfully combined the aids for the uncritical
reader with the textual evidence required for the scholar constitutes not the least of his claims to distinction.   The avowedly
popular aim of the edition, however, must be in some degree a
drawback to purely scholarly use.   The editor is forced, for
example, to pass judgment upon questions of dispute, because
for the purposes of such an edition a verdict must be rendered.
For this reason he was one of the first to admit the superiority
of the Cambridge edition, which came out from 1863 to 1866.
A perfect scholar's edition was most certainly still a desideratum;
although what a perfect scholarly edition should be was made
pretty clear both by the merits and the shortcomings of White's
edition.

The history of White's reputation as an editor is in part one of
misconceptions as to the critical value of his work, grounded
upon incorrect records of the facts pertaining to the edition itself.
The substance of these errors is that White issued two editions in
succession, one in 1857-60, and the second in 1859-65, in the
first of which he incorporated a large number of the emendations
from Collier's "Perkins folio," and in the second of which he
threw a large part of these "corrections" out.   In point of

fact there was only one issue; the comedies were published in 1857, the histories in 1859, the tragedies in 1862, and the introductory volume in 1866 [1865]. The originator of this error seems to have been Henry G. Bohn, who in his *Biography and Bibliography of Shakspere*, published in 1860, entered White's edition as a completed one, although only seven volumes of the edition had then appeared, and added the statement—wholly untrue—that the edition included one hundred and seventeen emendations from Collier's corrected folio of 1632. The source of the latter item of misinformation was in all probability the announcement of the edition in the *Athenaeum* for July 4, 1857, which assumed that the 117 of Collier's emendations which White had regarded, not as authoritative, but as both original and permissible, would be included in his forthcoming edition. The review of the first four volumes in the *Athenaeum* for November 13, 1858, credited White with having used "considerably more than a hundred" of the Collier readings in these volumes alone. White immediately pointed out in a letter to the *Athenaeum* that his indebtedness to the "anonymous corrector" was less than a quarter as extensive as had been asserted. It is not wholly clear where the impression arose that White issued a second edition immediately; but it is probable that since Bohn recorded White's edition as complete in twelve volumes in 1860, the edition which was generally known to have been completed in 1866, but, through Bohn's error, not generally known to be the only one by White then in existence, was assumed to be a second one. The idea that the non-existent second edition rejected many of Collier's emendations which were supposed to have been received into the assumed first edition, apparently has some indistinct connection with the disclaimer which White addressed to the *Athenaeum*, and also, in all probability, with the fact that White underwent a striking change of mind in regard to the need of general emendation between the time when he wrote his *Shakspeare's Scholar*, in 1854, and the appearance of his edition a few years later.

To-day there are a number of supposedly authoritative entries both of the inaccurate dates of the single issue which White brought out at this time, and of the exaggerated extent of White's indebtedness to Collier. Mr. Jaggard's *Bibliography of Shakspere* and Mr. Saintsbury's bibliography in the *Cambridge History of English Literature* both continue the fiction of the 117 emendations; and the Saintsbury bibliography, followed by Neilson and Thorndike's *Facts about Shakespere*, records the two editions which do not exist. Apparently under the influence of the tradition of the two editions, Mr. Jaggard, although giving correctly the dates of White's edition, states that White was the editor of an earlier eclectic edition in three volumes published by Martin, Johnson & Company, of New York, in 1854-6. This ascription seems to be unsupported by any evidence whatever; and the fact that the "competent Shaksperian scholar" referred to in the preface revealed practically no individual reaction to textual problems makes it extremely unlikely that he can be identified with White, especially when we recall the fact that at this moment White was advocating wholesale emendation in his *Shakspeare's Scholar*.

White returned once again to the editing of Shakspere in 1883, when he prepared the Riverside Shakspere for Houghton, Mifflin & Company. This edition is also a popular one, containing even less apparatus than the first, and in the preface dealing more in detail with methods of inference as applied to textual scholarship. Needless to say, the later edition, while it clearly shows that White had kept pace with Shakspere scholarship, is reworked largely from the previous one, and does not indicate any great advance in point of view or quality. An editor does not produce two remarkable editions of Shakspere in a lifetime. White's original edition has recently been republished after careful revision.

One might imagine that the distinctly scholarly plan and execution of the Cambridge Shakspere would check for some time the aspiration to produce a better. The Cambridge text was based upon a thorough collation of the folios, quartos, and all subsequent editions and commentaries, and was accompanied by a practically complete record of collation and history of emendation. Yet within five years of its completion, in 1866, an editor appeared who considered that the needs of Shakspere scholars were not yet fully satisfied. Furness's view of the

deficiencies of the Cambridge edition were that it did not give the
history of variant readings in the hands of successive editors,
and that it also neglected to record the first editor to adopt a
generally accepted reading.   These omissions were to his mind
important, because they deprived the student of a full opportunity to see the weight of judgment in favor of any reading.
We may also infer from what Furness *did* include in his edition
that he was not of the belief that a scholar's edition should present no more than the absolutely necessary evidence.

Furness's incentive to edit a variorum Shakspere came from
a genuine love of scholarly investigation.   We are told that in
his earliest undergraduate years he had made for his own gratification a variorum copy of Hamlet.   When because of his growing deafness he found the practice of law closed to him, he decided to undertake an edition which should collect the results of
fifty years' scholarship, already ripe for concentrated study and
judgment.   The Variorum was at first planned simply as a supplement to Boswell's Variorum of 1821; it was therefore to contain
all the notes of the 1821 Variorum, except where they were
judged valueless by succeeding editors, and to add the notes from
editions which had appeared subsequently.   As the magnitude of
the plan developed, however, Furness ceased to regard the 1821
Variorum as the starting point of his study, and worked up for
himself the history of scholarship prior to Boswell's edition.

Furness's first volume, Romeo and Juliet, was published in
1871.   The text of the first three volumes was eclectic, representing in the main, though not without exception, "the decisions of
the majority of the ablest editors."   In 'King Lear,' the fourth
volume, the First Folio text was, as Furness said, "virtually
followed, but without, it is to be trusted, an absolute surrender to
that modern Manicheeism, the worship of the printer's devil."
Beginning with the following volume, however, 'Othello,' the
First Folio text was uniformly adopted, on the ground that the
Variorum was a students' edition, and should therefore be based
on the text preumably nearest to the author's manuscript.

The scope of Furness's edition has been variously criticized.
The apparatus includes not only variant readings, but prefaces,
generally compressed, and at times a vast amount of editorial

opinion upon specific readings. There are also interpretative and expository comments on characters and situations given in the footnotes, and in the later volumes other aids, such as time analyses, notes on costumes, and acting traditions, including in some cases quotations from Edwin Booth's prompt-book. In all but a few volumes the prefaces are simply descriptive of textual sources and other facts connected with the history of the printed play.

In view of the growing antipathy to aesthetic criticism, so strongly voiced by Grant White, one must credit Furness with no little personal courage in venturing to make the collection and presentation of it a part of his plan. He defended himself with the observation that "the generality of us have not eyes to see what is written between the lines." It is inevitable that this part of Furness's work should appear the least profitable; yet the fact that the editor had an eye for the amusing as well as the useful made it possible for him often to find a breeze even in a desert of arid comment. The most imposing mass of critical quotation is, of course, to be found attached to 'Hamlet.' Here it occupies two hundred and fifty closely printed quarto pages. To a grateful student there must be some genuine comfort in the knowledge that his judicious selections give us the cream of what he found in literally "months spent in reading criticisms on 'Hamlet.' " Much must be said for the fact that because of his enormous knowledge of Shaksperian literature he could handle this mass of criticism not only with discrimination and good humor, but humorously. Yet with all his sense of proportion he was not disposed to minimize the importance of any work whatever that was inspired by intellectual interest; he had, for example, a kindly feeling for the intense seriousness of German scholars in the study of the problems of character in Hamlet, for he recognized that study to be grounded in German character. This point touches upon his own opinion of the work of German scholars, the value of which he thought to be greatly overestimated. Acquainted as he was with the bulk of German scholarship, he advanced his own authority for the fact that "although the opposite belief has pretty generally prevailed in Germany, the foreign editors are indebted at every step to the

English editors. Lessing revealed Shakspere to Germans, but not to Englishmen."

Furness himself edited fourteen volumes of the Variorum, his last play being 'Antony and Cleopatra,' issued in 1907. Even before he finally suspended his own work upon this edition, he made public acknowledgement of his indebtedness to his son, Horace Howard Furness, Jr. In 1908 the latter issued his first volume, 'Richard III,' a play from the textual standpoint extremely difficult. Two volumes have followed from his hand, the last, 'Cymbeline,' in 1913.

A study of Shaksperian editing is to a certain extent an investigation in the growth of good manners. Hudson had much, White some, of the harshness and blatancy of Steevens or Gifford. Furness was, on the contrary, the very incarnation of the decency of spirit to be found generally in modern scholarship. He was also reserved in his expressions of opinion, and almost if not quite skeptical with regard to what we have learned—either in or out of Shakspere's works—of Shakspere himself. Again and again he confronts us with a refusal to piece out an impossible passage or an obscure fact with approximations or guesses, because to his mind opinions have little significance in such junctures. His adoption of the First Folio text after he had already begun to publish his own, is simply one instance of his unwillingness to stand in the reader's light upon matters of judgment. Whatever one may say as to the absence of critical finality in such an attitude, it must at least be conceded that there is in it a scholarly ideal.

A publishing project of some interest and originality was carried through between 1888 and 1892 by the New York Shakspere Society. The society, incorporated in 1885, issued in August, 1886, a prospectus of the Bankside Shakspere, which was to present reprints of the texts of the plays originally printed in quarto, parallel with the 1623 folio. The society published twenty volumes of this series in the four years preceding the generally unstable financial conditions of 1893; and the twenty-first volume, 'Love's Labour's Lost,' was issued in 1906. The editing of the plays was assigned to various members of the society, thirteen editors standing sponsors for the entire series.

The society issued the textual portions of the volumes under its own guaranty of accuracy, but the introductions to the separate plays appeared with the customary disclaimer of collective responsibility for the facts or the views therein expressed. The general editor, Mr. Appleton Morgan, president of the society, edited in person five of the plays. The remainder appeared largely under the supervision of scholars of considerably less experience than is usually regarded as necessary for even so relatively simple an editorial project as a textual reprint; and naturally the inevitable traces of incompetency appeared most conspicuously in the introductions, in which the editors were not only allowed, but encouraged, to chase their own particular critical butterflies. Two or three of the editors of the series had in addition to their enthusiasms distinct editorial qualifications, but the rest of the number, including lawyers, physicians and clergymen, displayed, in some cases to an unfortunate degree, the characteristics of the amateur.

The introductions are elaborate and, as a whole, very badly proportioned. In some, large claims are made, and defended out of all relation to their importance in the history of the play itself. In Mr. A. K. Frey's introduction to the 'Taming of the Shrew,' for instance, the thesis is proclaimed that Shakspere wrote the 'Taming of A Shrew,' and that the 'Taming of the Shrew' was written not before the close of 1607. This entire introduction is a marvel of editorial ineptitude. Other examples of sadly disproportionate or irrelevant handling are to be found in Mr. William Reynolds' introduction to the 'Merchant of Venice,' the bulk of which he devotes to the legality and equity of the pleading and judgment in the case of Shylock v. Antonio, his particular purpose being to develop the fact that if Bacon had written this play, he would have handled its legal features in a way much more consistent with the practice of the time, but equally discomfiting to the plaintiff. In Dr. B. R. Field's 'Romeo and Juliet,' almost the entire introduction is devoted to exposition of the fact that Shakspere was no physician. An edition which aims, soundly or unsoundly, to give the reader an opportunity to form his own judgment upon the fundamental problems of the text, should in mere consistency give him the same basis of fact, the same premises of speculation, and nothing more, with regard to the external history of the plays. The faults indicated here may readily be seen to arise in part from the editorial policy which the society pursued. Mere division of labor among untrained scholars can be no adequate solution of the difficulties of a problem of the nature and magnitude of editing Shakspere. There still remains the question whether the part of the edition— the text itself—which is satisfactorily done, was wholly worth doing. The reprint would of course be useful in cases where a reader wished to consult the quarto and folio texts, and no others. Even for such a reader, however, a record of variants such as is given in any reputable scholar's text of to-day would be rather easier to use.

After the twentieth volume of the Bankside had appeared, the Society undertook to issue as the Bankside Sequel the sixteen plays printed for the first time in the 1623 folio. In this case it was planned to print parallel texts from the First Folio and the Globe edition. Only one volume, the Comedy of Errors, came out in this wholly unnecessary series. The Bankside Restoration Series, parallel reprints of Restoration adaptations with the Shakspere originals, published in 1907-8, includes Davenant's adaptation of Measure for Measure, Dryden's of Antony and Cleopatra and the Tempest, and Shadwell's of Timon of Athens. It also includes what must be, even for the most hardened student of parallel texts, excuse for a moment's surprise, the second 1604 quarto of 'Hamlet' opposed to "a conjectural text of the alleged Kyd 'Hamlet' "—in other words, a translation of Der Bestrafte Brudermord.

Professor Neilson has the modern fault of being more interested, at least editorially, in his text than he is in exploiting his own opinions. If it were otherwise, one might say much of his admirable edition published by Houghton, Mifflin & Company in 1906, in their series of *Cambridge Poets*. The qualities of the edition are largely negative—for that reason wholly commendable. Professor Neilson's text is based for each play upon either quarto or first folio, according to the merits of those editions. The editor has given his attention to some considerations which had been neglected in previous editions because of the imminent presence of more fundamental problems; he has, for instance, distinguished modern from contemporaneous stage directions, and has repunctuated the edition entirely in accordance with modern usage. The editorial policy is conservative, and the introductory material compact, yet sufficiently comprehensive, and devoid of groundless or unnecessary speculation. Since the history of conjectural emendation and exegesis has, for the study of Shakspere, practically closed, the merit of future texts must consist largely in just such small further advances toward the production of a mechanically perfect copy.

The needs of younger students have brought forth in the United States a number of school editions of varying merits. The pedagogical problem is, however, so distinct from that of the editor of the everyday Shakspere, either popular or scholarly, that it needs no more than casual comment here. The most familiar school editions are a reissue of Hudson's edition, published in 1871, and Rolfe's, issued from 1871 to 1881. Both of these expurgated editions have been frequently reprinted, and are at present in course of revision. The Tudor Shakspere, based upon Neilson's text, and edited by a number of representative American scholars, has the modern aim of introducing the student to Shaksperian problems, rather than giving guidance to his appreciation by aesthetic comment.

It seems as difficult to derive effective generalizations from this review of the work of American editors of Shakspere as Taine found it to deduce a political principle from the Jacobins' domination of France. One fact, however, seems to stand out: that our editors have been in the main conservative. It may be, of course, that they could be nothing else, since in the period of discovery and speculation, when the fever of scholarship turned a few first-rate European heads, our countrymen were not exposed to the contagion of spectacular scholarship. It is an interesting thing to find in the reviews of Verplanck's, Hudson's, and White's editions that these editors were considered pretty uniformly to err on the side of conservatism. There is matter for satisfaction, too, in the fact that our critical independence weathered admirably the Shaksperian controversies of the mid-century. It may be remembered that White was one of the first writers to dispute the claims of authority which Collier made for his "corrector" of the 1632 Folio, although White was not willing to believe at the time that the corrections were spurious. Both Hudson and White in their respective editions were indifferent to the cry of their reviewers that they had paid too little attention to the emendations of the mythical corrector—wherein it again appears that editors frequently know as much of their trade as their reviewers do. There can be little doubt that Americans have contributed a tangible something to the modern conception of Shakspere scholarship, and that such men as White and Furness have been of the first importance. We can say, at least, that American editors have left little for their successors to deplore. That, for the scholars of a nation given to dominantly radical views and pronouncements, is something to be said with gratification.

XVI

REALITY AND INCONSISTENCY IN SHAKSPERE'S CHARACTERS

By Ernest Hunter Wright

Assistant Professor of English

REALITY AND INCONSISTENCY IN SHAKSPERE'S CHARACTERS

We may begin with the familiar miracle of the reality of Shakspere's characters. During the three centuries since Shakspere held the mirror up to nature and drew from his most eminent literary friend the praise that "Nature herself was proud of his designs," critics have been emulating one another in an unexampled admiration of that miracle. Shakspere "is not so much an imitator," in the consummate phrase of Pope, "as an instrument of nature; and 'tis not so just to say that he speaks from her as that she speaks through him. His characters are so much nature herself that 'tis a sort of injury to call them by so distant a name as copies of her.......Every single character in Shakspere is as much an individual as those of life itself." And though with the last sentence Johnson may be in verbal disagreement, with the whole position he is in enthusiastic concord. "Shakspere is above all writers, at least above all modern writers, the poet of nature; the poet that holds up to his readers a faithful mirror of manners and of life. His characters....are the genuine progeny of common humanity....His scenes are occupied only by men who act and speak as the reader thinks that he should himself have spoken or acted on the same occasion.....This, therefore, is the praise of Shakspere, that his drama is the mirror of life; that he who has mazed his imagination in following the phantoms which other writers raise up before him may here be cured of his delirious ecstasies by reading human sentiments in human language; by scenes from which a hermit may estimate the transactions of the world and a confessor predict the progress of the passions."

Beyond such declarations from the critics of the century called classic it was scarcely possible for even the idolators of the romantic period to advance—there was almost nothing for them to add except adjectives. In all the pages of Hazlitt's 'Characters of Shakspere's Plays,' for instance, there is no syllable of admiration for the veracity of Shakspere's people finer than we have just found in the words of Pope, words which Hazlitt himself takes as a gospel text which his own comments upon various characters in the plays are to illustrate. And what Hazlitt did the romanticists could do in abundance. They expanded where they could hardly intensify; if they could add no cogency to the proclamation of the reality of Shakspere's people, they could copiously describe and interpret and illustrate the creatures in the plays, plucking after the heart of their mystery and sounding them from the lowest note to the top of their compass—and sometimes making "much music, excellent voice." Their work was as fervent as critics' work has ever been. They produced libraries of descriptions of Shakspere's people and created the all but universal habit of speaking about his characters in terms similar to those more usually reserved for actual beings—of talking about Hamlet as we talk about Napoleon. In this last respect they frequently went to an extreme that is comparable and similar to what, in another species of description, is known as the pathetic fallacy, and for this reason largely it is now in fashion to refer to their enraptured work a little condescendingly. But neither the validity nor the value of their work is properly in question here. It is a feeling underlying all of it, a feeling that it encourages in every reader of it, that is our concern: in fine phrases it tells the reader a truth the gist of which the reader has already felt—that the characters in these plays are as nearly living beings as any other characters to be found in books.

Can anything be added as to why this is true—any cause be given for the fact that these creatures who, after all, are only people in a play, should come to seem so uniquely lifelike? For after fulsome statement and illustration of the fact itself, the critics have usually laid down their pens. The classic school of them was gibbeted by the leader of the romanticists for seeming to consider the creator of such characters a species of "inspired idiot"—an "instrument" of nature in a perfectly passive sense, a magnificent voice without a mind; the leader of the latter school proclaims that the creator is possessed of wisdom always equal to his inspiration, of judgment and genius everywhere commensurate; with both doctrines nearly every modern critic is at variance. But in general the illustration of the evident reality of Shakspere's characters has been copious, while the attempt to find an explanation for the fact has been infrequent. Is it possible to give a reason as to why they are so verisimilar?

In the first place, it is evident that any work of art is made up of three elements: an object depicted, an artist depicting, and an audience beholding. Without the object there would be nothing to tell, without the artist there would be no one to tell it, and without the audience the work of art would enjoy the meaningless existence of a sound that no one is listening to. Of course, the artist may suppose an imaginary audience or may take himself as audience—two things which are possibly the same thing and which certainly do not alter the necessities of the case; for at any rate the work of art is that mental state aroused in the observer as he contemplates the picture that the artist shows him of an object in the physical or moral universe. It is true that a modern critic and his followers insist that in making the picture the object and the artist are not two but one; that what gets into the picture is not object *plus* artist as separate units, but a compound of object and artist which is indivisible—a mental state, an "impression" not separable into parts. But this might be admitted without damaging our thesis. For not only do common sense and psychology declare that if the artist had no object to contemplate his mind would be a blank and he would have nothing to communicate; but the spokesmen of the indivisible "impression" themselves call it a compound, in whatever proportions, of the object and the artist's mind; and if the two are both admittedly in operation, they may be quite indivisible in fact and yet separable enough in theory for the purpose of our discussion.

It is further true that any artist must stand between his object and his audience and must therefore get more or less in their way. The audience must see the object through him, and something of himself will of necessity illuminate or blur it. In the terms of science, the artist is a medium between the object and the audience and must more or less refract the light that passes through him, as all knowledge is refracted by its media.

So a work by any artist will combine in some proportion an image of the thing he is describing with something of his own state of mind as he describes it.   But there is an extreme variation in the proportions in which different artists make the combination. Of some it is the nature or design to keep themselves as far as possible invisible, to let the light shine through them as media all but utterly translucent.   Only in the slightest is their picture "sicklied o'er," or silvered o'er, "with the pale cast of thought." It may be that they have not much thought to display or it may be that they do not consider their thought the main thing to be displayed; the result is similar.   Perhaps Veronese, idealist though he was, is a good though not extreme example among painters.   There in his paintings are the lords and ladies, courtiers and warriors, Cupids and dwarfs, palaces and banquets, dogs and horses, which he saw and painted so clearly.   But there is hardly any message.   We are shown the things and we can make up our own minds about them.   The artist has a large segment of life to exhibit, but very little to tell us about it—or about himself.   For all that the pictures say, Paolo Cagliari may have been either a scoundrel or a saint.   He "seems to have come into the world to prove that the painter need have neither head nor heart, but only a hand, a brush, and a pot of paint."

At the other pole we have those artists about whose head and heart we are left in no dubiety; whose nature it is to be conspicuous in their own pictures, to tell us what they think and feel about the bit of life they reproduce before our eyes.   They tell us how to look at what they show us, and we see it not so much with them as through them, see it clarified by their own thought or colored by their own imagination.   The image they present us of the object is all compact with their own emotions inspired by it.   And thus unless we are technicians for the moment we may think less about the hand and brush of Turner as we look into one of his landscapes, and sometimes, possibly, even less about the landscape itself, than about the dream that was in the mind of Turner.   He is himself inseparably in the picture, and the result is a landscape conditioned by a state of mind. Perhaps of him, as of Chateaubriand, it might be said that he painted nature as he saw it, but he saw it as he loved it.   And it is a commonplace to say that in modern times all the descriptive arts have tended more and more to voice the artist's feeling, less and less to delineate the object merely. Thus it will be readily appreciated that in offering impressionists as obsolescent as Turner and Chateaubriand to illustrate the point, we are choosing artists who in certain modern circles would appear retiring to the point of self-effacement. In the hands of certain recent artists, the object has all but vanished and the soul-state remains all but unalloyed with anything from the gross world of fact.

Though possibly the poet is in general less likely to remain impersonal than the painter, we have in poetry also the same two extremes. The fact is so familiar as to need but little illustration, and again we need not take the more extraordinary examples. Certainly no one would say that the personality of a poet like Chaucer is left dim to us in his poems. And yet a description of the birds in Chaucer, for example, does hardly more than give us a delightfully neat picture of the "smale fowles," each set before us with an adjective or two defining his actual or suppositious character, each making his own melody rather than singing Chaucer's song, each telling unmistakably that Chaucer had listened to these carols, but evincing little more than this implies about the character of Chaucer. The celebrated passages about the mating of the birds in Thomson do not go much deeper in revealing the poet. They refresh us with a tender picture of the fluttering folk of grove and hedge indulging their amours, and direct our glance upward to the marvellous Spirit who controls their instincts. That Thomson loved the birds is most apparent; but to be eloquent of his own ecstacy (if such it was) in listening to them is far from his chief design. Now contrast either of these with the "shrill delight" not so much of the skylark as of Shelley's soul as it wings its way after the blithe spirit—"*bird* thou never wert"—into the heavens, or with the luscious grief of Keats which keeps up but a tenuous relation with the nightingale through the eight wonderful stanzas that mainly complain of the poet's own heart-ache, voice the longing for a draught of vintage that may aid him to forget it, lift him for a moment on the viewless wings of poesy into a realm above it, only to bring him back at last to his *sole self:* make this contrast and the difference is apparent between what used to be called the objective and the subjective in poetry. There is some evidence that Samuel Johnson was not averse to flowers; but of him, if of any English poet, it may be said that

> A primrose by a river's brim
> A yellow primrose was to him;
> And it was nothing more.

To Wordsworth it was all that another "flower in the crannied wall" was to Tennyson—it enveloped the whole mystery of God and man.

The bearing of all this upon our present subject is of some importance. It will probably not be disputed that among all English poets, perhaps among all poets, Shakspere is the least obtrusive. Presumably no one infers from this that Shakspere lacked passions and opinions of his own, for to have conceived such reason and such feeling as he has put into a hundred characters is evidence enough that much of both was in himself. That there must have been a great personality behind the plays, and even a great thinker, though not necessarily a thinker with a creed, we find it very hard to deny; but we also find it very hard to affirm a great deal more. The personality remains *behind* the plays; of his own opinions and his own passions the poet almost never speaks; and though in reading his book we know that we are in the presence of a great master, we feel this in something of the same way that we feel the electric current, conscious that a fearsome force is passing through us but unable to grasp and retain any particle of it. In this sense he is at once in his work and out of it. A Johnsonian might say that he is always circumjacent and never interjacent. And in this way he is possibly the most perfectly translucent glass that ever stood between an audience and nature. Of course all the characters in his plays, the reality of whom was the first point in our discussion, passed through his mind before they got into his pages, but in so doing they took on less bias and distortion than they would have suffered in the mind of almost any other reproducer. It was his gift in making characters to copy no apparent part of his own image. And hence a miracle of art, that whereas most authors get between us and their characters, Shakspere's own creatures get between us and him. We cannot see him for them.

In vain, therefore, all but entirely, have been the many efforts to deduce the character and moral system of Shakspere from the dramas. We do not see him because our eyes are filled by the things he is talking about. His ghosts and fairies are as palpable to us as is his Julius Caesar; but when we ask whether he believed in the existence of such creatures we can only answer that it is about as likely as it is unlikely. In the first half of his career especially, as has been noted, he made much of the pagan deity of Fortune, but it is impossible to say whether she was for him merely a poetic figment or a semi-real article of faith. His plays embody sentiment in plenty unembarrassed by strict reason, and also sense in plenty uninflamed by passion; but the proportionate parts the two played in his own life are but vaguely estimable. Joy triumphs in some of the plays and sorrow reigns in others, while in many the two are intermingled; but the man who would deduce the amount of joy or bitterness in Shakspere's own life will soon find himself in the sphere of fancy. To many questions in the moral realm the answers in the plays are vague, if not conflicting. Good and evil are equally abundant in the dramas, and often are inseparably fused; Shakspere's own solution of the problem of good and evil, if he had one, is as dark to us as that of Milton, for example, is clear. Thus the whole question of his religion remains almost a pure question. As clear-minded a critic as Bagehot, in the best of all attempts to divine the character of Shakspere from the plays, pauses in the discussion of this point—a discussion that makes the arguments, based on nearly nothing, that would prove Shakspere a Catholic or a Protestant, seem petty—because he is afraid of growing "mystical and confused." And so, to a score of other questions of importance that we might ràise, the dramas return inconclusive answers. Even as to the dramatist's political beliefs— the point on which the critics have usually been most confident— there can be considerable debate.

The truth is that we do not grasp the character of Shakspere in the plays, and further illustration of the fact is hardly necessary here. We need merely refer to another essay in this volume which gives an account of many efforts that critics have made to reconstruct his personality. Take all that the most searching critic therein mentioned has been able to discover from the plays, take all that the whole group of investigators have made certain or plausible, and the sum total could be stated in a paragraph or two. Think of the books that have been written about Dante's philosophy, about Spenser's moral system, about Milton's theology, about Pope's critical principles, about Wordsworth's "philosophy" of nature, and balance them against the paragraph or so containing all that the critics have discovered about Shakspere the man from thirty-seven plays, two poems, and a series of sonnets. But the books that have such meagre portraits of Shakspere are swollen with the portraits of his creatures, the men and women in the plays. His nature was to conceal himself and to reveal life.

Life is more puzzling than literature. It is scarcely a novelty to say that many characters in books are better known to us than are the people in the world around us. One of the chief uses of books would be gone if this were not the case. And the obvious reason is that the characters in books are simpler and more consistent than the characters in life. The simplest individual in life is many-sided. To begin with, he is one man to you and another man to me, because with each of us he sets up a personal equation differing according as our characters differently affect his. Neither of us will ever grasp the whole of him. For another thing, he has "moods"—he vacillates. He changes more or less from day to day, under multiple influences that bear in upon him. He may be following reason at one time in one direction and passion at another in a different direction. Again, and more important, a character in life is likely to embody a number of contradictions. Consistency is the jewel of little minds. It is very common to hear some Jones or Smith described as a "bundle of contradictions." And indeed if we think long enough about almost any of our friends, do we not come all too frequently to this genial conclusion about him—or about ourselves, if we have the gift? Do we not see frequent witness to the fact as we watch a friend debating between two or more courses of action, striving to combine a congeries of mixed motives into some single policy—"making up" his mind, we call it—and finally acting, at least in many cases, upon motives not entirely clear to him, and far less clear to us? And so it happens not infrequently that our best friend perplexes us, or we him, by some unexpected action; and the reason why we are astonished is that we know only part of his character, or that he is inconsistent, or both. He defies a single definition.

Is it permissible to give, with no intention of presumption, a personal illustration of these facts? For some twenty years now there has been before the people of America a man whose energy, exerted in an age enjoying unprecedented means for circulating news, has made him as familiar in the public eye, perhaps, as any man has ever been. During this period he has done all sorts of things. He has reformed New York City, governed New York State, and twice filled the presidency. He has waged war, hunted lions, and discovered rivers. He has been entertained by King and Kaiser, has discoursed at the Sorbonne and at Oxford, and has filled pulpits in small churches in the middle west. He has made thousands of speeches on every subject from the danger of mollycoddling students to the duty of bearing children, and he has announced his position on nearly every question that has come up in his time. He has published a dozen books, and helped to edit a magazine. He has created a new political party, has been almost assassinated, and has sued and been sued. And we may probably expect him to "breathe awhile and to't again." Meanwhile he has told us all about himself, and ten thousand other people have told us about him. Surely if there is any one we ought to know, this is the man. Well—ask a hundred people what they think of him, and you will get about a hundred different opinions. And by and large, the hundred opinions will fall into two groups, not strikingly unequal in number, but about diametrically opposite. Nor is the case exceptional. Rather it is universal. The same thing happened to Napoleon and to Caesar, to Socrates and to Rousseau. They defy a single definition.

But the first hundred people that you meet will give you the same definition of Mr. Micawber—for the very good reason that there is only one thing to see in him and that this is visible on equal terms to all. Let us confess at once that we are taking an extreme example for the sake of contrast. But what has been carried to an extreme in the case of Micawber has happened more or less with every character in fiction. It is a necessity that the author shall make life simpler. He cannot reproduce the whole of it, or even the whole of any person in it; his book would be an interminable worthless duplicate. So a character in fiction, whether painted from a single model or made up from many persons who remain unrecognizable, must in passing through the author's mind grow relatively simple. About the character the author tells us what is needed to explain completely the progress of the plot in hand, and leaves out all the rest—or he approaches this ideal. Thus he discards at once all the irrelevancies and immaterialities that distract our vision of life. And, furthermore, that part of the person which the author leaves in his pages must be relatively congruous within itself. The character must be consistent; even if inconsistent, it must be consistent in its inconsistency. And thus the author shapes the rough-hewn edges of people as we find them in the world, softens their incongruities and contradictions, and chisels off the freaks, vagaries, and caprices that cloud our view of life. It is obviously because the characters in books are thus made simple and consistent that we know them better than we know our friends. Now, Mr. Micawber is an excellent example of a character cut down to a single trait. There are no such folk in life, though there are plenty of them in literature, where they have a place; and it is because they are so unlifelike that we are unwilling to dignify them with the name of characters, and so we call them caricatures. One could trace the way up from this simplest type of reproduction through the various higher stages of characterization—through such creatures as the "lay figure," somewhat more rounded and less precise, through the "stock character," more or less faithfully conforming to tradition, through the secondary persons of a fiction who are more verisimilar without rotundity, to the complex fulness of a character like Chaucer's Criseyde or Meredith's Diana.

Thus, though the author must in some degree make simple and consistent every character that he creates, the limits between which he may work are still very liberal. If he shears down a character to a single attribute, his creature cannot fail to be perfectly comprehensible and perfectly consistent; and the creature will not be satisfactory, except for purposes of laughter, because in these two particulars it is unlike life. But with every trait the author adds, he increases the demand upon the reader's understanding and the risk of inconsistency in the character. And ever as the character grows more complex the increase continues. The nearer the character approaches to the full rotundity of life, the longer we must think to understand it, until in highly comprehensive creations like those last mentioned, we get to wondering about the meaning of the characters and the reasons for their doing certain things. They begin to puzzle us somewhat as life puzzles us and we debate about them as we debate about people in the flesh. Thus the argument as to just why Criseyde deserts Troilus or just why Diana gives away the secret of state will presumably go on as long as people read these stories. No point is to be made here as to whether it is good or bad art to leave such seemingly inconsistent actions only partially explained—it might possibly be good in one instance and bad in another; the only point is that such cases are very similar to cases which we often see in life and that we debate about them in similar language. Neither is it to be inferred that every complex character in art must exhibit a degree of inconsistency. It may, in the hands of an author who so wishes and who has the power, remain a perfect unity though highly complicated. But it is at least true that in the hands of any author the chances of symmetry decrease as the character approaches the complexity of actual human nature. These chances may be negligible for a writer like Racine, consciously refining into lucid order every character that he elaborates, but they are considerable with an unconscious master like Shakspere, whose genius, as we said, was to transmit with relatively little rearrangement the diversity of life.

"There are no straight lines in nature, or in Shakspere." And at this point we reach the combination of the two ideas that have been put forward in our study. For if, as we said, it was the way of Shakspere to efface himself from his own work and to function as the most translucent mind through which beings in the flesh were ever transmuted into characters of fiction, we should expect to find his characters so similar to beings in the flesh as to elicit such assertions as we quoted at the outset, assertions that they are the "genuine progeny of common humanity" and that in reproducing them Shakspere appears to be their mouthpiece, or, in the exact word, their "instrument," rather than their "imitator"; and if, again, the prime difference between people in the flesh and characters of fiction is that the one are complex and irregular while the others are simple and consistent, we should expect the characters in Shakspere, so similar to people in the flesh, to retain in their complexity some of the unaccountable irregularities, disparities, and inconsistencies which are usually removed from characters in books but which are always present in the people that we know. As this admittedly is what we have been finding for two centuries, during which critics have in one breath been marvelling at the reality of Shakspere's characters and in the next wondering at their meaning. Perhaps we may therefore turn back to our first statement of that reality with some added light: believing that a reason why the eighteenth century marvelled over the veracity of the people in the plays, and began to talk about them as of actual persons, is that they were copied with so little alteration by the poet from the population of the world; and believing that a reason why the nineteenth century, habitually speaking in the same familiar terms, sank itself in the interpretation of those characters and quarreled over definitions of them, is that such portraits, lacking the perfect regularity of most people in books, preserving in their complexity a little of the confusion and disarray that baffle us in the actual world, in a degree perplex us and defy a final definition just as people in life do.

Real people are baffling for their complexity and inconsistency. Shakspere's people are the purest copies that we have of real people. Hence, in an unusual degree, they too are baffling. Hence many of the arguments about them which it seems impossible to settle. This is of course very far from implying that Shakspere put into his characters certain random traits of inconsistency by way of mystifying us—that might possibly be argued of Shaw;—it is merely to imply that in copying his creatures from life he may unconsciously have reproduced more of the irregularity that life contains than most other artists do, and thus left us realities that puzzle. For there are two kinds of reality in characters of fiction. To illustrate them briefly we may suppose an author starting the creation of a character with a certain leading trait. To keep the character from being a mere abstraction, the author must give him other more or less subordinate and subsidiary traits. Of these, if he is shaping a well-rounded person, he may add hundreds. Now it is possible for him to make each of these entirely consonant with the central trait of character and with all the others; to have each one perfectly correlated with all the rest, and to make out of them all a whole entirely symmetrical. Not a single thing will the character do or say but will fit properly into his total line of action, his total body of thought and feeling. He is logically and psychologically a perfect unit. He is an integer, however large. And so he has one kind of reality. But it may be called the reality of art rather than of life. No man in life is a logical and psychological unit. The character we are supposing may have no single trait that is not lifelike; it is the perfect combination of his traits that is not lifelike. He has the reality of a straight line, which exists only in the mind, just as an integer exists only in the mind; in a word, he has the reality of an idea, and not of life. But another author, starting to build a complex character around the same central trait, may include among the many secondary and minor traits a number that are not strictly subsidiary to the main, that are even at variance with it, in strict logic, or with one another. He may do or say things not entirely consonant one with another; he will not be a unit. Every one of his traits may be entirely lifelike, *including* this trait of imperfect consistency. And this character may have another kind of reality if his creator has genius—for without something like that the character is likely to be contorted out of all semblance either of straight lines or of natural curves—a reality, not of the perfect idea, but of relatively wayward life, a reality enjoyed by all the "genuine progeny of common humanity." There need be no choice here between these two forms of art. It is a distinction, and not an evaluation, that is being made. The plays of Racine probably furnish the noblest examples in modern literature of the first kind of characters; those of Shakspere perhaps yield the supreme examples of the second.

Of all this, of course, the character of Hamlet is the excellent example. But in drawing from this character nearly all the illustrations now to follow, we are actuated only by desire of brevity; the reader may find in various other characters, to whom we shall make some reference, material altogether similar and sometimes nearly as abundant. Our illustrations will be of two kinds. In the first set we shall simply state, with the least interpretation that is possible, practically all that the play tells us about the character of Hamlet—what he does and purposes, what the other people in the play say of him, what he says about himself. When this is before us we shall find that out of all his actions, some of them not altogether explicable, others scarcely reconcilable one with another, and out of all the opinions, some of them vague and some of them conflicting, held of him by other persons in the play and by himself, no single definition has been found for him or in all seeming can be found for him; just as no single definition can be found for living people, and for the same reason. The second set of illustrations may then deal with certain of the vagaries caused in Shakspere criticism by this fact.

The only thing we hear of Hamlet prior to his own appearance is that he is "young." (Later we are given to believe that he is thirty.) To his uncle-father, when he enters, his attitude is one of avoidance, of brief contempt; to his mother he is somewhat distantly respectful, but somewhat oblique in answering inquiries, in snatching at one of her words to evade her question as to the true cause of his protracted grief by means of a poetic speech distinguishing between its visible appearances and its hidden reality. Finally, he is obedient to her wishes; and after acceding to them he is left alone—to talk about himself. Out of the confession he now utters, all the detail of which must be omitted here, three facts emerge: that he has been thinking of suicide, that his despair springs from the sight of a mother married in wicked speed to the unworthy brother of his father, but that though his reflections on self-murder have been serious, no purpose to carry them to action is impending—on the contrary, he meditates only inaction, for though his heart break he must hold his tongue. At this point in his thoughts Horatio and the two officers enter. Up to the moment when they divulge the secret of the ghost that they have seen, Hamlet shows himself a good companion, something of a democrat, also a wit—jesting somewhat bitterly about the things that most harrow his mind—and after they tell him of the apparition, he exhibits a shrewd mixture of detective questioning, agile thinking, and firm resolution, with a certain caution and a certain suspicion—the whole showing a mood strongly contrasting, though not incompatible, with that of the soliloquy he has just uttered.

In the next scene we do not see the prince, but we hear three opinions of him. These question his sincerity in love; we take them, unless, like many readers, we disregard them entirely, as we might take opinions, let us say, about the private life of a man whom we already knew fairly well in the public world: we fit the new facts, if we think them worth while, into our notion of the man's character already formed. Laertes is inclined to think Hamlet a mere trifler in love, and yet admits that he may be sincere. Polonius is more downright—cocksure that Hamlet's love is trickery inspired by a passing passion. Ophelia, like many an innocent girl at such a point, cannot be certain in her opinion: "I do not know, my lord, what I should think." It seems foolish to ask who is right about this, and yet if we were reading the play for the first time we should have to ask the question, and to wait for the answer. If we can by any possibility purge our minds of preconceived opinion on the matter, made up from former study of the play, or from some critic's opinion or some actor's interpretation—if we are naïvely rereading the play and looking solely for what is therein said about Hamlet—we must raise the question and look for an answer to come; and perhaps no unequivocal answer is coming; perhaps after the scene with Ophelia in the lobby and the demonstration at her grave, we shall still be among those who ask questions about the character of Hamlet's love.

The next scene is a test of character. Before the ghost comes, Hamlet is calm, satirical, tending to moralize. When it appears it finds him ready, unafraid, quick to act and to defy and foil those who would hinder—exhibiting one of those many moments

of firm resolution that so strongly contrast with the great ir-
resolution which is the most obvious trait in his character. The
ghost finds him "apt"; before the prince knows what he is to
do he is in haste to sweep to it "with wings as swift as medita-
tion." But the moment after the ghost has laid the duty on
him and vanished, Hamlet's resolution begins to dissipate itself. To let the ghost's commandment alone live within his
brain is indeed the central thought in the speech he now utters,
but it is diffused among invocations to heaven, earth and hell,
prayers that his nerves and sinews may not fail him, curses on
the most pernicious woman who is his mother, searchings for
words black enough to name his uncle—an effort running into
something like grim humor before the speech is finished. Then
follow "wild and whirling words" to Horatio and Marcellus;
fantastic insistings as to the form and manner of the oath of
secrecy they take; saucy snatches thrown to the revered spirit
of his father in the cellarage; an intimation that he is going to
play the madman; and finally, in a most serious vein, an impre-
cation on the "cursed spite" that has laid on him the duty to
which, a few minutes before, he was eager to sweep upon the
wing. And one who reads through all of this must form his own
opinion as to exactly what is going on within the mind of Hamlet; no one of the critics has put forward an explanation of this
varied discourse that has proved acceptable to all the others.

The next thing that we hear of Hamlet is that he has appeared
in a strange guise before Ophelia—hatless, with doublet un-
braced, stockings foul and ungartered, his knees knocking each
other, his face pale and piteously hinting horrors. He took
Ophelia by the wrist and held her hard; then, standing at arm's
length, he searched her face in silence and for long; he shook her
arm a little, waved his head thrice up and down, and without a
word, but with a piteous sigh, he left her, gazing back at her over
his shoulder all the way as he went out. And what does this
mean? It is very typical of the way Shakspere frequently
works. There are the facts for you—that is how Hamlet looked
and that is what he did—but there is not a single word as to his
reason or his purpose, and you can make up your own mind
about it. Not to travesty the situation, it is very much as if a

man whom you knew and who, as you were conscious, had made
advances of more or less sincere affection to an innocent girl,
and had been overtaken by deep sorrow, should by an accident
be disclosed before your eyes behaving to her in this way. You
would come away from the sight wondering just what it meant.
It might not seem an unnatural sight in the circumstances, it
might be entirely lifelike; only, out of half a dozen plausible
explanations of it, you would not be able to settle upon any one
that would be exactly and assuredly correct. Just so have the
critics come away from this scene, bearing half a dozen explanations no one of which is indisputably right. In the scene itself
there are two opinions as to Hamlet's behavior. Polonius will
wager his head that it is plain madness sprung from ecstasy of
love—but beshrew his jealousy if he can tell now whether the
love was honorably meant or not! Ophelia cannot be so sure of
Hamlet's madness: "My lord, I do not know, but truly, I do
fear it."

Polonius takes the news to the king. The king and queen are
already talking about Hamlet's "transformation," to Rosencrantz and Guildenstern, companions of the prince's youth whom,
we are told, he loves most dearly. Polonius comes to reveal
"the very cause of Hamlet's lunacy." Hamlet is mad because
Ophelia has repelled his love; as evidence of which the coun-
sellor reads some verses, written by Hamlet to her, of a quality
not markedly superior to the somewhat puzzling, inane rimes on
Shakspere's tomb. To test the theory they will bring Hamlet
and Ophelia together in the lobby—he is in the habit of walking
there "four hours together." As this plan is maturing, Hamlet
himself enters. It is the first time he has spoken to Polonius in
our hearing, and from the first he teases and befuddles the "tedious old fool" with sarcastic wit. The reason for this, again, is
not utterly clear; Hamlet never tells us exactly what he has
against Polonius. Unless we are content to think that his irrita-
tion proceeds solely from dislike of the old man's character in
general, we are tempted to assume that he knows more about the
machinations of Polonius than is revealed to him in the play—
which is what many a critic has consciously or unconsciously
presumed. A similar sarcasm he is finally going to vent upon

Rosencrantz and Guildenstern; but at their first meeting, which now occurs, he begins in good fellowship, approaching jollity, and proceeds gradually to evade their questions, to suspect their motives, to discover that they are the king's agents, to feign a marvellous confession of his own mental disorder, ending in a joke, and to moralize on the estate and prospects of child-actors. After some more foolery with Polonius, he welcomes the actors in cordial democratic fashion. He will have a speech from them immediately, he will have a play tomorrow, and it shall be "The Murder of Gonzago," with a few lines of his own written in—another instance of quick resolution. But now when he is left alone again, for the first time since he saw the ghost, he begins berating himself for lack of that very quality. The player could find tears for Hecuba; he, the son of a dear father murdered, can but unpack his heart with words and fall a-cursing with his deed undone. And all through a very long speech Hamlet is his own first critic in continually demanding of himself the reason for this thing; but he returns himself and us no certain answer —he does little more than call himself names.

We see him again on the morrow. The play is planned, the king is to be trapped, vengeance is to be ensured—and Hamlet comes forth thinking of suicide! This time the idea is still more serious, though to be sure it turns to a debate upon the pity of the human lot in general rather than upon his own problems. But there is no word of the play, of the king, of the deed. Ophelia now meets him, and there follows the scene between them which every one knows, but which no one can interpret in terms that every one will agree to. You may find several reasons for Hamlet's behavior in this scene, as in Ophelia's chamber, that are plausible enough, but you are likely to remain undecided among them. Ophelia cannot explain Hamlet's actions except as incoherent madness caused by love. The king is sure that love is not the cause, and expresses some doubt as to the madness. Polonius has no question as to the insanity, and still thinks it springs from love repelled.

As we approach the play that is to trap the king we first find Hamlet rather ignoring its prime purpose while delivering some very just dramatic criticism to the actors and delineating his

idea of manly virtue to Horatio. Then in a few words he tells
Horatio that the play is to decide the ghost's honesty and his
uncle's guilt, and bids Horatio watch. Before the play starts
and during its intervals he bandies fun, irony, sarcasm, and in-
decency with the king, Polonius, Ophelia, the players. The
play is given, the king is convicted, Hamlet is placed beyond
doubt; and there follows, no resolution to the deed, but certain
wild and whirling words to Horatio, certain sarcastic trickeries
played on Rosencrantz and Guildenstern, and on Polonius.
When these are finally gone, and he is alone again, he feels that
in this witching time of night he could "drink hot blood and do
such bitter business as the day would quake to look on." But
that business he does not face. He goes softly to his mother.
On the way to her he scorns a chance to do the business and he
gives his reason. It is the only time that he gives us a definite
reason and this one is only for the moment; and yet the world
has not wanted critics who have not credited this reason, even
for this moment, because, though natural, it is more revolting
than comports with Hamlet's character as they understand it
elsewhere in the play.

In the next scene, it is one Hamlet who enters to wring his
mother's heart with vituperation, and another Hamlet who goes
out promising to ask his mother's blessing when her own repent-
ance is fulfilled—two moods that are of course entirely compatible. She, in turn, considers him insane at the beginning of
the scene and at the end apparently believes his word that he is
only feigning madness—though we cannot be quite sure what
she believes. With instant resolution, in the meantime, Hamlet
tries to kill the king and slays Polonius instead. But a little
later the ghost enters "to whet his almost blunted purpose" to
the deed that he has just attempted. Hamlet knows that the
ghost comes to urge action, and is certainly impressed; but he
makes no promise, and no word would indicate that the visitation
has given a spur to his will. On the contrary, he mentions no
purpose of vengeance in the remainder of the scene, and at the
end of it, announces that he is off to England at the king's behest.
Of this, to be sure, he is apprehensive, but he is ready to play
the game of knavery if the king's messengers force it on him, and

confident enough of his ability therein. And after some embittered jesting with Rosencrantz and Guildenstern, and with
the king, as to the hiding-place of the body of Polonius, he is
ready to go—without a word, during the last three scenes, about
his purpose.

The sight of soldiers with a purpose brings his own crowding
back again into his mind. And there follows the self-searching
soliloquy in which, by common consent, the critics have agreed
that the heart of Hamlet's mystery must be discovered if it is
discoverable in anything that he says. It would require a considerable volume merely to repeat the various solutions of his
mystery that have been based, in all degrees of certitude, upon
one part or another of that soliloquy—upon his hint that his
revenge sleeps except when "occasions" arise to awaken it, his
statement that man is a creature of "such large discourse, looking before and after," his question whether his lethargy is mere
"bestial oblivion," or whether it comes from "thinking too precisely on the event"—and so forth. Why is it, if he has "cause
and will and strength and means" to do the deed, that he does
not do it? That is the question that all the critics have tried to
answer from this soliloquy. It is the question that Hamlet is
trying to answer in the soliloquy. From Hamlet's argument
about it and about, the critics have drawn many answers. But
in Hamlet's argument there is one answer only; one single positive statement on the matter. It is unsatisfactory to him, it
has proved so to nearly all his critics, who mainly pass it over
quickly or in silence. Yet this is the sole thing of which he is
certain; it is said in four words, but for the theory of this essay
they are priceless: "I do not know."

> *I do not know*
> Why yet I live to say, "This thing's to do,"
> Sith I have cause and will and strength and means
> To do't.

Without pushing this sentence too far, we may pause to say that
it reveals in miniature the whole idea with which we are dealing.
Perfectly honest with himself, Hamlet cannot diagnose his own
mind. Able beyond the average in the analysis of his own motives, he cannot say which of them, or what combination of them,

actuates him—all the more because of that ability. He is experiencing what all men experience many times in actual life, and in proportion to their thoughtfulness. And his critics, when they have been judicious, when—far from frequently—they have not felt it imperative that they should find some one explanation for Hamlet, have often been at as great a loss to define his psychosis as he was himself. They are experiencing what they experience often in observing actual life but encounter rarely in literature.

Hamlet cannot come to know his own stops, but he can make further resolutions. He ends the speech by devoting himself to thoughts of blood from this time forth—and straightway embarks for England! From this point on, not very much that is new and important is revealed about his character. There is plenty of shrewdness and quick action in his escape at sea; there is a non-committal letter to the king upon his landing. We are told that he is envenomed with envy at Laertes' skill in fencing, and that he will be ingenuous enough not to suspect the fraud in the rapiers; the ingenuousness we may believe, but the envy hardly comports with the idea of Hamlet that we have already formed, nor is it intimated later at the match. It is a detail, like his assertion that he has been in continual practice with his rapier recently, that we find it hard to fit in with the rest of his character. His half-humorous moralizing in the grave-yard is quite comprehensible; his spectacular leap into Ophelia's grave, with the bombast he hurls at Laertes, he himself explains as the quick execution of a fiery impulse. Perhaps we are not astonished when we find him once more arguing, this time with Horatio, as to whether he has not all-sufficient reason to slay the king, and determining to do it quickly in the brief interim that remains to him; though we may be justly surprised to find him giving for the act one further reason, of which we can hardly have seriously suspected him before, and with which we may find it hard to credit him now—namely, that the king has "popp'd in between the election and his hopes." He tantalizes Osric, as he does all fools, he begs pardon of Laertes like a gentleman, he plays the king's wager for him in good earnest, he discovers that he has been duped to his death, and—that the moment for his deed is come. In a certain kind of resolution and foresight he is instant to the end. He snatches the poison from Horatio, settles the kingdom on Fortinbras, and prays that his own name be cleared from stain. The rest is silence.

We have recited practically all that Hamlet does, and practically all that he says about himself or that others say about him. Now out of all these facts about him—and of course allowing for whatever contradictions may have come about in the revision of the play, for whatever inconsistent details may have arisen from mere carelessness, or from too closely following the sources at this point or that, or from confusion of the text—out of all these facts and opinions, or, better, out of the total play restudied for the purpose, can we frame a unitary and definable character? It is very doubtful whether any of us can or ever will. It is certain that no one so far has done so; none of the attempts so far to reduce the character to unity has satisfied all readers of the play, or even probably the larger number of the readers. No critic has made one perfectly comprehensible man out of Hamlet. And yet there is no question of his reality—no one denies it— there is only question as to whether we can grasp him as an entity, whether we can put him in a definition. We *know* Hamlet, in much the same way as we know our friends, in spite of the fact that we cannot entirely explain him. Or rather, it is the meaning of this essay that we know him in this way partly *because* we cannot entirely explain him.

This does not come from mere carelessness on Shakspere's part, though that may sometimes operate to our confusion. It does not come from the fact that for the purpose of a certain scene a character may take on a trait somewhat at variance with our idea of him in the remainder of the play, though that may sometimes be the case. Other dramatists of the period sinned in these respects without achieving Shaksperian verisimilitude. The reasons are deeper. For one thing, Shakspere is given to putting the actions of his people before our eyes, maybe with an opinion or two, not usually his own, about them, and letting us interpret their motives. Minutely and graphically he tells us how Hamlet acted when he came before Ophelia as if to speak of horror; he presents no syllable of explanation, except one from Polonius that we can scarcely believe, and leaves us the privilege of making up our own minds why, in the attendant circumstances,

Hamlet was inspired to act in this particular fashion. For another thing, when there is full discussion as to motives, it is frequently conflicting and inconclusive. He leaves us to conclude about the matter, if we can. Hamlet circles in debate a great deal around his motives, but he states very little positively about them; his very central statement about them being, as we have seen, "I do not know." When Othello comes to murder Desdemona, "It is the cause, it is the cause, my soul," that actuates him; and his next words are "Let me not name it." He has given us, not an explanation of the cause, but a text to set a hundred critics arguing about it. And for a third thing, in the characters thus left mainly to our interpretation, Shakspere copied a good deal of the wayward inconsistency that is seen in people in the flesh; copied it, not seemingly upon any deliberate theory of psychology or art, but because his genius led him by this natural pathway to reality; copied it all the more because he was not trying fully to explain his characters, or to make up characters who would be fully explicable.

If Hamlet has been used for nearly all the illustrations here, it is not because there has not been much debate of the same kind about many other characters, arising largely from the same cause. The interpretations of Shylock on the stage have varied all the way from the purely comic to the profoundly tragic; the debate as to what Shylock was meant to be is still going on and is perhaps just at its height at present. The explanations of Falstaff's character began a good deal over a century ago and are still continuing, at least one notable discussion having been contributed to the subject recently. And so with Lear, Macbeth, Antony, Cleopatra, Prospero, and many others; the discussions upon these characters will yield much material to illustrate the theory of this essay. Next to Coriolanus, perhaps Othello among the tragic heroes has seemed to have the most lucid and consistent character; but at the moment when these pages are being written, there comes Professor Stoll's book on that character, in which, after summing up in a long paragraph some of the traits that Othello possesses, the author opens his discussion with the question, "What is to be made of this great heap of contradictions?"

For our second set of illustrations, it may be interesting to give a few instances, out of thousands at hand, of certain results to which this species of reality in inconsistency has led in Shaksperian criticism. In three directions principally have the results been apparent. In all of these they have been natural and harmless so long as they have been kept within a certain bound of common sense, but in all the impulse to transcend reason has frequently proved overpowering. First, and already mentioned, the temptation has been nearly always irresistible, since Shakspere is himself so dim and his characters so palpable, to treat them as creatures of flesh and blood, with a heart and brain independent of Shakspere's, with a life not merely in his mind and in his play, but before the play and after it and in its intervals, with a life in the real world, or in our minds, or in God's mind, or in some ideal universe. In a measure this is tolerable; in an extreme it is a monstrous pathetic fallacy. Second—and exactly opposite—the temptation has frequently been too enticing to seek the hidden Shakspere in the characters themselves, to read his mind in theirs, to deduce him from them, to identify him with them—a tendency natural enough and inoffensive till it runs to that extreme from which, once started, it seems hardly restrainable. Third, and perhaps most striking, since the characters are so insusceptible of final definition, we have no end of conflicting opinions concerning them—hundreds sometimes of a single character, no one of them satisfactory to everybody, no two quite agreeing with each other, and many of them squarely and irascibly opposed.

As to the first point, it is of course legitimate to speak of Hamlet as a person without constantly reminding us that this man with whom we feel so familiar is nothing but a *dramatis persona*. In Hazlitt, for example, this method is usually unobjectionable. Hazlitt's portraits combine the skill of painter and psychologist and, as a rule, in speaking of the characters as of real persons, he indulges only such imaginative license as may cordially be granted; once in a while, perhaps, he trembles on the brink of the pathetic fallacy. About this Hamlet, "all whose thoughts we seem to know as well as we do our own," he says: "Hamlet is a name; his speeches and sayings but the idle coinage of a poet's brain.

What then, are they not real? They are as real as our own thoughts. Their reality is in the reader's mind. It is *we* who are Hamlet......" and so on for a long paragraph. The sternest materialist may listen equably to this manner of speech about Hamlet, though he could confidently challenge any one to find in Hazlitt's long life of Napoleon, that god of his idolatry, a passage showing half the familiarity that the critic assumes with the melancholy Dane. But it is when Hazlitt's example inspires certain of the more gushing sentimentalists among his many imitators that we are favored with the following species of rhapsody, supposedly popular among early Victorians but not yet altogether out of fashion in some quarters.

"Ophelia—poor Ophelia! Of, far too soft, too good, too fair to be cast among the briers of this working-day world, to fall and bleed upon the thorns of life! What shall be said of her? For eloquence is mute before her! Like a strain of sad, sweet music which comes floating by us on the wings of night and silence, and which we rather feel than hear—like the exhalation of the violet dying even upon the sense it charms—like the snowflake dissolved in air before it has caught a stain of earth—like the light surf severed from the billow, which a breath disperses—such is the character of Ophelia; so exquisitely delicate, it seems as if a touch would profane it...."

A nunnery would have besmirched this piece of virtue. Heaven itself, where Shakspere sent her, will be the purer for her presence. But if the mortal reader here below needs a sour pickle to take this saccharine out of his mouth he may find it in the pathetic fallacy of a German critic who argues that Ophelia was a scheming woman who led Hamlet on to seduce her in the hope of marrying him later and succeeding to the throne.

All this is bad taste. But the pathetic fallacy has gone farther and, psychologically at least, has made worse blunders. We read Goethe with interest, whether we agree or not, as he tries to pluck the heart out of Hamlet's mystery; we even follow him as he searches for every indication of what Hamlet was like before his father died, of what he might have been like if his father had not died. This may, we feel, be beyond the province of common sense, but we tolerate it in order to arrive at Goethe's explanation of the character; and when we have pondered this, we go on to find the great critic arguing as "incontestable" the fact that Hamlet was "fair-haired and blue-eyed," asking us if we "can conceive of him as otherwise than plump and fair." And here we feel that we have got well into the realm of the pathetic fallacy and are not far from the kingdom of Werther. But this is mild. Goethe is merely adding something to the play. So do all those who write books with titles like 'The Girlhood of Shakspere's Heroines,' or who promulgate notions like the one that Hamlet was really a woman and in love with Horatio. The plain trouble here is that the critic is not content with Shakspere's text and must contribute something of his own. But examples are not lacking in which a critic, having made up a Hamlet in large part his own, has then found that his Hamlet does not perfectly agree with the Hamlet in the play and has thereupon accused the Hamlet in the play of intentional or unintentional falsehood. The thing sounds impossible, but:

"The sentiments which Hamlet expresses when he finds Claudius at prayer are not, I will venture to affirm, his real ones. There is nothing in his whole character that justifies such savage enormity......He alleges, as direct causes of his delay, motives that could never influence his conduct; and thus exhibits a most exquisite picture of amiable self-deceit."

This is the very ecstasy of madness. But one sees how it comes about. Hamlet is so real that the critic takes him bodily out of the play, reshapes him according to church doctrine, then tries to put him back again, and when he will not fit, accuses the play of being wrong. And this is not the work of a romantic transcendentalist but that of a sedate critic of the eighteenth century; even as the effort to explain Hamlet as a phenomenon in a mother-complex of the Freudian variety is from a scientist of our own day.

This is not an attempt to raise a monument to critical aberration, but merely to give some examples of the moderate and the immoderate results of that reality of Shakspere's characters which is our subject. As to the second of these results—the reading of Shakspere into the characters—we may be briefer. Most people know the temptation to this, the danger of it, and the excesses to which it has sometimes led. It is all but inevitable for the novice, seeing with what apparent relish Shakspere drew the character of Mercutio, for example, to conclude that Shakspere must have been something like Mercutio; but as he goes on reading Shakspere he finds evidence of the same relish in Prince Hal and in his merry-maker Falstaff and his opponent Hotspur; in the melancholy Jaques, the brooding Hamlet, the winsome Rosalind, the heroic and luxurious Antony and his unmatched paramour, and in the magic Prospero, if not in the villain Iago, the doting Lear, and the swearing Timon. The novice ceases to be a novice in this matter when he sees that Shakspere cannot be all of these men, although each is drawn with a devotion which, isolated, would be very likely to suggest self-expression. If Shakspere had left us no character but Hamlet we should doubtless think we knew much more about him than we do with his full gallery of portraits before us. And yet, although the danger has been often indicated, we are all familiar with assertions old and recent, and in all degrees of confidence, that Shakspere drew his own likeness in Mercutio, or in Jaques, or in Hamlet, or in Prospero; or that one of these is his portrait at one period, and another at another. We are further familiar with the alleged life-histories of Shakspere, made up from the story in the Sonnets and supported by the demonstration that Shakspere has left us in the plays a series of portraits of himself and the dark lady that display from year to year the progress of his fortunes and of his philosophy, that explain everything about him from the reason why he wrote Hamlet's soliloquy to the reason why he left Ann Hathaway only the second-best bed. No two of these life-histories agree, and no one of them has ever been accepted in entirety, or frequently in any essential part, by any critic but its author. But these "biographies" we shall doubtless always have with us. Novices, like Baconians, are born every year, and some of them never grow up. The latest of them is the most confident and insolent of all.

But the most inevitable result of the reality of Shakspere's characters, and perhaps the most amusing and innocuous, is seen in the multiplicity of differing opinions that have been pronounced upon them. One could fill a book with variant definitions of Hamlet alone. As abbreviation is imperative, we may therefore shorten the discussion by confining it to certain questions about this one character, by giving only a selection of the answers, and first of all by neglecting all the most preposterous of these—such as the demonstration we once encountered that Hamlet was a spiritistic medium conforming to all the laws of the occult science. For nearly two centuries now people great and small, expert and untrained, have debated whether Hamlet was insane or not, whether he was a moral man or not, whether he loved Ophelia or not, why he treated her with such apparent cruelty, why he delayed in his revenge—and all of these things together, with twenty more questions about him. Most of the alienists tell us that he was insane, though some say otherwise, and even those who insist on his insanity do not always give it the same name or agree as to when it began; while most of the laity scout the theory of lunacy. One writer affirms that Hamlet is veritably mad, though only after the play within the play, but that he is himself unconscious of it; another that he has paroxysms of insanity, had them before he saw the ghost, and that his feigning madness is but the surest proof of a real malady; another that he is quite conscious of his madness and therefore endeavors to deceive his friends by saying it is feigned; another that his madness is so scientifically managed that but few alienists exist who might not learn by watching him; and another that though his insanity is real it is unscientifically handled. On the other hand, we are informed that he is only trembling on the brink of madness; or that he is not a veritable lunatic but a reasoning melancholiac; or that he feigns madness in order the more easily to get at the king; or that he feigns it in order to enter a plea of insanity after killing the king; or that he is afraid he will actually go mad and tells his friends that he is going to feign madness in order that they may not suspect the truth. In the last case he would seem to be both mad and feigning; but the prize solution comes from the critic who declares that he is neither mad nor feigning, but merely indulging a sardonic irony which some people take for real madness and others for feigned madness, but which Shakspere meant for neither. If Hamlet is not mad, says one critic, then he is a scoundrel; if Hamlet is mad, rejoins another, then the play is a chaos. "In plain terms, Hamlet is mad," says Hudson. "A

supposition so preposterous.....is worthy only of a madman,"
says Meadows. "It is not possible to settle this question," says
George Henry Lewes.

Now it is evident upon a moment's thought that Hamlet is mad
only if Shakspere meant him to be mad, and is not mad if Shakspere did not so intend him—Shakspere's Hamlet being the only
Hamlet there is. What Shakspere meant may not be indisputably
clear; but what Shakspere meant is about the rarest question that
seems to occur to these critics. They see the creature so much
better than they see the creator.

And so it is with every other question about Hamlet. Scores
of reasons have been offered for his strange behavior to Ophelia.
One critic would have us believe that he mistreats her because he
is mad; another because he wants the king to think him mad;
another because he has never really loved her; another because he
loved her so much as to wish her in a nunnery safe from other
lovers. Most critics agree that he had loved Ophelia, but argue
either that he now believes all women are as vicious as his mother,
or that he turns against her because her father had worked to
keep him from the throne, or that in trying to dissemble his love,
for higher purposes, he overacts the part, or that when she repels
him he is unaware that she is only following her father's orders
and believes her to be acting on her own heartless initiative.
More risible are the opinions that he has lost respect for her because she had allowed him to seduce her, or because she came to
him in the lobby without a chaperon. The whole thing is "a
blunder," according to one critic; "it is tender and worthy of the
poet," according to another, "to leave this a riddle."

Riddle it is. But the attempted answers to it are still few in
comparison with those presented to what has always been the
cardinal question about Hamlet's character—why he did not
sweep to his revenge immediately. No summary can possibly do
justice to the wisdom or the ingenuity or the absurdity that
abound in the opinions offered on this matter. Either Hamlet
does not quite believe the ghost; or he finds it hard to come at the
king; or he plans some worse punishment than assassination; or
he nearly forgets the king in his rage against Polonius, himself
scheming for the throne; or he is afraid that having no evidence

that will convince the court of the king's guilt, he will seem himself a common murderer, and perhaps be executed as such; or if he is not actually afraid of death, he wants at least to be above suspicion. Such reasons seem most ingenuous. Yet a too-celebrated book, reminding us that Hamlet cannot give convincing reasons to the court for his revenge and will therefore incur obloquy himself if he takes it immediately, argues that if we but remember these facts we shall see that Hamlet does anything except delay—that he "drives ahead in storm." Then there are more subtle theories. Hamlet's rage against the king is balanced by a sense of justice; to avenge his father is to murder his uncle and widow his mother; so the animal man struggles against the Christian spirit, and Hamlet's life passes as he vacillates between two contradictory duties. Goethe thinks he is too frail a spirit to perform the bloody deed—a kind of Prince Charming ordered to do Othello's work and unequal to it. Schlegel thinks that endless deliberation over all the aspects and possible consequences of the act has crippled Hamlet's power of acting. Coleridge is like-minded; Hamlet displays "a great, an almost enormous, intellectual activity, and a proportionate aversion to real action, consequent upon it"; and so he "loses the power of action in the energy of resolve." Hazlitt makes a kind of combination of Goethe and Coleridge: Hamlet is at once "a young and princely novice" and "a prince of philosophical speculators"; he is "the sport of circumstances" and "his ruling passion is to think, not act." These latter views have found much acceptance, though they have not passed unchallenged; and seemingly are now considered not so adequate as the various opinions which, in one form or another, have something like this at their center: Hamlet lacks neither will nor nerve to act, but either thinking too precisely on the event has brought about a hopeless conflict of opposing duties, or thinking too comprehensively about the problem has led him to the vision of a whole world out of joint which no one act of retribution will do much to set right.

If we pause, it is not for lack of instances. Here we are, then, after three centuries, with no sure key to Hamlet's character. We are not the poorer for it. Hamlet is just as real to us, and just as fascinating, as if we had found a perfect formula for him;

perhaps more so. Perhaps he is the more real because, consummate copy as he is of human traits, he embodies also, like all people in the flesh and like many characters in Shakspere, the human trait of indefinability. We need not stop to say at length what is apparent at a moment's reflection, that if Hamlet swept to his revenge Shakspere would have no play, and that therefore, in the manner of all writers of revenge plays, Shakspere had to delay the action. This obvious fact will not close the discussion, and it need not. For Shakspere may have had in mind some further explanation for the delay, or he may have had none; he may conceivably have thought out some reason in psychology for Hamlet's not acting, or he may never have dreamed of any one such reason; and according as he did or did not, there is an explanation or there is no explanation for Hamlet. But that again is the rarest idea that one meets in the discussions. To illustrate this—that the characters are so real as to have been all but universally divorced from Shakspere and studied for themselves—has been the aim in the examples given. And perhaps some explanation of the fact lies in our theory that Shakspere, most translucent of all authors, gives us characters that retain in their complexity enough of the irregularity of actual men and women to present to us some portion of the puzzle life presents, and to elicit from us such variant opinions as we shower on the Smiths and Robinsons, the Caesars and Napoleons, of the world.

XVII

SHAKSPERE ON HIS ART

By Carl Van Doren
Assistant Professor of English

SHAKSPERE ON HIS ART

Guesses as to what Shakspere thought of his art are easy to make and hard to verify. Studying the problem, one perceives at the outset that the evidence is much too scanty for dogmatism. There is no reason, for instance, to think that any extant word of Shakspere's represents his certain opinions concerning the merits or purposes of his own work. The comments of this or that character upon songs in the plays are clearly dramatic; the prologs and epilogs, when not dramatic, are in the conventional mode of deference to the hearers upon whose favor the success of the play hung. If in the dedication to 'Venus and Adonis' the author refers to his "unpolished lines" as so "weak a burden" and "so bad a harvest" grown from "so barren a land," or if he calls the 'Rape of Lucrece' his "untutored lines," he speaks only in the tone of humility due from a poet to a great lord. Even the 'Sonnets,' which might be expected to abound in revelation, reveal little beyond this same humility. He speaks of his "barren rhyme,"[1] "poor rude lines,"[2] "pupil pen,"[3] "blunt invention,"[4] "wit so poor as mine,"[5] "slight Muse,"[6] "tongue-tied Muse."[7] He compares himself unfavorably with other poets: "Desiring this man's art and that man's scope";[8]

> outstripp'd by every pen,
> ....
> Exceeded by the height of happier men.[9]

He yields the palm to the rival poet: "My saucy bark inferior far to his."[10] He admits that he lacks learning[11] and that he has not kept up with the new modes of poetry.[12] He is "shamed by that which I bring forth,"[13] and esteems his work as but "The barren tender of a poet's debt."[14] In all this one finds only pas-

[1] Son. 16.
[2] Son. 32.
[3] Son. 16.
[4] Son. 103.
[5] Son. 26.
[6] Son. 38.
[7] Son. 85.
[8] Son. 29.
[9] Son. 32.
[10] Son. 80.
[11] Son. 78.
[12] Son. 76.
[13] Son. 72.
[14] Son. 83.

sionate, or superlative, compliment to an excellence in the friend
which compels a sense of deep unworthiness in the poet. Compliment, too, lies behind the poet's show of pride. When he
boasts, with a Roman ring of confidence, that

> Not marble, nor the gilded monuments
> Of princes, shall outlive this powerful rhyme,[1]

or insures himself against the flight of time with the consolation
that "My love shall in my verse ever live young,"[2] he means
chiefly to commend himself, as the poets of the age often did, for
fidelity in reporting virtues which would render any verse immortal. This he makes clear again and again:

> The argument all bare is of more worth
> Than when it hath my added praise beside.[3]

> For who's so dumb that cannot write to thee
> When thou thyself dost give invention light?[4]

> But thou art all my art and dost advance
> As high as learning my rude ignorance.[5]

Whatever Shakspere may have thought of himself as poet, he at
least did not, in words that might reasonably be thought to
stand for his own feelings, relax the vigilance of habitual modesty.

The testimony of the plays fits well with this conclusion.
Only three poets, to begin with, appear as characters. Cinna,
who falls unhappily foul of the citizens in 'Julius Caesar,' comes
of course from Plutarch. He is torn to pieces almost as curtly as
in the original narrative, but Shakspere adds the savage jest of
the fourth citizen, "Tear him for his bad verses, tear him for his
bad verses,"[6] in which the only sympathy for the poet seems to
lie in the fact that the mob is thus made a kind of critic. The
same play has another poet, nameless, who breaks in upon
Brutus and Cassius with the officious design of reconciling them
and is promptly driven out. "What," asks the scholar Brutus,
"should the wars do with these jigging fools?"[7] Here there is
something gratuitous about Shakspere's unconcern for his fel-

[1] Son. 55.   [4] Son. 38.   [6] J. C. III. iii. 34-5.
[2] Son. 19.   [5] Son. 78.   [7] J. C. IV. iii. 137.
[3] Son. 103.

low craftsman.   In Plutarch the intruder is not a poet at all but a
fierce philosopher, one Marcus Phaonius, whom Brutus calls
merely "dog, and counterfeit Cynic."   Another poet made out
of mean stuff is that in 'Timon of Athens,' again unnamed, who
has as prototypes the parasite Gnathonides in Lucian and the
fiddling singer Hermogenes in the old Timon play.   By Shakspere he is introduced reciting a dedication to Timon, and,
when asked about it, characterizes it as

> A thing slipp'd idly from me.
> Our poesy is as a gum, which oozes
> From whence 'tis nourish'd: the fire i' the flint
> Shows not till it be struck; our gentle flame
> Provokes itself and like the current flies
> Each bound it chafes.[1]

Such stale coxcombry is quite suitable to the mouth of one who
has brought Timon a conventional piece upon the slipperiness of
fortune, but who will not have the meaning taken as in any way
personal:

> I have, in this rough work, shaped out a man,
> Whom this beneath world doth embrace and hug
> With amplest entertainment: my free drift
> Halts not particularly, but moves itself
> In a wide sea of wax: no levell'd malice
> Infects one comma in the course I hold;
> But flies an eagle flight, bold and forth on,
> Leaving no tract behind.[2]

Later, when Timon is raging in his cave, the poet, with a painter,
having heard their former patron is really rich and is only trying
his friends, goes to him as a friend in distress, hoping for future
benefits.   The poet has had time to write nothing, but he plans to
promise Timon "an excellent piece": "it must be a personating
of himself; a satire against the softness of prosperity, with a discovery of the infinite flatteries that follow youth and opulency."[3]
Timon, who overhears the plan, perceives its insincerity and
beats poet and painter from his cave.   All three of these poets, it
will be noted, come from Shakspere's sources; he invented no
poet himself, unless it was invention to give the title to a mad

[1] Tim. I. i. 20-5.   [2] Tim. I. i. 43-50.   [3] Tim. V. i. 35-8.

philosopher and a parasite. In no case is there the slightest disposition to defend the character. The two poets in 'Julius Caesar' are more sharply scorned than their originals, and the poet in 'Timon of Athens' is even more unworthy than Hermogenes or Gnathonides. There is the possibility that Shakspere thought the poet a figure which his audience would find clearer and fresher than the old academic types; possibly the player was taking a fling at those wits between whom and the players some spirit of rivalry existed; it is at least certain that no lurking sympathy for a brother in art betrays itself.

Nowhere, in fact, does Shakspere represent a poet with the sympathy he manifests for soldiers and lovers, although he allows both of them, on occasion, to practice verse. Glendower tells that he has been trained in poetry at the English court [1] and excites the quick contempt of Hotspur; the Dauphin, in 'Henry V', has written a sonnet to his horse,[2] a touch of malice which puts him in ridiculous contrast to the blunt Britons. The lovers, of course, slip naturally into rime as the age taught men of their condition to do. Even Benedick, tricked into love, tries valiantly to do his metrical duty until he decides he was not born under a riming planet.[3] Posthumus, shocked by the news of Imogen's faithlessness, vows to write against women.[4] Biron propounds a text for the matter:

> Never durst poet touch a pen to write
> Until his pen were temper'd with Love's sighs.[5]

In all these cases, however, poetry is presented as a kind of weakness. The soldier who cannot fight best, the lover who has not won, or who has lost, his lady, finds in poetry an outlet for energies which fuller action would exhaust.

If Shakspere allows the poets only trifling rôles, he is borne out in his position by the most vigorous spirits of the plays, who plainly regard verse-making as an unmanly, or at best a youthful, folly. The Duke of York complains of

> Lascivious metres, to whose venom sound
> The open ear of youth doth always listen.[6]

[1] 1H4. III. i. 123-5.
[2] H5. III. vii. 42-3.
[3] M. Ado. V. ii. 40-1.
[4] Cym. II. v. 32.
[5] LLL. IV. iii. 346-7.
[6] R2. II. i. 19-20.

Mercutio mocks lovers for their love of riming.[1] Hotspur

> had rather be a kitten and cry mew
> Than one of these same metre ballad-mongers;
> I had rather hear a brazen canstick turn'd,
> Or a dry wheel grate on the axle-tree;
> And that would set my teeth nothing on edge,
> Nothing so much as mincing poetry:
> 'Tis like the forced gait of a shuffling nag.[2]

Henry V, wooing Katharine, disavows the art of poets: "for these fellows of infinite tongue, that can rhyme themselves into ladies' favours, they do always reason themselves out again. What! a speaker is but a prater; a rime is but a ballad."[3] Rosalind and Jaques are merry over Orlando's verses. Posthumus, vexed with a certain lord, tells him:

> you are made
> Rather to wonder at the things you hear
> Than to work any. Will you rhyme upon 't,
> And vent it for a mockery?[4]

Even the famous speech of Theseus on imagination, examined with these, seems something less than a poet's tender analysis of his art, put casually into the mouth of a man of action. The whole context must be taken into account:

> *Hip.* 'Tis strange, my Theseus, that these lovers speak of.
> *The.* More strange than true: I never may believe
> These antique fables, nor these fairy toys.
> Lovers and madmen have such seething brains,
> Such shaping fantasies, that apprehend
> More than cool reason ever comprehends.
> The lunatic, the lover and the poet,
> Are of imagination all compact:
> One sees more devils than vast hell can hold,
> That is, the madman: the lover, all as frantic,
> Sees Helen's beauty in a brow of Egypt:
> The poet's eye, in a fine frenzy rolling,
> Doth glance from heaven to earth, from earth
>   to heaven;
> And as imagination bodies forth
> The forms of things unknown, the poet's pen
> Turns them to shapes and gives to airy nothing

---

[1] R&J. II. i. 6-10.   [3] H5. V. ii. 163-7.   [4] Cym. V. iii. 53-6.
[2] 1H4. III. i. 129-35.

A local habitation and a name.
Such tricks hath strong imagination,
That, if it would but apprehend some joy,
It comprehends some bringer of that joy;
Or in the night, imagining some fear,
How easy is a bush supposed a bear![1]

This is, of course, the fine and happy statement of a vivid idea; the large-minded Theseus, fortunate in his love, appears for the moment gracious to poets. But, exact as he may be in his knowledge of the poetic process, there is in his words nothing whatever of praise or apology for poets. He classes them readily with madmen and lovers, an old and conventional classification. Poets are not, to Theseus, divine madmen, as Plato would have it, nor, after the creed of Petrarch, souls ecstatic with love. They are persons so fully in the control of imagination, of which Shakspere's men of action are always chary, that they are a little suspected, a little condescended to. They write down what lovers and madmen only see. Poets might be held to speak with authority, if one were only sure their madness brought to earth some supernal thing. But Theseus has nothing to say about the source or the importance of their possession. There is no reason to think that, to him, the poet's frenzy is authoritative. As he does not believe "these fairy toys," which are more than "cool reason ever comprehends," so he can be under no illusion as to the reality of an "airy nothing" which has been placed and named. "The best in this kind," he says, speaking of plays, "are but shadows; and the worst are no worse, if imagination amend them."[2]

Among the less active, the reflective characters of the plays, one looks in vain for a more concerned attitude toward poetry than that taken by the friends of action. Holofernes, who knows of "the elegancy, facility, and golden cadence of poesy,"[3] is a grotesque pedant; the duke in 'Twelfth Night' merely prefers old songs to the

light airs and recollected terms
Of these most brisk and giddy-paced times.[4]

[1] MND. V. i. 1-22.   [3] LLL. IV. ii. 125-6.   [4] TwN. II. iv. 5-6.
[2] MND. V. i. 214-6.

Tranio has the general Renaissance notion regarding the place
of poetry in education. "Music and poesy," he advises Lucen-
tio, "use to quicken you."[1] Equally general, and conventional,
is the remark of the duke in the 'Two Gentlemen of Verona,'
who says "Much is the force of heaven-bred poesy,"[2] meaning
that his daughter can probably be won to the suit of Sir Thurio

> By wailful sonnets, whose composed rhymes
> Should be full-fraught with serviceable vows."[3]

This "heaven-bred" is the sole epithet in Shakspere which
ascribes to poetry any transcendental quality. Against this
may be set the position of Touchstone [4] and of Olivia[5] that
poetry is only feigning, of Apemantus [6] that a poet, having confessed himself such, has confessed himself a liar, and of numerous
characters that rime and reason, as the popular phrase has it,
are opposed. Let all these be as dramatic or as casual as they
will, it is at least clear that Shakspere was too little touched by
them, whatever his secret defence, to think it worth while to set
off against them, anywhere in the whole body of his work, any
direct or indirect praise of poetry such as, for instance, he gives
more than once to music. He seems, that is, to have taken in
his work about the same tone in speaking of poets as a reserved
and humorous poet might use with regard to his profession in
the easy gossip of a club.

The people of Shakspere's world think and talk little about
literature of any sort. Such literary allusions as appear are, in
the main, obvious, and they are not frequent. Shakspere could
probably not assume that his audience knew or cared anything
like as much about literature as about history or law, and he
obtruded no such knowledge upon them. Lavinia,[7] Benedick,[8]
Brutus,[9] Ulysses,[10] Imogen,[11] are shown reading. Gower [12] and
Bianca [13] are reported fond of it. Hamlet is a scholar, as is Prospero, whose books Caliban fears.[14] Caesar says that Cassius
reads much;[15] Iago despises Cassio as one who knows only the

[1] TofS. I. i. 36.
[2] TGV. III. ii. 72.
[3] TGV. III. ii. 69-70.
[4] AYLI. III. iii. 19-20.
[5] TwN. I. v. 208.

[6] Tim. I. i. 226-8.
[7] TA. IV. i. 13-14.
[8] MAdo. II. iii. 3-4.
[9] JC. IV. iii. 252, 274.
[10] T&C. III. iii. 92-102.

[11] Cym. II. ii. 3.
[12] H5. IV. vii. 157
[13] TofS. I. ii. 92-3.
[14] Tmp. III. ii. 99-101.
[15] JC. I. ii. 201.

"bookish theoric" of wars;[1] the Bishop of Winchester,[2] Cardinal Wolsey,[3] and Henry VI,[4] are scorned for their bookishness. The plot of 'Love's Labour's Lost' is laid to reveal the victory of life over study, to justify Biron's assertion that

> Small have continual plodders ever won
> Save base authority from others' books,[5]

and that there is no delight so vain as

> painfully to pore upon a book
> To seek the light of truth.[6]

There is but slight comment upon the terms of literature. Shakspere seems to have preferred the theory of a plain style, to judge by his parodies of such as make a flourish of rhetoric, Armado, Holofernes, Pistol, Osric, but the terms "rhetoric" and "style" are rarely and unimportantly mentioned in his world. It is notable that he refers to "rhymes" and "verses" more than six times as often as to "poem," "poesy," and "poetry," and that he never applies the prouder title to his own writings. Sonnets, for all he gave them, in his practice, a full weight of seriousness and wisdom, are spoken of in the plays smilingly, as the harmless ammunition of lovers. "Assist me," implores Armado, "some extemporal god of rhyme, for I am sure I shall turn sonnet."[7] Ballads, by which Shakspere almost invariably means vulgar broadsides, never come in for a good word except from Autolycus and the clowns he sells them to. "The world was very guilty," says Moth, "of such a ballad [the 'King and the Beggar'] some three ages since."[8] Bottom vows he will have Quince write a ballad on the bottomless dream.[9] Helena will venture

> Tax of impudence,
> A strumpet's boldness, a divulged shame
> Traduced by odious ballads,[10]

that she can cure the king. Falstaff threatens, as revenge for

---

[1] Oth. I. i. 24.
[2] 1H6. III. i. 99.
[3] H8. I. i. 122-3.
[4] 2H6. I. i. 259.

[5] LLL. I. i. 86-7.
[6] LLL. I. i. 74-5.
[7] LLL. I. ii. 189-90.

[8] LLL. I. ii. 116-7.
[9] MND. IV. i. 220-1.
[10] AWEW. II. i. 173-5.

his indignities, to have ballads made upon his roystering friends.[1]
In the cynic Jaques' world, the lover appears

> with a woeful ballad
> Made to his mistress' eyebrow.[2]

A Roman serving-man thinks peace is only "to rust iron, increase tailors, and breed ballad-makers."[3] To Cleopatra one
of the bitterest facts of her defeat is the thought that, when she
has been taken to Rome,

> scald rhymers [will]
> Ballad us out o' tune.[4]

In this unanimous contempt there seems to appear something of
that regard for the mob's entertainment which, according to the
same kind of evidence, Shakspere felt for the mob itself.

It may reasonably be objected that conclusions thus derived
from the speech of his characters cannot be thought more than
guesses, however close, at Shakspere's opinion. There remains
another species of testimony in his images, which might well be
studied, deeply and minutely, with the purpose of finding out the
matters which regularly, or under given circumstances, inhab-
ited his mind as a store upon which he could draw for illustration. The objection that it is not he but his characters who
speak, may be answered with the fact that he puts images into
the mouths of all of them with no painful concern for dramatic
propriety. The serious objection is that poets have been too
little studied in this fashion to warrant any very firm conclusions
or comparisons. Nevertheless, it is obvious that Shakspere is
enormously abundant, that he levies upon many provinces of
life for his images, and that law and sports and war, for instance,
are among his major tributaries, while astrology, say, and music
are less frequently called upon for this service. But, admitting
the impossibility of exact judgments on this point, it is at least
certain that literature is scantily represented. A considerable
number of images come from the acts of reading and writing,
such as Queen Elinor's question regarding Philip the Bastard,

[1] 1H4. II. ii. 48-9.   [3] Cor. IV. v. 234-5.   [4] A&C. V. ii. 215-6.
[2] AYLI. II. vii. 148-9.

> Do you not read some tokens of my son
> In the large composition of this man?[1]

or the gloomy suggestion of Richard II,

> Let's talk of graves, of worms and epitaphs;
> Make dust our paper and with rainy eyes
> Write sorrow on the bosom of the earth.[2]

A few are metaphors based upon forms of narration: Clarence refers to "old folk, time's doting chronicles";[3] Claudio, when Hero has swooned at his accusation, asks

> Could she here deny
> The story that is printed in her blood?[4]

Life, says Macbeth in passionate despair,

> is a tale
> Told by an idiot, full of sound and fury,
> Signifying nothing.[5]

The overwhelming majority, however, of the images of this class in Shakspere are comparisons of persons or things with books, as concrete objects. Some, very simply, picture abstractions: "the book of memory,"[6] "sour misfortune's book,"[7] "the book of forged rebellion,"[8] "the book of honour,"[9] "the bloody book of law,"[10] "nature's infinite book of secrecy,"[11] "the book of virtue."[12] Northumberland says of Morton:

> Yea, this man's brow, like to a title-leaf,
> Foretells the nature of a tragic volume.[13]

Iago calls Desdemona's handclasp "an index and obscure prologue to the history of lust and foul thoughts."[14] Suffolk tells Henry VI that his description of Margaret is "but a preface of her worthy praise."[15] "In what chapter of his bosom?"[16] asks Olivia, to the assurance that the text of Viola lies in Orsino's bosom. More frequent than any, almost a mannerism, is the

---

[1] John. I. i. 87-8.
[2] R2. III. ii. 145-7.
[3] 2H4. IV. iv. 126.
[4] MAdo. IV. i. 123-4.
[5] Mcb. V. v. 26-8.
[6] 1H6. II. iv. 101.

[7] R&J. V. iii. 82.
[8] 2H4. IV. i. 91-2.
[9] Son. 25.
[10] Oth. I. iii. 67.
[11] A&C. I. ii. 9.

[12] WT. IV. iii. 131.
[13] 2H4. I. i. 60-1.
[14] Oth. II. i. 263-5.
[15] 1H6. V. v. 11.
[16] TwN. I. v. 242.

image which sees a book in the person of one of the characters, especially in the face or eyes. Biron regards women's eyes as

> the books, the art, the academes,
> That show, contain and nourish all the world.[1]

Gloucester says he has made Hastings

> my book, wherein my soul recorded
> The history of all her secret thoughts.[2]

Lucrece foresees that the unlearned, incapable of reading, will yet "quote my loathsome trespass in my looks."[3] "Poor women's faces," she says later, "are their own faults' books."[4] Lysander finds in Helena's eyes "Love's stories written in love's richest book."[5] Richard II sees in his glass

> the very book indeed
> Where all my sins are writ.[6]

King John offers with Blanch a large dowry if the Dauphin "Can in this book of beauty read 'I love'."[7] Lady Capulet plays with the image elaborately:

> Read o'er the volume of young Paris' face
> And find delight writ there with beauty's pen;
> ....
> And what obscured in this fair volume lies
> Find written in the margent of his eyes.
> This precious book of love, this unbound lover,
> To beautify him, only lacks a cover:
> ....
> That book in many's eyes doth share the glory,
> That in gold clasps locks in the golden story.[8]

Juliet asks of Tybalt

> Was ever book containing such vile matter
> So fairly bound?[9]

Orsino says he has unclasped to Viola "the book even of my secret soul."[10] Hamlet will write the commandment of the ghost

---

[1] LLL. IV. iii. 352-3.
[2] R3. III. v. 27-8.
[3] Lucr. 812.
[4] Lucr. 1253.
[5] MND. II. ii. 122.
[6] R2. IV. i. 274-5.
[7] John. II. i. 485.
[8] R&J.I.iii.81-92.Cf.Lucr.101-2.
[9] R&J. III. ii. 83-4.
[10] TwN. I. iv. 14.

"Within the book and volume of my brain."[1] Othello, looking
at Desdemona, questions:

> Was this fair paper, this most goodly book,
> Made to write 'whore' upon?[2]

Lady Macbeth warns her husband:

> Your face, my thane, is as a book where men
> May read strange matters.[3]

Menenius declares he has been to Coriolanus "the book of his
good acts."[4] Akin to such images are those, like "the heavenly
rhetoric of thine eye,"[5] which suggest a less physical aspect of
literature, but, generally speaking, the variations are within
narrow lines.

One might, with the aid of a concordance, exhaust the images
derived from literature in Shakspere's works, to afford a broader
basis for the general judgment that he wore his reading with due
lightness. It would be possible, also, to extend the study to his
use of such terms as "nature," "art," "imagination," "invention," with the object of finding some clue to whatever principles of aesthetics he may have had or assumed. But to keep
the inquiry brief and specific, one may at least hold that Shakspere seems not to have demanded for himself, as poet, any great
place in the world which he represented as little interested in
poets; that he seems to have had no very vehement belief in the
divine inspiration of poets; that he seems to have smiled upon
youth driven to poetry by love; and that, though clearly
a reader of books, he seems to have drawn upon them for
images, and that not too often, less as spiritual than as physical
facts.

Such a position fits well the traditional character of the genius
who was also a plain man, competent in affairs, and gentle in
his outward behavior. It is interesting to turn from the poet,
bearing himself thus reticently, to the playwright and actor.
One might expect the craftsman to speak of his livelihood. As
dramatist, however, Shakspere keeps close behind the dramas.

[1] Hml. I. v. 103.   [3] Mac. I. v. 63-4.   [5] LLL. IV. iii. 60.
[2] Oth. IV. ii. 71-2.   [4] Cor. V. ii. 15.

While there are three poets among his minor characters, there is no writer of plays, and in prologs and epilogs appears the barest mention of "our humble author,"[1] or "our bending author,"[2] who writes "with rough and all-unable pen,"[3] and without confidence.[4] Yet he readily finds images in the terms of his profession and often puts them into the mouths of characters who can know nothing of the stage. 'Venus and Adonis' has the lines

> And all this dumb play had his acts made plain
> With tears, which, chorus-like, her eyes did rain.[5]

"He is a proper man's picture," says Portia of Falconbridge, "but, alas, who can converse with a dumb-show?"[6] Menenius tells the tribunes that "if you chance to be pinched with the colic, you make faces like mummers.'"[7] Hamlet wonders, when he hears the first player declaim,

> What would he do,
> Had he the motive and the cue for passion
> That I have?[8]

Buckingham informs Gloucester that Hastings was about to speak for the duke in the matter of the coronation:

> Had you not come upon your cue, my lord,
> William Lord Hastings had pronounced your part.[9]

Othello quiets the scuffle between his followers and the men brought to arrest him:

> Were it my cue to fight, I should have known it
> Without a prompter.[10]

Falstaff calls Shallow a "Vice's dagger,"[11] referring to the wooden sword of the traditional buffoon, and Hamlet names his uncle a "vice of kings."[12] It is just worth noting, though presumably an accident, that "epilog" is never used in any figurative sense, as is "prolog" again and again:

[1] 2H4. Epil. 27-8.
[2] H5. Epil. 2.
[3] H5. Epil. 1.
[4] T&C. Prol. 23-4.
[5] V&A. 359-60.
[6] Merch. I. ii. 78-80.
[7] Cor. II. i. 81-3.
[8] Hml. II. ii. 586-8.
[9] R3. III. iv. 27-8.
[10] Oth. I. ii. 83-4.
[11] 2H4. III. ii. 344.
[12] Hml. III. iv. 98.

We'll have no Cupid hoodwink'd with a scarf,
Bearing a Tartar's painted bow of lath,
Scaring the ladies like a crow-keeper;
Nor no without-book prologue, faintly spoke
After the prompter, for our entrance.[1]

Thus he his special nothing ever prologues.[2]

not so much as will serve to be prologue to an egg and butter.[3]

as sin's true nature is,
Each toy seems prologue to some great amiss.[4]

Two truths are told
As happy prologues to the swelling act.[5]

to perform an act
Whereof what's past is prologue.[6]

There is a technical implication in the use of some words which have also a general meaning. Aaron, abused by Lucius, says:

Some devil whisper curses in mine ear,
And prompt me, that my tongue may utter forth
The venomous malice of my swelling heart![7]

Calchas tells the Greeks:

Now, princes, for the service I have done you,
The advantage of the time prompts me aloud
To call for recompense.[8]

Ingenuous Miranda, about to confess her love for Ferdinand, seems to remember the theater:

Hence, bashful cunning!
And prompt me, plain and holy innocence.[9]

The Duchess of York asks Queen Elizabeth, "What means this scene of rude impatience?" and is answered, "To make an act of tragic violence."[10] Sebastian says of his father:

He finished indeed his mortal act
That day that made my sister thirteen years.[11]

[1] R&J. I. iv. 4-8.
[2] AWEW. II. i. 95.
[3] 1H4. I. ii. 22-3.
[4] Hml. IV. v. 17-18.
[5] Mcb. I. iii. 127-8.
[6] Tmp. II. i. 252-3.
[7] TA. V. iii. 11-13.
[8] T&C. III. iii. 1-3.
[9] Tmp. III. i. 81-2.
[10] R3. II. ii. 38-9.
[11] TwN. V. i. 254-5.

"Scene" Shakspere always uses in the theatrical sense, either literally, as when Richard II says that death allows kings only "a breath, a little scene"[1] of pomp and honor, or with the transferred significance of "setting," as in "And so our scene must to the battle fly."[2] The later use of the word to mean a piece of landscape does not appear. "Comedy," as might be expected, means nothing but a play acted on the stage—Falstaff calls his too brief interview with Mistress Ford "the prologue of our comedy"[3]—while tragedy may mean any fatal incident as well; Tamora refers to the death of Bassianus as a "timeless [i.e., untimely] tragedy."[4]

The number of such images, even if increased by every possible diligence, remains small in proportion to the whole body of Shakspere's tropes, but it is enough to show that the poet's allusions to the drama concern the actual theater, not the study whence the play came, and the acting not the writing of plays. When he complains of his dumbness in love, he compares himself to

> an imperfect actor on the stage
> Who with his fear is put besides his part.[5]

One figure calls for further notice. "All the world's a stage,"[6] says Jaques, and elaborates the metaphor. Serious Antonio holds

> the world but as the world, Gratiano,
> A stage where every man must play a part.[7]

Northumberland, raging against fate, cries out:

> And let this world no longer be a stage
> To feed contention in a lingering act.[8]

Ross says, on the ominous night of Duncan's death:

> the heavens, as troubled with man's act,
> Threaten his bloody stage.[9]

[1] R2. III. ii. 164.   [4] TA. II. iii. 265.   [7] Merch. I. i. 77-8.
H5. IV. Prol. 48.   [5] Son. 23.   [8] 2H4. I. i. 155-6.
MWW. III. v. 76.   [6] AYLI. II. vii. 139.   [9] Mcb. II. iv. 5-6.

Lear, in his madness, reflects that

> When we are born, we cry that we are come
> To this great stage of fools.[1]

And Shakspere himself reminds his young friend

> That this huge stage presenteth nought but shows
> Whereon the stars in secret influence comment.[2]

In another these comparisons might seem a dramatist's boast; they are rather the verdicts of disillusioned men upon the validity of the world, which they find an insubstantial, temporary dream.   The speakers might have found sufficient similes for life in a cloud, a flowing river, the sea, the sky, the lightning; but with Shakspere it was natural enough that the sense of transitoriness should seek an emblem in the pretense and brevity of the theater.   This mood, and with it perhaps a touch of histrionic self-consciousness, appears often when a character compares his, or another's, part in life with an actor's role.   Biron, objecting to the long probation set the lovers, says:

> the ladies' courtesy
> Might well have made our sport a comedy.[3]

The Duchess of Gloucester vows

> I will not be slack
> To play my part in Fortune's pageant.[4]

Warwick asks why they

> look upon, as if the tragedy
> Were play'd in jest by counterfeiting actors?[5]

Queen Margaret sees in the bloody events she has witnessed "this tragic play."[6]   York takes an illustration from the theater to explain to his wife the greeting London gave Bolingbroke and Richard:

> As in a theatre, the eyes of men,
> After a well-graced actor leaves the stage,
> Are idly bent on him that enters next,
> Thinking his prattle to be tedious.[7]

[1] Lear. IV. vi. 186-7.   [4] 2H6. I. ii. 66-7.   [6] R3. IV. iv. 68.
[2] Son. 15.   [5] 3H6. II. iii. 27-8.   [7] R2. V. ii. 23-6.
[3] LLL. V. iii. 885-6.

Philip the Bastard is furious that the citizens of Angiers

> stand securely on their battlements,
> As in a theatre, whence they gape and point
> At your industrious scenes and acts of death.[1]

Juliet, about to drink the poison, thinks "My dismal scene I needs must act alone."[2] Henry IV, on his death-bed, tells his son that

> all my reign hath been but as a scene
> Acting that argument.[3]

The Archbishop of Canterbury urges Henry V to remember that the Black Prince "on the French ground play'd a tragedy."[4] Rosalind, hearing of the courtship of Silvius and Phebe, decides to "prove a busy actor in their play."[5] Cassius, having murdered Caesar, thinks

> How many ages hence
> Shall this our lofty scene be acted over
> In states unborn and accents yet unknown![6]

"If this were played upon a stage now," says Fabian of Malvolio's folly, "I could condemn it as an improbable fiction."[7] Hamlet explains of Rosencrantz and Guildenstern that

> Ere I could make a prologue to my brains,
> They had begun the play.[8]

And again, dying, he speaks to the bystanders as "but mutes or audience to this act."[9] Enobarbus laughs at Antony's challenging Octavius to single combat:

> Yes, like enough, high-battled Caesar will
> Unstate his happiness, and be staged to the show
> Against a sworder![10]

Coriolanus says that his feigned humility before the people

> is a part
> That I shall blush in acting.[11]

[1] John. II. i. 374-6.
[2] R&J. IV. iii. 19.
[3] 2H4. IV. v. 198-9.
[4] H5. I. ii. 106.
[5] AYLI. III. iv. 62.
[6] JC. III. i. 111-3.
[7] TwN. III. iv. 140-1.
[8] Hml. V. ii. 30-1.
[9] Hml. V. ii. 346.
[10] A&C. III. xiii. 29-31.
[11] Cor. II. ii. 148-9.

Later, overcome by the supplications of his mother and his wife, he answers them:

> Like a dull actor now
> I have forgot my part, and I am out,
> Even to a full disgrace.[1]

When he has yielded he exclaims:

> Behold, the heavens do ope,
> The gods look down, and this unnatural scene
> They laugh at.[2]

Posthumus is maddened when Imogen, as a page, speaks to him in his grief over his fancied loss:

> Shall's have a play of this? Thou scornful page,
> There lie thy part;[3]

and he strikes her. Cymbeline, after Imogen has been identified, asks his daughter:

> What, makest thou me a dullard in this act?
> Wilt thou not speak to me?[4]

The 'Winter's Tale' abounds in such comparisons. Hermione tells Leontes that she is unhappier

> Than history can pattern, though devised
> And play'd to take spectators.[5]

Camillo promises Florizel

> To have you royally appointed as if
> The scene you play were mine.[6]

Perdita forgets her reality in her happiness:

> Methinks I play as I have seen them do
> In Whitsun pastorals.[7]

When she must disguise herself for the escape, she says:

> I see the play so lies
> That I must bear a part.[8]

[1] Cor. V. iii. 40-2.　　　[4] Cym. V. v. 265-6.　　　[7] WT. IV. iv. 133-4.
[2] Cor. V. iii. 183-5.　　　[5] WT. III. ii. 37-8.　　　[8] WT. IV. iv. 668-9.
[3] Cym. V. v. 228-9.　　　[6] WT. IV. iv. 602-3.

Of her reception by Paulina it is said that the "dignity of this act was worth the audience of kings and princes."[1] Leontes feels that, should he marry again, Hermione's ghost would appear "on this stage."[2] And the last words of Leontes seem to make out the whole action as only a comedy:

> Good Paulina,
> Lead us from hence, where we may leisurely
> Each one demand an answer to his part
> Perform'd in this wide gap of time since first
> We were dissever'd.[3]

All these but conduct to the powerful valedictory of Prospero:

> Our revels now are ended. These our actors,
> As I foretold you, were all spirits and
> Are melted into air, into thin air:
> And, like the baseless fabric of this vision,
> The cloud-capp'd towers, the gorgeous palaces,
> The solemn temples, the great globe itself,
> Yea, all which it inherit, shall dissolve
> And, like this insubstantial pageant faded,
> Leave not a rack behind.[4]

It is worth pointing out that the similes founded on books are rather more frequent in the earlier than in the later plays, and that the later show more instances of comparison, in the 'Winter's Tale' amounting almost to confusion, of the universe of fact with the universe of fiction. As this shift corresponds to no known change in theatrical fashion, and seems a little too marked to be mere accident, reasons may possibly be looked for in Shakspere's mind. Perhaps his sense of the unreality of existence grew upon him: perhaps, becoming more assured, he became less careful not to remind his audience that the play was only a play: perhaps, with the passage of years, his mind came to be more and more full of his profession. One thinks of the sonnet, so often regarded as direct revelation, in which he complains of the "public means" which have bred "public manners" in him and have branded his name:

> almost thence my nature is subdued
> To what it works in, like the dyer's hand.[5]

---

[1] WT. V. ii. 86-8.   [3] WT. V. iii. 151-5.   [5] Son. 111.
[2] WT. V. i. 58.   [4] Tmp. IV. i. 148-56.

Did he feel himself being mastered by a calling that he could not respect? And yet the plays do not make light of players as much as they do of poets. The companions of Holofernes and Bottom are, of course, amateurs, and so fair game for laughter. When Macbeth calls life

> a poor player
> That struts and frets his hour upon the stage
> And then is heard no more,[1]

he is but using Shakspere's repeated symbol of impermanence. The greatest scorn for actors appears in the words of Ulysses and of Cleopatra, at the thought of dignity mimicked. Ulysses is telling Agamemnon that Patroclus takes him off in Achilles' tent:

> like a strutting player, whose conceit
> Lies in his hamstring, and doth think it rich
> To hear the wooden dialogue and sound
> 'Twixt his stretch'd footing and the scaffoldage,—
> Such to-be-pitied and o'er-wrested seeming
> He acts thy greatness in.[2]

Cleopatra dreads not only the balladists of Rome:

> the quick comedians
> Extemporally will stage us, and present
> Our Alexandrian revels; Antony
> Shall be brought drunken forth, and I shall see
> Some squeaking Cleopatra boy my greatness
> I' the posture of a whore.[3]

Such speeches are warranted by the nature or position of the speaker; they seem less gratuitous, and they are less numerous, than those passages which make light of poets. The players in 'Hamlet' and in the induction to the 'Taming of the Shrew' Shakspere presents without special qualities. Brutus advises his fellow conspirators not to show in their looks any sign of the deeds they plan:

> But bear it as our Roman actors do,
> With untired spirits and formal constancy.[4]

Presumably, "English" might as well be put for "Roman," but in any case the words represent a certain respect in which Brutus

[1] Mcb. V. v. 24-6. [3] A&C. V. ii. 215-20. [4] JC. II. i. 226-7.
[2] T&C. I. iii. 153-8.

holds the profession. Caesar counts it against Cassius that he "loves no plays,"[1] as Antony does. The current opposition to the theater is not reflected in the dramas; prudence may have kept Shakspere from that mooted point. His world of fiction does not emphasize the difficult social status of actors in his age, partly, perhaps, because such emphasis would have to be laid by actors on themselves. Whatever the explanation, it remains the fact that in Shakspere's world the poets stand, as in the actual world, a little misty, a little remote, a little ridiculous, by virtue of their very calling, while actors, as persons engaged in a visible and tangible business, Shakspere's own, are taken as a matter of course and come in for comment only when they perform their function badly. That function is stated, in broad terms, by Hamlet: "they are the abstract and brief chronicles of the time."[2]

It is on this basis that Hamlet utters the most deliberate piece of artistic criticism in the plays. He counsels actors, as the world knows, to be temperate in delivery and gesture: "suit the action to the word, the word to the action; with this special observance, that you o'erstep not the modesty of nature: for anything so overdone is from the purpose of playing, whose end, both at the first and now, was and is, to hold, as 'twere, the mirror up to nature."[3] Here Hamlet makes a phrase which has been taken to fit all art, though he himself, of course, applies it only to acting. Elsewhere he characterizes "an excellent play" as being "well digested in the scenes, set down with as much modesty as cunning. I remember, one said there were no sallets in the lines to make the matter savoury, nor no matter in the phrase that might indict the author of affectation."[4] These judgments come from the plain code of nature. The mood Hamlet enjoins in the artist is modesty, that nothing may step between truth and its reflection. There is no simpler theory of art; it is as easy to hold as it is hard to follow. The Chorus of 'Henry V' had apologized for

> The flat unraised spirits that hath dared
> On this unworthy scaffold to bring forth
> So great an object.[5]

[1] JC. I. ii. 203. [3] Hml. III. ii. 18-24. [5] H5. I. Prol. 9-11.
[2] Hml. II. ii. 548-9. [4] Hml. II. ii. 460-5.

When Shakspere put principles of realism into Hamlet's mouth, he himself was probably, to judge by the plays of that period, deeply concerned with the problem of truth to life, whether in his deliberate creed or in the instinct by which his imagination worked. He was no longer so young as not to see truly; he was not yet so old as to feel that there is little to choose, after all, between the twin shadows of life and art. If there is a change in this respect from his earlier to his later work, it may lie in some shift of his power to perceive nature; but at any stage of his career he could have held the principle that art is purely nature's mirror. All poets have held some such principle. The incredible matter is that Shakspere should have been able to blur his reflection of nature so little, by any intrusion of himself, that one may search his work through and through and come upon only faint traces that he was even conscious of the process of reflection. He could discuss, penetratingly and finally, the technic of an art, as 'Hamlet' shows; but he kept his own artistic principles implicit in his art. The only mark which his calling seems to have left upon him, so far as the works reveal it, is a few images which almost any one might have picked up, and which make it appear that certain details of the stage may have found their way into his language a little more readily during his later years than they had done at an earlier date, when he had drawn more frequently upon books. He refused, so far as can be determined, to be drawn into the war of the theaters; he hardly mentions contemporary poets; he is utterly reticent about himself. This is an example of that modesty which Hamlet urges upon the players and which he remembers in the piece he commends. It does not mean that Shakspere thought ill of himself in comparison with other poets or that he thought ill of poets in general; it means that he gave, for whatever reason, to the act and technic of mirroring reality only the slightest trifle of the attention which he gave to reality itself. With inscrutable blandness he seems to have taken precisely the tone of the ordinary world, ignorant and casual, with regard to the art of which he knew the secrets. The ordinary world looks askance, a little scornful, and yet a shade credulous, at the theory that poets are, in some way or other, divinely inspired; the ordinary world laughs at perceiving that youth, in love, must rime; the ordinary world entertains itself with art but gives it few serious thoughts; the ordinary world, naturally, sees less mystery in actors than in poets; the ordinary world thinks more of finished works of art than of the artists who make them. It is such a world which Shakspere reflects to itself. He makes no effort to correct the reality in its reflection nor to teach his audience better. Being a poet could not make him a partisan of poets.

XVIII

SHAKSPERE AND THE MEDIEVAL LYRIC

By Frank Allen Patterson

Assistant Professor of English

SHAKSPERE AND THE MEDIEVAL LYRIC

Gaston Paris was among the first to notice that the prolonged and reluctant parting between Romeo and Juliet is an example of a distinct type of the medieval lyric, the *aube*, well known in Provence, Northern France, Italy and Germany.[1] Curiously enough, among the songs of pre-Shaksperian England there seem to be left no lyrics that more than distantly suggest the *aube*, though there have been preserved several first lines, such as

> Lemman, dawis it nocht day?[2]

which seem to indicate that Shakspere may easily have known English poems of this type, and that medieval lyric tradition was still surviving in Elizabethan England. It seems worth while, therefore, to attempt to determine Shakspere's inherited knowledge and use of the medieval lyric in its various forms and in its content.

In order to avoid needless confusion, it may be well to remind ourselves in the start that medieval lyric verse consists of two large divisions: first, the sophisticated, courtly lyric of which the *aube* is an example; second, native popular poetry, sung by the folk at winter gatherings in the hall or chanted at Mayday dances on the green. Shakspere's contact with the courtly lyric will be considered in the first part of the present paper, his knowledge of popular poetry in the second part.

Before passing on to other reminiscences of lyric tradition in Shakspere, we may direct our attention to the care with which the dramatist has met the conventional demands of the type already mentioned, the *aube*. In accordance with the earliest popular poetry, the protest against parting and the

[1] *Les Origines de la Poésie Lyrique en France* in *Journal des Savants*, Mars, 1892, p. 163. The next year appeared a study by Ludwig Fränkel, *Shakespeare und das Tagelied*, Hannover 1893.

[2] Mentioned in the *Tale of Cowkelbe* as a popular dance tune. Quoted by Sibbald, *Chronicle of Scottish Poetry*, I, 379.

fault-finding with envious day and the lark that sings so out of tune, come chiefly from Juliet; it is she who insists that the nightingale sings on the pomegranate tree; it is she who sees in the first streaks of dawn, the light from some meteor acting as a torch-bearer for Romeo; and it is only until Romeo has argued with her, stating the truth plainly, yet gladly resigning himself to death, that she, against her inclination, urges him hence. To have mistaken the lark for the nightingale was, Paris thinks, a primitive convention, derived finally from the earliest French lyrics, now non-extant, and indeed, perhaps, in the sense of the written lyric, never extant. More primitive, though, is this passionate expression of feminine love and the pacific resignation of the lover, who clearly sees that he 'must be gone and live, or stay and die.'

Another detail, not noticed by Paris, is the use made of the nurse to take the place of the watchman in the conventional poems. He it is who in the lyrics calls out to the lovers, warning them that a suspicious parent is near, that day is dawning, that caution is needed. In Shakspere it is the friendly nurse who enters the room in haste, crying:

> Madam....
> Your lady mother is coming to your chamber:
> The day is broke; be wary, look about.

One other convention of the *aube*, which seems to fit into dramatic exigencies, and of which Shakspere made full use, is the placing of the scene in a garden on an elevated porch, a balcony, or in a tower. When Romeo declares, 'One kiss and I'll descend,' he is but repeating the sentiment of every preceding lyric lover about to depart and using practically the same words. Promises of fidelity similar to those in the play occur, of course, in most lyrics of the genre.

In one other place, Shakspere has a hint of the *aube*, though here the characteristics of the type are not fully developed. In 'Troilus and Cressida' there is a scene where the two lovers are forced by the approach of morning to part.[1] Here again the

---

[1] *Troilus and Cressida*, IV, II. The corresponding scene in Chaucer's *Troilus and Criseyde* somewhat resembles an *aube*. The most important trait here is that both lovers curse cruel day, 'calling it traytour, envyous, and worse.' III, 1695-1701.

'busy day' has been 'waked by the lark'; the lover declares that
he would stay were it not so; upon which Cressida comments,
'Night hath been too brief'; and Troilus exclaims in good lyric
fashion, 'Beshrew the witch!', declaring that usually she stays
tediously enough. Cressida in reply prays him to linger, saying,
'you men will never tarry' and breaks off her speech with,
'Hark! there's one up.' They are then interrupted by the uncle
who acts the part of the watchman, with a difference, it is true.
Thus there are several traits of the conventional lyric found here,
almost all except the one necessary, for there was never an *aube*
which had so little true, sincere emotion and generous love as has
this scene between Troilus and Cressida.

Shakspere's knowledge of courtly lyrics was not limited to
conventional songs of lovers parting at dawn, as is proved by the
experience of Ferdinand, king of Navarre.[1] His court was
'haunted with a refined traveller of Spain,' who had a 'mint of
phrases in his brain' and the music of whose 'own vain tongue'
did 'ravish like enchanting harmony.' The first time that we
hear directly from this knight, Armado, is when the king reads a
letter from him, describing a recent experience of this literary
courtier. Armado's diction reminds us at once of that Elizabethan euphuism which came ultimately from Spain; but the
details which the visitor chooses to relate and all the attendant
circumstances of the incident described, show that the writer
had given some time to the study of approved poetry of an older
generation. It is no less than an 'adventure' which he reports
in the fashion of the *chanson d'aventure*, except that he is constrained to use prose, perhaps because of the urgency of his business.

It seems that this poetical knight, apparently the evening before, was 'besieged with sable-colored melancholy,' and determined to take 'most wholesome physic' of the 'health-giving air.'
Accordingly, at 'about the sixth hour, when beasts most graze,'
and 'birds best peck,' he betook himself to walk. The place he
chose was the park belonging to the king, and there in a spot
'north-north-east and by east from the west corner' of the king's
'curious-knotted garden,' he discovered Costard, 'that low-spir-

---

[1] *Love's Labour's Lost*, I. I.

ited swain... sorted and consorted... with a child of our grandmother Eve, a female.'

Eavesdropping and spying upon the love-making of a rustic couple, usually a shepherd and his lass, formed, of course, the subject matter of many typical medieval *pastourelles*. The ridiculous parody which Armado innocently gives us of this type of lyric can hardly be other than intentional on Shakspere's part, for the conventional details are retained in surprising fullness. Like the medieval poet, Armado is driven forth by melancholy to take the air; very properly he chooses the sixth hour, but instead of hearing the songs of birds on briar, he reminds us that this was the hour when 'beasts most graze' and 'birds best peck'; like the medieval poet, he discovers the pair in a secluded place in a wood, or, rather, a park; and likewise finds the couple a country swain and his sweetheart. The king showed good judgment in choosing this 'child of fancy' for his minstrelsy.

Another form of the medieval lyric of which we find more than a trace in Shakspere, is the *reverdie* or nature song celebrating the coming of spring. The *reverdie* in its purest form is simply a song expressing the joy which birds, flowers and trees find in the newly awakened earth; seldom, though, it fails to suggest that the joy of mere living has entered also the poet's life. Such a song is a Latin lyric found in the 'Carmina Burana,[1] the first stanza of which runs:

> Iam ver oritur.
> Veris flore variata
> tellus redimitur.
> Excitat in gaudium
> cor concentus avium
> voce relativa
> Iovem salutantium.
> In his Philomena
> Tereum reiterat,
> et iam fatum antiquatum
> querule retractat.
> Sed dum fatis obicit
> Itim perditum,
> merula choraulica
> carmina coaptat.

[1] J. A. Schmeller, *Carmina Burana*, Breslau, 1904, p. 117, no. 33.

Already spring is at hand. The land is adorned with summer's variegated flowers. Birds singing in harmony, each in its own tune, saluting Jove, stir up the heart to joy. Among these Philomena now tells over and over the story of Tereus and now complainingly rehearses the ancient tale. While she mourns Itys lost, the blackbird joins the song with flute-like melody.

In this instance birds not able to sing were yet able to make known their joy in spring by the use of wings. To the singing birds were added:

> Mergus aquaticus, aquila munificus,
> bubo noctivagus, cygnus flumineus,
> phaenix unica,
> perdix letargica, hirundo domestica,[1]

and some eight others.

One is instantly reminded of the numerous birds in the 'Parlement of Foules' and the song[2] which they sang as a salute to approaching spring:

> Now welcom somer, with thy sonne softe,
> That hast this wintres weders over-shake,
> And driven awey the longe nightes blake!

Chaucer's long poem is not, of course, a pure *reverdie*, nor even a lyric, but the *rondel* which the birds sing, answers the requirements of the type. Closer, though, to the *reverdie* in its narrowest sense, in that the names of various birds are woven into the lyric, is the song which Bottom sings:

> The ousel cock, so black of hew,
> With orange-tawny bill,
> The throstle, with his note so true,
> The wren and little quill,
>
> The finch, the sparrow, and the lark,
> The plainsong cuckow gray;
> Whose note full many a man doth mark,
> And dares not answer, nay.[3]

Most of these birds figure in the numerous *reverdies* printed in various collections of Latin, Old French, and Middle English

---

[1] The water-loving diver, the generous eagle, the night-wandering owl, the river-haunting swan, the phoenix, only one of its kind, the drowsy partridge, the domestic swallow.

[2] Ll. 680-692.

[3] *Midsummer-Night's Dream*, III. II. 128ff.

lyrics. Doubtless Shakspere was not consciously following a model in this poem, but was merely writing a song that would fit in with fairies and the outdoor life that fills his play, yet the fact that innumerable songs of this type had been sung in France and England for centuries before, is significant. Literary tradition once firmly established has a habit of turning up in unexpected places and in unaccountable ways.

Often in medieval poetry there is attached to the *reverdie* a love theme of some kind. Sometimes the poet, sitting in a shaded wood, enjoys the flowers around him, observes the leaves beginning to grow green, and finds in nature almost the Wordsworthian 'universal joy.' But, like the greater poet, he, too, feels a sadness in the air; it comes from the singing birds and especially from the nightingale, who, complaining of her misfortune in love, suggests in allegorical fashion the plight of other true lovers. The anonymous poet of that golden treasury of medieval lyric song, the Harleian manuscript,[1] has given us several poems of this type. The following well illustrates the union of the *reverdie* nature song and the lover's complaint of his unfortunate passion:

> Lenten ys come wiþ loue to toune,
> Wiþ blosmen & wiþ briddes roune,
>   þat al þis blisse bryngeþ;
> Dayes eȝes in þis dales,
> Notes suete of nyhtegales,
>   Vch foul song singeþ.
> þe þrestelcoc him þreteþ oo;
> Away is huere wynter woo,
>   When woderoue springeþ.
> þis foules singeþ ferly fele,
> Ant wlyteþ on huere wynter wele,
>   þat al þe wode ryngeþ.
> . . . .
> Mody meneþ, so doht mo,
> Ichot ycham on of þo,
>   For loue þat likes ille.[2]

More briefly had another anonymous English poet expressed this not unusual condition of lovers:

> Foweles in the frith,
> The fisses in the flod.

---

[1] No. 2253.

[2] Fol. 71b; printed by Böddeker, *Altenglische Dichtungen*, Berlin, 1878, p. 164.

> And I mon waxe wod;
> Mulch sorwe I walke with
> For best of bon and blod.[1]

Shakspere's Passionate Pilgrim in one of the phases of his emotion had an experience similar to that of many medieval poets.[2] Once he found himself sitting in a pleasant shade in the merry month of May, while around him

> Beasts did leap, and birds did sing,
> Trees did grow, and plants did spring;

all was happy 'save the nightingale alone,' who complained of her griefs in so lively a fashion as to find in the poet a sympathetic listener. The subsequent portion of the poem, with its moralizing upon the evils of life and the fickleness of fortune, is quite in the medieval manner.

Autolycus, who in his knowledge of medieval lyric poetry is Armado's only rival, introduces himself by singing a song in praise of spring.[3] All the time-honored details reappear, the joy in flowers, like the daffodils, and the songs of birds, 'the lark that tirra-lyra chants,' the thrush and the jay. Many an anonymous English poet had been using this theme of joy in flowers and birds in spring for centuries before, sometimes devoting an entire poem to the celebration, as did the author of the famous cuckoo lyric, sometimes using it for a conventional opening, as in the following:

> When þe nyghtegale singes,
> þe wodes waxen grene,
> Lef & gras & blosme springes
> In aueryl, y wene.[4]

The nature lyric reached its highest literary development in two of Shakspere's songs: the first in 'Cymbeline,' 'Hark, hark! the lark at heaven's gate sings'[5]; the second, the song of Ariel in the 'Tempest':[6]

> Where the bee sucks, there suck I:
> In a cowslip's bell I lie;

---

[1] MS. Douce 139; printed here from Chambers and Sidgwick, *Early English Lyrics*, p. 5.
[2] *The Passionate Pilgrim*. No. XXI. This particular poem is usually ascribed to Richard Barnfield, from whom Shakspere may have borrowed it for the occasion.
[3] *Winter's Tale*, IV. III, 1-22.
[4] MS. *Harleian* 2253, fol. 80 b; printed Böddeker, p. 174.
[5] II. III, 21-30.
[6] V. I, 88-94.

> There I couch when owls do cry.
> On the bat's back I do fly
> After summer merrily.
> Merrily, merrily shall I live now
> Under the blossom that hangs on the bough.

Paris has remarked of one of the most delicate of the French *reverdies*,[1] that it is 'full of charm and bizarre poetry, very rare in our literature, reminding one, by its graceful and vague fancy, of the most aerial bits of Shakspere.'[2] It is possible that the dramatist himself owes much to poems now lost belonging to this type. Several French *reverdies* are filled with fairy creatures like those in Shakspere's plays, who live under the blossom that hangs on the bough. Thus Ariel's song has a twofold resemblance to a *reverdie*, in its joy in nature and in its suggestion of fairy life.

A large number of Shakspere's other songs may be classed as nature lyrics, and are thus, even when not distinctly salutes to spring, more or less intimately related to the medieval *reverdie*. Poems in praise of nature are, of course, not unusual in all literatures and in nearly all ages. But the vigorous nature songs of Elizabethan poetry, whether translated from some Italian poet of the Renaissance, or written out of the poet's own experience, owe most to the nature poetry of western Europe in the Middle Ages.

In the last scene of 'Love's Labor's Lost,' the Owl, representing winter, and the Cuckoo, standing for spring, hold a 'dialogue that two learned men...compiled.' Armado, who introduces this diversion, thus gives further proof of his scholarly knowledge of ancient minstrelsy. The *debat* was, of course, a well established form of poetical exercise in the Middle Ages,[3] and of *debats* one of the most popular was that between two birds, such as the owl and the cuckoo or the owl and the nightingale. Winter and summer were also constantly at odds. Usually, it is true, the

---

[1] Printed in Bartsch, *Altfranzösische Romanzen und Pastourellen*, Leipzig, 1870, No. 28.

[2] Gaston Paris, *opus cit.* November, 1891, p. 687. The original reads:....mais elle est pleine d'une charmante et bizarre poésie, bien rare dans notre littérature, et qui fait penser, par sa fantaisie gracieuse et vague, aux morceaux les plus aériens de Shakspere.

[3] The debate, in the widest sense, lasted long after the Middle Ages, and is a good illustration of the persistency of literary custom. Andrew Marvell has a 'Dialogue between the Soul and Body' which may be considered an evidence of inherited tradition, a deliberate return to the past, or the eternal persistence in poetry of a natural human motive.

debat took more the form of a sprightly dialog, a repartee and a quick exchange of wit, running on indefinitely, rather than, as here, of a single song by each participant. The two learned men displayed thus a moderation unhappily not known to their predecessors. The first song, mingling love and nature in celebration of the delights of spring, readily reminds one of many *reverdie* songs like those already mentioned. In England the cuckoo was to lyric poetry what the nightingale was in France. From the time of one of the earliest secular lyrics with its refrain

> Sing cuccu nu! Sing cuccu!
> Sing cuccu! Sing cuccu nu![1]

to this song of Shakspere's we have references to the herald of the English spring. To find a parallel for the owl's vigorous praise of winter is more difficult. The learned man who wrote the song condensed a whole manuscript and more into two stanzas. One may search in vain through medieval literature for poems expressing such rugged delight in the time 'when milk comes frozen home in pail' and 'birds sit brooding in the snow.'

Another contest should be noticed in this place, the Passionate Pilgrim's praise of youth 'full of pleasance' and dispraise of 'crabbed age,' a theme done justice to long before his time by many a poet expanding the *carpe diem* text and many a serious monk urging a worthier end. In fact, medieval Europe was as full of contrasts as our modern Macaulay, and about as moderate in using them. Shakspere could not easily have escaped; no more could his fellow Elizabethans.

One other contest, this time in love, the Pilgrim relates.[2] He tells us there was once, presumably in medieval Europe, a 'lording's daughter,' the fairest one of three sisters, who was courted by two lovers, a gallant knight and her master, perhaps her teacher of languages. Those who are acquainted with similar poems of the thirteenth century need not read to the end to discover the outcome, for of course the 'trusty knight was wounded with disdain.' 'Alas! she could not help it!' 'The silly damsel'

---

[1] MS. *Harleian* 978. The cuckoo was the favorite bird in Anglo-Saxon poetry as references in the *Husband's Message* and the *Seafarer* show.

[2] *The Passionate Pilgrim*, No. XVI.

had to abide by the precedent of three centuries and more. It was the learned man who carried away the 'lady gay.'

Shakspere in other ways has shown us that he could use inherited literary customs when he desired. Throughout the Middle Ages a poet about to give up his courting in despair, apparently wrote a lyric celebrating the ugly and unhappy qualities of the woman whom he had loved in vain. This unattractive kind of poetry, or better, literary exercise, reached in England a culmination in a lyric [1] the first two stanzas of which are given here:

> I haue a lady where so she be
>   That seldom ys the souerayne of my thought;
> On whos beawte when I beholde and se,
>   Remembryng me how well she ys wrought,
>   I thanke fortune that to hyr grace me brought; .
>   So fayre ys she but nothyng angelyke,
>   Hyr bewty ys to none other lyke.
>
> ffor hardely and she were made of brasse,
>   fface and all she hath y nowgh fayrenesse;
> Hyr eyen byn holow and grene as any grasse,
>   And rauynnysshe yelow ys hyr sonny tresse;
>   Therto she hath of euery comlynesse
>   Suche quantyte yeuyne hyr by nature,
>   That with the leest she ys of hyr stature.

This custom of ironical praise of a woman lasted well into the Italian Renaissance. Shakspere in the sonnet printed below[2] may have been following contemporary foreign influences, but it is more probable that he acted upon a hint and more found in Lydgate and other post-Chaucerian writers.

> My mistress' eyes are nothing like the sun;
> Coral is far more red than her lips' red;
> If snow be white, why then her breasts are dun;
> If hairs be wires, black wires grow on her head.
> I have seen roses damask'd, red and white,
> But no such roses see I in her cheeks;
> And in some perfumes is there more delight
> Than in the breath that from my mistress reeks.
> I love to hear her speak, yet well I know
> That music hath a far more pleasing sound;

[1] MS. Trinity Coll., Camb., R. 3. 19. fol. 205 a. Hitherto unprinted.
[2] No. CXXX.

> I grant I never saw a goddess go;
> My mistress, when she walks, treads on the ground:
> And yet, by heaven, I think my love as rare
> As any she belied with false compare.

The detailed description of the lady here given is also quite in the medieval manner. There are other passages in Shakspere that suggest this favorite method of medieval poets in beginning with the eyes, and describing with weary minuteness all the lady's charms. Olivia ironically proposed to give out divers schedules of her beauty.[1] She promised to have it 'inventoried, and every particle and utensil labelled.' The list was to include 'item, two lips indifferent red; item, two grey eyes with lids to them; item, one neck, one chin, and so forth.' Fortunately, Viola did not encourage the proceeding. Shakspere may easily here have been glancing at the numerous medieval poems of this class, represented even by Geoffrey Chaucer in the following attempt to portray beauty:

> Madame, ye ben of al beaute shryne
> As fer as cercled is the mappemounde;
> For as the cristal glorious ye shyne,
> And lyke ruby ben your chekes rounde.
> Therewith ye ben so mery and so iocounde,
> That at a revel whan that I see you daunce,
> It is an oynement unto my wounde,
> Thogh ye to me ne do no. daliaunce.[2]

More typical, because much more commonplace, is the following:

> Ichot a burde in boure bryht,
> ....
> Wiþ lokkes lefliche & longe,
> Wiþ frount & face feir to fonde,
> Wiþ murþes monie mote heo monge,
>   Þat brid so breme in boure,
> Wiþ lossom eye, grete ant gode,
> Wiþ browen blysfol vnder hode;
> He þat reste him on þe rode,
>   Þat leflich lyf honoure![3]

---

[1] *Twelfth Night*, I. V. 262-268.
[2] *To Rosemounde. A Balade.* Skeat, *Minor Poems*, 389.
[3] MS. *Harleian* 2253, fol. 72 b; printed Böddeker, p. 168.

When the fairies in 'Midsummer-Night's Dream' are about to sing, we have the invitation:

> Come, now, a roundell, and a fairy song.

Those of us, though, who are hoping to find in the forthcoming song a genuine *rondel* like those which Chaucer imported from France, are to be disappointed in spite of Furness's note in which he quotes Skeat's definition of this kind of lyric. The *rondel* of the courtly school of lyric poets, as given us by Chaucer and Occleve, consists of a lyric in which, among other characteristics, the first lines are used as a recurring refrain. The fairies' song is simply a round or dancing song, far removed from the more sophisticated *rondel* and closely allied to indigenous song, such as we may imagine being sung at the May dances mentioned by Lydgate and others.

Armado, learned in minstrelsy, uses the term 'l'envoy'[1] and excites our hope that perhaps he knew also of the later highly conventional courtly lyrics, such as the *ballade*. His definition is somewhat to the point, for he declares that an *envoy*

> is an epilogue or discourse, to make plain
> Some obscure precedence that hath tofore been sain.

When he attempts to 'example it' though we are mystified. Either the author is deliberately making fun by parodying the *envoy* or else both Shakspere and Armado are hopelessly lost in the mazes of technical usuage. In several other places Shakspere uses the word 'ballad,' but never is there a hint that a rhyme can be anything but a ballad.[2]

Nearly all the reminiscences of the medieval lyric in Shakspere, thus far noticed, have been concerned more with the later development of the courtly lyric than with primitive popular song. The *aube*, the *chanson d'aventure*, the *reverdie*, when it departs from its oldest form, the original bird and flower spring poem, the *debat*, especially when it becomes a strife in love between a knight and a clerk, are forms of the lyric that were elaborated and conventionalized from earlier popular poetry by poets who placed art above originality and the usual in literature above the actual. But while

[1] *Love's Labor's Lost*, III. I. 72ff.
[2] *Henry V*, V. II. 166.

courtly poets were celebrating fictitious love affairs and listening
to the allegorical complaints of the nightingale, there existed an
indigenous poetry in the homes of the people and among their
teachers, the clergy, simple indeed, though often not unaffected
by the sophisticated lyric.

The contest, previously mentioned, belonged originally to the
folk, as did most other literary types; and as folksong, it persisted throughout the Middle Ages alongside the more complicated and sophisticated debates, Shaksperian examples of which
have just been given. Shakspere was the inheritor, also, of these
folk contest lyrics, doubtless handed down by oral tradition.
In 'As You Like It' is the lyric celebrating the winter wind and
man's ingratitude. This song, medieval enough in scope and
tone, has the refrain:

> Heigh-ho! Sing, heigh-ho! unto the green holly:
> Most friendship is feigning, most loving mere folly:
> Then, heigho-ho, the holly:
> This life is most jolly.[1]

Lyrics in praise of the holly, emblem of winter's festivities and
Christmas revels, were unusually popular in England during the
last centuries of the Middle Ages. Most often the celebration
took the form of a contest between holly and ivy, in which 'sory
ivy' came off the worse. Such a song is that preserved in MS.
Balliol 354, the refrain of which will give an idea of the spirit of
joyous contention which pervades the lyric:

> Nay, nay, Ive,
> It may not be iwis!
> For holy must haue ye mastry,
> As ye maner is![2]

In another Oxford manuscript is found a poem in the likeness of
a Christmas carol that sings the praises of holly without feeling
obliged to disparage 'jentyl ivy,' though even here there are
wishes of ill for those who may secretly feel disposed to take sides
with ivy:

---

[1] II. VII. 174-190.
[2] MS. Balliol 354; printed by Flügel, *Anglia* xxvi, 279.

Alleluia, alleluia!
Alleluia, now syng we!

Her commys holly, that is so gent,
To pleasse all men is his entent.
Alleluia!

But, lord and lady off this hall,
Who so ever ageynst holly call;
Alleluia!

Who so ever ageynst holly do crye,
In a lepe shall he hang full hye!
Alleluia!

Who so ever ageynst holly do syng,
He maye wepe and handys wryng!
Alleluia![1]

In Shakspere's youth and probably much later, country and town must have rung at Christmastime with traditional praises of this plant, welcome even yet to us in midwinter, though no longer celebrated in popular song.

Equally dear to the mind of the unpretending folk as the standing quarrel between holly and ivy, must have been the Christmas carol, which, judging from printed collections of medieval poetry, seems to have flourished most vigorously on English soil. Here it developed a form peculiar to itself consisting usually of from four to eight stanzas of three to four lines, rhyming often aaaa and furnished with a chorus or burden of one or more lines, rhyming BB. Often the refrain was simply the exhortation, 'Be merry, be merry!' Sometimes these carols were of a sacred nature and were used, doubtless, for religious purposes by the folk at their frequent gatherings; sometimes they were far from having any pious function.

The religious Christmas carol is well illustrated by the following poem:[2]

Be merye, be merye,
J pray yu euery chon!

---

[1] MS. Eng. Poet, e. 1, Bodl., Oxford. Printed by Wright, *Songs and Carols of the Fifteenth Century*, Percy Society Publications, 1847, p. 84.
[2] MS. Corpus Christi Coll., Camb., No. 233, fol. 95 b. Hitherto unprinted.

A pryncypal poynth of charyte,
It is so mery for to be,
In hym þat is but one.
      Be merye!

He þat is but on in blys,
To vs haue sent hys sone, I wys,
To saue vs fro our fone.
      Be merye!

Mary, for youre sonnys sake,
Saue ye all þat mery make,
& lengest holdyn vppon.
      Be mery!

For þei þat make mery here,
In gladness & in very goode chere,
To blys þan mote þei goon.
      Be mery!

That the sacred Christmas carol was not unknown to Shakspere, is proved by two lines in the 'Midsummer-Night's Dream', where we read:

The human mortals want their winter cheer;
No night is now with hymn or carol blest.[1]

Yet Shakspere not only knew about the medieval carols, but could write songs very similar to the secular carols when occasion demanded. In the fifth act of the second part of 'Henry IV' are to be found two carols genuine enough to have issued directly from a medieval manuscript. It is, of course, possible that Shakspere may have borrowed them from an unknown source, but it is much more likely that he wrote them himself. Indeed, the first one, though it answers strictly the requirements of the type in matters of form and meter, has in its content a Shaksperian ring not to be found in many of its medieval predecessors. The second carol Master Silence must have learned at some jolly gathering of festive souls:

[1] II. I. 101-102.

> Be merry, be merry, my wife has all;
> For women are shrews, both short and tall:
> 'Tis merry in hall when beards wag all,
>   And welcome merry Shrove-tide!
> Be merry, be merry!

We can have no hesitancy in agreeing with Master Silence that he must have 'been merry twice and once ere now.' Doubtless he could have given us the following poem, modelled upon a Christmas carol, had he happened to think of it:

> All that I may swynk or swet,
> My wyfe it wyll both drynk and ete,
> And I sey ouȝt, she wyl me bete;
>   Carful ys my hart therfor.
> Care away, away, away!
>   Care away for ever more.![1]

Evidently Silence's cause of joy, the fact that his wife had all, was known also to singers of preceding days, nor was his opinion of womankind vastly different from that of his ungallant ancestors.

The drinking songs in Shakspere demand a word, if only to call attention to Middle English drinking songs of scarcely less merit. Feste, the clown in 'Twelfth Night,' was not the only soul who knew and loved a song of good life.[2] The medieval convivial song did not assume any peculiar conventions, and it would be useless to attempt to establish any strict connection between Shakspere's lyrics of this class and those sung a century before his day. Yet it may not be amiss to remark that in general tone and substance there is an indefinable resemblance. The utter simplicity of thought and construction, the numberless repetitions, and the fact that the lyrics were written for singing, differentiate Shakspere's drinking songs from many classical convivial lyrics, such as Horace's *In Bacchum*, and from many songs of his contemporary dramatists.

In these respects the drinking song sung by the boy in 'Antony and Cleopatra':

---

[1] MS. Eng. Poet, e. 1., Bodl., Oxford. Printed, Wright, *opus cit.* p. 26.
[2] II. III. 34.

Come, thou monarch of the vine,
Plumpy Bacchus with pink eyne!
In thy fats our cares be drown'd,
With thy grapes our hairs be crown'd:
Cup us, till the world go round,
Cup us, till the world go round![1]

may well be compared with the following medieval song, full of
repetitions and a similar simplicity:

Tapster, fille another ale!
Anonne have I do!
God sende us good sale!
Avale the stake, avale!
Here is good ale ifounde!
Drinke to me,
And I to thee,
And lette the cuppe go rounde.[2]

There is a certain resemblance of hearty good cheer between
Iago's song,

And let me the cannakin clink, clink,
And let me the cannakin clink![3]

and the anonymous lyric with the refrain,

Bryng us in good ale, and bryng us in good ale!
For owr blyssyd lady sak, bryng us in good ale![4]

Iago's assertion that he had learned his excellent song in England
may be considered further evidence that Shakspere's drinking
songs belonged to the native soil.

In the later medieval England the 'jolly forester' occupied a
considerable place in lyric poetry. We have preserved three or
more songs which celebrate this officer, his skill, and the honor
of his occupation. More than one lyrist in the Middle Ages
declared:

[1] II. VII. 120-125.
[2] MS. Selden B. 26, Bodl., Oxford. Here printed from Chambers and Sidgwick, *opus cit.*
p. 226.
[3] *Othello*, II. III. 71-75.
[4] MS. Eng. Poet, e. 1. Printed, Wright, *opus cit.* p. 63.

> I am a joly foster, I am a joly foster,
> And haue ben many a day;
> And foster will I be styll,
> For shote ryght well I may,
> For shote ryght well I may.[1]

Shakspere in the forester's song, 'What shall he have that killed the deer?'[2] was carrying on the tradition of a previous day.

There are other proofs that Shakspere was rich in the inheritance of the common people of his age. Mingled with foresters' songs and those of good life, we find in medieval England invariably commonplace poems of every description. The dramatist was not slow in fitting these or their like to his own uses. When Apemantus in 'Timon of Athens' asks a grace, he does so in rhymed octosyllabics, speaking in poetry for the first and last time. Compare his short prayer:

> Immortal gods, I crave no pelf;
> I pray for no man but myself:
> Grant I may never prove so fond,
> To trust man on his oath or bond:
> Or a harlot, for her weeping:
> Or a dog, that seems a-sleeping;
> Or a keeper with my freedom;
> Or my friends, if I should need 'em.
> Amen. So fall to 't:
> Rich men sin, and I eat root.[3]

with such a grace as we find in MS. Harleian 2339:[4]

> Lord, wiþ þis sustynaunce,
> Ʒeue us good contynnaunce
> Þine heestis forto kepe;
> And neuere aftir to do amys,
> Bi which we mone lese heuen blis,
> But þere to haue oure seete;
> And þat þis bone þus grantid mai be,
> Seie we a pater noster & an aue.

Apemantus manifestly reworked an ancient metrical grace into a parody sufficiently disgusting.

---

[1] MS. Add. 31922. Printed, Flügel, *Anglia*, XII, 245.
[2] *As You Like It*, IV, II. 11-19.
[3] I. II. 63-72.
[4] Fol. 122[b] ; hitherto unprinted.

Well-intentioned clerks in the Middle Ages had a habit of advice-giving somewhat comparable to Polonius's custom, except that they never said commonplace maxims quite so splendidly, fitting their advice to the recipient. They almost always delighted in using one monotonous system of assonance, illustrated in the following piece of wisdom, handed down to us in numerous manuscripts:

> Aryse erly,
> Serve God devowtely,
> And the worlde besely,
> Doo thy work wisely,
> Yeve thyn almes secretely,
> Goo by the waye sadly,
> Answer the people demuerly,
> Goo to thy mete apetitely,
> Sit therat discretely,
> Of thy tunge be not to liberally,
> Arise therfrom temperally,
> Go to thy supper soberly,
> And to thy bed merely,
> Be in thyn inne jocundely,
> Please thy love duely,
> And slepe suerly.[1]

The Fool in 'Lear' had learned of his masters, as witness:

> Have more than thou showest,
> Speak less than thou knowest,
> Lend less than thou owest,
> Ride more than thou goest,
> Learn more than thou trowest,
> Set less than thou throwest,
> Leave thy drink and thy whore,
> And keep in-a-door,
> And thou shalt have more
> Than two tens to a score.[2]

In fact, the epigrams and scraps given forth on every occasion by the Fool in 'King Lear' are echoes of similar bits of wisdom, which instructed and delighted the moral populace of pre-Shaksperian England. On the margins of Latin manuscripts, scribbled on the fly-leaves of illuminated prayer books, embedded in medieval

---

[1] This particular version is taken from MS. Lansdowne 762, fol. 16[b], hitherto unprinted.
[2] *King Lear*, I. IV. 131-140.

sermons, everywhere in the Middle Ages, we find pieces of wisdom such as this exceeding wise fool of Shakspere's uses to instruct his king. England was filled with an accumulation of common wisdom, tersely crammed into couplets. The following fourteenth century sound moral statement, typical of medieval epigrams,

> He is wys þat kan be war or him be wo;
> He is wys þat lovet his frend and ek his fo;
> He is wys þat havet inow and kan seyn, 'ho!'
> He is wys þat kan don wel, and doeth al so,[1]

is similar in tone to the fool's declaration,

> He that keeps nor crust nor crumb,
> Weary of all shall want some.[2]

Equally in the Fool's vein is the following:

> He that spendes myche and getythe nowghte,
> And owith myche and hathe nowghte,
> And lokys in hys purse and fynde nowghte,
> He may be sory, thowe he seythe nowghte;[3]

or this sage bit of advice:

> If thow art young, then mary not ekit;
> If thou art old, thou hast more wite;
> For young mens wifes [may n]ot be taught
> And olde mens wifes be good for naught.[4]

Not only are the moral epigrams and scraps of fourteenth century literature represented in Shakspere, but the longer moral poems of that didactic century, also, find at least an echo there. When Hamlet and Horatio encounter the gravedigger they find him singing a song, which, in spite of Hamlet's feeling that the man should not be singing at his work, is unusually fitting for one of his business.

> In youth, when I did love, did love,
>   Methought it was very sweet,
> To contract, O, the time, for, ah, my behove,
>   O, methought, there was nothing meet.

[1] MS. *Harleian* 2316, fol. 25a.
[2] *King Lear*, I. IV. 217-218.
[3] MS. *Harleian* 2252; printed in *Antiquae Reliquiae*, I, 316.
[4] MS. *Harleian* 3835; printed in *Early English Text Society*, 109, xlix.

But age, with his stealing steps,
   Hath claw'd me in his clutch,
And hath shipped me intil the land,
   As if I had never been such.

A pick-axe and a spade, a spade,
   For and a shrouding sheet:
O, a pit of clay for to be made
   For such a guest is meet.[1]

In reading this song we are instantly reminded of the many moral poems of the Middle Ages, dealing with old age and its deformities. In some of these, regret for a misspent youth forms a theme, as in the first stanza above, and in all there is an insistence on such details as crippled limbs, failing eyesight, and lost powers. In fact, we are rather surprised at getting off so easily in Shakspere's song as we do in the last stanza. Now it happens that we know something of the history of these verses of the grave-digger, and this history is suggestive of a process that may have gone on with the anonymous poets from whom Shakspere in a very indefinite way drew.

This song of Shakspere's, which has a decidedly medieval tone, and yet is not quite medieval in its moderation and restraint, is, it seems, a portion only of a longer song by Lord Vaux, first published in *Tottel's Miscellany* in 1557. This poem of Vaux's written probably fifty years or more before it was used by Shakspere, is in its entirety considerably nearer the Middle Ages than the three stanzas which Shakspere excerpts and retouches. In the earlier poem we are told:

The wrinckles in my brow,
   The furrowes in my face:
Say limpyng age will hedge him now,
   Where youth must geue him place.

The harbinger of death,
   To me I see him ride:
The cough, the colde, the gaspyng breath
   Dothe bid me to prouide

A pickeax and a spade.....[2]

[1] *Hamlet*, V. I. 69ff.
[2] *Tottel's Miscellany*, edited by Arber, p. 174.

Vaux was clearly following in his ideas similar poems of medieval preachers. 'God sende us patience in oure olde age', fervently prayed many a medieval clerk, and with delight proceeded to declare the reason why.   Vaux, imitating older poetry, forms a link between Shakspere and the Middle Ages, and suggests how the dramatic poet happened to know so many medieval traditions.

It is indeed somewhat startling to find Shakspere in the full tide of the English Renaissance using literary forms known two hundred years before to Chaucer, living in a different civilization and in another England.   One is at a loss to explain just how Shakspere knew about the *aube,* or why he chose to parody the *chanson d'aventure,* or how he chanced to strike the medieval note so accurately in his nature songs—one is surprised at all this till a study is made of Elizabethan lyric poetry, and then one begins gradually to see that Elizabethan England was still in some measure the England of Chaucer.   The Englishman home from Italy and enthusiastic about song, did not attempt entirely to introduce foreign models: often he found at hand material to work with, songs of older generations still current.   Conservative England yet clung to its own past.   Shakspere, perhaps more than his contemporaries, modelled his lyrics upon those of former times. With him it was no far cry to write a *debat.*   That he wrote a perfect *aube,* is no sign that he studied literary movements. Rather we may infer that in using these artistic forms he was employing types well known, though a little old-fashioned, just as in the carols and the holly poem he turned popular poetry to his own purposes.   This is but saying that Shakspere, who as a dramatist reworked magnificently the plots which others had devised, as a lyrist took the poetry that England had bequeathed him and made of it songs not unlike those of his predecessors, yet unapproached.